MW00979561

You Never Really Know
'Til You Get There

By Andy Bishop

You Never Really Know 'Til You Get There

By Andy Bishop

Copyright © 2009

Published by S.D. Myers Publishing Services
180 South Avenue
Tallmadge, OH 44278

First Printing, May 2009
Printed in the United States of America

All rights reserved. No part of this publication may be reproduced, stored in a retrieval system, or transmitted in any form or by any means—for example, electronic, photocopy, recording, internet—without the prior written permission of the authors. The only exception is brief quotations in printed reviews.

Editing by: Larry Weeden, Katie Sobiech and Scott Myers.
Book design by Michael Grimes and Jeanette Kilchenman.

ISBN: 978-0-93920-18-9

All scripture quotations, unless otherwise indicated, are taken from the New King James Version®. Copyright © 1982 by Thomas Nelson, Inc. Used by permission. All rights reserved.

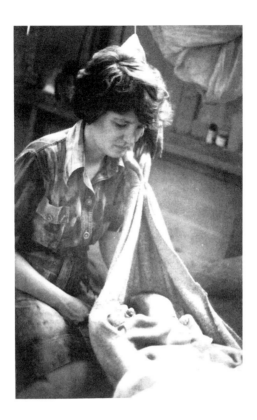

The LORD had said to Abram, "Leave your country, your people and your father's household and go to the land I will show you.

"I will make you into a great nation and I will bless you; I will make your name great, and you will be a blessing.

I will bless those who bless you, and whoever curses you I will curse; and all peoples on earth will be blessed through you."

GENESIS 12:1-3

TABLE OF CONTENTS

CONTINUED

Chapter 1
Getting There

Chapter 1.
Getting There

Some dreams seem to end before they even get started. That certainly appeared to be the case on a November day in 1965, when Beverly, my wife, and I were living in Seattle and preparing – we hoped – to become missionaries.

I was a senior at Seattle Pacific College, studying microbiology and public health. Bev had finished her bachelor of science in nursing at Whitworth the year before and worked as an emergency room nurse at St. Cabrini Hospital.

We were on track to become missionaries but did not know where we might serve. We had applied to several groups, but medical missions were not plentiful. We also applied to the U.S. Public Health Service to serve with the Inuit in Alaska. I worked nights at the King County Juvenile Court. Drew, our first son, was two.

On that fateful November day, Bev had been at a luncheon with her classmates from nursing school. As she headed home across the Evergreen Floating Bridge, a car entering the freeway forced her into the divider. Her Corvair jumped the divider and hit two other cars head on. She was gravely injured, while Drew, sleeping on the backseat, got only bumps and bruises.

A series of miracles followed. An ambulance came by, and the paramedics removed her from the wreckage. She had a critical head injury. Since the accident was half a mile from the University of Washington Hospital, they decided to cross the divider to take her there. The driver recognized her from the ER at Cabrini and was eager to help. However, as he bumped across the divider, he dislodged his gas line. As he entered the hospital parking lot, the ambulance stalled. They rolled Bev the rest of the way to the ER on the gurney.

The intern who received Beverly pronounced her "dead on arrival." An older doctor, however, detected a heartbeat. Her skull had been badly fractured, pushing bone splinters into the brain, but the chief of neurosurgery said, "Let's try to save her."

He canceled an elective brain surgery and went to work on Bev.

When the police finally contacted me with the grave news, I had no transportation of my own, so a neighbor drove me to the hospital. I prayed, "Lord, we are planning to serve You. Please restore Bev completely for Your service. But if not, don't let her suffer. She's in Your hands."

Both the doctor and state trooper treated us kindly. I held Drew and listened to the grim report. She was in surgery for seven hours, and they could make no promises that she would survive.

Some tough days followed. Bev stayed unconscious for about three weeks. Her brother and family helped by taking care of Drew. When not working my way through finals, I sat by Bev's bed and prayed.

Bev's friends from nursing school had become her 24-hour volunteer nurses. They took great care of her. When she began to wake up, she couldn't speak, so she wrote a note saying, "My leg and back are broken." A flurry of x-rays and treatments followed. Although awake, she didn't know exactly who I was. Our families and I both prayed. Later they discovered she had a broken jaw as well.

Through it all, we never gave up the dream of missions; Bev never suggested we do anything else. She reread her nursing textbooks. The speech area of her brain had been damaged, so she had to relearn how to speak.

But she refused to give up the dream, so how could I? And God never left our side.

Five and a half years later, on the gray afternoon of April 1, 1971, our family stood at the rail of the motor vessel Albertville, on the river Schelde, as it flowed through Antwerp, Belgium. We were en route to serve as medical missionaries at the Paul Carlson Memorial Hospital in the remote Equator Province of what had been known as the Belgian Congo.

We had spent the previous seven months learning French and researching our destination deep in the African jungle. We read books, visited museums, and talked to veteran missionaries, some of whom had escaped the murderous Congo rebellion of the 1960s. Now we were going to take the next step to serve there ourselves. In fact, we would work at a hospital named after Dr. Paul Carlson, who had been killed in that uprising.

Getting this far had been a journey in itself, even before Bev's accident. Bev had been a pastor's daughter. As a child she gave her life to Jesus, and she decided to become a missionary while attending King's Garden High School in Seattle. A missionary came to speak at one of the assemblies and closed his presentation by saying, "If God calls you to become a missionary, would you go? If so, stand up."

Bev thought, No problem, I don't have the right stuff; God won't call me, so she stood up. She remembers instantly feeling that she was going to be a missionary. Right away she began to bargain with God: "You know I'm not a leader. I've seen single missionary ladies, and I can't do it alone; I need a husband." So from then on when she dated, she always asked, "What are your life plans?"

After high school, she enrolled in a nursing school in Spokane to prepare her life for missions.

I, too, had been raised in a Christian family and at a young age gave my life to Jesus. Later at a summer camp, I responded to an invitation to commit my life to missions.

At a camp meeting in 1959, the Lord reminded me that I had done little to prepare my life for missions. I had dropped out of high school after the tenth grade and joined the Air Force. While the aircraft mechanic's training came in handy years later, I needed a lot of work to qualify for any meaningful international missions service. So I knelt and rededicated my life to Christ's service.

Two months later, a friend invited me to go on a blind date. He told me that his girlfriend was so shy that she always brought a friend on their dates, so he needed someone to even up the sides. We went to the Deaconess Hospital nurses' dorm in Spokane and met two nursing students, one of whom was Bev Dean. She immediately sat with me, and in our first discussion she asked, "So, what are going to do with your life when you finish the Air Force?"

I had about a year left on my enlistment. I responded, "I'm going to become a missionary."

Bev later told me, "You were the first person with that response, and at that moment I decided I would marry you."

Now, I'm a bit slow, so it took me two and a half more years to get the message and pop the question. We got married in August 1962.

After our wedding, Bev and I moved to South Dakota, where I attended a small junior college in Wessington Springs. They accepted me with a tenth-grade education and a GED certificate. It was a great way to start our marriage. I went to class each morning and each afternoon hunted pheasants or caught fish. We ate well! Bev was a nurse at the small hospital. We loved the life there.

Bev continued to work as a nurse while I worked part-time and took summer jobs, sometimes helping her dad, Percy Dean, build houses and sometimes driving a farm truck. One summer, some friends took us to Whitehorse in the Yukon, where I served as a fishing guide. However, due to the earthquake in 1964, I actually spent most of the summer driving a tour bus for Alaska Highway Tours. It taught me how to deal with the public.

In preparation for missions service, we enrolled in and attended graduate school. During the first five years of Bev's recovery, I worked in environmental health. Graduate school wasn't high on my list, but the Lord knew it would be needed, and He has a sense of humor.

In the fall of 1967, I attended a public health conference in Yakima, Washington. One afternoon, as I went for a swim, I noticed a group of older men from the conference examining a spot of algae on the side of the pool. They were trying to figure out why the algae appeared only in that one spot.

I laughed and said, "You guys really don't know, do you?"

One asked, "Do you?"

"Yes," I replied.

"Why?" They asked.

I said, "I'll show you." I picked out the largest man and instructed, "Go jump off the diving board."

After exchanging puzzled glances with his colleagues, he climbed out and, after a quick walk, did a cannonball. The resulting wave swept down the pool, and as it approached the spot of algae, it struck a skimmer, which caused it to miss the spot as it continued on. I said, "No chlorinated pool water hits there, and so algae can grow."

They looked amazed, and we all laughed.

Later one of the men came to me and said, "I'm Dr. Oswald from Berkeley. How would you like to come to Berkeley graduate school? We're doing research that has space applications, and your kind of thinking would be welcomed."

Surprised, I said, "Send me more information. Graduate school, eh?"

At dinner, another of the pool group came over and said, "I'm Dr. Mytinger from the University of Hawaii School of Public Health. I like the way you made your point about the algae. Would you like to come to our graduate school?"

"Well," I said, "I'm married and have a son, so we would have to get financial aid."

"That can be done," he said.

I responded, "Send me the papers."

By the next year, I had a full grant to attend the University of Hawaii School of Public Health Graduate School.

They paid all my expenses, including my rent and so on, but I needed to earn extra money to take Bev and Drew along to Hawaii. At that time in 1968, I had been serving as the First District Court probation officer in Whatcom County in Bellingham, Washington. One of my jobs had been setting up a job release program for first-time offenders. While helping a young man sign up as a cook on a fishing tender in Alaska, I noticed how much he would be paid for the summer; it was substantial. I thought, What better way to get the money for Hawaii?

I worked for very helpful judges, and soon I was en route to Bristol Bay, Alaska, as a cook for the M.V. Cachalot. When I arrived at the boat, the little Norwegian captain, Louie Lee, looked at me and said, "Kid, can you cook?"

"I grew up in a big family and sometimes took a turn at the stove." I replied. "But not to worry, I bought a cookbook."

At this point, I pulled out a dog-eared paperback entitled The Can Opener's Cookbook. Stunned, Louie said, "Oy! It's going to be a long summer."

It was in fact a great summer, punctuated by bouts of seasickness in rough storms, but I survived and earned the money to take our family to Hawaii. The school year passed quickly, and on a summer day in 1969, I defended my master's thesis as Bev gave birth in Seattle to our second son, Matt. I graduated with a masters in health services administration.

For the next year I worked in medical care administration. I also helped to start the School of Public Health at the University of Washington. In February 1970, while working as director of health care delivery research for the Veterans' Hospital in Seattle, I attended a men's missions luncheon put on by our InterBay Covenant Church. Art Lundblad from the Congo spoke. He talked about the terror of the rebellion and the hope for recovery that had begun. He emphasized the need for professionals to help the Africans learn to run their schools and hospitals.

Sitting by Pastor Ostrom, I said, "Too bad they don't need a team like Bev and me. We have been praying for something like this for years."

He said, "See me afterward."

I felt a chill. The only other time I had felt like that was when I said "I do" seven years earlier. Things were about to change!

After the luncheon, he introduced me to Art Lundblad and gave me applications for the Covenant medical project known as the Paul Carlson Medical Center in the Equator Province of the Congo.

I said, "I'd better talk to Bev."

I called my office to let them know I wouldn't be back that day and drove home. When I arrived, Bev said, "Are you playing golf this afternoon?"

"No," I said, "we need to talk."

Now, if you want your wife's attention, just say, "Dear, we need to talk." Bev stood very still and blurted out, "About what?"

I responded, "Umm, make coffee and--"

"No," she interrupted, "I want to know what we're talking about."

"Umm, well, what would you think if some day we might go to Africa?"

Bev didn't hesitate. "When do we leave?"

"Well," I said, "get out the typewriter. We have paperwork to fill out."

We never did make the coffee.

The next few weeks were a flurry of letters and interviews. Dr. Arden Almquist, the medical director for the center, came to Seattle for an interview. He carefully reviewed Bev's medical history and said he could handle any health problem she might have.

We began to realize that not only had our door to missions been opened, but we were also going through it. We stopped at Belgium next, to study French.

The Lord confirmed along the way that this was the way we should go. Even small things like selling our nearly-new car were no obstacle for the Lord. Packing and shipping supplies, disposing of unneeded items, plus storing of things we would want later all took time.

Our families had varied reactions to the announcement that we were going to Africa. It horrified and angered Bev's mom at first. She said, "After all she's been through, you can't take her to that place." Her dad kept quiet, but he let me know he wasn't happy.

My parents said, "God bless you. We'll be praying for you."

As the spring turned into summer, Bev reminded me that she had an obligation to serve as the camp nurse at the Covenant camp.

"But," I said, "that's the last week before we leave for Belgium. Can't they get someone else?"

They tried, but no one else was available. So we adjusted the schedule some, and Bev took the boys to camp. I finished packing and cleaning up.

I said good-bye to Reed Clegg, the hospital administrator. He was a Mormon and fully understood going on a mission. "Come back when you're done," he said. "We'll always have a job for you here."

After a final check on things, I drove to the campground. While I sat on the porch of the infirmary, a man came over to look at our Toyota. He saw the "For Sale" sign and said, "It's new. Why are you selling it?"

I replied, "We're leaving as missionaries to Africa in a few days and can't take it with us."

"I'll buy it from you," he said. "I'll bring you a check tomorrow, and you can drive it until you get on the plane."

I was amazed and thankful! Just another step in the journey God took us on.

The seven months we spent in Belgium were fascinating and enjoyable. We had arrived on Pan Am from Seattle via London. While the boys and I collected the bags that day, Bev headed for the ladies' room. When she came back she said, "I need money. There's a lady at the bathroom door. She won't let me in without money, and she doesn't speak English."

This began our multicultural experience. Dan and Anne Ericson, former Congo missionaries, welcomed us, and their staff helped us set up our apartment, as well as manage everything from furniture to French classes. We also studied the history of missions in the Congo. We visited Paris and found that our French was Belgian, not real French. We also found that French and Flemish people in Belgium didn't like each other much. Shock! Here in a small country were two distinct languages with clashing cultures. It prepared us for the Congo, though, where there were many tongues and tribes.

We visited Holland and England and finally got down to visit my brother Dave, who lived in Spain with his family while serving in the U.S. Air Force. We toured museums and castles and soaked up history. We also visited West Berlin, where we saw the stark differences between freedom and communism.

⌁

As the Albertville entered the mouth of the Congo River, a military patrol boat met us with laundry drying on radio aerials and the small pilot's launch. The pilot, being Belgian, knew the river and would guide us past sand bars and shallows to the port of Boma, where we spent our first night.

The next day we moved upriver to Matadi, the main port for the Congo, while the cargo got off-loaded. We walked the dusty streets, and people gave us "Mbotes." The town looked tired and down at the heels. Buildings were in poor repair, the streets teemed with people, and our noses got introduced to the hot, humid smells of the tropics.

I thought of stories about the first missionaries who came to the Congo. They wore pith helmets and wool suits with wool cummerbunds, supposedly to ward off disease. As they wandered about the villages, they tried to mimic the African linguistic sounds and make connections to their meanings. The Africans knew that the Germans came for the iron, the French for rubber, and the Belgians for copper. The British came to organize and the Portuguese to trade…but who were these people?

One day a young man went to the chief. "I know why they're here," he said, "they are here to buy eggs!"

Considered the only safe local food, the missionaries still bought eggs when we got there.

The next day, after finishing customs paperwork, we headed for Kinshasa. The sights fascinated us: mud houses with grass roofs, bare dirt yards with people waving, and kids cheering as we drove by. We saw palm and papaya trees, and goats and chickens wandered everywhere. It was all a dream come true.

Kinshasa had been best described as a "village" of more than a million, with few stores and only a limited variety of goods. I found my way to the open markets where they had a greater variety of goods. The heat and humidity, along with the dust and the crowds of people, astounded me.

I went to a market to buy cases of canned goods of every variety. I had fun bargaining with the traders, who were mostly Portuguese, East Indian, and African. We bargained in French, with some English. The French was uniquely African, and we loved it. The market offered not only business, but also a great social and cultural experience.

At the mission guest compound, we met other missionaries and African pastors. We began to feel "at home." The boys discovered a monkey at the guest house and enjoyed playing with him in spite of a few nips.

Two weeks later, all our goods and luggage arrived, including our huge case of goods shipped from America the previous year. We were ready to head to our hospital on the Loko River. The large, Belgian-built facility, located in an extremely remote part of the Congo, had sat empty for several years. Now the government had given it to the Covenant mission to reopen and operate.

Getting to it from Kinshasa was no easy trip. Drew and I went up the Congo on the riverboat Colonel Ebaya. It carried more than 250 passengers, mostly on barges pushed by the big push boat. We loaded our goods, plus supplies for other people at the station. We knew that by traveling with our goods, we probably wouldn't lose them. Bev and Matt would fly up country with Mission Aviation Fellowship (MAF) and land at the hospital airstrip. Art Lundblad, the man who introduced us to this adventure in Seattle, was the mission business agent and a great help.

Drew and I spent the next five and a half days on the river. We saw it as few do, an experience we will never forget. We saw villages on little islands, dense jungle right down to the water, and, of course, animals and people.

Among the passengers were hundreds of traders selling everything from pins and needles to brassieres. The villagers would paddle out in pirogues and grab onto the passing boat. They loaded these little boats with dried meat, vegetables such as manioc, woven goods, and carved items. Some had fish, both fresh and smoked. It amazed Drew to find a catfish over five feet long and weighing more than 100 pounds. The traders would buy the products, and people would use the money to buy other goods. Once all the transactions were finished, they climbed back into their pirogues and paddled down the river to their village.

On the second day, Drew rushed into my room in the afternoon shouting, "Dad! Dad! Come quick. They're going to eat the monkey."

Some of the trade goods were live animals. I said, "They do that here, son."

"But," he said, "I want it for a pet."

So down to the barbecue pit on the aft deck we went. I approached the man holding a young colobus monkey. It was a pretty little animal and very gentle.

After exchanging "M'botes" and handshakes, I said, "My son would like your monkey."

"Will he share it with us?" He asked.

"He doesn't want to eat it," I replied. "He wants it for a pet."

"Oooh," the monkey owner said.

So we bargained. Finally he said we could have the monkey for my short-sleeved coverall. Deal!

Now I had Drew and the monkey for roommates.

The riverboat also stopped at small ports along the way to unhook a barge load of people and cargo, then continued up the river. When the boat came back down the river, the crew would collect barges loaded with fresh cargo and passengers bound for Kinshasa.

At last we arrived at Lisala, the port where we debarked for Loko. Dick Farquhar, the hospital station mechanic, met us driving a Fiat two-ton truck. We loaded up and headed north, a 12-hour drive through the jungle and occasional villages.

At each village, kids rushed out and cheered us as we passed. Drew and his monkey waved, shouted, and enjoyed the trip. The Africans said, "Ah, new customers for our products."

As we drove, Dick, a midwest farmer, brought me up to speed on conditions and progress at the hospital. He was glad I had brought the parts to overhaul one of the generators -- our only source of electricity -- as well as a load of their personal goods from America.

We finally arrived after averaging about 20 miles per hour on really rough roads. Bev and Matt gave us a joyous welcome. We had finally reached the destination Bev and I had dreamed of ever since we married almost eight years before.

1970 Africa Bound

Our family studying French in Belgium 1971

Chapter 2
IMELOKO

Chapter 2.
IMELOKO

The Paul Carlson Hospital in the Equator Province of the Belgian Congo sat just four degrees north of the equator. As colonialism was pushed back, the name of the country was shortened to "Congo." It was Africa's largest country, and King Albert of Belgium had considered it to be his own private farm.

The hospital was situated on beautiful rolling hills at about 1500 feet of altitude. As we looked around us in every direction, we saw rolling plains covered with sobe grass, three to five feet tall. Interspersed patches of jungle filled the ravines and ran down to the swamps and river bottoms, and a double canopy jungle with trees 100-200 feet tall spread over vast areas.

A large number of croton bushes and their colorful foliage added a nice feel to the station. We also had lots of papaya and palm trees, as well as guava, mango, tangerines, and limes.

Several varieties of monkeys and the small gorilla known as the bonobo populated the forests. A vast array of birds populated the area, including hornbills, partridges, parrots, and a myriad of small, beautifully colored birds, as well as hawks and owls. There were also many varieties of ants -- everywhere!

Several kinds of small cats, along with leopards, prowled the forests. Wild pigs, antelope, and different varieties of buffalo roamed around as well. We also saw crocodiles, hippos, and elephants. And of course, snakes. Black and green mambas were the worst, but we also had two or three varieties of cobras and several types of viper. Pythons, some over 20 feet, were seen, but we had very few encounters – thankfully.

The hospital, laid out in a cruciform pattern, contained a main building for surgery, outpatient care, pharmacy, lab, and some storage. A number of wards stood adjacent to the main building, with an outpatient building that served as a church next to the shop.

Several multiplexes for nurses and a 10,000-gallon water tower sat between the main facility and the airstrip. The water system ran well, but like everything else, depended on electricity. A village for workers and their families lay beyond the tower.

European-style houses for the doctors and a guest house sat on the other end of the station.

Built as a tuberculosis hospital by the Belgians, the facility was unusually well done for Africa. Because it had been built for tuberculosis treatment, it was isolated from population centers. The nearest trading post was Businga, 40 kilometers away.

Once we got acquainted with the hospital staff, we moved to G'bado, a station 20 kilometers away, to begin Lingala study. This introduced us to another language and another culture. Our house made of mud brick had walls three feet thick and a sobe grass roof. Surrounded by a wide veranda, it stayed cool even on the hottest days. A snake lived in the ceiling, and we could hear him at night as he slithered about looking for rats, mice, and bats. Welcome to Africa!

With water being a problem during dry season, we took very different evening showers. We had a two and a half gallon bucket with a shower head in the bottom. This had to shower the whole family at the same time, as we had only two and a half gallons for bathing the four of us.

So, Bev would warm the water, I would hang the bucket, and then we would disrobe and get ready. I would hold Matt and turn on the water, and we would dance about. After that we would turn off the shower while we soaped and scrubbed, and then we would have about a gallon to rinse with. We followed this daily bathing routine for two months. Years later, when we saw the bumper sticker "Save water; shower with a friend," we had a good laugh.

We loved the people. Their warmth and openness allowed us to relax with them as we had seldom done before. The reduced social pressure was a breath of fresh air for Bev as she continued to recover from her car crash.

The people were also amazingly resourceful. They collected our empty cans and turned them into kitchen utensils. They worked hard to find food and to make their own clothing. Some of the tribes had special hunting skills, some gardened well, and others wove mats, baskets, and so on. We found one tribe to be especially good with metal and mechanics, while the other had good organizational skills. They traded things like meat, vegetables, baskets, and knives with one another. It made quite an economic system, and everyone seemed happy.

Because the people viewed us as a potential source of income on several levels, initiation into the system of employment began right away. We hired a yard boy to cut grass, kill snakes, and tend the garden once we had seeds to plant. We also had an egg boy. People knew we wanted to buy eggs, so they had a system already in place.

Our major home staff member was our cook, Simone. He could make bread, cook any kind of a critter, and make sauces and gravy that we loved. His daughter, Georgina, became Matt's babysitter, because we needed Bev at the hospital to be the pharmacist and nurse.

I wanted to work but had only a first-grade vocabulary. Learning the second language frustrated me. So one day the older missionary who sensed my frustration asked me about it.

"I can't even teach a basic Bible study yet," I complained.

"Andy," she said, "you've already told them everything you know about Jesus."

"How?"

She replied, "The way you treat your family and your workers says everything. You will be known by what you do more than what you say. So far you're doing a good job."

This taught me a vital lesson, given the range of countries and cultures that we would serve over the coming years. Let them see Jesus in you!

Once we finished language study, we moved to our comfortable house at Loko, which had just been painted. I built a wood stove on the back porch, using an old steel safe for the oven. It made great dishes and bread, as it held an even heat for a long time.

∽⌒

Tukia, one of our neighbors, had been trained as a nurse 20 years before we came and did a lot of surgery as well. During the several years when the Congo rebellion was on in the early 1960s, he was the only source of medical care because all foreigners had to leave when the rebellion began. We saw him as a great example of Christian love and action in a dangerous time.

He had a dozen kids, and they took Matt in as one of their own. It was fun to watch him play soccer, climb trees, or whatever. He was the only white sheep in the pack, but he didn't think he was any different.

Because we had gone on a short-term assignment, Tukia needed training in order to become the hospital administrator. Teaching him the mysteries of management and logistics was crucial.

Bev was trying to teach the pharmacist the system for ordering medicines so that they would arrive in time to keep the pharmacy from running out, but her student said, "We still have some on the shelf."

The thought that it took two or three months before more would arrive seemed too complicated. Finally Bev painted a red line on the shelf and taught them that when the supply reached the line, they needed to order!

Bev spent the first few months going through barrels of donated medicines, most of which contained samples. She always had a pharmacy book on hand, which she used to sort and classify drugs. This took days! She also had to mix medicines from chemicals. With their names being in French, she worked hard. She soon found out that expiration dates didn't mean much.

One day she said, "We need something for the terrible cough going around. I have the suppressant powder, but no syrup to mix it with so they can take it."

I remembered some items in our small warehouse. We used a lot of Metrecal, which was for dieters but could help re-hydrate patients. We also froze it because it made fair ice cream. However, the syrup I had in mind was Hadacol, a form of "cure all" for the elderly that our FDA had taken off the U.S. market. Being made up of 40 percent alcohol, it made the elderly a little too happy! The company pulled the product off the market and donated cases of it to Africa for a healthy tax write-off. Bev mixed in the suppressant, and voila, cough syrup. It was a hit. People walked miles for Madame Beverly's cough syrup, even when they didn't have a cough!

Bev always had good, imaginative solutions. One time I discovered about 1,600 pounds of Swedish long woolen underwear in our storage. A mission committee in Sweden thought they would be helpful to the Africans, but woolen underwear on the equator? When I told Bev, she said, "Let me have it. I'll sell it at the market."

"Why would anyone buy it?" I wondered.

She replied, "They'll buy it for the buttons."

She was right. Because of our distance from a source of things like buttons. they bought it all. They sold for about ten cents per suit. However, after removing the buttons, they put the underwear to other uses. When it got cool, or below 80 degrees Fahrenheit, they'd wear it. I called it "bun city" because they didn't have the button for the trapdoors on the underwear.

I once showed a movie featuring Apollo 11 on the moon. The people loved it. Afterward we sat by the fire and drank tea. A huge African moon shone down, and I remarked, "Isn't it amazing that those men walked on that very moon and flew back here?"

Some discussion followed, then one fellow said, "Yes, that is good, but you go to a place called New York, and we can't see that, ever."

Our son Drew went to boarding school at Karawa, about 80 miles from our station. He would go for three months and come home for two weeks. He loved it there. Eight kids made up his third-grade class, and they learned to function as a family. They kept their rooms up and did a variety of chores to keep things clean and orderly. One of their jobs was shelling peanuts. Each grade school child had to fill a soup can with shelled peanuts, and the older kids would roast and grind them into peanut butter for the sandwiches in the coming week. No peanuts shelled meant no peanut butter!

Both of the boys had pets. Drew's first was the colobus monkey we got on the riverboat. The Africans said, "Ah, they buy animals."

So soon we had another monkey…for Matt! Next came a mouse deer, which was a tiny, beautiful creature about the size of a small puppy. Then we had a cat, which was afraid of mice, goats, and chickens. Matt even had an owl at one time.

I'll never forget the day a group of men came into our yard carrying a large, covered basket. "We have caught you a wonderful pet," they said.

I thought, Hmm, perhaps a wild pig or a small gorilla.

I wondered what Bev was thinking, although she had always been pretty longsuffering when it came to the zoo.

"Voila," they said and lifted the lid. The basket was filled to the top with a big python. "No, thanks!" I said.

"Oh, but we worked so hard to catch this for you, and we need the money."

"Look, fellows, that snake will eat the monkeys, the goats, the deer, the chickens, and then the neighbor kids -- and I'll be in deep trouble. No, thank you!"

Then I had an idea. Missionaries always needed snake pictures to show the folks back home, so I called all our foreign staff to the doctor's home for a photo session. I remembered that we had received a big kerosene refrigerator and still had the box, so we could put the snake in the box. I explained to the snake men, "We'll photograph the snake and each pay you some money. Then you have the money and the snake. Sort of like having your snake and eating it too."

They loved the idea.

We gathered around the box and began clicking away as they emptied the snake from the basket to the box. Now, the men hadn't mentioned that while catching the snake they stuck him with a spear, which he was still angry about. So as soon as they got the snake in the 6'x4'x4' box, he lifted his head to take stock of the situation. He raised his head four or five feet and then took us all in as snacks!

Suddenly all 12-plus feet of him darted out of the box and slithered across the lawn, quick as a little garter snake. Dr. Arden Almquist shouted and ran ahead of him. I gave Bev the camera, thinking, This isn't going as planned. As missionaries shouted and scattered, I grabbed a big stick and went after the python. As I caught up, he suddenly reared and struck at me. I deflected his huge, gaping mouth with a quick backhand, and before he could strike again I broke his neck. I had killed many rattlesnakes and a few vipers, but nothing like this. It took a number of heavy blows to dispatch him.

Well, damage the snake and you've got to buy the snake. I made a deal. If they butchered the snake and tanned its hide for me, I would pay them about five dollars. That plus the photo money made them happy. Not only did our team get great photos, but they each got a big chunk of snake to cook. Bev pressure cooked it, but it tasted like whitefish. A few months later they brought another snake. I just shot it and gave the meat to the Africans and the skin to a visiting doctor.

As the hospital picked up the tempo of treating the sick and doing surgery and related activities, so did the demand for space to give care, house families, and store supplies.

We solved getting the space we needed by building African style. First we determined the size of the needed structure. Then a crew cut and set support poles from the jungle. After that, another group wove a lattice work of branches and vines for the walls and the roof. Finally, a crew arrived to do the mud. The boys loved this part. A spot was chosen for dumping water, and the men and women worked it with their feet till they had a big mud hole. After that, the mud was stuffed into the lattice work until it was four to six inches thick. Matt squealed with joy and got plenty of red mud all over himself. Bev was not amused, but Georgina scrubbed him clean.

While the mud set, another crew arrived with sheaves of sobe grass and bundles of vines. They wove and tied the grass in a thick thatch which would shed water.

I was filming the process one day when suddenly a man gave a shout, "Nyoka!"

The men flew in every direction as they discovered a small viper had gotten into a grass bundle. They killed him with a "coup coup" -- a big, long knife used to cut grass. Afterward everyone stopped for tea.

Finally we brought mud from big termite hills that dotted the region. They defied even the strongest rains. When we plastered the mud over the regular mud walls, it dried to a cement- like finish. All one had to do was add doors and windows, and for about $400 to $500 have a storage building or cook house. We built several places for families of patients to use while they cared for their family member. When people came for treatment, their families had to follow the system which stated that a family member had to provide food during their stay. If they didn't have money, their family member would have to do some work on the hospital compound.

For this purpose they set up a small market so that people could buy food. It consisted of a collection of tables with palm frond roofs. Matt loved to browse and readily accepted snacks of peanuts and even certain dried bugs. Drew always watched for a spear or knife in the market.

Travel was always an adventure. A bridge might be out, a tree might be across the road, or, as happened one time, the road might collapse. One day on a trip with our Fiat 2.5 ton truck, I drove southeast to the town of Bumba, on the Congo River, to try to buy fuel. It took me at least two days to get there. Fuel had been scarce due to low water that kept boats from making it up the river.

It was a tough road, and there weren't any service stations or trading posts during the 24-hour drive. Sand was often a problem, and as I crossed an uphill sandy stretch, the side of the road gave way and the truck sagged over on its side. I got discouraged knowing that there probably wouldn't be any other vehicles coming along and no AAA to pull me out. Two of our African mechanics accompanied me, and we had some 55-gallon drums, as well as a saw and a 12-foot plank. I prayed for an idea and then remembered some farm situations from my childhood. We could pry the truck upright.

We cut some long poles and used the barrels for fulcrums to pry and crib the truck upright. Once it was on its wheels, we jacked up the wheel in the ditch and slid the plank underneath. I continued to pray for help, and shortly after, a man stepped out of the forest. He didn't speak French or Lingala, but one of the mechanics knew his dialect and soon had an agreement. He disappeared and quickly came back with his entire village of about 30 people.

Continuing to pray, I stepped into the truck and it started right up. Then the villagers grabbed hold and began a rhythmic chant. Whenever they hit a beat, they would rock the truck. As they rocked, I'd let out on the clutch. As they sang and pushed, we got the truck up and out of the stretch of sand and back on the road. This answered our prayer and cost us just a few dollars! As Dick Farquhar would say in similar situations, "This sure is a hard way to serve the Lord!"

We experienced this type of "road service" from time to time. Once someone asked President Mobutu, "Why don't you fix the roads? If attacked, you couldn't even get a tank to your border."

He replied, "Well, tanks roll both ways."

If one could average 20 miles per hour on a trip, they considered it a good speed. Taking a trip to see Drew 80 kilometers away was always an adventure. The roads usually ran through villages consisting of collections of round mud thatched huts teeming with kids, dogs, chickens, pigs, and goats. We had to exercise caution, as the kids loved to cheer and run along the road as we drove by.

We enjoyed our team. Our cook, Simone, would come at about 6:00 a.m., and Matt would jump out of bed and run to meet him while shouting, "Simone, Simone, Na linge pannecake...pannecake."

Simone was a good hunter, too. He would bring in delicious critters and cook them with gravy over rice. Many of the men hunted with home made shotguns, and though they killed mostly small game, they occasionally shot a buffalo.

They said, "We wait till he's sleeping, and then the gun man and two spear men creep up and attack." Hearing a loud "click" meant trouble, because if the gun misfired, the huge buffalo would wake...angry!

Malaria, a common problem, often killed children and adults. Amoebas and hookworm were there also. When Bev asked one of the mothers how to prevent the kids from getting these diseases, she told her, "Have them take their anti-malarial, and when they get worms, treat them. It's like a cold or flu at home…you'll always get them."

One time our team planned a weekend of fun and ministry for about 80 African kids. The first evening we butchered a goat, and I cooked rice with goat gravy. My days as ship's cook came in handy, and they loved it.

After dinner they sang for hours and finally quieted down at about midnight. My bed was a piece of cardboard on the cement floor. Bev had been left to run the station at Loko alone, but we prayed and she did a good job.

I awoke at about 1:00 a.m. with a high fever and a terrible neck and headache. Soon 'pulu pulu' (diarrhea) came. By morning I couldn't even hold down the malarial treatment meds or aspirin. The Belgian nuns at their small hospital didn't have any medicine either. I do remember the Portuguese trader who went into his house and got me a cold Coke and some aspirins from his kerosene cooler. By afternoon I began vomiting and passing blood, so Mary Wickstrom loaded me into the truck and drove me to Loko. Dr. Ron Tolls had just come in from Wasolo and quickly diagnosed cerebral malaria.

He placed me on the cool floor and covered me with wet cloths to bring the fever down. We talked and discovered that he had spent summers working at Point Roberts, Washington, where I spent some time as a child. As we talked, he prepared two big syringes of Camolar, the only treatment that worked for my malaria, especially since I could not swallow anything.

Finally his wife said, "Dear, treat him. If he lives till morning, you can carry on the conversation." That had to have been the worst case of malaria I ever had. It took a couple of weeks to get back up to speed. Bev, Matt, and Drew experienced malaria regularly, which was always a drag - especially since the anti-malaria meds we took did not prevent malaria entirely. It was just part of the cost of being there.

After several attacks, they diagnosed me with chronic malaria. That meant every other week or so I would get a fever, chills, and pulu pulu, but Bev would quickly give me the shots and I'd only be down a day or two. It was not a good situation because the anti-malarial drugs did not work in my body; they only made me sick.

Bev, who everyone had worried about, seldom got sick with anything!

Our two nurses from the U.S., Karen and Carolyn, lived next door. Karen Gammelgard had come to serve from California. She was in her twenties and adapted quickly. Carolyn was older and an experienced public health nurse. She traveled with the public health team to the village clinics we established through the region.

Karen loved the people and would let the ladies braid her hair African style. She loved to travel out to join Dr. Teddy and nurse Gerde on their mobile clinic that operated in very remote areas. Once she went hunting with our sentinel, Andre, and me, helping us carry a big colobus monkey that I shot back to the house. It weighed over 40 pounds. Simone served the monkey in gravy.

Andre was smitten. "Oh!" he told me one day, "you must negotiate for me with Karen's father. I must have her for a wife!"

Unfortunately for Andre, the romantic affection was not mutual. "Not ever!" she growled when she heard I was discussing the situation with him.

Before long, Andre announced he'd found a 15-year-old in a village, and he could get her for 12 chickens, 2 blankets, a hoe, a shovel, a bucket, and a machete. But after the wedding, the bride's family started back to their village…with the bride. "Andre," I asked, "didn't you just marry that girl?"

"Yes," he said, "but I still owe five chickens."

"Well," I responded, "get five of mine from the chicken coup and claim your bride!" Sadly, she only lived about eight more months and then died suddenly of one of the mysterious fevers common in the region. By custom, Andre got 75 percent of the bride price refunded. Early death or no children was grounds for a return and a refund.

Anna and Mokanda, an older Christian couple who showed the love of Christ in their lives and faces, had not followed custom after being unable to have children. Instead they stayed married and raised ten orphaned kids. For us, it confirmed that God loved and honored them.

At the hospital, we had a lot of equipment breakdowns, and since repairs were hard to make with no spares readily available, it meant no electricity, water, or transport until repair parts were sent in from Kinshasa, Europe or the United States. During one bad period, the African Christians decided that evil spirits had come because they had developed "bad hearts" or "spiritual coldness." So they held special services, a revival took place, and prayers got answered. They found parts that had been missing, put a new diesel pump motor in place of the electric, and we had clean water. God had answered our prayers.

Getting medicine was always a challenge. We were supposed to get some from the government, but that seldom happened. Because people died for lack of medicines, we had to go get them ourselves.

As the hospital administrator, one time I needed to make a trip to Kinshasa. With all the political tension in the country, we needed to know what to do, as well as get supplies. After a day and a half drive to Gemena, where a plane occasionally came in, I found the airport -- a dirt field near a dilapidated shed that functioned as the terminal. Several hundred African traders from the north, mostly Senegal and Niger, camped out in the field.

I watched the government round them up and expel them. A group had been caught with the corpse of a dead relative, which they planned to take to his home country for burial. When the customs agent looked closer, he found a bunch of diamonds in the body cavity. Because of this, all the traders from those regions got arrested and expelled. That was my first experience with refugees.

They camped in the open, waiting for a military plane to take them out of Congo. Having waited in the open under guard for days, they grew very hungry and thirsty.

After a day or so, the old DC-4 came rumbling in, and I flew off to Kinshasa. I had a list of medicines to secure, and I needed to get our station radio repaired; it had been hit by lightning. The radio was our quickest link with the outside. Through our daily radio checks with the central station, we were able to contact the MAF station in Kinshasa.

It had been vital for emergencies. I also had paperwork for a truck shipped from America a year before. It had been unloaded in Matadi, taken to Kinshasa, and put on an upriver barge...then it disappeared.

After I dropped off the radio at the repair shop, the medicine order got handed into the government pharmacy, and another list was given to a Belgian drug supplier.

At the shipping office, I went over all the papers on the truck. The agent found that it had been put on a barge but had been sent up the wrong river. Several months later, he was waiting for it to come back to Kinshasa. As we spoke, I looked out into the yard by the river and saw the truck. "That's it!" I exclaimed.

"Oh," he said, "so that is your truck. It's been here a while, but the papers were lost." Time and details were never important in the Congo.

I made sure Art Lundblad knew about the truck and would get it on the next boat to Lisala. After one more good soak in the guesthouse tub, I loaded all my goods into boxes, made a call to my family in the United States, and headed back up country. It had been a busy ten days, but I finished the entire list - a rarity in Africa!

Back at Loko, things were in flux. Carolyn, the older nurse, had read various Congo martyr books and got distressed after becoming more aware of the increasing political unrest in the country. She remembered that several missionaries had been killed by their workers in the rebellion of the '60s. She grew increasingly apprehensive and reluctant to go to the villages with the public health team. Paranoia began to set in.

Matt and Drew had a very rascally monkey. He loved to swipe manioc, and Matt would get a small can of peanuts and they would hide in the goat shed and munch. The monkey figured out how to undo the latches I put on the veggie box and even tried to pick the lock when I put a padlock on it.

One day, Carolyn came to Bev quite upset and said, "You've got to do something about that monkey."

"Oh," said Bev, "is he stealing your veggies?"

"No," she exclaimed, "he's been watching me while I undress!"

A few days later, she announced that if she weren't sent out of Africa, she would commit suicide. I needed to arrange the travel. Once she knew she could leave, she calmed down. Even though it took two weeks, the thought of leaving calmed her.

One evening we sat on the porch, looking over the savannah. For miles we could see lightning storms, grass fires, and a rising African moon. A road cut across one stretch of savannah, and the lights of a vehicle could be seen in the distance. It took half an hour for the car to get to Loko.

I said, "Carolyn, you worked in rural Kentucky on dirt roads and hard places. How is Africa different?"

"Oh," she said, "I would go on dirt and up a creek in my Jeep, but then I'd come down the dirt road, then to a hard top road, then to a town where there were lights and restaurants and people, but that road…" she said, pointing in the distance, "that road doesn't go anywhere!"

She was right, our isolation was complete. We often said you couldn't go any farther into Africa there because when you left Loko in any direction, you were going out!

A few weeks later, she arrived safely back in Chicago.

The political unrest in Kinshasa grew. Copper prices went down, and money was tight. Most people blamed Europe for the problem. Mobutu announced that everyone would get a 20 percent pay raise, hoping to calm them down.

At the morning staff meeting, one worker asked, "When do we get our raise President Mobutu announced on the radio?"

I thought fast and said, "Well, he has to sign the decree, then the paper goes to the minister of the interior. He checks it, signs it, and sends it to the sub-ministers, who do the same. Then it's sent upriver to the province administrator, and he sends it to Businga, to the local administrator." By now their eyes said it all – bureaucracy would delay their raise for another two months or more.

"However," I said, "most of your raise has been given away in the form of medicines and treatment to your family and friends. Their I.O.U.s fill the cash box, and if they are not paid, there won't be enough money to pay your raise."

A spirited discussion followed, and then Louie, the office clerk and Tukia's son, stood up. "May I borrow your motor bike for a few days?" he asked.

"What for?" I responded.

"I am going to take the I.O.U.s to the people and collect the money they owe. Most of them have it."

We had a system that if you didn't have money, you could work on the grounds and cut grass or keep the airstrip maintained. But in their culture, one couldn't deny a loan if family requested it.

"Okay," I said, "go to it."

Louie was gone for a week, but he came back with most of the money! The workers got their raises, and fewer I.O.U.s were approved thereafter.

By this time, there was rioting in Kinshasa. Mobutu targeted the Europeans and continued to blame them for the country's economic woes. People tore down statues and destroyed European street signs and billboards. Tukia came to our home and said, "Don't be alarmed. We will care for all of you. This will pass."

The next day, Mobutu renamed the country "Zaire" and ordered whites to begin turning over all management to Zairians. As this had been our intent from the start, we began to make plans to speed up the process. The timing wasn't bad, either. My chronic malaria had triggered high blood pressure, and the Atabrine I took was hard on my body and didn't mitigate my malaria attacks much.

Bev had the pharmacy well organized, and the pharmacist finally learned to order medicine even when he still seemed to have lots on hand. He observed Bev's red line as a guide.

Our family wasn't too excited about leaving Africa. Drew loved his school and the joy of whizzing about on Bev's motor bike. Matt loved everything and everyone. He could chatter in a couple local languages and loved his bananas. We enjoyed Simone, Andre, and Georgina, as well as the whole hospital team.

When Tukia and I discussed the turnover, he said with tears, "Well, I'm losing a brother, but I am gaining my job."

I felt he was ready to be the administrator and would do a good job in that role.

We flew to Kinshasa from Gemena. As the old DC-4 droned along, I could see the screws on the engine cowl unwind from the vibration. When we landed at Mbandaka, the mechanics climbed up and tightened them down. Then we flew to Kinshasa while they unwound again. We always landed just before they gave out. Africa!

To catch the 8:00 a.m. Air Zaire flight to Nairobi, we had to check in at 4:00 a.m.! Amenities like coffee couldn't be found. Just darkness and confusion. Finally we got on the Air Zaire DC-8, ready to fly to Nairobi. The air conditioning came on, and they passed out candy. We welcomed the lovely air conditioning. Finally I heard the engine begin to start…then thump! The pilot had missed the moment, and the engine would not start.

After all the confusion, they told us to go back to the terminal and have breakfast.

Good luck…there wasn't any. We were exhausted, and both boys were limp. Finally at about 11:00 a.m. they said, "Come back tomorrow morning, we'll try again."

Once we got to the mission guest house, I called David Lundblad. "Please get us any flight but Air Zaire. If they can't start the plane, I'm not too sure they can fly it." We canceled the Nairobi stop.

The next day we flew to Athens on Sabena Airlines. After a fascinating visit to Israel, we visited my brother Dave in Spain and then arrived in Chicago at last. We had tears in our eyes as we saw he American flag flying. We had made it back to the USA!

Mission truck Congo 1972

IMELOKO

Comparing babies in the Congo 1971

Chapter 3
ELLENSBURG

Chapter 3.
ELLENSBURG

Chuck Sebastian, the chairman of the board of the Paul Carlson Foundation, and his wife hosted us in Chicago. Chuck was eager to be brought up to date on all the happenings in Zaire. Our hospital report was delivered to the board meeting in Wheaton, Illinois, and they were pleased with the progress.

We talked about our future. Some of the board members were eager for us to settle in Wheaton and work for the Medical Assistance Program there. They assured us that we wouldn't find any work out west, so we should stay there. However, after two years away, we felt eager to get back to Washington to see our families. We prayed about it and decided to go. We loved the good roads and the freedom of being home, but we wondered what kind of work we would find in Washington.

Once in Seattle, we had a great reunion with our families. Their prayers for our safe return had been answered. Bev's two brothers fed us salmon and the boys loaded up on fresh fruit and ice cream while we brought them up to date on our two-year, 25,000-mile odyssey.

After a few days, I called a friend at the state health department. I had a master's degree in public health and health services administration, which made the health department a logical place to start. After exchanging greetings, he welcomed me back from Africa and said, "There are two county environmental health director jobs open just now, one in Bellevue and one in Ellensburg. Which one would you like?"

We discussed the various aspects of the jobs. Given the rural environment and the lower population density of Ellensburg in Kittitas County, I chose that one. My friend said, "I'll arrange for you to meet the county commissioners right away."

Bev and the boys were happy with the choice, and we headed to Ellensburg for an interview with the commissioners. It went well. Being a farm boy from north central Washington helped me fit into the community, as well as understand how to deal with the area's environmental health needs.

We rented a small house near a hospital that hired Bev for a nursing position. It had been seven years since her car crash, and she no longer needed to take any medication. She began driving again, thankful for the full recovery God granted her.

I still took some Atabrine for my malaria. Because of the medicine's effects, people made comments on my strange yellowish tan. My health had definitely been mending.

Selecting a church became a priority. The nearest Covenant church, the denomination we chose after moving to Bellingham in 1967, was over 40 miles away in Yakima. We visited a Church of the Nazarene, the denomination Bev grew up in, and a Free Methodist church, the denomination I had grown up in. Neither one had the atmosphere or missions commitment we were looking for.

One day we dropped in at the Sunday service of the local Christian and Missionary Alliance (CMA) church. About 35 people filled the place. Most of them looked young, and it had an informal atmosphere. The pastor, Tim Owen, was pretty laid back, and we loved his preaching. He wore jeans and a red flannel shirt and interacted with the people informally. He knew his Bible and communicated it effectively. The people warmly welcomed us, and we left feeling pretty good about attending there. It also helped that we knew the CMA had a serious commitment to missions.

When I asked Bev what she thought, she said, "Well, it's kinda like summer camp -- you wonder how long it will last."

We had found a church home.

We found adapting to America to be easier in Ellensburg than if we had been in a more urban setting, but it still had its moments. Drew didn't have any problems. Though he missed his friends in Africa, he found new ones in Ellensburg that he loved to play with.

Matt took a while. He loved to communicate, but because of his limited ability to speak English, making friends proved difficult. On our way home we took a 747 en route to Israel, with several African gentlemen sitting behind us. Matt stood up and greeted them in Lingala. After getting no response, he tried Baka, then Banza, the languages of his playmates. When he got no response in French, I used English.

"He's been living in rural Congo and isn't sure what language you speak," I explained.

With a big smile, one of the men responded, "Well, we're from Nairobi, old chap."

Finally Matt stopped speaking and just listened. Then after a few weeks he began to speak English. He would still respond if I gave him directions in Lingala or French, but with a stern look he would say, "They don't speak that here, Dad."

Drew retained his French and later had many opportunities to use it in his own missionary career.

Bev with her Scotch heritage had loved bargaining in the African markets. One day while in a department store, she saw a leather-covered bottle in the shape of a turkey. She thought it cost 45 cents because it was on the sale table, but the clerk rang it up $4.50. "Oh!" Bev said, "I wasn't going to pay that much."

"Well," the clerk said, "how much would you pay?"

Bev thought for a moment and said, "Maybe 50 cents."

The manager came by and heard the conversation. Interested in Bev's reasoning, he joined the bargaining, which ended when Bev agreed to pay two dollars. When she told her mom about the deal she had made, her mother responded, "Oh my dear, we don't do that here in America."

"Well," Bev said, "you should. It's fun and it saves money."

I settled into my role as director of environmental health. I had a good staff, and while health standards in the county needed to be upgraded, the people were friendly for the most part and good to work with.

I also kept the campus at Central Washington University healthy and taught public health there. Some of my students became interns and environmental health officers later. We had fun no matter what we did. Whether we went on a field trip to the Olympia brewery to see food microbiology in action or tried solving the problem of a skunk trapped on campus, it didn't matter. The students loved the active participation -- not that it all came out as planned. Two of the boys dealing with the skunk succeeded in the live trapping, but they had to take time off after they put the trap in their car trunk. It took a long time for them to get rid of the smell.

We loved our church. Bev became the children's ministries leader and worked with Child Evangelism Fellowship. The group consisted of only four or five kids at first, including Drew and Matt, but as the church grew under Tim's leadership, more families came.

One of the new couples was Gordon and Jane Kelly. Gordon interned with the health department as he completed his master's degree in environmental health at Central Washington University. We drove around the county a lot, and he asked a lot of questions about our faith and our motivation in the area of missions. He had a genuine interest. They ended up coming to the church a few times, and one morning at work Gordon said, "Well, we did it."

"What?" I asked.

"Last night Jane and I discussed believing in Jesus and then got up, knelt by our bed, and did it!"

I was overjoyed to know that our mission career had not ended!

We hadn't been in Ellensburg long when someone invited us to a party to introduce new faculty at the university. At the party I met Dr. David Lundy, the new campus medical director, and his wife, Linda, a nurse. As we spoke, déjà vu overwhelmed me. I knew Linda from somewhere, but where? Then it came to me.

"You're a nurse?" I asked.

"Yes," she responded.

"Did you ever work in the ICU at the University of Washington Hospital, say in 1965?"

Her eyes widened, "Yes, oh, your wife...?"

"You took care of her!" I exclaimed.

She hesitated and said, "Did she, uh…survive?"

"Oh, yes, and we just got back from two years in Europe and Africa, where she was a nurse and pharmacist. We now have two boys as well!"

Her mouth hung open. "Where is she? I would never have believed it."

"Right over there, drinking coffee!" I indicated. It became quite a reunion!

The boys continued to grow and enjoy life in Ellensburg. Bev transferred to work at a clinic, and I did some hunting and fishing. We lived 100 miles from Bev's parents and 70 miles from mine.

One day Bev's mom said, "I'm so glad you've got the missionary business over with. Now you have a new home and a good, permanent job."

Bev looked at me. We both knew our "missionary" business had not ended. We just didn't know where or when it would begin again.

Each year our church had a missions convention, and on that particular year it started quite casually. A missionary from one of the CMA countries came to report and teach missions, but I already had an introduction to Alliance missions in the field. Gordie Fairley, our Missionary Aviation Fellowship (MAF) pilot in the Congo, had been a missionary kid raised in Gabon, and we knew a bit about the CMA through him.

One day at the university, I sat in on a discussion about how to get the school involved in international learning opportunities. I made some suggestions on what could be done. "How would we grade them?" Someone asked.

"Well," I responded, "if they go and return in one piece, give them a C. If they survive and can write a coherent description of the experience, give them a B. If they actually made a contribution to the situation, can write a coherent paper, and volunteer to go again, give them an A."

After some merry discussion, Dr. Claire Lillard, the chairman of the international program, said, "Well, Andy, when can you go set this up? Our partner country is Ecuador, and we want you to go there and negotiate a program in your field, public health!"

Shock! "Well," I said, "you'll need to convince the county commissioners to let me be away for two or three weeks."

In short order, I found myself on a plane headed for Quito, Ecuador. The Partners for the Americas had been established to increase contacts with partner countries in South America. Because of its being a U.S. Department of State program, good contacts had been put in place before I left. They liked the idea of an exchange between Central Washington University and the Ecuadorian Public Health Department. I enjoyed the flight, especially seeing the whole Panama Canal from 35,000 feet. I arrived in Quito on February 14, 1973.

After meeting Sam Height, Chief of Family Health Division for USAID, I was given a diplomatic escort and a chauffeur. A very nice start to the project! As I walked into the hotel, I got excited about being overseas again. The hotel was brand new and comfortable, which made it nice.

Language wasn't a problem during negotiations with the minister of health and the medical school. My French and some high school Spanish helped me navigate, but most of the officials spoke English. In no time we had an agreement for the first group of students to come for the summer of 1973.

I also had time to look around. JAARS, the Jungle Aviation and Radio Service, had a DC-3 flight going to Limoncocha at the headwaters of the Amazon, so I went along. After flying over the Andes at 19,000 feet in the unpressurized 1940-era plane, we splashed down on the rain-soaked jungle airstrip. The station was huge and had its own phone service and a short-wave station that reached their home base in the United States. I had a good visit with their clinic staff.

We had an interesting flight back to Quito with it being at 10,500 feet altitude and on the equator. While there, I visited a Spanish hospital that had opened in 1565! Later I visited the Spanish "Mitad del Mundo." This equator monument reminded me that we don't know everything. The Incas had designated a hill a few miles away as the middle of the world, or equator. The Spanish Conquistadores disagreed, saying that the equator was where they had built their monument. When astronauts measured from space, they found that the Incas had been right all along.

After more meetings with public health officials and seeing more CMA missions, I found myself feeling the "missionary itch."

One night at dawn in Guayaquil, I woke with my bed bouncing around the room – earthquake! I prayed, "Lord, I'm ready to meet You, but I'm not in a rush, and I have a family to go back to! Please let this pass."

It did. The next day Carl Eckdahl picked me up. We saw noticeable damage in the city, but few injuries. We met with the dean of the medical school and completed our plans for the student exchange.

On the way to the airport with Carl, we rounded a crowded corner on a green light -- bam! A drunk had staggered out of the waiting crowd, and we hit him so hard that he put a dent in the hood. Soldiers appeared. Carl said, "Pray. This may not go well."

He began to speak with the soldiers, and the drunk stood up, bleeding. Refusing any help, he staggered away to meet a friend for another drink. The soldiers shrugged their shoulders and waved us away. We praised God and drove on to the airport.

The plane took off for the United States shortly after. My head and heart were full. Not only had all the goals for the university exchange been met, but I had a very favorable impression of CMA missions in the field. Their "self governing, self-financing, self-propagating strategy" had planted a vibrant, growing, and impressive Ecuadorian church. This also pleased Bev.

The university immediately took steps to select and send the first contingent of public health students to Ecuador during the summer. The program developed very well, and our first group of students went to Ecuador a few months later.

That fall another event occurred. Chuck Fowler, a CMA missionary from Hong Kong, came as a missionary speaker. He was about my age, and I really enjoyed spending time with him. He grew up on the mission field in China and Hong Kong, a third-generation CMA missionary. After the convention, Pastor Tim and I drove him to Yakima to catch his flight. Tim wanted to go into the terminal with him, but I said firmly, "No Tim...drive!"

Later he said, "Why the reaction?"

"Tim," I said, "when I smell the jet fuel, I want to get on the plane and go!"

The Lord began setting the stage for our next step.

In 1973 World Vision started building a children's hospital in Cambodia. They asked the CMA to staff and operate the new facility. The CMA began to seek staff, starting with veteran missionaries Dr. and Mrs. Dean Kroh from Zaire.

The project came to our attention in an article placed in the March 13, 1973, issue of our denominational journal, the Alliance Witness. What caught my eye was, "Come to Cambodia. We need the following staff for the Phnom Penh Children's Hospital." It included a photo of Dr. Kroh and a couple of nurses who had already been appointed.

That evening as I sat at dinner with the family, I had Cambodia on my mind. "Did you see the article about Cambodia in the Alliance Witness today?" I asked Bev.

She looked at me for a moment and replied, "Yes! What are we going to do about it?"

"Well," I responded, "I'd better call Tim Owen."

Our Pastor Tim had seen the article, too.

"I'll contact New York," he said. "I knew this town wasn't big enough for both of us, so you should go to Cambodia."

In November 1973, we wrote to Dr. Roy Johnston, the personnel secretary of the CMA in Nyack, New York, inquiring about CMA mission opportunities like Cambodia. The more we prayed about the possibility, the more the Lord confirmed that He was leading us in this direction.

After my dad, Ray Bishop, became a Christian, the Lord pointed out a problem. He had lived as a hunter and fur trapper and loved the woods. In fact he said, "I loved hunting even more than the Lord, so He made it clear to me I should not hunt anymore."

Dad agreed and sold all his hunting equipment.

Years later he became a Free Methodist pastor in Blaine, Washington. With a large family, a small salary, and World War II just beginning, it became difficult to get by. Food was scarce, but the Lord gave my mother a solution. "Daddy," she said, "I believe you should hunt. Meat is so scarce, and these children need to eat."

My dad said, "No, I promised the Lord I wouldn't do that anymore."

Then one night he dreamed he had gone hunting near Everson. As he got out of the car, a deer stepped out. Dad shot it, and it ended up making a good meal!

The next day he told Mother about the dream, and that same day someone came to the door and gave her some money. "Daddy," she said, "here's the money for a hunting license. Now go get a license and get a deer."

Dad didn't even own a gun, so when he went to the city clerk's office to buy the license, he asked if he could borrow his .30-.30 and some shells. The clerk agreed, and Daddy got into his Model A and drove east. Near Everson he saw a logging road and followed it to a clearing. After he stepped out of the car and loaded the gun, a deer stepped out of the brush. He shot the deer. A little later, when he returned the gun to the amazed clerk, he knew the Lord would let him hunt as long as it didn't interfere with the Lord's work. God had given him clear confirmation.

We had similar feelings as we began the process that led us to Cambodia. At that time the war in Cambodia had reached a high level of action, and people avoided going there at all costs. Our friends asked us, "Why for God's sake go there?"

We responded, "Well, it is for God's sake!"

We told our families. Everyone supported us except for Bev's mom, who did not encourage us at all. But as time passed, we knew we should go. We had physicals, filled out the questionnaires, and corresponded with Dr. Kroh and Grady Mangham.

By then we knew the hospital in Phnom Penh needed to be a 50-bed facility for phase I, with supporting facilities, and a planned phase II with 74 additional beds.

By March 1974, we had finished the application process. In early

April we received a visit by Dr. Johnston and Grady Mangham, the area secretary who would be our boss if we got appointed. After our interview, Bev and I drove them to Seattle. Somewhere on the road, while Bev interrogated Dr. Johnston in the backseat, I asked Grady, "Since I'm a fairly key official in the county government, I should begin to prepare them if we are going to Cambodia. What do you think about our qualifications compared to others you are considering?"

Grady sat quietly for a bit and then said, "If you two are serious, you're the only ones qualified!"

On May 8th, Dr. Johnston confirmed by phone that we had been given an appointment to the hospital in Cambodia, contingent on our passing the physical exams. The possibility of getting malaria still concerned me, but confirmation from the Lord came one day while in the office. We received a report from the World Health Organization that Phnom Penh had become malaria free. One less concern!

World Vision contacted me and asked me to meet Dr. Warner, their medical director, at the Weyerhaeuser warehouse in Tacoma, Washington, to select equipment for the hospital. I selected 9 tons of equipment and suggested they sell the other 18 tons for scrap. We had dinner with C. David Weyerhaeuser, and he invited Bev and me to come to Tacoma to speak to his church group.

We began getting calls to speak, and I had a meeting with the county commissioners. They gave me a warm endorsement for our plans and told me to work until I left and that they would pay me for any vacation accrued. We agreed that if Gordon Kelly could finish his master's degree by the time we left, he would be the one most likely to get my position. On June 20, 1974, we were appointed to Cambodia with a January 1975 departure date. I would be the hospital administrator, and Bev would be the nurse and pharmacist.

When the CMA had their annual church council in Atlanta, I asked Tim Owen to go with me. I wanted to see more of the CMA since we were going to serve in Cambodia under them. We sold our car to get the money, and the church sent Tim. I took him out to buy a new sport coat and tie.

In Atlanta we met Chuck and Midge Fowler and a number of other missionaries, as well as Dr. Nathan Bailey, president of the CMA, and Dr. Louis King, vice president for overseas ministries. We enjoyed all the meetings and discussions and invited the Fowler family to come visit our family in Ellensburg. I knew Bev and I would both get a lot of questions answered, and our boys would benefit from talking to their kids about life in Asia and the boarding school.

We sold our home, moved into an apartment at the university, and Bev and I made a trip to New York to have a final sit-down with Grady Mangham, Dr. L.L. King, Dr. Johnston, and the others we planned to work with. They had some questions about Bev's health and medical history, but thankfully she was cleared for travel. We began correspondence with Cambodia Field Chairman Gene Hall and Dr. Carl Roseveare at Dalat School in Malaysia, where our boys would go to school.

Outfit lists and packing and shipping instructions flowed in. Drew even got a photo of the style of haircut the government required him to have in Malaysia.

Finally in late October, just after my 37th birthday, our travel itinerary arrived. As requested, we had a stopover for a few days in Hawaii and Hong Kong. The war brought a high level of hostility, both in Cambodia and via war protesters in our nation. Everyone filled out and sent in their visa applications and prepared to fly out of Seattle on January 6. We filed our "Last Will and Testament" and proceeded on faith in spite of some feelings of disquiet. News of the war flooded radio and television, but we knew that the safest place for us to be was in the center of God's will. This challenged us to put the truth of that statement to the test.

As the Lord led us on our journey, He confirmed it in various ways. We sold our house, paid off all our debts, and even received unsolicited financial gifts as people came to know about our destination.

During our final Christmas service, Pastor Tim Owen said, "This year, give your very best gift to the Lord. The best you have."

We were only days from heading into the war zone, and I knew my ability to protect my family wouldn't be enough, so I took Drew and Matt up to the altar and dedicated them to the Lord, placing them under His protection. I felt a great sense of God's relief and confirmation that He had indeed accepted the gift and would care for all of us. Bev wasn't able to attend the service due to work.

A few days later, with a wonderful send-off by our Ellensburg friends, we boarded the train for Seattle. We spent some time with our family and then boarded Northwest Airlines flight 95 bound for Hawaii. Our journey had begun.

Rev. Fred King met us in Hawaii and invited us to speak at a Bible study for military officers at Pearl Harbor. We said, "Okay," and then spent time on the beach and visiting places we knew from my time at the university eight years before. Matt loved it! Drew did, too, since he had gone to kindergarten there.

Not only was Fred the CMA pastor, but he was also the chaplain for the Honolulu police force. When he came to take us to Pearl Harbor for the Bible study, he arrived in a police car. This amazed the boys! We had a great evening, and our willingness to go to Cambodia impressed the officers because they had been doing all they could to stay away from Asia. One officer, Duane Wheeland, had been so moved that he offered to be the hospital financial officer. We heard more from him later.

Chuck Fowler met up with us in Hong Kong. We had a great time and loved the city. From the very low approach through the city to the landing field, to the ferries and sampans in the harbor and the restaurants with great food and stores bulging with exotic goods, we loved every moment!

We received a lot of help from David Sensmeier, the mission business agent. He helped us purchase the washing machine and refrigerator that we shipped to Cambodia.

After a few days there, we went to confirm our onward travel to Cambodia on Air Cambodge. Chuck Fowler had designated them "Air Pandemonium." They said, "January 17, perhaps."

As the war closed in on Phnom Penh, anticipation filled our hearts.

Leaving Ellensburg for Cambodia

Chapter 4
PHNOM PENH

Chapter 4.
PHNOM PENH

It was a beautiful morning on January 17, 1975, in Hong Kong. As we sat on the Air Cambodge Caravel, we waited for clearance to depart for Phnom Penh. Unbeknownst to us, the "slight delay" the captain announced had been a rocket attack going on at the Pochentong Airport.

We sat in the back of the plane and saw boxes strapped to the floor ahead of us, as well as crates of cargo filled with items that the people in Phnom Penh desperately needed.

Air Cambodge was the only international airline servicing Cambodia at that time. The U.S. state department explained that other airlines did not want to subject passengers to the potential dangers of landing at the Cambodian airport unless they actually wanted to go there.

That was an understatement.

When clearance came, we didn't waste any time getting airborne. As we climbed out over Hong Kong Harbor, we wondered what awaited us in Phnom Penh. We flew down the coast of Vietnam, where heavy fighting raged. We knew the country would not hold out much longer. Our government had decided that further resistance was no longer a U.S. problem and voted to cut off involvement. Then we turned west over Saigon.

As we followed the Mekong River toward Phnom Penh, we passed the river port of Neak Leung and saw smoke from the fighting below. Then suddenly we went into a tight descending spiral and saw the sprawling city of Phnom Penh where the Bassac River joined the Mekong River below us. Gunships escorted us along the steep descent, and the pilot came on the intercom as we leveled to land.

"We'll taxi into a bunker, deplane quickly, and go to the terminal," he announced. "We will get your luggage to you when we can."

The plane quickly parked in a huge, blast-resistant enclosure built of ammunition crates filled with sand. People scrambled off and ran for the battle-scarred terminal.

Instead of having a lineup to get passports stamped at a window, everyone crowded into a windowless terminal where a small group of Cambodians wearing steel helmets peered over sandbagged enclosures. "Go, go," they shouted, "we will see to your passports later!"

Gene Hall, the missions director, welcomed us in the customs room and then quickly ushered us to the mission car and drove to the city. Buildings by the terminal had gaping holes, some still smoldering. "It's from the rocket attack," Gene explained matter of factly. "There are more of them all the time."

We thought, Where was that information in the description of the ministry site in the application?

In the center of God's will is the safest place ran through my mind, as it would many more times in the coming days.

As we drove into town on a road filled with shell holes, we passed ponds covered with huge water lilies. We saw bamboo and thatch shacks everywhere. Gene explained that the normal one million population had grown to over two million as refugees fled the battle-scarred countryside. The city had become extremely over crowded.

Phnom Penn's buildings had an art deco, French colonial flare much like Kinshasa, complete with patches of mold, but in spite of the war the city remained in much better condition than the African cities. The streets were cleaner and always crowded with vehicles of all kinds, including army trucks, tanks, and cyclos (the three-wheeled personal taxis peddled by their drivers). You could feel the sense of urgency in the people moving around the streets.

We made a brief stop at the hospital, where we saw workers busily finishing the roof, building the generator room, clearing brush, and exerting more effort than was usual in Africa.

Suddenly a gaggle of naked four- to six-year-old kids rushed through a hole in the fence to scrounge the trash pile. "Oh, look," cried Matt, "streakers!"

We ended up seeing thousands more of these kids. Some came in as refugees, some as orphans, but all kept busy scrounging to survive.

Finally we arrived at the Alliance guest house at 72 Norodome Street. They took our bags to a big, airy room with several beds and mosquito nets on the second floor. We had a late lunch, and then Gene gave us a grim briefing. He explained, "The Khmer Rouge, or the communists, hold a lot of the east bank of the Mekong River. That makes us in line for rockets fired into the city. Fortunately, they're so close the rockets fly over us and impact farther in town. You will hear swooshing, whistling sounds tonight because the rockets come at 1:00-2:00 a.m. to terrorize the city. Don't be alarmed; they usually don't land here."

We found ourselves filled with mixed emotions. Dr. Kroh, the medical director, came in and told us about the ongoing work. He and several nurses had been doing mobile medical work in the refugee camps that surrounded the city and filled every open space. They did all they could, considering the terrible conditions.

Bev and I needed to get settled and push ahead on the completion of the hospital. I had to finish writing the policies, procedures, and job descriptions and begin the interviews for staff. Bev needed to prepare the pharmacy, and we both had to help push the construction. All of us worked together to select a hospital board.

Dr. Kroh and the nurses conducted a crash course in nursing for a group of 21 Cambodian men and women. Once they graduated, we put them to work practicing among the refugees while others completed the hospital construction.

Sure enough, the rockets came at about 2:00 a.m. Wheee...osh... crash! I prayed as they kept going over us. "In the center of God's will is safest...?"

Yes! We experienced this night after night and never got used to it. Seeing the sun come up always made us happy!

We got a tour of the town the next morning and saw flowering trees and palaces. The port, choked with small boats that had been blockaded in Phnom Penh due to the fighting, fascinated us. The small ships and barges that made it through the gauntlet of communist ambushes were battle scarred. We saw that their bridges had been heaped with sandbags and wire netting to set off rocket-propelled grenades before they could penetrate. The big Japanese bridge built over the Bassac River had the middle spans missing.

We drove by the U.S. embassy, which also had wire nets and sandbags for rocket protection. We saw bunkers at every main intersection, with machine guns poking out and very serious soldiers manning them. We began to realize that the city was fighting for its life.

The open markets had produce and piles of fruit, while the little street restaurants and food carts sold noodles, rice, and soup. We soon learned not to ask too much about the origin of the meat in the noodles. As the number of critters in town decreased, all creatures became fair game. We just made sure to cook the food well.

In the evening of our second day, the mission team welcomed us. This included Dr. Dean and Esther Kroh, Gene and Carol Hall, Ruth Patterson, Norm and Marie Ens, Mr. and Mrs. Jean Jacques Piaget, Barbara Neath, Mary Lou Rorabaugh, Lynn Walsh, and Carol Weston. They came from many places, including the U.S., Canada, and Switzerland, but were united by service in Cambodia. A hymn sung by the group, Work for the Night Is Coming, was more prophetic than we realized. We had an optimistic outlook that somehow things would work out and that we would see everything through.

Other missions came under the auspices of the CMA. Overseas Mission Fellowship (OMF) had Alice Compain, Rose Ellen Chancey, Don Cormack, and others. All were keenly aware that the night was coming, so everyone stayed focused on teaching, training, and preparing the Cambodians for the future.

Cambodia had been experiencing a movement to Christ unlike any other since the first missionaries, the Arthur Hammonds, came in 1923. American missionaries had to leave for a while in the 1960s, but French CMA missionaries had permission to stay. By 1971 they worked together with the U.S., Canadian, and European missionaries, and many people turned to Christ.

Mass evangelism by people like Stan Mooneyham of World Vision and Ravi Zacharias of the CMA had packed the Olympic Stadium. Thousands had stood outside in a religious response unseen in the history of normally Buddhist Cambodia.

All the missionaries immersed themselves in teaching new believers, training pastors, and printing and distributing Christian materials. Others busily "dispensed" Christ through the mobile medical outreach.

Cliff Westergren, who had spent nine years in Cambodia setting up the CMA Cambodian publishing business, came in from Hong Kong to assess needs and make arrangements with the Bible Society and the Gideons to procure more Bibles. In fact, one of the last boats to make it through the communist blockade carried a large shipment of Bibles, which got distributed quickly.

At the hospital, we sorted through the equipment and supplies that made it through. At some point our washer and refrigerator from Hong Kong got flown in from Kompong Som. We left the refrigerator at the hospital because World Vision had purchased it from us, and the washing machine went to our home because we had been washing clothes by hand.

Being only five and a half years old at the time, Matt stayed close to Bev. He had figured out that because of her being totally deaf in one ear, she could not tell directions, so when rockets or bullets flew, she didn't know which way to duck. Matt became her range finder and quickly learned the difference between incoming and outgoing fire, and even the type of weapon being fired, by its sound. The soldiers guarding the hospital gave him a helmet with a big Red Cross symbol on it.

Drew and the other MKs prepared to leave for their four-month stay at Dalat School in Penang, Malaysia, and Bev busily sewed name tags in the clothes he planned to take. He loved to travel, and he couldn't wait to start. He had his KLM carry-on bag and a three-foot piece of sugar cane to snack on as they waited to fly to Bangkok to join a larger group of MKs en route to Dalat.

We had a "no tears until the plane is gone" policy. When the plane took off, the eyes could start leaking. That helped us deal with the separations over the years.

After this, we moved into a two-story house at 207 Hem Cheav. It was about a mile from the guest house, out of "rocket alley," and several blocks from the U.S. embassy -- where most of the artillery and rockets went. There was a fire base about six blocks away, near the Independence Monument, with the counter-fire radar and big 155 and 105 cannons that fired at communist positions across the Mekong. When they launched rockets into the city, the cannons thundered their response, shaking the house. It was classic arrows by day and terror by night.

Sometimes Matt would wake us and say, "They're coming. We need to get in the shower."

The shower was in the middle of the house, and many cement walls separated us from the outside. Bev cowered with us as rockets flew and artillery pounded. "I can't take anymore! We must leave in the morning," she would say.

But in the morning the sun would warm our porch, Sopha our helper would make coffee, and a boy with fresh-baked bread would ride up banging the metal bread box with a stick and yelling "Pain, pain" (French for bread).

As we ate the fresh bread and drank the fresh coffee, Bev would say, "Well, let's stay one more day."

After breakfast I would climb onto the flat roof, three stories up, and check on where the smoke from fighting was. Then we would head out for another day at the hospital.

At that time the hospital board included Gene Hall, Dean Kroh, John Kwong, Son Sonne of the Cambodian Bible Society, Major Taing Chhirc of the national church, and Minh Thien Voan of World Vision. Al Gjerde, the World Vision builder, was a wizard at scrounging supplies and materials in the war-torn city, so the construction work moved quickly.

On January 26, Drs. Bob Beck and Chuck Folkestad arrived to swell our ranks. They had finished medical school and were waiting to start their internship. Rather than vacation, they chose short-term service in Cambodia, where people desperately needed their help.

Bob was a Vietnam War veteran and knew what to expect. Chuck, built like a professional linebacker, came to serve in spite of the danger. At 6'6", Chuck became known as "two Cambodians tall." Both men set about helping unpack and install the x-ray and surgical equipment and helped Bev with the pharmacy. They also pitched in with Dr. Kroh and the nurses to help the mobile team deliver care in the refugee camps. Our days were full, and we always had more work than time to do it!

As the communist noose tightened around the city, river traffic became more sporadic, and rice and ammunition had to come by air. The approach to the airport brought planes over the hospital, where we worked in the morning. We could often hear shelling in the distance and subconsciously waited for the first Flying Tigers DC-8 to pass over to land. It always encouraged us. If we heard them flying, we knew that things would hold on for the day.

More than 500 people were killed by rockets in January 1975. The workers covered the bodies with a grass mat until a pickup crew came to carry them away. Then someone would scrub away the blood, and life would go on. Holes in buildings were quickly patched and painted over, part of a concerted effort to keep some level of order in the city.

The battle for the river continued. On one particular night, we could hear it clearly at our house. A ship pulling a barge, escorted by heavily armored gunboats, fought through the blockade set up only a few miles down the Mekong from Phnom Penh.

The next morning, I stopped by the floating dock where they tied up the gunboats. I went on board and heard a Cambodian sailor's tale of point-blank fighting. He told it while washing the blood of a slain shipmate off the deck.

Kaboom! The explosion came so close that water splashed on us. As we hit the deck I thought, Oh, no! The Khmer Rouge have the boat's range. Kaboom! More water over us, but I had not heard any incoming sounds. Cautiously, I peeked over the side. There, floating on an eight-foot piece of a Styrofoam box used to ship bombs, sat two kids about nine and ten years old. Half a dozen hand grenades lay at their feet. As they pulled the pin to drop the next grenade into the water to kill fish, the Cambodian sailor shouted, "Stop, go somewhere else!"

They calmly put the pin back in the grenade, collected their dead fish, and paddled away to a less-populated fishing spot.

Drs. Bob Beck, Chuck Folkestad, Dean Kroh, and the medical team were exhausted. All day long, block-long lines waited with dying children and very sick adults trying to get medicine. By the end of the exhausting days, the lines seemed just as long, and more kids died in spite of everyone's best efforts. The national church workers gave out food, mats, materials for building shelters, mosquito nets, and cooking utensils. Refugees came in all sizes, usually with just the clothes on their backs. They told of genocide being committed by the troops of Pol Pot, the Khmer Rouge leader. No one was spared. When a village fell, everyone died.

The city was surrounded, the river route had been cut, and people could travel only by air. The airport got hit by rockets, mortars, and artillery on a regular basis. With fuel being scarce, electricity needed to be rationed, and each section of the city got an hour or two at a time. Yet no one wanted to think about leaving.

At night we left the light switch on when we went to bed so that if electricity did materialize, we would wake up and Bev could do the laundry. More than once she washed clothes and hung them on the line on our roof while rockets shrieked overhead. Then when morning came she would say, "Well, one more day."

However, we began to get letters from the U.S. embassy. They wrote, "The embassy wishes to express its concern for your well being and safety. As you are aware, hostilities are now taking place only a few kilometers from the city, and rocketing of the airport has curtailed flights."

Air Cambodge came in sporadically, and the Flying Tigers, Bird Air, and a host of "one plane airlines" (usually old DC-3s) supplied the city. One of the planes had so many bullet holes that we nicknamed it the "flying harmonica" as it wailed over us.

On February 14 we received a letter informing us that the embassy had evacuated all its dependents to Bangkok and urged others to do the same. They offered space-available travel on the embassy cargo plane. It did not seem like Valentine's Day. We prayed and stayed one more day.

Student anti-government marches and Khmer Rouge infiltrators entered the city, so we could feel the heightening tensions. One afternoon as I approached a checkpoint, a motorbike with two young Cambodians on it sped past me, not even slowing for the soldier who tried to stop them to check their documents. When he realized they weren't stopping, the soldier drew his gun and began to fire. I swerved out of the way while the motorbike raced around the corner amid flying bullets.

Another night we were late getting back to our house from the guest house. Suddenly a blinding light from a helicopter above pinpointed our car. I stopped at once. Bev, Matt, and Lynn Walsh froze as a screaming soldier ran up and said, "You're late. There is curfew! I almost shot you. Go home!"

Then he called to the checkpoint ahead to clear the way, and we got home safely. One more day.

Finally a registered letter that Bev had to sign for came, advising her to leave ASAP. We discussed it with Dr. Kroh and Gene Hall, and they agreed that Bev and Matt should go. I decided to continue on at the hospital as long as possible.

On February 22, we loaded into my VW Beetle and drove to the airport. Lynn Walsh, a nurse who lived upstairs in our home, came along. The plane, a Curtis C-46 built in 1943, was a tough old bird. We said our good byes and watched it depart for Bangkok in a cloud of dust.

We had just seen 21 nurse assistants graduate from the program Dr. Kroh and his team had taught. It felt like a race against time to put them to work in the refugee camps and clinics while we finished the hospital.

Bev and Matt arrived safely in Bangkok on a Saturday. We had planned a wheelchair church meeting at our house the next day. Bev had wanted to stay to fix a meal for the soldiers from their military hospital, but she'd had to leave. We sent out the small taxi trucks as planned. Rev. Reach Yea, assisted by Yourng Soth, a young pastoral student, stayed at our compound with Yourng's family. More than 40 amputees attended. The church had grown from a Bible study at the nearby military hospital.

One Sunday night, Gene Hall summoned all of us to the guest house. With a trembling voice, he read the telegram that ordered all personnel under CMA responsibility to temporarily depart from the Khmer Republic to Bangkok. After a special security briefing, Drs. Nathan Bailey and Louis L. King decided that we all needed to leave. This especially shocked those who had spent so many years in challenging ministry. They had seen the "Son rise." Within four years, the number of churches had grown from 4 to 23, with more than 8,000 new believers. Yet now we had five days to get ready to go.

The desperate need of the people, especially the refugees, weighed heavily on the medical staff, and all we could do was pray. Gene Hall called Dr. Kroh and me into his study. We could hear rockets landing in the city. "Dean," he said, "do you know where I put that emergency evacuation plan? We looked at it a while back, but I can't find it."

I thought, Oh boy, they don't have a plan?

"Well," Gene said, "Andy, you go to Air Cambodge tomorrow and get tickets. Dean, you and I will meet with the church leaders."

The church leaders were in full agreement with the directive from our leaders. They said, "You should go while you can. You have prepared us for this time. We want you safe. We live here, and besides, the communists won't know that we know you if you are gone when they come."

I went to the Air Cambodge office, and the line at the office door was literally a mile long. People desperate to leave the city offered to pay anything. The Khmer riel had gone from 400 per dollar when we came to over 11,000 riels to the dollar. You could only purchase tickets with dollars, and even then there was no guarantee the flight would leave. Time for plan B. I went to the U. S. embassy.

The embassy had said in its "go letters" that they would "assist Americans with transport as far as Bangkok for a limited time." I spoke with Mr. John Rieger at the embassy. He listened as I explained the evacuation order and looked at his list of places available during the next five days. "Twenty-six people…CMA, OMF, Campus Crusade. How about Thursday, the 27th? You could have the whole plane!"

We discussed logistics and security, and he said we shouldn't come to the airport until we received a notification. Then we were to come and get aboard quickly. We would save a lot of money because the embassy flight would be free.

From 1960 on, when the French had eliminated missionary visas as they expired, a number of temporary evacuations had taken place, but this one seemed more final. The communist night began to close in.

On the 27th we assembled at the OMA guest house, and once the word came we raced to the airport and into the sandbagged bunker that had become the "departure lounge." Camouflaged C-130s of Bird Air roared in and out nonstop, bringing ammunition and other essentials. Great Flying Tiger DC-8s screeched in, unloaded tons of rice and other essentials, and then made seemingly impossibly short takeoffs, climbing at impossible angles to escape the enemy gunners. In between, T28 fighter bombers and helicopters roared out with loads of bombs to attack the enemy.

All the action was punctuated by a siren that announced incoming ordinance! We knew a brave soldier was in a deep bunker off the end of the runway. When he heard a rocket fire or a mortar go off, he pressed the button on the siren that gave 15 to 20 seconds for us to duck behind sandbags.

The morning that the embassy C-46 came in was quiet, thankfully. We quickly loaded our light luggage into the plane and got aboard. It seemed we all held our breath while the plane roared down the runway and off to Bangkok.

After arrival at the guest house and a reunion with Matt and Bev, we learned that Betty Mitchell, the Phillipses, and several others had been captured by the North Vietnamese at Ban Me Thuot in Viet Nam. We didn't know anything of them at the time. This no doubt had influenced the decision to bring everyone out. Years before, Archie Mitchell and two others had been taken at Ban Me Thuot and disappeared. No one ever found Archie.

The days following our arrival in Bangkok were special. The CMA sent all of us to a wonderful hotel, The Rose Garden. We had 24-hour electricity, hot water, ice cream, and a very restful decompression. We also had times of Bible study and prayer. Matt loved the animals at the Garden, especially the baby elephant -- just his size.

We did not receive good news from Phnom Penh. Several more cities fell to the communists. Cargo planes got shot down, and the needs in the city escalated.

One night we had a big loud Thai thunder and lightning storm. Matt came in rubbing his eyes and asked, "Dad, are they throwing rockets again?"

"No," I replied, "it's only a thunderstorm."

"Okay," he said as he headed back for his bed.

On March 20, 1975, the U.S. embassy requested that some of us return to Phnom Penh to try to complete the hospital. An enormous number of people needed medical care.

Drs. Folkestad and Beck left on the embassy plane, and when we agreed, the embassy scheduled us for Saturday, March 22. Due to the danger, only Gene Hall, Jean Jacques Piaget, and I went. In a letter to my friend Gordon Kelly I said, "I'm scared, but this is where I'm to be."

Bev and I prayed a lot.

When the C-46 touched down in Phnom Penh on the 22nd, we saw Drs. Beck and Folkestad waiting. I took a few steps down from the plane then heard "Siren!"

"Down!" Bob screamed.

I threw my bags toward the car and dived under it. Jean Jacques and Gene hugged the tarmac. The rocket landed 50 yards away, and shrapnel buzzed overhead. Bob Beck had rolled in under the car from the other side. "How's it going, Bob?" I asked.

Boom! Another rocket landed nearby. "A lot like this," Bob replied.

When we got the all-clear signal, we crawled swiftly out from under the car and crowded ourselves into it. Hulks of burned-out or scavenged aircraft littered the airfield. The car we leaped into sped out of the target area and wove around gaping craters. We hoped we could avoid a flat tire from the razor-sharp shrapnel that lay everywhere.

Things moved rapidly at the hospital. World Vision and the Red Cross hoped to get surgical teams in, and the Olympic Stadium became the medical triage and emergency surgery center.

When we drove there to see how things worked, it looked like a scene from Dante's Inferno. I climbed onto the bleachers to get a better perspective. A teenaged Cambodian lay beside me on the bench. A breeze ruffled his hair. He looked peaceful, perhaps asleep. I realized he had died, but they had left him unmarked. He had been brought in on a med-evac helicopter from Neak Leung and had a thumb-sized hole under his armpit from shrapnel. About a hundred more lay in the makeshift morgue. Helicopters disgorged the wounded on the soccer field. At the side entry, Jeeps with piles of stretchers unloaded their suffering cargo. The silence made it seem like an old movie.

On the center court, medics moved among the wounded. Using felt tip pens, they wrote instructions on foreheads. They selected some for immediate surgery in the locker rooms, sent some to an aid station that could stitch and patch on site, and assigned others to get transported to different medical facilities. They moved the rest onto the bleachers, where family members stumbled among them trying to find the body of a loved one. They pronounced some "dead on arrival," and others died soon after being deposited on the bleachers. You could hear the sound of rockets, artillery, and helicopters outside.

We had to get the hospital open. We still needed some things, but we could use a few of the rooms to treat children right away.

I attended meetings of the emergency medical committee. The loud fighting came very close to us. Cambodiana, Prince Sihanouk's unfinished luxury hotel on the riverbank, became a six-story refugee camp for more than 7,000 refugees. They had a daily clinic there, as well as in a number of other places.

Drs. Penny Key, Folkestad, and Beck worked nonstop to aid the endless stream of dying humanity. Word came that the World Vision team and the Red Cross surgical team could not come into the country. That left the Catholic Relief Service (CRS) people as the only ones who could use the hospital. After lengthy discussions, they agreed to employ our staff. I became head of the hospital for CMA, and CRS put their doctors into the mix. Beck and Folkestad eagerly waited to help. Our last meeting to finalize details was held under a heavy conference table at the CRS office while shells rained down and plaster and glass flew. We knew time was running out.

Jean Jacques and Gene Hall worked hard to get the church leaders ready. They had been instructed by CMA headquarters in New York to send a few leaders out of the country until it was safe again. Some pastors already had death threats sent to them. However, after a meeting among themselves they said, "You must go, but we must stay. When the wolf comes upon the sheep, the shepherd cannot leave."

This deeply moved me. Most of them would not survive the coming holocaust.

Rumors told us the enemy was at the gates and could take the city at any time. A big thunderstorm brought a pause in hostilities. The wind slashed the city, and monsoon rains flooded the streets and the region. Trees got ripped out of the ground and fell in the streets. As the storm lessened, people swarmed the fallen trees with all kinds of cutting instruments. The city was out of wood, gas, charcoal, and any other cooking fuel. The flooded roads and rice paddies kept the Khmer Rouge from entering the city for a few more days.

On the last Sunday of the wheelchair church, more than 100 men came, plus 50 or so kids. Yourng Soth and his wife helped Gene Hall and Reach Yea with the service. It was Easter, April 6. We brought all the wheelchairs and crutches from the hospital to give to the soldiers who needed them.

I gave all the storehouse keys to Pastor Soth and told him to give away what was inside to anyone in need. Things such as canned goods and clothes were given to the Christians for distribution.

We had a blessed Easter service. We didn't know for sure, but we suspected it would be our last week in the city. It was the soldiers' last service. Within 10 or 12 days, most would be butchered by the victorious Khmer Rouge.

The next day, Al Gjerde came by the hospital. We were nearly ready for the opening. "I'm leaving; my work is done," he told me.

Flying Tigers flew over on its way to deliver the rice we needed. The lifeline was still open.

The shelling went on. One landed in the yard of the French school, killing and maiming dozens of kids. A rocket hit the World Vision compound, narrowly missing Dr. Penny Key. Another hit the fruit market, killing many. Ambassador Dean upped the security briefings and urged nonessential staff to begin an orderly departure.

I had lunch with Gene Hall and Jean Jacques Piaget. We talked about departure. Boom! A rocket hit the house next door. Kaboom, another hit the street. "I think you should set up our departure for Friday," Gene said.

Jean Jacques said, "Well, I'm Swiss, so I think I can stay."

"Remember Maria and your children," Gene said.

After lunch, I stopped by the embassy to put our names on Friday's departure list.

In another meeting held under tables, Dr. Dee Garcia of CRS and I worked out a final plan for joint operation of the hospital even after we had gone. We continued to believe optimistically that the communists would at least let the hospitals continue to operate. Dr. Garcia said they would staff the hospital beginning on April 15. We would remember those meetings years later as we again teamed up to deliver medical care to refugees.

Thursday afternoon, as the tempo of fighting increased, Jean Jacques told Gene Hall, "I think I must go now, too."

"What can we do?" Gene asked me.

"He will take my seat tomorrow," I said. "I'm here under the embassy's care, so I'll get out okay."

Bob Beck, Chuck Folkestad, and I played Risk that evening. It's a game where you move armies and try to conquer the world. The "real world" war could be heard in the background. Helicopter gunships swooped over the guest house as they fired at the communist lines a little over a mile away. Chuck showed us a large shopping bag of colorful Cambodian money, which he announced would be used with his Monopoly set when he got home. Home seemed a long way away.

I left to get home before curfew. Not long after I arrived, a terrific barrage of artillery and rocket fire descended on the city. The guest house got shaken, but my area did not. The next day, as we sent Gene Hall and Jean Jacques off to the airport, I asked, "Who won the game last night?"

"We didn't finish because when the shelling started, we had to spend the rest of the night under the cement stairs. How about you?"

"They left my area alone and I slept," I said.

Bob advised, "Tonight move over to where we're staying, at World Vision, because they have guards."

I agreed. The radio announced the convoy to the airport was starting out for the airport, so Gene and Jean Jacques left.

We had another busy day. We ate dinner in a small restaurant with a mixed group of relief workers and discussed how much time remained. Suddenly, while listening to the embassy channel on the radio, we heard "Tango, Tango, Tango." Silence filled the room. This code told us the evacuation of all personnel would begin the next morning. One of the men left immediately to get details from the embassy.

I went back to 207 Hem Cheav. Bev had made one request before I left Thailand. She'd said she couldn't find any underwear in Thailand that fit right and remembered that she had left her good underwear at our house in Phnom Penh. So I packed my carry-on bag with Bev's underwear. It was a loud, long night, and someone stole the rear window out of my VW Beetle.

The heat and humidity at the airport felt oppressive. We huddled in the sandbagged bunker with its sign saying, "Welcome to Phnom Penh." A cargo DC-6 got hit by the runway, but they pushed it out of the way so that other aircraft could continue to arrive and depart. In the military area one-half mile away, C-130s loaded with supplies continued to arrive and depart. A Flying Tigers DC-8 got hit by one of the shells landing in the area of frantic activity. It completed its unloading and, with fuel streaming out of a wing tip, roared off to Saigon. A big four-engine Carvair cargo plane roared off amid exploding shells. Smoke streamed from one engine as it climbed away.

Finally the trusty embassy C-46 rumbled to a stop. The load master began to call out our names. We climbed in and found a seat. I sat next to Time magazine correspondent David Aikman. Bob Beck and Chuck Folkestad sat behind us.

They overstuffed the plane, and as we roared down the runway, shells landed nearby. The plane staggered off, sank back, lifted again, sagged back to the tarmac, and finally gained enough altitude to raise the landing gear. Trees and flooded rice paddies flashed under us as we lumbered off, trying to gain altitude. Some cheered. One of the World Vision guys left his seat to pour coffee from a Thermos as I rose to take a photo. Rinngg! A warning bell sounded. "Everyone sit," shouted one of the crew. "We are overloaded and not well balanced with 53 people on a 38-passenger plane." We weren't home free yet.

Later, though, as we descended to the Bangkok airport, my mind turned to the thought, What will customs think if they open my bag and see all of Bev's underwear? But I cleared customs with no problem.

At the guest house I was told, "Bev and Matt are in Penang with Drew." So I took the train to join them that same afternoon.

That night as I slept on the train, I suddenly heard boom, boom, boom! I woke up trying to get under my bunk. Turns out the train was only crossing a bridge, but it sounded almost like mortar shells exploding nearby. I went back to sleep exhausted, as well as thankful to be safe and en route to my family. God had protected us as He had promised, and He proved to us that the safest place to be truly was in the center of His will.

Dr. Bob Beck and Andy waiting for evacuation
from Phnour Penh airport in April 1975

Cambodia Rev. Yea The wheelchair church Easter 1975

Phnom Penh 1975, Hotel Cambodiana, a refugee camp of 7000⁺

Matt and friend at the Rose Garden in Thailand 1975

Lynn Walsh, Bev and Matt waiting to board
the evacuation flight, Feb. 22 1975

Chapter 5
A New Thing ~ Part 1

Chapter 5.
A New Thing ~ Part 1

Many of the kids whose parents lived in harm's way attended the beautiful Dalat School in Penang, Malaysia, on the shore of the Strait of Malacca. It was a long way from the war.

We heard of the embassy staff evacuation by helicopter from Phnom Penh and of the Khmer Rouge's entrance into the city. The terror for Cambodia was underway. At Dalat we enjoyed the quiet, the food, uninterrupted electricity, and fellowship with the Halls, the Ens, and other missionaries who visited their children during Easter break. We had not received any word from Betty Mitchell and the others taken captive in Vietnam. Their children attended Dalat School.

One of the teachers, Mr. Klippenger, got sick, so for a couple of weeks I became a 7th grade teacher. Drew remembers that they saw lots of movies and heard stories. On the last day, they didn't even have a teacher. I thought Klippenger was going to be there, and he thought I was, so neither of us showed up. The kids loved it!

At that time, we weren't sure of our next step. The collapse of Vietnam meant that the CMA had to evacuate two of its major mission fields, and suddenly refugee missionaries scattered every direction. Word came from New York that we could go home or stay until our next assignment. Grady Mangham mentioned helping with Maranatha Clinic in northeast Thailand. They had problems that our experience might help solve.

Someone said, "Did you misread God's directions? You sold everything to come to Cambodia, and now it's all gone."

We did not feel that way. In fact, one devotional in Isaiah 43 stood out: "Forget the things past… for behold I'm going to do a new thing." That resonated with Bev and me. We didn't know what God was going to do, but we wanted to be where He was working.

Matt asked Bev, "Mom, how did you, me, Drew, and Dad all get together?"

"Andy," Bev said, "you need to explain this to him."

"Well, Matt," I began, "after your mom and I got married, we…"

"No, Dad, I know that," he said, tears beginning to come. "Are we always going to be together? I don't ever want to be alone."

"Ah," I replied, "that's why we have Jesus. Even after your mother and I get old and pass on, you will have Jesus if you ask Him to be with you always."

As we knelt by the bed, Matt asked Jesus to be his Savior and to always be with him. In all the uncertainty, he had gained one constant to depend on.

We waited for the issuance of visas so we could go back to Bangkok to work out the next phase of our missionary lives.

We soon received a telegram from "Ting Verplanke." The phone number on the telegram was from a Bangkok hotel. It was May 9, and Bev planned to go back to Bangkok with Matt the next day. Their visa was already issued, so we decided she should go and make the contact with Ting. My visa was ready the next day, so Gene Hall and I flew to Bangkok.

I met "Vim," not Ting, Verplanke from "The Dutch Committee for Helping South Vietnam." His group had worked with the CMA among the Vietnamese hill tribes and was ready to help with more refugees. I remembered a conversation with Gene Evans from the CMA in Penang. He vaguely mentioned what our next work might be, but he didn't know for sure because he was a refugee, too. Now here was a Dutch committee who thought this was to be my work.

"We want you to be our representative in Asia," he explained.

"I'll have to phone my boss in New York," I told him, "as I've not received definite word on this yet."

We talked more, and I suggested they change their name to "Committee for Helping South East Asia," because there would be refugees from all over and we couldn't focus on just one group. We agreed to meet again the next day, when I would hopefully know more.

That evening I went to Bangkok Telephone Center and called New York. I called person-to-person to Grady Mangham -- collect. Since the calls in those days cost $50 for three minutes, I decided that if they accepted the call, they were interested in what I had to say. As I waited for the call to go through, I prayed, "Lord, is this the new thing?"

When Grady answered, I sketched out developments and my meeting with the Dutch. Grady listened and then said, "Wait a moment."

About a minute passed, then he came back and said, "You have been appointed the director of CAMA Services."

I had heard the name in meetings in Phnom Penh, but I didn't know much about what it meant. "What is CAMA Services?" I asked. "Do you have any guidelines on expectations for it?"

"Not yet," he replied. "It's up to you to decide."

"Ah, I'll need some money," was my next comment.

"We will pray for you," he replied.

I thought a moment, then said, "I'll need some staff."

"We will assign Beverly, too," he offered.

An army recruitment poster says, "Be an army of one." That describes Beverly. She is wife, friend, mother, nurse, teacher, bookkeeper, and secretary. She never allows anyone or anything to keep her from giving 100 percent. It has always been a blessing to have her on the CAMA team.

"Well, I'll do a survey of the refugee needs and develop a plan," I said.

"We'll be praying," Grady said as he rang off.

When I got home, I told Bev, "We're now CAMA Services."

"What's that?" She asked.

"Ask me in a couple of weeks," I replied. "I don't know yet myself. But we now know what to pray for."

When I told Vim Verplanke about the CAMA Services appointment, he said he would give me money to start. "Let me get a plan and open a bank account first," I replied.

He agreed and said he would go back to Holland to get the name change done and send me an official letter of appointment so I could get started. Grady Mangham did the same thing. I found out later that the CMA had talked about having CAMA Services for a number of years. They used the name in Vietnam and Cambodia but had not formally begun CAMA Services programs yet. Dr. King said he had seen "CAMA" on a Dutch airline list in Indonesia that stated their services for the CMA, so he appropriated their airline designation for us.

During the following weeks, we traveled to various parts of Thailand. Paul Undheim, the CMA field chairman of Thailand, took me to Maranatha Clinic, which was in the throes of labor unrest. Grady needed to know what to do with it. Gene Hall and I visited refugee concentrations on the Cambodian border. Refugees had fled in all directions from Cambodia and Vietnam, crossing the Mekong River from Laos. Some CMA missionary refugees went to Singapore, Guam, and the Philippines. They helped process the people seeking asylum as they fled the communist takeovers of their countries. They performed a very valuable range of services for the refugees and those processing them for resettlements in third-world countries.

The CMA began "Operation Heart Beat" as a response not only to physical needs, but also to deal with the refugees' spiritual needs. No one seemed willing to come help us in Thailand, partially because conventional wisdom expected that it would fall to the communists. Another factor had been that missionaries suffered from post-traumatic stress syndrome. Because of my training in public health, I knew how to evaluate the needs (e.g., food, water, shelter, and sanitation) for the refugees' survival in the ad hoc camps that were arranged by local Thai officials. There was much confusion over what would happen. All the government officials said, "The refugees can't stay here."

Gene Hall had not gone home yet, so he helped me search for any Christians who might have escaped Cambodia. We found very few.

I phoned Grady again and told him, "We need to provide food supplements like fish, fish sauce, etc., blankets, and mosquito nets, as well as cooking utensils and building materials. I need $20,000 per month."

"Well," he replied, "now we know how much to pray for."

"Can I use the hospital money I brought out of Cambodia to start?"

"Yes," he agreed.

Our colleagues gave us mixed reactions when we began the refugee aid efforts. Refugees became a hot political topic in Thailand. The groups with ongoing activities in Thailand grew wary of any refugee involvement. Some missionaries wanted the refugee money to go to poor Thai church members. Some didn't think CAMA should exist in the CMA and even passed a resolution forbidding us to operate in Thailand. "After all," they said, "the CMA doesn't do these things. You and Bev are inexperienced junior missionaries. Who would supervise you?"

When urged to help only Thai people, we said, "When you are locked into refugee camps, we will be there to help you. For now we must help the refugees."

Grady said, "Complete the Maranatha study, make your recommendations, and move on with the CAMA work. You are under my direction, not the field. Follow your plan. An official letter authorizing you is on the way." After careful study, my report recommended that Maranatha Clinic close, a reorganization be carried out, including clear job descriptions for all positions, and a clear organizational chart be drawn up. This should be approved by the national church, and workers should be hired as needed, but only if qualified for the job positions.

The clinic closed and never reopened.

Money for CAMA began to come in. The Cambodian hospital money opened a Bank of America account, and the newly renamed South East Asia Committee, or ZOA, began to send money from Holland. One day Carl Harris phoned me from World Vision to say refugees were too hot a political issue for them, so they sent me the Cambodian money they had on hand -- about $10,000. We didn't have time to raise money in the way most groups did. We just prayed and worked, and God supplied the means. Everything we did was considered unorthodox.

We needed help and transportation to cover the many needs. We had to hire people locally and lease transportation. People said, "We never did things this way."

Bev did a great job at being secretary and bookkeeper, but I needed help with translation, purchasing, and distribution once we secured the materials. We also needed to solve the visa problem. The Thai government granted a one-month visa that might be extended once or twice, but we didn't have a permanent solution.

We read the book of James and made our requests known. We did our best to act when God gave us clear direction, but we definitely had uncertainties. Would Thailand hold in the face of mounting communist pressures? Should we operate from a neighboring location, like Singapore or Hong Kong? We did not question that it was the work God called us to do, so we worked out each problem as it came up. We decided to operate from Bangkok rather than the mission office in Khorat.

One day a young Korean presented himself. "I am Jimmy Rim," he said.

He was a martial arts instructor and had been training Cambodian soldiers. As a believer, he began to see the needs of wandering refugee children and soon had an orphanage of boys in Phnom Penh. He was out of Phnom Penh when it fell to Pol Pot's communist troops, so he could not get his kids out. He had told them, "If anything happens, come to Thailand. I will find you."

Jimmy wanted to help with refugee needs and look for his orphans along the border. We needed hands, feet, eyes, and ears on the border, so we agreed to work together. World Vision had helped him while he stayed in Cambodia and was happy for him to get their funds through CAMA Services. Our team grew.

John and Jean Ellison were CMA missionaries living in northeast Thailand among the Cambodians. John was born in Cambodia and grew up there as a CMA MK. He and Jean had started out as missionaries in Cambodia in 1950, but they were rerouted to Thailand in 1951 due to the Korean War. They always dreamed of being in Cambodia, but they settled in the Surin province in Thailand, where they became part of the community. Surin had a large Cambodian-speaking population and was situated on Cambodia's northern border.

One day John called me to ask, "Can you help us with Cambodians in Surin?"

It was a pleasant surprise because the Thai mission leadership had made it clear that CAMA had not been an approved activity for any missionary to become involved in.

We made an effort to understand their position and even put money into a couple of small development projects done by individual Thai missionaries. Another missionary lent us an old Land Rover, and we carefully paid the mileage and so on. I told John I would drive up to Surin and see what we could do. John and Jean took us to the refugee camp. We also took a load of milk powder, mosquito nets, grass mats, tea, sugar, and rice. The Cambodians, overjoyed to see John and Jean, had a committee to ensure proper distribution of the goods. It was the kind of grass-roots organization that needed to be encouraged, and we felt it was a good way to use CAMA funds.

John took us to see the provincial governor. He was gracious and thankful for CAMA's interest. As a Buddhist, he could not condone the refugees' suffering; but as a government official, he could not encourage the refugees or allow them to roam free as illegal aliens. John and Jean's help solved his problem. The refugees would be our guests on his territory.

As John and Jean began to minister, they told me, "We wanted to go to Cambodia, but God brought Cambodia to us."

We committed $5,000 to get them going and headed back to Bangkok.

Wayne and Minnie Persons, along with Ollie and Winnie Kaetzel, were CMA refugees from Laos. They were trying to decide what to do while waiting for their kids to finish their school term at Dalat. Their experience in Laos could be a valuable asset for our CAMA efforts.

The Kaetzels were due for furlough, but the Persons wanted to stay on to try to help with the Hmong hill tribes who had fled the highlands of Laos into northern Thailand. The Persons had spent over 30 years in Thailand and Laos. They, with the Sawyers and others, had ministered in Xiangkhoang near the Plain of Jars. Not only had they done refugee work during the war, but they were also fluent in Thai, Lao, and both Blue and White Hmong dialects. When told he could not be in the Thai Mission and go near the Hmong, Wayne said, "No problem, I'll resign and join CAMA Services."

In a phone call with Dr. King, vice president of the CMA, he was authorized to be the "Lao Mission in Exile" and work with CAMA. As the team grew, the Persons finished their work on the Hmong Bible that was being printed.

Katanyu Pongstaphone sat across from me one day and said, "I heard about CAMA, and I wondered if you could use some help?"

Katanyu was married to an American girl and part of a Thai-Chinese business family. He had contacts in many areas and had been a supplier to the U.S. forces in Asia. As they pulled out, he needed a new customer. When we talked, I explained the Christian basis for our action and our commitment to sharing Christ's love in both spiritual and material ways.

He said he attended the Baptist church with his wife and was quite content with CAMA's philosophy. We didn't have money for a salaried position at the time, but he agreed to use his contacts to get us the best prices for everything and include delivery to any site we selected in Thailand. I agreed to pay him the cost plus two percent, and we were in business.

The CMA still had teams of missionaries who served as translators for people processing refugees for the U.S. in many areas of the refugee world. In America, Dr. Nathan Bailey challenged the churches to become sponsors for refugees seeking to resettle in America. Several thousand CMA church members from Vietnam and Laos were of special interest. Very few made it out of Cambodia. There was some pressure to move us into refugee processing in Thailand, but Grady Mangham agreed that our best role would be in refugee care while they were in transit. During the next few years, under Dr. Bailey's leadership, CMA churches took in more than 10,000 Asian refugees.

Grady asked me to go to Khlong Yai Trat to look for a Vietnamese highlander named Hyar Lieng Hote, about five feet tall, with dark hair, and so on. It took me 12 hours to get there from Bangkok. The rainy season had begun. Driving a car Katanyu leased for me, I headed for Trat. I touched base with the local Southern Baptist missionary, Ron Hill. He had been in Thailand many years and was willing to help with refugee needs. CAMA committed resources to get him going while the Southern Baptists worked on a budget for him.

Khlong Yai Trat is a dangerous place located at the tip of a long, thin peninsula bordering Cambodia. The Khmer Rouge could easily cross the sparsely defended border and rob and pillage before running back to the forest in Cambodia. It was also the site of a growing group of refugees from Cambodia, as well as a few Vietnamese. After hours of plowing through rain and mud, I reached the area.

I stopped at a new camp under construction before heading on to Khlong Yai Trat. A man named Sok Thong Doeung greeted me. He spoke English very well. As he explained their situation, I told him CAMA would help through Dan Cobb and a Korean, Jimmy Rim. This made him happy because they had many needs. As we spoke, I learned he had graduated from the University of Florida with a degree in forestry. He was dean of the School of Tropical Agriculture in Phnom Penh. As the Khmer Rouge executed all the educated people, he barely escaped with his life.

He later became the regular translator for Dan Cobb and Jimmy Rim. One day while translating the gospel for Jimmy, he realized the message was for him, too. He said that he had already tried to appease all the gods, but that day he came to know the one true God through His Son, Jesus Christ. He began to study the Bible and shortly after started preaching and teaching on his own.

I drove on to the wat (temple) at Khlong Yai Trat where the refugees stayed, praying that I would find Hyar Lieng Hote somehow among the hundreds of refugees there.

As I walked into the camp, a group of Cambodians greeted me. I had met them when Gene Hall and I visited there on our survey trip. A group of refugees gathered as they gave me a list of their current needs.

"I'm looking for a young Vietnamese named Hyar Lieng Hote," I said.

We heard a shout from the back of the group. "That's me!" cried a young man, jumping up and down.

Finishing my conversation with the group, I took Hyar aside and explained that the Bridges family in New York wanted to sponsor him. He was ecstatic! His escape from Vietnam had been an odyssey that left him worn and thin. I bought him noodles while asking questions and filling out the papers I had received from the U.S. embassy. He told me he also had a brother in the States.

"It will take a few days," I said, "but you'll go to America."

Over the years, we heard thousands of stories all confirming the horror that took place in Cambodia. Sadly, the world looked the other way. The Khmer Rouge drove two million people into the countryside, emptying Phnom Penh. They killed leaders and soldiers, even making doctors leave patients to die on operating tables. They would be responsible for nearly two million deaths of their own people during the coming four years.

We needed to solve our visa problem if we wanted to be effective in CAMA's work. A story in the Bangkok Post caught my eye. The headline read, "Huge Refugee Camp to Be Built at Sattaheep."

In the accompanying story, the refugee situation was described, along with the needs of the refugees in several border locations. Refugees could not go home because the communists executed them immediately when they went back to Cambodia. The article quoted Chief of the Foreign Affairs Division of the Ministry of the Interior, Kamol Prachuabmoh. He emphasized the fact that they would need outside help if Thailand planned on helping these unfortunate people.

I wrote Kamol a long letter at once. I described CAMA Services and my background in public health and detailed the work we had begun in the border areas. A couple of days later, at an embassy-sponsored discussion of refugees, I met a young Thai from Kamol's office. When he heard my name, he set up an appointment for me with Kamol the very next day.

At six feet, Kamol Prachuabmoh was tall for a Thai. He was a lieutenant colonel in the army, assigned to foreign affairs and also the new chief of refugee affairs. He had been trained at Fort Bragg in the U.S. and had served with Thai troops in Vietnam, Cambodia, and Laos. He spoke clear English and was open and direct in his conversations.

We got along well from the start. I took Katanyu along to translate, but he wasn't needed. Kamol gave me as clear an explanation as he could of the problem the refugees posed for Thailand. He said, "If we're too easy, they will all leave their countries to come here. The communists already say we're encouraging people to leave Cambodia, and they are angry with us. The communist armies are too busy at the moment, but when they finish subduing their people, they will try Thailand. The United Nations is not yet organized and won't be ready to help for a while. We need groups like CAMA now."

He knew I had helped in Surin and Khlong Yai, as well as some other areas. "You will hear a lot of anti-American speaking in the press and TV, but do not believe them. Our government wants you here."

His meaning was clear.

I explained that CAMA was part of the Siam Mission of the CMA who had come to Thailand in the 1920s. While we had mainly been involved in "teaching religion," we also did medical work and some rural development. I said, "Now we are going to be doing refugee work in Thailand and the U.S., as well as making arrangements for the refugees to go there. However, we have taught Christian religion in Vietnam, Cambodia, and Laos and would like to continue this teaching in the refugee camps here."

Colonel Kamol thought for a moment and then replied, "As long as your refugee work is as good as your teaching of religion, you will have no problems."

Then he added, "If anyone demands a bribe to allow you to help us here, don't argue, just come to me."

We talked ways and means, and he took me to the cafeteria for lunch. "We are working on a visa procedure that will recognize humanitarian workers here," he explained.

He thought a moment and asked for my passport. He wrote a note in it about our work and then phoned a general at the immigration office. "Take your passport and your wife's to his office at once, and come again tomorrow."

I did as instructed. We never had to get another temporary visa in Thailand. God cleared the way for CAMA, and we rode the crest of His wave of provision.

With Dr. Richard Wurmbrandt 1976

With Dr. Richard Wurmbrandt. An early donor
at the Bangkok airport 1976

Matt's birthday party in Bangkok July 1975

Don Cormack and Jimmy Rim delivering rice to the camps 1975

John and Jean Ellison Surin 1975

Drew and Matt leaving for school in Malysia.
No tears till the plane leaves

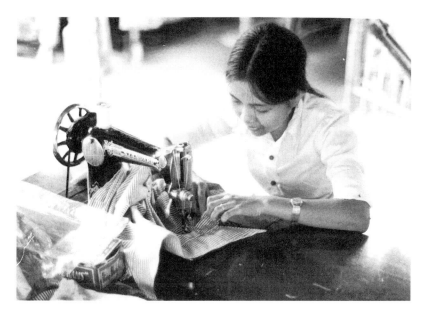

Refugee making clothing in Cambodian camp 1976

Early refugee housing for Cambodians in Surin, Thailand

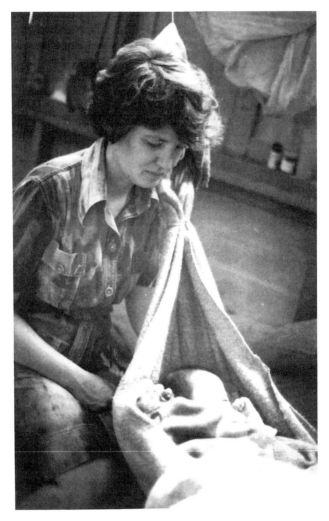

Bev with a refugee baby in Sikiew camp 1975

Sending a rice convoy on its way, 1975

Col. Kamol in Prachuabmoh

Col. Kamol was a constant help over the years

Dr. L.L. King, Vice President of CMA and Dr. Nathan Bailey,
President of CMA visiting in Surin. They decided CAMA should live on!

Chapter 6
A New Thing ~ Part 2

Chapter 6.
A New Thing ~ Part 2

Refugees came in all shapes and sizes and had a variety of needs. Since the borders on both sides were being patrolled more frequently and with more troops, the refugees had to find ever-more-remote places to cross. The U.S. had flown General Vang Pao and his troops to a secure base in Thailand and arranged to take his whole military group to the States. Hmong family members swam the Mekong, seeking asylum and reunification. Many died in the process. Refugees came in small groups, some in very remote areas all along the border with Cambodia and Laos, and the Vietnamese arrived in fishing boats.

The U.N. High Commission for Refugees (UNHCR) negotiated for a role, but the Thai government was reluctant to accede to their demands that would allow the refugees to live indefinitely in Thailand. In 1954, the Thai had allowed 50,000 Vietnamese fleeing communism in the north to "temporarily" enter northeast Thailand. Over 20 years later, they were still there. The Thai government said refugees would be allowed "transit status" only and would be confined to "transit camps" until they could be moved to a new country. The UNHCR reluctantly agreed.

While negotiations continued, the number of refugees grew. There was a serious need to somehow coordinate the work of the groups like CAMA to assure that help went to all the refugee groups. The Royal Thai government did its best to avoid being seen as taking ownership of the refugee situation, so I suggested to Col. Kamol, "CAMA will invite everyone you know of to an informal discussion of the refugee problem. We can meet at the CMA guest house. They have a hall big enough for a neutral group meeting where we can get acquainted and learn how to work together."

We contacted all the voluntary agencies, embassies, the UNHCR, and Col. Kamol. We set the meeting for Friday, September 19, 1975. Bev and Minnie Persons were the hostesses and made banana bread for everyone.

We had a good turnout. Col. Kamol represented the Royal Thai government, and Dr. Cesare Berta represented the UNHCR. Officials of the International Red Cross came. A dozen or so came from World Vision, Food for the Hungry, Overseas Mission Society, and the Southern Baptists. YMCA, YWCA, CAMA Services, and a few others who were beginning to give aid to the refugees came as well. A representative from the U.S. embassy and some others who took refugees to their countries also attended.

I opened with prayer, and everyone told about his or her group and work. At the end, we all had a much better understanding of where the refugees were located, their numbers, and the resources they needed. Some, like YMCA and YWCA, had infrastructure but no funds. Others had funds but no people. We agreed to share, with the goal of meeting all the refugees' needs as best we could.

The Royal Thai government agreed to implement a visa system, clearance into sensitive areas, and clearance into the provincial camps being set up.

The U.N. said they would soon have people and money to provide basic food and shelter, as well as to advocate for new homes for refugees.

Everyone agreed we needed to meet regularly. We did not become a formal organization, and Col. Kamol reminded us that the term refugees was still sensitive. "Well," I said, "in Europe after WWII, the millions of homeless people were called displaced persons."

Kamol liked that, so we became "CCSDPT," or the "Committee for Coordinating of Services to Displaced Persons in Thailand." It was a model that worked for the next 15 years and was used by the U.N. in other countries such as Ethiopia. Agencies did not have to belong, but to get visas and access, they needed the committee's approval.

I was elected chairman, and we agreed to meet weekly until we had things working as smoothly as we could. I opened and closed meetings with prayer, explaining that the problem was bigger than all of us and we desperately needed God's guidance to get the job done.

CAMA had already determined we would do all we could to couple humanitarian efforts with the active proclamation of the gospel. On one visit to Pua in the far north of Thailand, I met a Scottish Overseas Mission Fellowship (OMF) missionary, Doris Whitelock, who traveled to and from the Hmong camp by taxi. After telling me of the spiritual progress, she asked, "Do you think someone would help me get a wee little motor bike? It would make my work so much more effective."

CAMA got her the bike and a "wee budget" to help with other needs.

CAMA determined we should do all we could to secure Christian materials for the refugees to read and funds to get missionaries into the camps. We brought Cliff Westergren from Hong Kong to find out what was available in print in the various languages. He toured the camps, preached in Cambodian, and came back excited about the possibilities he saw in the camps. Spiritual thirst was great. Our prayers for Bibles got answered when I received a call from the Bangkok Gideons. They said, "We have Bibles in Vietnamese, Cambodian, and Laotian that were printed but can't be delivered. We don't have money to store them, and we don't want them destroyed."

I promised to send a truck at once. Another answer to prayer.

After receiving a supply of Cambodian New Testaments, John Ellison headed out to the Surin Cambodian camp. They gave a wonderful response. Being confined in camps with no utilities, no newspapers, or anything else in their language, it was nice to have a Cambodian book. Classes were organized to teach the children to read and write Cambodian, and the adults would read and discuss the Bible at night. "Look, John," they said, "it's speaking to us. Tell us what it's saying."

John began to teach them and led the camp commander and his staff to Christ that day. John saw more response to Christ and the gospel in the first weeks in the camps than he had seen in 40 previous years of ministry. One man told him, "Many years ago I heard this story from a man in Cambodia. I did not believe, but now when I see you doing what the book says, helping me in my trouble…I believe."

After they prayed, John asked him where and when he had met the man so many years before in Cambodia. As the man described the time, place, and person, John exclaimed, "That man was my father!"

We reaped a harvest from seeds planted over the years with great dedication by missionaries and national pastors in tough times. Sometimes we felt the strain. One day Richard Wurmbrandt, the author of Tortured for Christ, and his wife stopped in Bangkok. I gave him a report and thanked him for the funds he had sent. He listened and said, "Young man, you are worrying too much."

"Well," I said, "there's a lot to be worried about."

"But," he responded, "worry is God's work. He doesn't want us to try to do the worrying because we can't affect anything but our health! He worries and things happen. You have to learn like Martin Luther to go to the window at night and say, 'Lord, I'm tired. I'm going to sleep now. You take over.'"

"Thank you," I said. "I'll try to learn to do this."

He replied, "And I will pray for you."

God supplied just what we needed time and again. This is one lesson I keep relearning.

Not only did CAMA finance materials, but we also invested in radio broadcasts that covered Asia. One refugee from Vietnam said that for God's special reason, FEBC (Far East Broadcasting Company) had been omitted from the communists' list of forbidden stations in Vietnam. They heard the gospel daily from FEBC from Manila.

As the CCSDPT developed, we began a series of joint inspection tours of refugee camps by helicopter to make sure all went as planned with the refugees. It had exciting potential. One morning the security detail had been sent in ahead of the group. Col. Kamol, UNHCR, U.S. embassy, and the CCSDPT all waited for the "all clear" to fly in to Ban Vinai refugee camp. When the helicopter landed, the pilot ordered a different helicopter for our flight. He was an air marshall I knew, and I asked, "Why the switch?"

"Look," he said, pointing, "we got 16 bullet holes on the trip this morning. There are some communist insurgents in the hills by the camp. We will take another route to the camp with you!"

"Thanks!"

On another trip, they requested that we fly to a schoolyard near Chanthaburi. As we landed in the yard, we saw a Huey helicopter with Vietnamese markings. We met the Vietnamese pilot, his family, and a Vietnamese mechanic and were quite amazed because it's a long way to travel by helicopter from Vietnam to Thailand. He said, "When the communists took over, all of us in the military got sent to a re-education camp. A week ago they came to me and said, 'We need to know how much rice is growing, and flying is the best way to survey the crop. You have been a good student of communism, so we want you to come fly one of these helicopters for us.'

"'Okay,' I told him, 'but I need a good mechanic.'"

They let him secure one he trusted and then went to a base in the Mekong Delta. There were six brand new helicopters left by the U.S., each with fewer than 50 flying hours. Since they had been there for several months, the pilot said they would need a thorough checkout. And because the crop survey would cover a large area, he told the officials they needed to install long-range fuel tanks, with two spare 55-gallon fuel drums lashed in the cargo area. Again the officials agreed. When they finished, he convinced them he needed to take a test flight with the full fuel load on board. Again they agreed. He set the flight for the cool of the next morning and told his wife, "Do not speak to anyone. In the dark of the morning, go to the rice field at the edge of town and wait for me."

When he took off he told the mechanic, "I'm going to fly to Thailand. When I land, you can get out while my family gets in, or you can go with us."

"I'll go," he responded.

So they flew out over the Delta and off around the Cambodian coast. The mechanic used a hose to siphon fuel from the drums into the tanks as they flew. When they made it into Thailand, they landed at a gas station. "We're looking for the Americans," they told the startled attendant.

The attendant replied, "You're too late; they have already gone home!"

The U.S. embassy representative said, "No worries, you'll be in America in a week."

Wayne Persons finally got access to the Hmong who had been on a secret Thai base at Na Pho. The CIA took Vang Pao and his staff to a ranch that they bought for him in Montana. He also took his five wives listed by the U.S. government as one wife and four cousins.

The Hmong were eventually moved to Loei Province. We drove there to meet with local government officials, and as we walked the streets of Loei city, a shopkeeper recognized Wayne. He had not been there for 16 years, but the shopkeeper remembered him. A bit later, a man from the governor's office came to ask us to join him for dinner. People remembered the Persons as good missionaries who knew the language and culture like no others. Word spread fast that he was back.

At the governor's home, we discussed what was needed to settle the Hmong in Loei until they could go on. Building materials, equipment, and so on would be purchased locally. I recommended he urge the farmers to plant extra crops. We planned to buy the food there and did not want to drive the prices up after the supply got used up. About 30,000 refugees eventually lived there.

We visited the remote site for the camp. Wayne said the refugees loved it because of its being in the hills like Laos.

During one of our meals at a restaurant, the owner came out and welcomed Wayne. He would not let us pay for the food. Wayne explained that when the Japanese came to Thailand in WWII, some CMA missionaries tried to escape to Burma by elephant. They had been detained in Loei, and the restaurateur took them food at the jail. It was great to be part of a group that had such history and respect in the country. Someone told me that when Wayne speaks Thai over the phone, people cannot even tell he's not Thai.

When Maranatha Clinic finally shut down, I was asked if CAMA would buy their medicines for the refugees. "Of course," I said.

Joy Boese was the nurse who helped load and itemize the materials. Bev and the boys came with me. She knew what was useful. Joy took me aside. Her face was red. "In the supplies we were given when the U.S. military left Thailand are a number of boxes of, um…eh, male birth control devices," she said. "Can the refugees use them?"

"Sure," I said, "load 'em in."

Some time later Col. Kamol told me, "CAMA did a good thing. When I took the UNHCR officials through the refugee camp, we saw condoms that had been washed and were being dried for reuse. Since these people reproduce like rabbits, you have helped slow down the population growth."

I traveled many miles by car, plane, helicopter, bus, and train during these early days of CAMA services. We saw continuous growth of refugee numbers and heard horrible stories about Khmer Rouge atrocities. The refugees told of torture and execution by ax, club, and hoe. They saw fields that were covered with unburied bodies. The communists in Vietnam and Laos were less violent, but people by the thousands still voted for freedom with their feet, and often with their lives. At the time, we heard about some Christians who were still alive in Cambodia.

One day a refugee came to the CMA guest house in Bangkok. "I've come for the book," he said.

Ruth Patterson, who had served in Zaire and Cambodia, spoke with him. "Tell me where you heard of the book," she asked.

"I was a teacher in Phnom Penh. When the communists took us to the countryside, I was made to pull a plow like an animal. Children with guns would kill anyone who objected or did not work hard. I was angry, but my plow mate was not. One night I whispered to him the question, 'Why?'

"He told me about Jesus and said, 'If you ever escape, go to the CMA in Bangkok. They have the Jesus Book in our language.'

"I'm here for that book," he said.

Ruth led him to Christ and gave him the Cambodian Bible.

I went to Hong Kong several times to meet with Cliff Westergren and fund the printing of Christian materials. We air shipped any materials we could find in the refugees' languages, and they were put to good use. When Hmong Scriptures arrived, the customs officers got concerned about what the Bible might say. Wayne Persons read it to them until they were satisfied and released the shipment.

Jimmy Rim had collected a group of Cambodian orphan kids. They had been sent to Kompong Som, Cambodia, when the Mayaquez incident happened and had been spirited out to Khlong Yai by a Cambodian navy boat, barely escaping the communists. Leakhena Kong was the oldest and, at 16 or so, served as a surrogate mom for her two brothers and nine other children. Peter, the oldest boy, was in a severe traumatized state due to having been forced to be a soldier for the Khmer Rouge. CAMA gave Jimmy funds for the children's food and care and worked out a "parole" with the Thai government while we sought sponsors to adopt them. We moved them to Bangkok.

A number of groups and individuals offered to help. One family we met at the Soi 10 Sukhumvit, CMA International Church, was Charlie and Sue Morton. Charlie was the regional vice president for Pepsi Cola. He helped with our communication needs from the start. Telex was a new way to communicate in 1975, but difficult to access because it was fairly new. Charlie volunteered his telex for our use. For several years our Asia address was CAMA PepsiCo. His wife fell in love with the orphans.

Robert Ashe and his sister came from England to operate the orphan house CAMA set up, but Sue Morton took the roles of being manager and mom to the kids. All of them did a fine job of caring for the kids and finding them homes in the U.S. and Canada. The Mortons adopted and educated Peter. The Lewises, a Canadian business couple, adopted Leakhena and her brothers and sent them to Paris for school.

Funding was always an answer to prayer. When I submitted my budget of $20,000 per month, Grady Mangham responded, "Now we know how much to pray for."

God did the rest. Richard Wurmbrandt, Mike Scholar, the World Relief Commission, World Vision, Samaritan's Purse, CMA, and Dutch ZOA all sent money. All of them got involved with the refugees via CAMA Service. I wrote biweekly reports to Grady Mangham and the donors, then spent my time on the road meeting officials, refugee leaders, embassy personnel, voluntary agency representatives, and anyone else who sought to help the refugees.

The CCSDPT became a very effective vehicle for meeting refugees' needs, and we did our best to remain neutral. We did not accept money, but we did handle goods donated by dividing them and getting them shipped to the various camps. At one meeting, the U.S. embassy donated 350 tons of rice. CAMA and the Southern Baptists financed the trucks to move the rice from Sattahip to camps along the borders. We also joined with others to purchase building materials for new camps. The Thai government gave land, we supplied materials, and the refugees did the construction under Thai supervision.

The big Hmong camp at Ban Vinai was a good example. Wayne Persons got a group of Christians to go there first. Not only did they work honestly, but Col. Kamol also said, "When they built their church, they did it with their own money. They are good people."

It was the largest church of any kind in Thailand.

As the needs developed, we bought more sewing machines and sewing materials, first for a YWCA-sponsored clothes-making initiative, and then for similar CAMA projects. We bought looms for Cambodian and Lao cloth-making, and silkworms and mulberry plants to begin silk production. We also bought chickens, fish ponds, and pigs, seeds, agricultural and blacksmithing tools, and whatever was needed to facilitate care for the refugees during their stay at the camps. We were especially eager to support any self-help initiatives, as encouraged by the Thai officials.

Our CMA partners, the Persons and the Ellisons, were faithful friends, as were some of the other missionaries including the Woods, Mack Sawyer, Gene and Carol Hall, Clem and Maddie Dreger, the Pratts and Gunthers, Mabel Hartman, Ruth Patterson, and the Undheims. The Lord used them to go to the camps and help, and CAMA paid their expenses. We did get some heat over bringing Cliff Westergren in from Hong Kong, but it was worth the hassle.

Our expenditures ran up to $5,000 per week. One Friday when we should have been buying for Monday's shipping, I did not have the cash needed. I was about to begin telephoning when I felt a strong prompting by the Lord to wait. At devotions on Saturday, Bev and I had read Philippians 4. The advice to be joyful in hardship just didn't seem possible considering the situation. Then the verse that says "Make your requests known with prayer and thanksgiving" struck me. We had been so busy every day that we had not stopped to thank God for all His provision. We did then, and afterward had a quiet weekend. We prayed, "Lord, if it's all over for CAMA, so be it. We just thank You for the months of Matthew 25 opportunities and the hundreds of refugees who have come to You as a result of CAMA's work for You."

Monday I was at the guest house for the mail. We had moved into an apartment at the Oriental Mansions and had good fellowship with our neighbors, Jim and Doris Pratt and George and Elsie Wood of the CMA mission. We even had a pool, where the kids spent a lot of time when they were home from boarding school.

The guest house phone rang and was handed to me with the comment, "They want to know about refugees."

As CCSDPT chairman, I often had "visiting firemen" referred to me by the Thai government or other entities.

"This is Bob Pierce," the voice said. "The embassy said you could give me a briefing on the refugee situation here. Can you come to the Florida Hotel now?"

I owed Bob; he had spoken to Bev on the phone when she was evacuated from Cambodia and alone at the CMA guest house. It really helped comfort her at that moment. So I went to the Florida Hotel at once.

At his hotel, I explained the overall situation in the dozen or so refugee camps. "World Vision should be there!" he exploded. "I started it for times like this."

"Well," I explained, "the politics are complicated just now, but they do give some."

I said that CAMA was short of funds at the moment as well. "I'll get on the phone now," he said. "We'll get a boatload of food from America on the way right now!"

"Thank you," I responded, "but we don't need American food. We need rice, fish, fish sauce, vegetables, and so on. In fact, we have several tons of Canadian cheddar cheese from Food for the Hungry, which refugees don't eat. We sent some to the Hmong refugees, and they sent a note back saying, 'Thank you for the soap, but it doesn't wash well.'"

After Bob stopped laughing, he said, "Buddy, I think God knew you needed this money. Here. I was on my way to India, but they closed the country due to an emergency."

He handed me $11,000. What an answer to prayer, and what a lesson! Bob had been en route when CAMA ran out of money. I had needed a reminder that CAMA was God's program, which He would provide for in His way and in His time. We had two weeks' operational funds right there.

Our work continued to grow. CAMA financed visits to refugee camps and opportunities for mission and national church involvement.

We also made trips to camps to find specific refugees whom CMA churches or individuals wished to sponsor. My parents, in their 70s, wrote and asked for a Cambodian family they could sponsor. John Ellison knew just the family. He sent Col. Po Than, a former military governor from Battambang, Cambodia, to live on our ranch in Washington. It's quite remote, and after arriving they wrote, "Now we live where no people are."

They adapted and eventually sent their kids through college. We remain friends today.

Our CMA missionaries preached, held short-term Bible training, and did theological education by extension in the camps as the number of believers grew. We contracted with George Heckendorf at Khon Kaen to make picture rolls to enhance the telling of Bible stories and had them laminated so any language title could be written with grease pencil on the bottom of the picture.

In October, we received word that Hanoi would release our missionaries. Dr. Bailey, CMA president, and Dr. King flew out to receive them. They were all brought in on a U.N. plane from Hanoi via Vientiane, Laos.

Drs. Bailey and King came a couple of days early. Although CAMA had better relations with the mission, we were informed that Bailey and King were fully booked, so Wayne Persons and I could not see them. However, as Dr. Bailey was checking in at the guest house, I came in for the mail. "You're Bishop, aren't you?" he asked.

"Yes," I said.

Dr. Bailey responded, "We need to see you tomorrow morning, my room at 8:00 a.m."

"I think the mission has scheduled interviews for tomorrow," Dr. King said.

"Well, I'm president," said Bailey with a twinkle in his eye, "and you and I are busy tomorrow."

Our discussion of CAMA's work and role lasted several hours. The books were examined, and finally Dr. Bailey said, "I'm amazed! Do you write reports?"

"Yes, every other week I send a report to Grady Mangham."

"Where do they go, Louis?" Dr. Bailey asked Dr. King.

"Umm…" he thought a moment… "into someone's desk drawer."

"From now on," Dr. Bailey said, "you send me direct a copy of everything! I'm also president of the National Association of Evangelicals."

He continued, "I want to see Cap Jeung, where John Ellison works."

"It's six or seven hours from here," I said, "but I can get Wayne Persons to drive us there in his Volvo. Can you be ready to go at 4:00 a.m. tomorrow?"

"For sure," Dr. Bailey responded, "just have me back to Bangkok in time to preach at Soi 10 Church on Sunday morning."

On Saturday morning, Wayne Persons chauffeured us to Surin, talking nonstop about what was happening in the camps. Dr. Bailey had a lot of questions. Dr. King and I sat in the backseat. He hadn't said much, but finally he asked, "How did you do all of this CAMA Services work here? The old Asia hands said it couldn't be done."

"Well, sir, my experience has been that when people don't want to do something, they either say it's not God's will or the government won't approve of it, so they never try. I never believed either proposition. After all, in these camps are hundreds of believers to whom the CMA ministered in their home countries. Why should we stop now?"

In Surin we met John and Jean Ellison, who accompanied us to the camp. Drs. Bailey and King were amazed, especially by the new believers. After lunch with the provincial governor, we headed back to Bangkok, with a stop in Khorat for Elmer Sahlberg's pancakes. It was a kairos moment for the CMA leadership and CAMA Services. We now had full support from the top leadership. We still got some grief from the middle-level bureaucrats about our operating without "oversight" and committees, but Grady Mangham ran interference, which freed us to do whatever needed to be done, whenever it was needed.

The Vietnamese finally freed the prisoners, who were then flown from Hanoi to Bangkok. CAMA, having become known at the airport due to seeing so many refugees off, was asked to set up a reception. Family members flew up from Dalat for the arrival, and although the press were excluded, I did make an exception for David Aikman from Time. We had gotten acquainted in Phnom Penh and evacuated together.

After their arrival, CAMA Services hosted the newly released missionaries, along with Drs. King and Bailey, at the Bat Boat restaurant in Bangkok. When they served Lillian Phillips her personal butter dish, she said, "Oh, my, is all this for me?"

"Yes," I said, "and you can have as many as you want."

After seven months on the Ho Chi Minh trail, freedom took some getting used to.

Our family adapted quite well in the face of all the activity. During the summer, the boys enjoyed getting to know other M.K.s and traveled with us to the camps. In August they packed their bags and headed for Dalat School in Penang. Matt was going to the first grade. Bev said they had been rather naughty the last few days before they left. It was probably their way of showing their feelings about going away.

The "no crying till the plane takes off" rule worked pretty well until Matt, in his little safari suit, reached the passport window. He was too short to be seen, so when he stood on his tiptoes and slid his passport into the customs office window, all they could see was his tiny hand and a passport. The officer stuck his head out, looked down, and with a smile stamped Matt's passport and handed it to him. Then he and Drew marched off in eager anticipation with the rest of the M.K.s to board the plane. Everyone was happy, but it was a long four months. We had mixed feelings, but in the middle of each semester, one of us would make a long weekend visit to see them.

CAMA used various approaches to educate local churches about Matthew 25:34 - 42, which says, "Then the King will say to those on his right, 'Come, you who are blessed by my Father; take your inheritance, the kingdom prepared for you since the creation of the world. For I was hungry and you gave me something to eat, I was thirsty and you gave me something to drink, I was a stranger and you invited me in, I needed clothes and you clothed me, I was sick and you looked after me, I was in prison and you came to visit me.' "Then the righteous will answer him, 'Lord, when did we see you hungry and feed you, or thirsty and give you something to drink? When did we see you a stranger and invite you in, or needing clothes and clothe you? When did we see you sick or in prison and go to visit you?' "The King will reply, 'I tell you the truth, whatever you did for one of the least of these brothers of mine, you did for me.' "Then he will say to those on his left, 'Depart from me, you who are cursed, into the eternal fire prepared for the devil and his angels. For I was hungry and you gave me nothing to eat, I was thirsty and you gave me nothing to drink." When a church in Chiang Mai said they would do a fund raiser for refugees, we agreed to match them. They raised $2,500, and we gave $2,500. It all went to Doris Whitelock of OMF, who worked with the Hmong. When they finished the project in early December, our whole family drove to Chiang Mai to present the check and take time for some tourism. It was watermelon time, and they sold the dark, round melons in piles along the road. Bev's first reaction was, "Oh, look at all the bowling balls for sale."

The boys howled with laughter. Sometimes we went by bus, sometimes by train, but it was always interesting to see Thailand. We even got to see the elephant roundup in Surin. There was a tug-of-war between a huge elephant and 100 Thai soldiers, and an elephant soccer game. Because of the many tourists, John Ellisondid the English translation on the loudspeakers.

Christmas of '75 found us in Surin for the refugee Christmas program. Drew, Matt, and their friend Stan Ellison gave out gift packets of food, candy, and clothes. We shared a Cambodian feast, and the Cambodians acted out the Christmas story. Although the camp was only about three miles from the Cambodian border in what was considered a security risk zone, with occasional border fighting, the refugees were thankful and happy to be free.

We heard of the cruelties being inflicted only a few miles away, which included executions, torture, and slavery, but here the survivors worshiped God and enjoyed the celebration of His Son's birth. They kept the story in culture. When the guard challenged the wise men as to who they were "he said, let me see your I.D. cards." After asking them for a bribe to see the King the guard, the wise men said, "but the king sent for us." The guard said, "Oh forget the money." When one guard said, "I can't kill two year olds," the other guard said, "Okay, I'll do it for you."

By December 31, I ordered an audit of the CAMA books by a reputed CPA organization. They were thorough and showed that from May 26 to December 31, we had received $153,462 and had spent $118,726. This was over the $20,000 a month we had prayed for and a comfortable surplus to begin 1976. Their only criticism was that Bev and I had received, recorded, spent, and receipted the funds, which they considered to be too much for one couple. "Put it in the report," I told them. "We need help out here."

CAMA's aid had built housing, provided water and sanitation, funded medicines and visits to the camps by medical personnel, cared for orphans, provided food and cooking utensils, clothes, blankets, and mosquito nets, as well as grass mats and many other vital items. We provided a range of self-helps, including materials for camp schools, projectors and films, and even vehicles to take missionaries to the camps. We supplied materials and equipment to make cloth and sew clothes, bought Bibles and training materials for Christian education, and paid to host workers at conferences and to plan meetings.

One action that got some good press in the Thai papers was the "family pack" -- a box that contained things a destitute refugee would need to get a start in camp life. It included things such as canned fish, rice, salt, tea, fish sauce, a cooking pot, a pakkama, mosquito nets, dishes, and eating utensils. We assembled and distributed thousands of them, which impressed the government and the press.

Our working partner agencies included the Laos mission in exile, Church of Christ in Thailand, YMCA, YWCA, and several other small groups who had people to do the work, but no funds. Our CCSDPT group had also grown and begun meeting every other week at the YMCA. The embassies had worked out most of the bugs in the system for taking refugees to their countries, but the problem went on for 15 years. Communist activities in the countryside had caused several Thai groups to step back after accusations of being tools for the West, but backing from Col. Kamol and the Royal Thai government confirmed we were doing God's work. Our team's relief work was as good as their teaching about Christ. They were so integrated that both could easily be seen.

New Year's of 1976 reminded us it had been only a year since we boarded the train in Ellensburg en route to we weren't sure where...but God had been waiting for us to show up! He never left us without what we needed to accomplish the work He set before us.

The Royal Thai UNHCR and NGO refugee camp inspection team

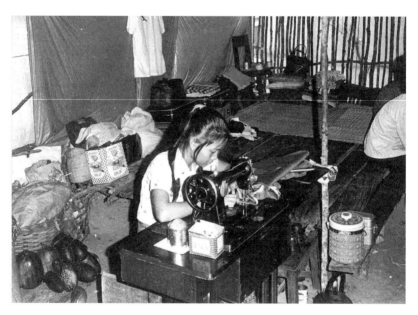

As the refugee camps grow, 'self help' becomes very important

Sami, Paul, Andy, Kerr, Matt, Marilyn and Bev in Aintoura, Lebanon

Bev conversing with a camel in Petra, Jordan 1977

Jimmy Rim with an orphan baby 1975

Bev organizing medical care at the Sikiew Vietnamese camp, 1976

Jimmy Rim with Leakhena and Peter

CAMA boutique in Paris

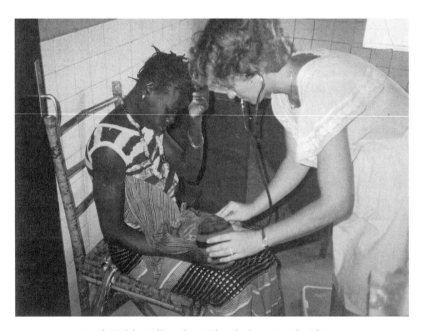

Beth Tebbe Albright with a baby in Mali Africa

New ways mean better crops in Mali

CAMA France turns One in Paris

Chapter 7
The Beat Goes On! ~ Part 1

Chapter 7.
The Beat Goes On! ~ Part 1

The year 1976 began with a lot of action: more border fighting, more refugees, and some visits from agency leaders who were rethinking their stand on refugees. It was clear that more were coming than going, and that the situation was getting worse. It caught international media attention, which for some agencies translated into fund raising opportunities.

The Vietnamese refugees had been placed in a low-security prison called Sikiew, halfway to Khorat. CAMA gave materials to help enlarge the living areas and build offices. George and Elsie Wood held church services, and Bev organized a group of ex-pat nurses from the embassy and women's club to go to the camp to help with medical needs. Captain Ban Han, the camp commander, explained that due to pressure from the communists and the Vietnamese refugees in Thailand, it was thought best to keep them "under control" at Sikiew.

Trouble was afoot in Thailand. Students marched and complained loudly about the money spent on the refugees when everyone knew that the communists would be angry about the refugee aid and the simple fact that Thailand was accommodating them. Some reports told of students who had gone into the forests to receive training from the Chinese on how to overthrow the Thai government.

There were usually incidents of violence at night along remote roads, so people advised us not to drive at night. That wasn't bad advice at any time, because Thai truckers had a nasty habit of driving at high speeds in overloaded trucks. They drank "high energy" drinks that contained caffeine and alcohol, and they often caused terrible accidents. Overnight buses were dangerous, too. They would literally race to Bangkok from remote areas and often wreck, hitting water buffalo, motorcyclists, cars, trucks, or each other. Highway deaths were all too common, and the story usually ended with the unknown surviving driver running away. No one ever got charged with anything. Sometimes we questioned which was more dangerous, the roads or the war, so we avoided night travel!

The war in Southeast Asia had evolved. It became Russia versus China, using Vietnamese and Cambodians, and the fighting was vicious. The Khmer Rouge also killed and filled the fields with those deemed unsuitable for their new Marxist society. Pol Pot declared that they would take Kampuchea back to year zero: "We won't have any technology. We will be a total farming society. Anyone who doesn't agree will be liquidated."

Some individuals and groups who just could not accept the changes wrought by war put forward wild schemes. For example, a group of Cambodian air force pilots living near Aranyaprathet, Thailand, became convinced that since they had not been involved in the war, they could go home. Besides, they thought the Khmer Rouge would need pilots. So after negotiations, the Khmer Rouge sent a truck to pick them up and drove them into Cambodia. They took the young pilots about five miles beyond Poipet to a Buddhist temple, where they executed all 54 of them.

We learned that the North Vietnamese had taken full control of the south, and Saigon had become Ho Chi Minh City. Another report told us that the southern Viet Cong leaders were disappearing, and China was threatening the Vietnamese as well. The refugee flow continued to grow. More than 200,000 people had been expelled from Vietnam to China.

One day I spoke with a small group of Cambodian students who had spent more than 40 days walking from Phnom Penh to Cap Jeung camp in Thailand. They had just killed a dog to cook, so I got them some rice to go with it. "Why did you leave?" I asked.

"We used to march and demonstrate against the government," they replied. "Then when the communists came, we marched to welcome them. We told them we were glad they came and that we were their friends. For a while they accepted us, then they changed. They made us go to the countryside and work like animals. They said, 'We don't trust you. Soon you will march and demonstrate against us.' So we waited and finally escaped. Soon there will be aut Cambodia."

Aut is the Cambodian for "no" or "none." "Aut te meat," "Aut te bread," "Aut te electricity, food, clothes, shoes, towns, cities…" "Aut te freedom" was the worst part of Pol Pot's revolution, and the students had been betrayed, so they voted with their feet. Some even voted with their lives.

The Khmer Rouge set mines and ambushes to kill anyone trying to escape. Some refugees told about dreams in which they were shown the way to safety. One lady told of being near death when "a being in white" gave her fruit juice and led her to Thailand. When the refugees experienced the physical help given by CAMA in the camps and heard the gospel from John and Jean Ellison, they made the connection and accepted the God of a faith that reached out to them in their need. In the first ten months of working in the camps, more than 4,000 refugees expressed having faith in Jesus.

We enjoyed the relationship with our Dutch companions, the ZOA. Henk van der Velde, the committee chairman, had appointed me their "executive official representative" in the refugee situation in Asia. They came out to Thailand, excited by CAMA Service's role and the progress made on the refugees' behalf. They mentioned that a lot of refugees chose to resettle in Europe, which we knew. CAMA Services gave the Christians a note with the mission address in the country to which they went. It stated that they were CMA church members from the refugee camp of origin.

In March 1976, Grady asked me to go to Gabon, Africa, to look at a planned medical program expansion that the CMA had under discussion. Dr. David and Becky Thompson had been slated to come to work with us in Phnom Penh. When that destination was no longer possible, they were told to finish French language study for deployment to Africa.

Africa? Well, when duty calls, we answer. After working out some details with Bev so she could manage CAMA while I was gone, I headed for Gabon via Europe. After a night in Frankfurt I went to Paris, where Don Dirks, the field director for CMA, helped me get a visa for Gabon. He also told of an increasingly complicated problem with refugees coming to France. They had little CAMA cards with his address, but he could not communicate with them. "Let's talk about it when I come back from Africa," I said.

Little did I know what that comment would generate.

Mel Carter, business agent for the CMA in Gabon, met me in Libreville and explained the problems I would face in getting the clinic enlargement program changed. Basically, the national church wanted a hospital just for the Christians. Several of the missionaries were against the project, seeing it as an unneeded complication in their lives. If we wanted to see the program develop as a base for evangelistic outreach, we had to negotiate.

Memories of our first stay in Africa flooded my mind as I flew to Mouila. The road was as bad as any I remembered in the Congo. At Lebamba, we took a pirogue across the river to Bongolo, where the clinic was located. Being situated 200 miles farther back in the jungle than Dr. Albert Schweitzer's hospital at Lamberene, it was primitive, but it had promise. We had talks with the church and the mission. The differences between them were clear, but the clinic expansion was needed. After I prepared a preliminary report that was translated and given to the church and the mission, we agreed on the need for further development of the plan, especially the evangelism component. I flew back to Europe to meet Don and discuss the refugee needs in Europe.

In Brussels, I got some rest and phoned Donald Dirks. He said a meeting in Amsterdam had been arranged and that he would pick me up. Dr. King, ZOA, and some others came to discuss the need for a CAMA Services refugee resettlement aid program in Europe. I was tired, and the discussion was going on and on. I made some suggestions, and suddenly Dr. King said, "Well, that settles it. The Bishops will move to Paris and manage this joint operation!"

What! Move to Paris? Suddenly I was wide awake. Henk van der Velde said, "Andy, how soon can you write up this project?"

"Well, let's see," I answered. "I'll need to bring Bev with me to Paris to work out the details. I can have the program and the budget ready by the end of May."

Everyone agreed, and the meeting ended.

"Dr. King, we need to talk," I said.

"Okay," he answered.

We went to a quiet corner. Now, in those days, management was sort of a Dr.-King-heard-from-God-and-let-you-know kind of thing, and you just said "Amen" and went to work. So I carefully expressed my feelings of surprise.

"CAMA Services is a major partner in the refugee efforts in

Thailand," I explained. "To walk away so abruptly doesn't seem wise."

He responded, "Oh, don't worry, we won't. I'm sending Reg Reimer to replace you in Thailand at once. He doesn't know it yet, but he will come soon."

Amen!

My mind raced as I flew to Bangkok. I needed to explain the change to Col. Kamol and make sure the CAMA operational plan was clearly defined so Reg wouldn't have any problems. I knew Reg had been deeply involved in refugee processing and resettlement in Guam and Canada. With him being a veteran of two terms as a missionary in Vietnam, I was thankful to have an experienced replacement.

"Bev, we're moving to Paris," I announced on my return.

After a moment of silence, she replied, "What for?"

She was perplexed by the news, especially the plan for a quick return to Paris. "The two of us will be involved in the evaluation and planning phase of the European project," I said.

She enjoyed our time in Thailand, as did I, and we felt fulfilled in the ways God had answered our prayers for new direction after being forced to leave Cambodia.

The two weeks turnaround went fast. I met with Wayne and Minnie Persons and John and Jean Ellison. I laid out the changes coming as I understood them and assured them that CAMA's commitment to the refugees in Asia would not diminish. I explained to Col. Kamol that this represented an expansion of CMA's commitment to solving Thailand's problem. Not only did the CMA, and even my parents, take as many refugees in for resettlement as we could, but we helped to expand refugee resettlement in Europe as well.

We flew back to Amsterdam on April 30, 1976. In Holland, the ZOA had arranged a series of interviews with newspapers and magazines designed to raise the Dutch people's awareness of the problems in Southeast Asia and to highlight ZOA's partnership with CAMA Services.

After a few days we moved on to Paris, where Jean Jacques Piaget met us. He gave us a clear picture of what was needed to help refugees in France. It ranged from helping with jobs, to housing, to language study and the gospel. Don Dirks had us stay at a small hotel near the mission office in Boulogne to set up meetings with key people in the CMA and various agencies we would work with.

Jean Jacques knew the European missionaries and Christian agencies we could cooperate with once we moved there. The CMA went to France for evangelism and church planting. Daniel Bordreuil, the French leader of the mission, made it clear that his involvement was crucial to any work CAMA might attempt there.

After nearly two weeks, we sat down to write out a program called "CAMA/ZOA Open Heart." We envisioned CAMA Services as a central point of interchurch cooperation and funding for travel to refugee concentrations to help with sponsorships, for small loans to set up living and working arrangements, for language classes, and so on. We became a team made up of refugee leaders, one from each language group, and missionaries with Asian language and service experience. We also funded children's summer camps, literature, and evangelism efforts. The budget called for more than $120,000 for the first year. We submitted the budget to CMA's headquarters in New York and ZOA in Holland and headed back to Bangkok.

The boys were excited about the impending move to Europe. At that time, we hadn't yet found out where they would go to school in Paris. We worked things out as they developed, and since we were sure God was leading, we hurried to follow.

Bev struggled with an ear infection, so Gordon Kelly sent medicine for her from Ellensburg. The embassy doctor said the medicine would help, but she needed care beyond his skills. She had only been back from Paris a short time when she discovered a marble-sized lump in her right breast. This, plus a funny-looking mole on her leg, caused me to push her to see a doctor at the Seventh Day Adventist Hospital in Bangkok. After a preliminary check, the doctor referred her to the surgical clinic.

Things piled up. I had covered 50,000 miles in the past three months, and that included stops in five countries, plus our trip to Paris. We planned on our boys coming home from Dalat on June 16, and Reg Reimer was scheduled to arrive in late June. I was scheduled in Hong Kong on the day before Bev's appointment with the surgical clinic. We prayed, knowing that surgery might be needed. Bev's mom had survived cancer after a radical mastectomy. It was pretty scary, but we committed it to the Lord. We agreed that should surgery be required, we needed to get it done before the kids came home from school. "Schedule it for the time I get back from Hong Kong," I said. "That way you'll have two weeks to heal before the kids get home."

On June 2, 1976, Bev went to the clinic and I flew to Hong Kong.

The surgeon was alarmed after checking Bev. "Check into the hospital now," he instructed. "There are more lumps and a mass from your chest extending into the armpit. We'll do the surgery in the morning."

Bev did her best to reach me, but she couldn't find me, so she prayed and again committed herself to the Lord and checked in. The hardest part was signing a release to allow a radical mastectomy if the tumors were malignant. She had complete peace from God over the situation, however, and was grateful that before starting the operation, her surgeon prayed, asking God for a miracle.

God answered. After extensive removal of lumps on her leg and breast, and taking biopsies of the mass on her chest and armpit, all were pronounced benign! Bev had committed to give God the glory if prayers were answered, and she started with the nurse in the recovery room.

When I got home from Hong Kong, a note told me Bev would be ready to leave the hospital that day. I had no idea the surgery had already taken place! I had to borrow money to bail her out of the hospital, but she made it home and gained her strength back by the time the boys got home. We kept up a hectic schedule getting ready to move to Paris while making sure the work could continue moving ahead in Thailand.

David Andrianoff came to see me one day. He grew up in Laos among the Hmong and had come to Thailand with World Relief (WRC), hoping to spend part of his time with the Hmong. He spoke the language, and Wayne Persons was in favor of his joining CAMA. However, his boss, Jim Gustafson, had forbidden any contact with the refugees. I called Grady Mangham and the Covenant Church headquarters that sponsored him through WRC. Would they object if David transferred to work with CAMA Services? No one objected, so

CAMA added David and Jean Andrianoff to the team.

Minnie Persons had recruited Bev to help the hill tribe women find a place to sell their unique handcrafts. CAMA Services planned to buy the items and then sell them at the monthly hill tribe sale in Bangkok. We also sent some items to Holland, where ZOA marketed them in craft shops. Jean Andrianoff took over the project from Bev, and as she and Minnie worked to improve and expand the products, CAMA CRAFTS came into being. Jerry and Rose Torgerson, former Lao missionaries, were sent to join CAMA Services, too.

When Reg and Donna Reimer came in late June 1976, Reg got excited about what he saw. CAMA Services' prominent role in the refugee work gave us real confirmation that the CMA was on the right track vis-à-vis Matthew 25:34 and our founder, A. B. Simpson's, commitment to the poor and needy.

Mr. Damrong Saengkaweelert, a Thai undersecretary of state, gave us a farewell lunch. The UNHCR attended, as did the Red Cross and U.S. embassy representatives, as well as several key volunteer agencies with whom we worked. Finally, we completed packing for Paris.

We arrived in Paris during their annual "les grandes vacances," the month when everything is closed down. We couldn't even rent an apartment, so we stayed with the Piagets for a few weeks. When we did get an apartment, it was bare! We had to supply everything from the light fixtures to the furniture, stove, and refrigerator. We knew what the refugees must feel!

Not long after we began to settle in, Don Dirks sat down with me. He was worried because Daniel Bordreuil told him CAMA Services could not operate or even have a bank account without his name on everything. Don had been dealing with this roadblock to progress ever since he had been assigned to Paris from Gabon. Daniel claimed that every organization or committee had to have a French citizen as its legal head.

"CAMA Services is an American nongovernmental organization," I said, "so I'll ask the bank about the best way to proceed." Then I continued, "God did not bring my family and me here only to be told that we can't do this work. I've heard that before, and it was not true."

Don said, "Daniel feels CMA is here for French people, not these foreign refugees."

I did not respond.

When I met with the manager of the Bank of America in Paris, I handed him a letter of introduction from the Bank of America in Bangkok and a $10,000 cashier's check. He was eager for our business and explained the ease with which CAMA Services could register as a foreign group with no restrictions, and we certainly did not require a French national as a partner.

A couple of hours later, I showed Don my new checkbook with the full cash balance available, as well as transfer instructions for CMA, ZOA, and others who sent donations. In amazement, he registered the CMA mission with its own bank account right away.

In the next few months, we set up refugee church organizations for the Cambodians, Lao, Vietnamese, and Chinese. Missionaries from France, England, and Switzerland soon joined the CAMA Services project. We opened a refugee center in Boulogne, a suburb of Paris, and used it as a base for everyone's work. We funded one pastor and a helper for each ethnic group. Things moved quickly, and we saw answers to our prayers.

Bev set up a home school program for Matt and Drew, as other options seemed too expensive. She worked out a study schedule, and the family settled into a routine. The CMA explored a job description for me that included "coordinator for medical programs in Africa." Paris was a good place from which to cover all the needs for CMA.

CAMA Services also funded an evangelism team to tour Cambodian settlement clusters. The Piagets and Cliff Westergren joined a gypsy evangelist, François Celier, who had a van named Resurrection and a trailer loaded with a tent and chairs, as well as Bibles and song books. They had great spiritual responses among the Cambodians. The refugees in France were said to have numbered 250,000 and had a growth rate of about 1,100 per month. The French government had experience with the Indochinese groups, as it had spent several centuries governing them as colonies. Its refugee agencies appreciated CAMA's aid to the people and were always very cooperative.

I traveled to Holland and England a lot. The boys went along if they completed their lessons. They loved to get fresh bread from the local bakery in the morning and usually ate the top off the loaves while walking home. Bev competed with them, as she loved it, too. They rode the metro all over Paris, and Matt became skillful on a skateboard. He did get run down by a hit-and-run motorcycle one day. I took him to the emergency clinic. The x-rays showed no fractures, but two teeth had to come out. I explained it to Matt, who was still dazed. He looked at me solemnly and asked, "How much under my pillow for each tooth?"

I thought quickly and responded, "$2.50."

With tears in his voice, Matt said, "Okay."

They gave him the ether, removed the teeth, stitched his lip, and he survived five dollars richer.

We now had a staff of six refugee workers. CAMA Services covered a stipend for their support and expenses, as well as travel expenses that took the CAMA team members all over France and other countries where the Asian refugees settled. We also had eight missionaries from France, Switzerland, and England. Their churches supported them, but CAMA covered their operational expenses.

It was cold in France. The refugees arrived with only lightweight clothing, so we discussed ways to help them get warm clothing. During one team meeting at the CAMA Centre d'Accueil, Josianne Matthys said a man in her church in Switzerland did dry cleaning, but some customers never came back for their clothes. Instead, they spent their money on new fashions.

I thought perhaps we could get a carload. Anything would help. "Call him," I recommended.

Two weeks later, Josianne phoned to say that the clothes had come and they needed help. When I got to the Centre, I saw a double semi truck loaded with beautiful, freshly cleaned clothing on hangers and in plastic bags. We quickly began to unload them in an underground garage. We also rented a second garage space to install clothing racks for hanging and sorting the clothes. Bev and Josianne, along with Harriet Irwin, began what we called the "CAMA Boutique." We purchased sewing machines and set up to alter the clothes to fit the small Asian refugees. It made a great project, since Josianne's friend owned a dry cleaning plant. He cleaned thousands of pieces every day and had many unclaimed items. He supplied us with loads of clothing while the CAMA Boutique was in operation.

"How soon can you leave for Lebanon?"

It wasn't exactly a call from nowhere. We had talked about Lebanon before. A serious civil war was going on, and all the missionaries had been evacuated. Grady Mangham asked me to go and see what role CAMA might play in helping the fledging CMA national pastor Sami Dagher respond to the needs of the thousands of people who were displaced by that war.

I had still been involved as a liaison for CAMA Services in Thailand, where Reg Reimer was now in charge. Col. Kamol Prachuabmoh and Under Secretary Damrong had visited us in Paris and proclaimed CAMA's overall performance outstanding. The resettlement activities in Europe impressed them as well. Dr. King warned me that I could be his troubleshooter for a wide range of problems the CMA had been dealing with in an ever-more-dangerous world. I had already been busy with the African needs. Now it was "another new thing."

"There's a lot of fighting there," I responded.

Grady said, "Oh, well, you're used to that."

So, I flew to Amman, Jordan. After some time with missionaries who had been evacuated from Beirut, we set out for Beirut in two cars. Norm and Bonnie Camp rode in one car, Betty Howard and Colleen Johns in the other, with me as the driver. We crossed into Syria and on to Damascus, where we contacted the local CMA pastor. Convoys of trucks, tanks, Jeeps, and armored cars crowded the road from Damascus to the border crossing. The Syrians were moving into Lebanon as part of the Arab peacekeeping force, seeking to enforce a deal between the Lebanese and the Palestinians, who were trying to take the country for their own.

Nothing clears traffic like a Russian tank driven by a Syrian. The road checks we stopped for were interesting. We saw lots of guns, pointing, and shouting until they saw our American passports; then it changed to "Kief," or "Welcome." It pleased them that Americans still came back to Lebanon even though shooting was taking place.

When we got to Beirut, the electricity was off and street signs were scarce. The night was lit by tracers fired by the various groups, and the explosion of a shell or a rocket punctuated the dark night. Shades of Phnom Penh, I thought. Even in the dark, Norm knew the way to Sami Dagher's place, and after climbing five flights of stairs, we entered Sami and Joy Dagher's apartment in the Achrafieh section. It was about 9:00 p.m. "Welcome," chorused the group of 16 seated on the living room floor around a candle.

"Praise God!" they said. "We knew when you left Damascus, and we have been praying for you all afternoon."

I thought, I don't know what CAMA can do in Lebanon yet, but these people know how to pray, and God will do the rest.

Over the next few days, we moved carefully around the shattered city. A cease fire had been arranged, but people got shot at the roadblocks, as vengeance was taken by people on all sides. The port became a shattered shell, with ships of various sizes sunk and washed up on beaches. The warehouses had been looted. Huge luxury hotels turned into empty shells. The Holiday Inn had an outside elevator stuck halfway up the building. A burned-out armored car sat in the lobby. The Phoenicia Intercontinental Hotel had been destroyed, as well as many buildings in the city center. Office buildings, apartments, and department stores all had gaping holes in their walls and roofs. Unburied dead bodies still lay in the rubble, but land mines had been set to keep rescuers away.

It was horrible, and it wasn't over yet. The peacekeepers were a mixed group of soldiers, mostly from Arabic-speaking African countries. They seemed confused about what they were to do and did not know what to ask us at roadblocks. Sami took advantage of the opportunity. When asked if he had explosives, he would reach into the glove box for a Bible and say, "This is the most explosive book you can read."

With guns pointed from every angle and nervous fingers on the triggers, I found the exercise rather disconcerting. But the soldiers would click the safeties on their guns and step back with a relieved smile when they saw the Bible. They always accepted Sami's tracts or Bibles.

As we traveled, Sami told his story of having been a food service manager at the luxury Phoenicia Intercontinental Hotel. He had met Christ through CMA missionaries Harry and Miriam Taylor, and after a series of Bible studies and prayer, he felt led to preach. "You have a family to feed," he was advised, "and no training as a pastor."

"That is God's responsibility," he responded.

He had a retirement fund at the Phoenicia Hotel. They had already told him to soften his evangelism of staff and guests. "I was employee of the year several times," he said, "and my division made more money than any other. One day the manager confronted me about my witnessing."

"Are you asking me to leave?" he asked his boss.

"No, no," his boss said. "Just leave out the Jesus stuff."

Sami explained, "If I stay, Jesus stays."

"Well," his boss said, "not so aggressive, please."

Sami finally said he must preach and trust God for the details. When he withdrew his retirement money, they told him he was crazy.

"You'll be back in a few months, begging for food, and we will laugh at you," his boss said.

Sami began to study and teach the Bible, and people responded. Then the war broke out, and the Phoenicia Hotel was one of the first to be destroyed. It wasn't long before his former colleagues came to his door, seeking food. Sami was happy to bring them in and share Jesus with them, along with the food. It was a beginning, and CAMA Services joined Sami in his outreach to his fellow Lebanese.

After three weeks of ducking the fighting from area to area, we began to get a clear picture of what the church could do. Sami had picked out a badly damaged building in the Karantina area. The name Karantina came from the historical fact that when people who had, or might have had, a disease came into Lebanon by boat, they were confined in quarantine until cleared and released. Sami thought the building he chose could be CAMA's base, as well as provide space for the church to meet. It was a wreck, but Sami said he could repair it.

Besides helping the displaced Lebanese with food, temporary shelter, and medical needs, Sami wanted to rebuild a village in the mountains as a way to engage them for the gospel. To develop a budget, we devised a "repair need sheet" that included things like windows, wiring, plaster, and plumbing. In each home, our goal was to provide a kitchen, bathroom, sleeping area, and family room. We also wanted to provide each family with a Bible and Bible study to explain our interest in them with a biblical perspective. Our first year's goal was 100 homes in the village of Aintoura, with a budget of $700,000.

When I flew to Switzerland, where Bev and the boys had spent Christmas with the Piaget family, I had the plan in hand. Bev and the boys enjoyed a Swiss Christmas with all the trimmings, including a live tree with lighted candles. They also skied and played in the snow.

After returning to Paris, Bev typed up the plan for distribution to funding agencies. I phoned Grady Mangham. "We need $700,000 for the first year in Lebanon," I explained.

"Well," he replied, "we know how much to pray for. Send me the program proposal."

I added, "We will need someone to help Sami with the administration as well."

"Okay, we'll discuss it," Grady said.

Dr. David Thompson stopped by for the New Year's celebration in 1977 in Paris. The Thompsons did well in language study and tropical medicine. We also had a good time with our French team and did some planning for the coming year. Our family had been away from home in Ellensburg for two very busy years, and we were looking forward to two more.

We had visitors. The Chuck Kellers, who had been Bible translators in western Cambodia, came to France to visit some of the refugees. They wanted their help so they could continue to work on the Cambodian translation for the tribe they had worked with. They stayed in our home, as did many visitors over the years. Our team gave them names of refugee Christians and leaders to contact.

We had become acquainted with George Hoffman, founder of TEAR

(The Evangelical Alliance Relief) Fund in England. He was eager to be involved as a partner with CAMA Lebanon. Jan van Barneveld, their director in Holland, became a lifelong friend. Jan was a hyperactive, hard-working individual with a wide range of contacts at all levels of Dutch government and nongovernmental organizations. He was committed to seeing the "household of faith" equipped to fulfill its biblical imperatives. TEAR Fund had begun to fund some of CAMA's programs among the refugees in France. They, as well as Scripture Gift Mission in England, not only helped with Bible and gospel tracts in the refugees' languages, but also funded reprinting a French-Cambodian dictionary. The only change we made was in the flyleaf. I replaced Sartre's quote, "If you would gain wisdom, spend an hour with me," to "The fear of the Lord is the beginning of wisdom. Proverbs 9:10."

Grady called to say they had decided to respond to Lebanon by seeking help from some U.S. nongovernmental groups and sending a couple to work with Sami in Beirut. Andy and Marilyn Kerr had recently married. They received a sort of congratulation from Grady on their marriage and news that CAMA wanted them to enjoy a two-week honeymoon in Paris, after which they would go to Beirut. Andy was Bonnie Camp's brother and had been an MK in Thailand. He had spent time at Beirut University and knew what was going on and what they would face. His wife was up for the challenge, as well as the opportunities.

After prayerful consideration, they came to Paris, where we hosted them. I filled them in on the plan for Lebanon and what we hoped would be accomplished. We had a nice two weeks. As we drove them to Orly airport to catch their flight to Lebanon, Andy asked, "So...when does the money come?"

My response was, "As far as I know, it's still in God's bank account. He will send it when we're ready. For now, get set up in an apartment, start Arabic study, and help Sami with the church."

They flew to Beirut trusting, as I was, in God's provision in His time and way.

Andy, Franklin and the team in Georgetown, Guyana

Taxi? Matt the camel driver with Andy in Petra, Jordan, 1977

John Ellenburger with an air lift of food in the Baliem Valley

Picnic on the road in Lebanon

Moving to Holland with WRC

The inspection team in Guyana

Chapter 8
The Beat Goes On! ~ Part 2

Chapter 8.
The Beat Goes On! ~ Part 2

One of our team members in Paris was David Soquier Chan, a Cambodian-Chinese pastor. He came to Bev one day feeling perplexed. "Beverly," he said, "I don't know what to do about Samuelle. She is a good choir leader, but she's always borrowing my pen and never remembers to give it back, so I must find her. She's a Ph.D. candidate in computer engineering and can't even keep her own pencil." Like David, she was Cambodian-Chinese.

Bev remarked, "David, it's not your pen she wants, it is you!"

David answered, "Oh my, my, what to do? Her family is dead, so is my father; there's no one to help us arrange a marriage!"

Bev joyfully responded, "Andy and I will help," and we agreed to meet the next week at the Pub Renault on the Champs-Elysées.

Thus began a "chaperoned date" relationship. It was fun to be with them and watch as they quickly became serious about the future and sharing their lives. Months later, when they married, they asked, "Do you want to go on the honeymoon with us?"

"Thank you, but no thank you," I said. "The lessons are over!"

We noted that over the next few months, several other young Chinese couples got married. David explained that after each of our "dates," they met with the other young couples to explain the next step in their relationship. Their church grew.

A Dutch reporter came to Paris to do a story on the work. I had written stories for the Dutch Telegraph newspaper in Amsterdam, which generated interest at several levels in Holland, including the Dutch government foreign aid section. I made rounds of the offices in London, The Hague, and Doorn, where Jan van Barneveld lived. They were all very encouraging. Now the reporter wanted to see firsthand how CAMA worked. We took him all over France, and the team had him interview refugees from each ethnic group. The reporter wrote a great story that was read all over Holland.

Andy Kerr contacted me from Beirut and said, "We're ready. We have an apartment, we're in language study, and we can start work whenever the funds arrive."

"Keep telling that to the Lord," I said.

A week later, Grady phoned to say, "We have a grant of $100,000 for Lebanon. Praise God! We can start."

Then Jan van Barneveld contacted me to say the Dutch government would send $200,000! It truly was time to start the work.

I flew to Beirut to help with the implementation of the plan. "Who knows best how to do this type of building?" I asked.

We had already selected the village of Aintoura as a place to begin. Sami said, "I led a builder to the Lord. He has been growing spiritually and doesn't have work."

"Let's take him to Aintoura," I said.

Afif handed us a repair sheet. He had been asked to evaluate a house we had looked at several weeks earlier. We wanted to see how accurate our estimates were. His cost was significantly below the one on which we had based the proposed budget. "How can you do the work so cheaply?" we asked.

"When the war started, I hid tons of cement and building supplies in a cave," he told us. "You can have them for the pre-war price."

What an answer to prayer! A lot of work had already been done. Sami became known for effective work among the needy in Lebanon. The church gave help to everyone regardless of their beliefs. The building in Karantina had become an office, church, and distribution center for clothes and food packages. It sat next to an empty field that had been the Tel Zaatar refugee camp. During one battle, over 20,000 people were killed and the buildings razed. The area became an empty field where you could find human bones among the broken tiles and glass. It amazed me to see the church grow on the border of that field of death and terror.

As the project went on, people's houses got repaired, Bible studies were held, and other aid was given. People came to Christ as they saw

His love in action. The U.N. was eager to help and gave 700 square meters of glass. We found a local glazier. He had lost his tools, but CAMA replaced them, which put him back in business, cutting and fitting the donated glass. We needed metal work. A local blacksmith was re-equipped with tools and a portable welder. He made door and window frames, as well as many other metallic objects that people needed to repair homes. We did the same for carpenters and stonecutters.

Sami was everywhere, making sure it all worked and God got the glory! By the end of the first year, we had completed 100 homes in Aintoura and started others. Amazingly, it had cost only $350,000, not $700,000. God had made it work with what He provided. Best of all, the church grew! It's a pattern that continues 30 years later.

I made regular trips to Holland to meet with Henk van der Velde of ZOA and Jan van Barneveld of TEAR Fund. They encouraged me, and I always enjoyed the meetings. The trips were often on my favorite "Train Blue" from the Gare du Nord in Paris. On one trip the border guards took a long time with my passport but finally shrugged and handed it back. The next morning as I checked my tickets and papers I understood... I had Bev's passport! I got back to Paris in spite of the mistake.

George Irwin came in to see me at the CAMA Centre. He and Harriet had spent their lives in Vietnam. They went to first grade together at Dalat School, grew up there, and served many years there after getting married. They now served the Vietnamese in France. George gave extra help to one of the families that they dealt with. The grandmother of the family of ten had committed suicide. Depression had become a common side effect for those who had fled their countries.

Their story became a reminder of what drove the refugee crisis. They had been a large, wealthy family in South Vietnam who decided they could stay and live under the communists. At first things continued fairly well. The North Vietnamese came and soon began asking for small bribes. Then the bribes got a bit larger. The family started quietly selling off possessions to get cash. Then they sold land and orchards. They eventually decided to leave secretly, which would cost $5,000 in gold per person.

The day for departure arrived, and as evening settled in, the family got on board the escape boat. Everyone but the old grandfather was there. He wanted to see his former home and businesses just one more time. Finally the captain said, "The tide is starting to turn, and the boat must sail."

At last the old grandfather came walking down the dock, clutching a briefcase with cash and gold, the remains of their fortune. As he approached the boat, his family urged, "Come on, Grandfather, we must go!"

Then suddenly a communist official stepped out of the shadows. "You may go," he told the old man, "but the briefcase must remain."

The grandfather looked at his family and then at his briefcase. He paused as the sailors untied the boat, and then, without looking back, he turned with head bowed, clutching his briefcase, and walked slowly back into the dark town. The boat sailed without him. The family never saw or heard from him again. George said the children needed help with a rent down payment and funeral expenses. CAMA helped.

By this time Drew was going to school at Black Forest Academy in Kandern, Germany. He worked well with correspondence courses, but he preferred the stimulating fellowship at Black Forest. He enjoyed playing soccer and making excursions to Basel, Switzerland with his friends. We made some weekend trips to see him at school and always enjoyed the experience.

Matt, being six years younger, enjoyed home school with Bev but always liked to see his brother at his school. On one trip he stayed overnight while Bev and I went for some business in Bonn, Germany. When we came back a teacher told us, "Yesterday at lunch, Matt came in and sat down. Drew and some others were missing. 'Where's Drew?' someone asked. 'Oh,' said another, 'he's chasing our sheep that got out again.' 'Sheep are really dumb,' said another. 'Well,' one boy said, 'when God created animals, He didn't make anything dumber than sheep.' After a quiet moment Matt said, 'Well, Jesus said we're all like sheep!'"

I continued a busy schedule of travel, so Bev did a lot of managing on her own. We didn't prefer life this way, but we accepted the situation as part of the price of service. Bev was alone when she got word that a dear friend, a nurse she had gone to school with, had committed suicide. As she cried and prayed for the family, the phone rang. It was Leakhena, our Cambodian refugee friend. She sensed Bev's sadness and asked, "Aunt Bev, what's wrong?"

Bev poured out her story, and Leakhena said, "When I get sad about the death in my family I play my Christian music, sing the songs, and pray. Then Jesus comforts me."

It was a wonderful reminder that although we had come to assist and comfort the refugees, when Bev needed comfort, a refugee comforted her.

I needed to go to Africa again. My itinerary was long and complicated. The first stop was Kinshasa, Zaire, followed by an MAF flight to Boma, Zaire. By road I went to visit Dr. and Mrs. Kroh, who, after Cambodia, had returned to Kinkonzi Hospital in Zaire. Then Dorothy Thomas drove me to Buku Tembe to meet refugees from Cabinda, Angola. The war there drove them into Zaire, and the CMA eagerly wanted to do a CAMA Service response for them.

I enjoyed seeing the Krohs and touring the hospital. They did a great job in a remote jungle setting. At dinner Esther said, "Dean, have Andy check our water tower; the water tastes funny."

When we climbed to the top of the tower, not only did we see leaves floating in the water, but also a dead mouse. "Oh, no," said Dean, "don't tell Esther! We'll have to drain the whole tank and scrub it, and I don't have the time."

"Do you have any Chlorox?" I asked while scooping out the mouse and leaves.

"Yes!" Dean replied.

"Good. Put a gallon in the tank, stir it, then run the faucet until you smell chlorine. Let it set overnight and you'll be okay."

We did the chlorination while Dean explained to Esther the taste was from some floating "stuff" that the chlorine would deal with. That answer satisfied her.

At the camp for Cabindan refugees, I asked the refugee camp leader, "What are your main needs?"

"Oh," he replied, "we need guns, tanks, ammunition, and things to get our country back from the communists."

Dorothy Thomas looked shocked. "Actually," I replied, "we are from the CMA, and we provide seeds, food, blankets, and tools. I'm sure the other group will come sometime."

Dorothy located some believers among the 9,000 refugees and set up a committee to hand out the aid once it came. She also found some Bible school students and arranged for them to continue their studies and handle the church as it began to form. We made a plan to submit to CMA headquarters in New York. The refugees did have freedom to hunt and forage, and with our seeds they busily planted gardens. They had a good outlook, and Dorothy found medical people to set up a clinic for them.

After meeting in Kinshasa with UNHCR officials, we planned to stop in Gabon. In Libreville, Mel Carter picked me up. We toured government offices and discussed the upcoming CMA expansion of the Bongolo medical program. Dave Thompson busily organized the program details and studied the local language. He got excited about the future there.

Then it was on to Abidjan, Ivory Coast. Fred Polding met me and we took the train, the Gazelle, to Bouake, where we attended some meetings of the Alliance World Fellowship. Drs. King and Bailey came, as well as CMA pastors from all over the world.

Fred and I decided to phone our wives. Bev had been holding down the program in Paris, which entailed hosting the Alliance Youth Team that had come for the summer and helping with David and Samuelle's wedding. Fred said we would need go to the Telephone and Postal Center and wait in line for at least two hours. "But we can pay a person to stand in line for us while we do something else," he explained.

On August 3, after making the arrangements, we went to the mission office. During our discussion, I noticed a new phone book on the desk. It announced direct dial service to the world, starting in May of that year, 1977. "Why are we standing in line, Fred?" I asked. "It says that we can dial direct there!"

"Oh, WAWA!" Fred laughed. "West Africa Wins Again. It means they say lots of things, but it never works."

I looked up the proper codes and began to dial Bev in Paris. Soon I heard her voice saying, "Hello."

It was great to hear her! She caught me up on things in Europe and told me that seven people had been staying in our apartment. The hot water provided by the city got turned off in August, so she heated water on the cook stove for baths!

Fred was jumping up and down. "My turn! Hurry up!" he said.

He made his call while David Arnold, the mission chairman, looked on in amazement. "We never tried it 'cause we didn't believe it," he kept saying.

It provided a good example that I used in several sermons years later.

Drs. King and Bailey, a few others, and I took the Gazelle from Bouaké to Bobo-Dioulasso in Upper Volta (later the country's name was changed to Burkina Faso). We discussed medical needs in the country as we drove to Koutiala, Mali, for dedication of the new mission headquarters, followed by a visit to the clinics the CMA operated there. Dr. Bailey said, "Well, I'll get a lot of ceremonial goats from the village churches. Then I'll say, 'Let's eat it together.' More Africans get my goat than you can imagine."

I made it home to Paris for our fifteenth wedding anniversary on August 18. I had been away for seven weeks, and Bev and the boys had done well. She excitedly told me of an answer to prayer. When I left, I had given our 12-member team money to carry them through August. Then I explained that it was the last of the money, and it would be up to the Lord whether or not we continued into September. "Pray," I admonished them. "I must go to Africa!"

While I was gone, Bev ran out of money due to the extra company she hosted. She prayed, "Lord, I need $200."

Shortly after, Bev got a call from Leakhena. She told Bev, "I've just come from visiting the Mortons in Japan. They sent you a letter."

When Bev opened the letter, there was a check for $200 along with a note of encouragement. "I should have prayed for more," she said, laughing.

CAMA faced a bigger need. I grew up in a family with seven kids and parents who prayed. My mother's favorite song was Trust and Obey. One year my dad cleared a new field for wheat. Mother and he committed one half of the expected yield to an Indian mission in Arizona. The crop looked good, but then a dry spell came. Dad prayed one day as he sat on a hill looking over the field. "Lord," he said, "our fields, Yours and mine, need rain. If not we'll not have much of a crop. But Lord, if You are satisfied with half of a poor crop, I'll be satisfied with the other half."

As he committed the outcome to the Lord, a breeze began to blow from the south and a small cloud appeared. As Dad watched, it came over the field and rained -- only on the wheat. The Lord got one half of a very good crop.

I needed rain, too, as the team headed back from their August vacations. We needed money for CAMA to continue, so we all prayed. A phone call from Grady Mangham soon after was the breeze-blown cloud we sought. "Someone has given CAMA $25,000," Grady said.

"Send it ASAP," I responded, "it's an answer to prayer."

The project never missed a beat.

Bev's brother Ed and his wife, also named Bev, arrived for a tour of Europe. Drew headed off for Black Forest Academy. The team had funds for their work. Things in Lebanon had been going well, as well as the program in Thailand, so we enjoyed a great two-week vacation showing her family the sights that had become part of our life.

Jan van Barneveld, from the TEAR Fund in Holland, reviewed my African program report and concluded that the Dutch government might be interested. He was right! He had once suggested that we use Dutch survival food. During the Cold War, European governments stored emergency supplies, including high-protein biscuits. They had to be replaced every ten years, even though they were still good. Jan proposed that they send the food to the hungry in Africa and Asia, so we sent out several containers. Twenty tons went to Zaire. They told us that when the Africans saw that the food was already ten years old, they grumbled but reasoned, "We can use the five-gallon tins for buckets and stoves."

But when they opened the sealed cans and tasted the biscuits, they said, "Wow, those Dutch bakers are really good. Even after ten years, these are still tasty with tea!"

Over the next few years, we shipped hundreds of tons to Asia and Africa. They saved a lot of lives. TEAR Fund also provided funds for agricultural projects like metal plows in Mali and wheels and axles to improve the donkey carts. They always enjoyed working through CAMA because we were linked into a grass roots infrastructure unlike most, and the Europeans had no problem with what are now called "faith based" organizations.

After travel to London and Amsterdam, we needed to return to Beirut again. This time Bev and Matt went with me. Norm and Bonnie Camp met us in Amman, Jordan. We enjoyed their hospitality and a fantastic trip for a picnic in Petra! Matt rode horses and a camel and got his own Arabian headdress.

Sami and Andy Kerr met us at the airport in Beirut. All the guns, roadblocks, shattered buildings, and other reminders of her Cambodian experiences alarmed Bev. But as before, the warmth and friendship of the people overcame her fear, and we had a great time with the Lebanese. We visited Aintoura and met several families who had become believers and begun attending the CMA church in Karantina. We also looked at targets for future work in Tarshishe. We saw individual houses being repaired, all of which were paid for by CAMA and its partners.

The U.S. Agency for International Development (USAID) and the U.N. became interested in our ability to mobilize the people so well. We explained that the church, with Sami as the motivator, was the key, as well as God's provision. On the way back to Beirut, we stopped at Byblos and saw the place where Saint Paul had set sail. We really enjoyed seeing all the biblical sites. The Kerrs did a good job and began talking of going back to the States for seminary. Overall, the project performed beyond our expectations, and God got all the glory.

Back in Paris, one of our favorite times was the team meals at CAMA Centre. They were usually after business meetings and often included the Dirks, Piagets, Penfolds, Dave Soquier, Nguyen Xuan Tinh, Thao Thongsouk, Josianne, Bev and me, and the boys when they were home. They always enjoyed those occasions. We loved the fellowship and stories of how the refugees adapted to France.

We had one special meeting that Grady Mangham attended to dedicate the CAMA Centre. The service was held in five languages, and the place was packed with refugees from various ethnic groups. Grady would speak a line in English, Daniel Bordreuil would translate to French, Ung Davy would translate to Cambodian, David Chan would translate to Chinese, and Nguyen Xuan Tinh would finish in Vietnamese. A "standing room only" meal followed. We saw our answered prayers in action, and I wondered what the final translation actually said.

Our work on behalf of the medical projects in Africa began bearing fruit. Money to upgrade the program had been granted with $10,000 from TEAR Fund, and the Dutch government had given $25,000 plus the high-protein biscuits. Dave Thompson busily studied language in Gabon as we sought funds for a mobile clinic and a builder to begin the Bongolo program.

We had also been seeking funds for a clinic building and a mobile clinic in Upper Volta. Mali had been granted $29,000, and our missionaries were excited about the new growth they had experienced. Dr. King was very pleased with the overall progress from the CAMA Services' efforts in every area.

Bev's parents came to visit. They had been reluctant to see us follow a missionary life, but they finally agreed to come see firsthand what we did. Ed, Bev's brother, had given them a good report after his visit, so they came to Paris.

We enjoyed two weeks of visits to various refugee centers and families, and to sights like Mont-Saint-Michel, the walled city of Carcassonne in France, Spain, Monte Carlo, Italy, Switzerland, Austria, and Drew's school in Germany. At every stop they were enchanted by the sights, and especially by the refugees who honored them for having their daughter serve the way she did. While on the autobahn in Germany, I suddenly noticed tears in Percy's (Bev's dad) eyes. "What's wrong?" I asked.

After a moment he replied, "I finally understand why you and Bev are over here. All those lovely refugees whom I did not know. What do

I do now? I am 63 years old, and I have lived my whole life with the wrong priorities!"

He had been a pastor for many years -- and now? "Well," I replied, "tell the Lord that and offer Him the rest of your time and talents for whatever He directs you to do."

He did, and over the next few years, Percy went with me several times to use his skills, such as building and electrical wiring, for missions.

❧

One day Leakhena excitedly told us, "My mother is alive!"

During the three years we had known her, she always requested prayer for her mom. She knew her dad had been killed, but she always prayed for her mom. Now, after three years, her mom had walked out of the forests of Cambodia into Thailand. She was very malnourished, but alive! When her mom got to Paris, she told us her story.

"When I escaped from Phnom Penh, I hid and lived in the forest," she said. "I had a picture of my children and a picture of Buddha. Daily I would pray to Buddha for my children. One day I lost Buddha's picture. I was worried, but then I had a dream. I saw a man in white with a beard. He comforted me and I realized it was Jesus, and now He was protecting my children."

From then on she prayed to Jesus for her children's care. Leakhena had the joy of leading her mother in prayer to faith in Christ.

❧

Don Dirks and I spent several days with Dr. King, the CMA vice president who was soon to become president. Bev and I began thinking about the end of our first four-year term. As Don and I discussed the future, we agreed that the CAMA program should become part of the mission's responsibility after we left. We discussed the subject with the team, and some wanted to change CAMA Services to a French name. "Let the refugees decide," I suggested.

After some discussion, the refugees said, "The CMA sent missionaries to us in our countries, and they told us of Jesus. When we became refugees, they sent CAMA Services to the camps and showed us Jesus. Now they are in France helping us. Refugees know CAMA Services, and it's a name they trust. If you want their cooperation and trust, keep the name of the center CAMA."

We encouraged Dr. King to raise the French mission budget by $20,000 for the year, explaining that there were nine refugee churches. "So," said Dr. King while fixing his eyes on Don with a severe, no-nonsense look, "will they become CMA churches after the Bishops leave?"

The question left Don speechless, so I said, "There are others watching them, and you can be sure they will move in to make them Baptists or Assembly if Don doesn't have the money to keep the programs operating."

After a moment, Dr. King said, "Okay."

By this time, Reg Reimer had become chairman of the CCSDPT in Bangkok. He and I spent time there with Dr. King, Evelyn Mangham, and Dave Andrianoff, evaluating CAMA and planning for a visit by the ZOA board to see the work. We signed a church mission CAMA agreement that Grady Mangham prepared to facilitate better cooperation.

We were amazed by the growth at the Ban Vinai Hmong refugee camp. Wayne Persons and Jerry Torgerson even had a check-cashing project for refugees whose families had gone abroad. In 1977, they had processed over $100,000. Dr. King preached to a group of more than 1,000 Hmong. We held meetings with Col. Kamol about moving refugees to countries in South America, and Reg preached at the Lam Sing boat people's camp. It was great to see the Vietnamese and Cambodians worshiping together, while only a few miles away their countrymen were at war.

When ZOA arrived, we had a great time. They all had cameras and would shout "Moment please!" while they stopped and snapped a photo.

We became the "Moment Please Tour!" Everyone was excited with the progress in the camps, and ZOA pledged to continue the partnership.

Col. Kamol hosted a dinner and told his guests, Dr. King and Grady, "God sent CAMA to us. Your work has saved many lives. CAMA never hid who they were and always did good work. Many groups came to me and tried to hide their Christian origins, but I am on the National Security Council and knew who they really were. In fact," he said, "I went to Bangkok Christian High School. I can even sing all your hymns."

Gen. Trasak Dhamaraks, the new under secretary of state for the Ministry of the Interior in Thailand, also attended the dinner.

By letting our lights shine, people saw the good works and gave God all the glory.

At Dr. King's request, I flew on to Djakarta, Indonesia. Richard Drummond met me and talked about the problems there. Tribal fighting in the Baliem Valley had destroyed churches and gardens. People of the Baliem Valley were hungry. I flew down to Irian Jaya from Djarkarta and met with the missionaries at Sentani. John Ellenberger reported that due to security concerns, travel to the valley had become dangerous and restricted, but he had been able to get us a two-day pass.

The next day, John and I flew in on MAF. We visited stations with grass landing strips, some of which were just short patches of grass going up a hillside. One was very short, with about a 40 degree grade. When we finished surveying the need, we roared downhill and off the cliff, gaining air speed just in time. There was never a dull moment in that valley. The Stone Age people had few coverings, the men only a gourd. I saw one woman nursing a baby on one breast and a baby pig on the other.

They used a helicopter to airlift food into needy areas, but they needed a place to store it. Most of the churches had spear holes in their roofs. "Let's put money in the budget request for food storage and distribution," I said. "That way, you can repair the churches and use them to store and distribute food and blankets."

We saw burned-out villages, and desperate people waiting near airstrips for food, all over the valley. We saw a small clinic at one stop where a long line of people waited for care. The needs included food packets, seeds, tools, and more medical help. We spent the night with Tom Bozeman and met with Tom, Jim Sunda, Dr. Myron Bromley, and Virgil Adams the next day. We wrote out a plan and asked Nita Fowler to type it. I flew to Ujung Pandang, where I presented the plan to Drs. King and Bailey and Bill Kerr, who were all pleased. The next day I flew back to Djarkarta and Singapore, then on to Bangkok, and then to Amman.

After spending the night in Amman, I continued on to Beirut for operational discussions. This time Rev. Harry Taylor, back from furlough, was there. I saw him as a missionary icon. He had served in Cambodia, been a prisoner of the Japanese for years, and after spending more time in Cambodia, came back to Lebanon!

Sami told me that the work team going to Tarshishe had been robbed on their way to the village. However, Mansour Raidy, a church member, had an uncle who was chief of the Phalange militia, which had done the bad deed and controlled the area. We climbed the stairs to the office of Salim Raidy. "Let Mansour go in first," Sami whispered. "If there's lots of kissing, it will be okay."

Well, there was, and we were welcomed with enthusiasm and coffee. "You Christians must help us," he said. "The Muslims want to drive us out of Lebanon like they did the Christians out of Damascus 500 years ago. They stop us at their roadblocks and kill us and exult as they drag our bodies behind their cars!"

"Yes," I replied, "but they disappear at your roadblocks, too."

"Yes, we do kill them, but it's with regret and shame that we must."

"To us in America, they are just as dead, and now you even rob our workers trying to help you." He looked surprised, and Sami explained the robberies. "I promise you it will cease at once," he said, and it did.

The fighting continued, some being very serious. Sami brought me up to date on the work and gave me the audit of the books to pass on to donors.

Back in Paris, things went well. We arranged everything so that we could turn the work over to Don Dirks before heading back to the U.S. for furlough. On Sunday I spoke at the American Cathedral in Paris. It was a beautiful facility, and in the afternoon it hosted the Lao and Hmong churches. After I spoke on the subject ,"They that wait on the Lord," from Isaiah 40:31, I went back to shake hands with the people as they left. Among them was the American ambassador. "Was that 'waiting poem' in the Bible?" he asked.

I smiled and gave him the reference.

Col. John and Barbara Hocker had dinner with us. We enjoyed their friendship and their help time and again with refugees. They had spoken for the Lao and Hmong using the cathedral. We considered the Hockers CAMA partners. Elizabeth Preisig was another unusual team member. She had been a Swiss missionary to Laos and helped us greatly by setting up projects and representing CAMA to Swiss churches. She delighted in smuggling refugees into Switzerland in her little Deux Chevaux car.

She also helped arrange a retreat for Cambodians in Switzerland, along with Josianne. Gene Hall and Norm Ens were selected to be the speakers. The Ens decided to come for a week, maybe two. They had been pastoring a church in Canada.

By that time, Ung Davy had married a nice Swiss girl and was excited about the retreat. He had become the leader of the Cambodian Christians across France.

The retreat went well, but a small delegation of Cambodians huddled in the Ens' room at the end. "Why are you in Canada?" they asked. "You can teach Jesus so well in our language, and we are so thirsty for God's Word. It's like when we were escaping Cambodia in the forest, our children cried for water and we had nothing to give them but our tears. Please stay and help us."

Norm and Marie broke down. "They were right," he said later. "We belonged with them."

They phoned Canada and got their church to release them for ministry in France, and they decided to return to France a couple of months later. A few days after making their decision, Ung Davy and his wife were killed in a car crash. The news shocked the Cambodians, but they took comfort in knowing Norm and Marie Ens planned to come and pick up the work.

Our time in Paris would soon come to an end, and CAMA Services was about to face a new challenge.

Food for work. Reforestation in Africa

A well equipped African kitchen

In limbo behind the wire. Refugees wait for sponsorship

A well dressed refugee/resistance fighter

Chapter 9
Home and Abroad ~ Part 1

Chapter 9.
Home and Abroad ~ Part 1

One key to CAMA's success was that we encouraged and facilitated direct contact between people in the field and the donors. It gave donors a level of participation that fostered their generous giving. One such trip brought Reg and Donna Reimer to Paris from Bangkok so they could make a personal connection with European supporters.

The Reimers really added to the team. Their experiences in Vietnam, in helping people escape in the final days of the war, and then on Guam and in the U.S. as they assisted the CMA and the refugees, gave them great credibility. Many of the refugees were members of the Tin Lanh CMA church in Vietnam, and the Reimers had been instrumental in finding resettlement homes in the States and Canada. They were presently keeping up the pace with CAMA in Thailand, so people listened when they spoke for the refugees. After Paris, I took them to Holland, where we made the rounds of TEAR Fund, ZOA, and other organizations.

Reg told me about some discussions going on between the CMA and World Relief (WRC). He said some in CMA were nervous about CAMA's growth, and they would rather use WRC for CMA's relief and development activities than have an in-house program.

He continued, "I want to go to the U.S. and get on the council floor and demand they recognize CAMA Services and give us their support!"

I quickly responded, "Reg, that could get us fired."

"They can't fire us. We're the generals," he snapped.

"Have you ever heard of Patton and MacArthur?" I asked.

"Working for this outfit is like wearing a dark suit and wetting your pants," he grumbled. "You get a warm feeling, but nobody notices!"

I chuckled and replied, "God knows, and when it's His time, He will make CAMA Services known in His way."

Jerry Ballard, the incoming director of WRC, phoned to say he would be in Geneva, Switzerland, on his way to meet with Francis Schaeffer. "I'll meet you in Geneva and go along," I said. "I want to meet him, too."

Schaeffer was warm and relaxed during the meeting, as he carefully listened to Jerry's comments. Basically, Jerry's said that the church had neglected the most-important part of the gospel -- feeding the hungry, caring for the sick, developing better living, and advancing justice. Schaeffer was patient in his explanation, and he later sent us the following letter:

Chalet les Melexes,
1861 Huemox,
Switzerland
29th April, 1978

Mr. Jerry Ballard
World Relief Commission, Inc.
P.O. Box 28
Wheaton, Ill. 60187 USA

Mr. Andrew E. Bishop
1, Allee de Norvege
91300 Massy,
FRANCE

Dear Jerry and Andrew,

Please pardon me for sending this as a carbon copy to you, Andrew, but I just finished the script and I am leaving again at once but wanted to send this letter to you, and this was the only way I could squeeze it in.

First, I want to tell you that I was glad we could talk the other day in Montreux. After we finished our conversation, I felt that we had left something unwrapped and I am writing to you. I hope it helps.

I do not think we can have two equally perspective points. I am sure God can, but we are finite and can't. One thing will be primary and another thing to some degree subservient to the primary. Thus, in what we were talking about – the Gospel and Social elements (especially when we got into "development") will not both be equal. One will be predominant and the other will tend to take a secondary position. I think this is true no matter how hard we fight against it. I, of course, think the Gospel should be first and then the Social elements (including development) must I hope be allowed to be minimized.

If the Social things are made primary, the Gospel will be secondary. This will be especially so if the Bible is being weakened as it is in evangelical circles. I think for example of the leading man, you, Jerry quoted, the leading man in relief work as saying that the N.A.E. should not have a doctrinal statement but welcome all evangelicals. The problem, of course, is the word 'evangelical' today means nothing, and certainly has decreasingly doctrinal content in regard to our base, the Bible.

I do not think we could have two equal perspective points even if the Bible is not being weakened but the need I think is obvious. As I quoted Billy Graham, I do believe he is right that we are where the ecumenical movement was in 1910 at Edinburgh. They had a weakened Bible even then, and thus the "Social Gospel" became everything and the Gospel nothing.

I do not think by any means that it will take 60 years for us to go from where they were in 1910 to where they are now. The spread of everything is faster today.

Nor do I think we can minimize the pendulum effect which has always operated in human thought and endeavor – including the church. We have been overwhelmingly weak in stressing the compassionate use of accumulated wealth in the past. The pendulum effect will certainly mean there will be a tendency for the pendulum to swing now to the other side. This would be true in the past conditions. Add to it the weakening of the Bible and the lack of a conscious decision to make the Gospel perspective first with Social things second and I do not think we have to guess where it will quickly end.

As I say in thinking over our conversation, it seems to me I did not answer you on this when you, Jerry, raised it, and thus I felt I should write to you.

I will be praying for both of you in this regard and ask you to pray for me. Do feel free to share this letter to anyone that you wish to, but if it was to be used in any written form in any way I would want to clear it up because I am dictating and not feeling too well on a very rushed Saturday afternoon.

With warm personal greetings,
    In the Lamb,
    Francis A. Schaeffer

After our discussion, Dr. Schaeffer said to me, "You in the CMA understand the importance of keeping the gospel the main thing uppermost in ministry."

As we drove back to Geneva, Jerry outlined his dream for WRC. I still did not know what had been transpiring at Nyack, but I said we would be happy to cooperate in any way we could.

Back in Beirut, I had the privilege of attending Sami Dagher's ordination. You could still hear fighting outside the city as militias and the PLO continued to struggle for control. The machine gun and mortar fire lent background sound to the ceremony. After getting details and budget projections to pass on to the donors, I returned to Europe.

After a farewell picnic with our team, the family and I went to London for a few days. We enjoyed seeing the sights and driving through the English countryside. Dr. King and Grady Mangham had gone to England for a CMA workers conference. We discussed the conditions of the CAMA/WRC merger, and I had concerns that I made clear. We did not want to sever our CMA relationship. Dr. King agreed. He later appointed me overseas representative for CAMA, to secure my help as needed for specific CMA needs.

On Saturday, August 5, 1978, we flew to New York. We went through the activities the CMA had for all returning missionaries, which included a seminar for those going on tour. Tour is an institution experienced by missionaries of the CMA. We call it the "CMA trial separation experience" because husband and wife/children are apart for weeks of public speaking assignments in churches all over America and Canada. We tell the story of God at work overseas. This educates and informs, as well as raises the money needed for funding missions. The seminar was to reacquaint us after four years with conditions in the churches we would visit. We heard about how to dress, act, and present our material.

Don Dirks in Paris had given me some good preparation for this experience, so I assembled a slide show titled "Round the World with CAMA Services."

Gene Evans, whom I had talked with almost four years earlier, conducted the seminar on the presentation of materials. He said he wanted us to "perform" and have the group critique the material. No one moved, so I said, "Here's mine," and showed "Round the World…"

When I finished, there was a stunned silence. "Well," Gene said, "don't you think it's a bit long? I timed it at 45 minutes."

Then an older missionary from India rose and with emotion said, "Don't change a thing. It's wonderful. I had no idea that CAMA Services existed. We need to hear more about this!"

A chorus of agreement rose from the group. My apprehension about being a public speaker subsided somewhat.

Discussions with WRC continued. I flew to Chicago and met with Jerry Ballard, and then back to Nyack to meet with Dr. King.

Finally we flew back to Seattle and Ellensburg. Between things like getting a house rented and driver's license renewed, we had a week of salmon fishing with Bev's parents at their summer home in Ilwaco, Washington. We enjoyed being home and also had fun on the ranch. My parents were happy to see us and brought us up to date on the Cambodian family they had sponsored. The Cambodians had moved to Seattle, where they now had a pizza restaurant and some of their kids enrolled at the university.

We had speaking engagements and newspaper interviews and got the boys settled in the schools they would attend. Our friends treated us wonderfully. They set us up in a comfortable home, and I even got welcomed back to Rotary. They said I would be their member at large.

Suddenly our tour time came, and I flew to Akron, Ohio, to start my tour. Bev did some part-time work at the health clinic and became a full-time parent at home. From September to early November, I showed slides and spoke in churches, schools, service clubs, youth groups, and small group gatherings. I found it to be a wonderful experience. It amazed people to see what God had been doing through CAMA Services. People most often asked, "How can I join?"

One day I sat with Gordon Blossom, the Kittitas County Engineer, in his office at the courthouse. I listened to him grumble about his problems with the latest edict from above. The courthouse was running out of space. The bureaucracy had grown during the four years we had been away, and Gordon had to make space for more offices. Among other things was a "packaged disaster hospital" stored there in case of a nuclear attack. "We can't just dump it," he complained; "it has to go to a nonprofit agency."

Knowing the county elections were coming up, I said, "I have an idea. Who's running for office?"

Gordon said, "Roy Lumaco up in Cle Elum is running for county commissioner."

I continued, "Let me call him. Better still, I'll go see him!"

We had a good visit at Roy's place of business, Star Cleaners, in Cle Elum, Washington. He had been in office when we left and became a good friend. "How would you like to be photographed giving that old disaster hospital to the new hospital we're building in Gabon, Africa?" I asked. "The doctor, Dave Thompson, is the son-in-law of Betty Mitchell, whose brother-in-law Vern owns the air service in Ellensburg! We can use our new connection with WRC to get free shipping, and the Alliance Men and Alliance Women will even remove it from the courthouse storage, saving the county money and freeing the needed space!"

"Done!" he cheerfully responded.

It made the paper, photo and all. Once it arrived in Gabon, Dave Thompson got many years of good use out of the equipment.

During our year in Ellensburg, Bev took a course in accounting at Central Washington University; she needed the skill to help in the field. She also kept busy with projects at the CMA church, now numbering over 400 attendees. While we were away, they had begun to build a new building. The pastor, Tim Owen, told me, "We needed a lot of dirt to fill the property. One day I was at the site where they were beginning the city's new pool facility to replace the one you condemned and closed before you left for Cambodia. They were complaining about the cost of dumping the dirt they were to excavate. 'Well,' I told them, 'you can dump it at our church site for free.' Our new church was built on that dirt!"

Bev and I helped put the finishing touches on the new building.

The negotiations between the CMA and WRC had progressed to the point that we were close to signing an agreement. At my insistence and with Dr. King's confirmation, we planned a two-year trial period. Half our support would come from CMA, the other half from WRC. I thought this would give both organizations the motivation to cooperate.

In January 1979, I made a trip around the world for CAMA Services and the WRC. The final steps of the merger were explained to everyone in the field, and CAMA committed to seeing that our long-term refugee commitments were kept. When I arrived in Bangkok on January 8, Reg told me that the Vietnamese had just captured Phnom Penh and were moving west. Reg had assembled a great team, and Dave Andrianoff had been making significant progress with the Hmong. Gary Johnston, son of a CMA missionary in Thailand, had taken leave from Houghton College to join the project, "In Time of Need."

They estimated that 6,000 Hmong would cross the Mekong River during the low-water season and that they would need to be there to offer help on the riverbank. Reg figured they would need four dollars per person, or $24,000, to provide each refugee with an emergency aid kit much like the one we had in 1975. WRC staff had come to visit, and when they saw what Reg's team needed, they gave him a check for $20,000. Reg then phoned Jan van Barneveld at TEAR Fund concerning the project and needs, and Jan arranged for a Dutch businessman to buy the needed pickup truck. After it arrived, the new, yellow CAMA pickup raced up and down the Mekong delivering the badly needed aid as refugees were herded to police stations for processing. The agony of the traumatic escape from the horrors of war changed into smiles of relief and gratitude as Dave, Gary, and other volunteers handed them the kits and promised to see them in the refugee camp.

Reg said that by the end of that season, they had helped 6,000 refugees and the costs were as estimated, $24,000. I was so thankful for God's provision.

Next I stopped in Manila, where Rev. LeRoy Josephsen met me and explained the growing refugee problem there. He had been a missionary in Vietnam and had helped with the evacuation and the CMA Heart Beat resettlement program in the U.S. Five thousand boat people had been staying in a makeshift camp outside Manila, plus 2,500 on a boat in the harbor. He had already led more than 100 to Christ and was excited about what the Lord was doing. He introduced me to others who worked with the plan as well, in order to build a larger camp up at Bataan. We pledged CAMA/WRC's participation.

Back in Thailand I flew to Nan, where Jerry Torgerson and his wife, Rose, had been working with refugees in the country's remote northern corner. They showed me agricultural projects, the CAMA craft sewing projects, blacksmith shops, and woodworking. I also enjoyed seeing Doris Whitelock still riding her "wee little motorbike" while faithfully ministering to the refugees.

Returning to Bangkok, I discussed the upcoming CAMA/WRC merger with Reg. Grady Mangham had joined WRC to head up their new U.S. refugee resettlement program. We worked on a proposed budget and then added a contingency for new refugees we expected from Cambodia later in the year, as well as more boat people from Vietnam.

I went to Hong Kong. Betty Arnold, another former missionary to Vietnam, had already come to the city to help with the boat people coming north. She took me to Macao to see refugees there. In each area, the message was the same. As we gave help based on the gospel, people responded to the message of Jesus Christ.

From Hong Kong I went to Tokyo to talk with Sue Morton. Her Refugee International project had met with good success. Everyone in Holland was thankful for the progress and for the planning for the expected numbers of new refugees coming over to freedom. They reminded me that they expected Bev, the boys, and me to move to Holland later that year. I had still been trying to convince Jerry about the need for such a move.

The spring tour began in the pacific northwest, which allowed me to see the family from time to time, and made being away less disagreeable. In between trips, consultations with Jerry Ballard continued. He still did not know how everything would come together.

In April, a trip to Beirut took me back to meet with Sami Dagher and the team. The Syrian army had moved into Aintoura. One of the new Christian families had been warned to stop the Bible studies at their home. Isabel led the study, and her husband, not yet a believer, pressured her to stop. Reluctantly, she obeyed. When fighting began in their area, a Syrian soldier came into their home. He ordered the family, including her mother-in-law and her three children, into their kitchen. He then threw a phosphorus grenade into the room and bolted the door. It exploded, and the intense flames burned Isabel's mother-in-law to death and crippled Isabel and her children. It scarred her face and body, and her hands got burned so badly that she could barely use them. She was, however, victorious in that she had memorized most of the book of James and was proving faithful in persevering under trials. Later we helped by giving her the opportunity to have plastic surgery on her face and hands.

Sami and the church had been under a lot of pressure. They had decided to build the village of Tarshishe next. Because of its being half Muslim, the challenge was getting the two groups to talk and agree that their village would live again.

The church prayed, and Sami finally got the two factions to meet in the village. Sami noted the cool reserve on all sides. "What," he said, "no embraces?" It was a custom to show friendship this way.

"Perhaps later," one leader responded, "but this is the first time in two years we have met without trying to kill each other."

Soon more than 20 houses had been repaired. But Satan did not give up. One house got blown up as a warning to stop the work, and someone trying to extort money threatened Sami. The church prayed, and an outbreak of fighting intervened. The church was spared. In spite of harassment by snipers, shelling of the area, and even a farmer killed by a mine planted in his orchard, the Karantina church continued to be a strong base for CAMA in Lebanon, and Tarshishe lived again.

Visitors like Bob Pierce, George Hoffman, and Franklin Graham added funds, as did Billy Graham's organization, and a larger sanctuary was built in the old Karantina building that the church owned. Many of the young men in the church had been trained to expand the scope of Christian outreach in Lebanon.

From Beirut I traveled to Bangkok for more review and planning, as the war in Cambodia inched even closer to Thailand. Col. Kamol said that preliminary contacts with the Khmer Rouge suggested there would be a serious problem. The communists wanted a safe hideout from which to fight the Vietnamese. Thailand said no, but the concern was for the civilians trapped in the middle.

While there I also received The Red Cross Medal of Merit. CAMA's prompt action in 1975 had mobilized support for the refugees and saved lives. It was the first medal of its kind awarded in eight years. Reg Reimer got one, too.

Back in Ellensburg, after a brief time with the family, my next step was an 11-day tour of Canadian CMA churches. Then, at a meeting in Nyack, we finalized the agreement between CAMA and WRC. It insured active participation by the CMA in the ongoing projects and WRC's intention to keep them in operation.

Our family was finally able to take a couple of weeks for vacation with some friends. The Harold Holters from Richland, Washington lent us a nice motor home in which we toured our own state of Washington. We fished, camped, and later visited my sister, Coralie Durden, in Bellingham, Washington. At 2:00 a.m. one morning, my sister's phone rang. It was Sue Morton calling from Tokyo. "Andy," she said, "we need $5,000 to start an action to help the boat people from Vietnam. All the world leaders are here for a summit, and we want to put an advertisement in the Japanese Time magazine and the Herald Tribune to challenge them to act in helping the boat people. If I can find $5,000, the owner of World Airways will give $7,000."

Our new connection with WRC helped, and the ad worked to bring aid to the thousands of Vietnamese then flooding the ports of Asia. Sue's Refugee International project grew.

On my previous stop in Hong Kong I met with Dr. Tom Stebbins, another former Vietnamese missionary. After helping with the U.S. resettlement, he had gone to Hong Kong. In a meeting to bring me up to date concerning the situation with the boat people, he asked for help.

"What do you need?" I asked.

He responded, "How much money can we have?"

I continued, "That's not the question. The question is what tools do you need to do the work?"

I got out a sheet of paper and began to write a list. We wrote down

Bibles, literature, clothing, blankets, and other tools. "Now," I asked, "how will you minister?"

We added a projector, P.A. system, screen, and so on.

"How will you move from camp to camp?"

"Well," he said, "a van would be best."

We added that to the list and then began to total estimated costs. When we got the total of over $250,000, John Bechtel, the Hong Kong field director, said excitedly, "We have needs, too!"

"What?" I asked.

"Well," he said, "we need a radio studio. How much money can we have?"

"John," I said, "let's make a list."

Now, I had no idea who to ask for the funds. From my experience, though, once we went through the process, "then we knew how much to pray for!"

Bechtel's list totaled $100,000. I had an idea. "Who will this studio prepare messages for?"

"Chinese," John answered.

Seeking more detail, I asked, "Be more specific, where and what group?"

John said, "We focus on south China."

To clarify I asked, "And what has recently happened down there?"

When he didn't respond, I pointed out, "The Vietnamese expelled 200,000 Chinese a while ago, so there are a lot of refugees there. Target them, and we can ask the people who are concerned with funding refugees for this money."

John had a big smile. "We'll do it," he said.

When I got back to Ellensburg, Don Dyk, a good friend and supporter, asked if I had anything special he could help with. We had written up the Boat People Hong Kong project and the radio studio project, and I had forwarded them to ZOA and TEAR Fund in Holland and WRC. I showed Don the radio studio project, and he wrote a check for $1,000, which got sent to John Bechtel with a note that said, "Keep on praying, only $99,000 left to go."

∽

"Andy, can you come to Holland right away?"

Jan van Barneveld had called to announce that the boat people project had become a great interest to the ZOA and the Dutch government.

I flew to Chicago, where Jerry Ballard joined me for the flight to Amsterdam. "The Dutch will have a full schedule from the time we hit the ground on," I warned him.

"Not me," he explained. "I like to rest for one night before I enter negotiations."

Sure enough, Jan was eagerly waiting at the airport. He had scheduled a meeting with a Dutch foreign aid official in The Hague, along with Tom Stebbins from Hong Kong. Jerry left for the Hilton; I left for The Hague. The meeting didn't take long. They reviewed the project and were impressed by the years of experience, as well as CMA's on-the-ground infrastructure. They knew Jan van Barneveld's reputation, and in a short time they committed over $250,000 for Hong Kong. Jan called the aid packets "Love Buckets," as the materials, packed in plastic pails that had many uses, got handed to the refugees as they got off the boats.

Henk van der Velde from ZOA then came and said we needed to leave for a ZOA meeting in Groningen, where they had been discussing further aid. I phoned Jerry to explain the progress and told him we were driving to Groningen. Astounded, he made arrangements to come with us. The meeting with ZOA provided further commitments for funds, and we finally convinced Jerry that our family should come to live in Holland.

In Utrecht we met with Clem and Maddie Dreger, former missionaries in Thailand and Laos. As CMA representatives in Holland, they were of great help to our family when we moved there a few months later. After we completed our work, Jerry headed back to

Wheaton, and I went to Paris for a meeting with Don Dirks and the CAMA Centre refugee committee. Thankfully the Lord provided, and everything moved along well. Back in Doorn, at Jan van Barneveld's, we completed some details for the Love Buckets. Finally on the 4th of July, I caught a Scandinavian Airlines flight via Copenhagen to Seattle.

The last weeks in Ellensburg involved cleaning out the house, getting Matt and Drew to our church's youth camp -- Camp Wooten -- packing our belongings, and shipping them to Rotterdam, Holland.

Drew had his sixteenth birthday, and on the last morning he went to take his driving test. Al Johnson, a game warden and friend from church, went with him as I helped Bev and Matt get our things to the airport. Earlier Vernon Mitchell, Betty Mitchell's brother-in-law, had asked me, "How are all of you getting to Seattle Tuesday?"

My response was, "I don't know yet. I'm giving our car to the Johnsons, as theirs is shot."

"I'll take you," he volunteered.

What a deal! He was flying a beautiful King Air twin turboprop to Seattle for the owner.

The plane was packed with our goods, and we waited for Drew. Suddenly we heard the horn honking, and up raced Al and Drew. Drew's smile said it all. Al explained he failed the first test, but Al had convinced the state examiner to let Drew take it again instead of waiting the usual two weeks. When the examiner understood Drew would be away for a long time and couldn't come back, he relented.

At 15,000 feet, we cruised past Mount Rainier with Drew in the copilot's seat. Matt lounged in the executive easy chair. "Dad," he said, "this missionary life isn't bad!"

Indeed God is good and had been waiting at every bend in the road to point the way with great assurance.

In Holland, we got some rest with the Dregers in Utrecht. Clem helped me buy a car, and Henk helped find a house. Housing is pretty tight there, so it was an answer to prayer when we found a place in the village called Saaksumhuizen, just outside Groningen. It was a wealthy family's "summer house," but they agreed to rent it to us.

As we settled in, we found the Dutch people warm and helpful. The small village housed only 40 people when everyone was home, and it didn't even have a grocery store. If we needed groceries, we hung a small flag on the gate post. Then three times a week, when the mobile grocery store drove through, the driver would see our flag and stop. Another village a short distance away did have a few stores. Matt saw a photo on our wall of a helicopter lowering food when the village had been snowed in years before. One day he said, "Mom, when are we going to get our winter emergency supplies?"

Thankfully we had very little snow that year and the helicopters didn't come, which left Matt disappointed.

With another school year about to begin, Bev decided to home school Matt, and Drew planned to return to Kandern to live in a dorm and attend the Black Forest Academy. Life in Holland got underway. ZOA rented an office, and Janni Loman came to work as secretary. We had lots of answers to prayers. Don reported that TEAR Fund England had taken on the main funding for the CAMA Centre.

Jan van Barneveld needed more information as soon as possible. He taught me that not only is time equal to money, but that timely information equals more money. To get it I had to go to the site of need and bring back firsthand reports. ZOA felt the same. My travels for this trip began in Ouagadougou, Upper Volta, Africa, to have dinner with the president of the country. He thanked us for the effective development assistance we had provided. While there I met Moise Napon, a fine believer who had experience with African development. "I'm going to need a person who can travel freely, understand the difference between wants and needs, and lead us to the heart of the problem," I explained.

"Will you listen to me?" he asked.

"Yes," I affirmed.

Thus began a great friendship and partnership in Africa.

From Ouagadougou, to Paris, to Bangkok, I lived on airline food. After meetings in Bangkok came meetings in Hong Kong. The boat people piled up, and they needed more staff to respond to the ministry opportunities. John Bechtel took me to see Mr. Courtland of the Hong

Kong government. They were strapped for places to hold refugees for onward travel and thankful for our help providing refugee assistance and finding places for resettlement.

En route to Wheaton, I spoke at Alliance Men's meetings in Victoria, Vancouver, Kelowna, 10th Avenue in Vancouver, and Kamloops, all in British Columbia, Canada. The trip had been arranged by Martin Hartog, a wool salesman and native of Holland. He was eager to know if there was a place for him in CAMA or WRC. We prayed about it, and then I headed for more meetings in Wheaton. We spent a lot of time planning and considering how to meet all the refugee needs. At this point, WRC had people seconded from several church groups and had been working on how to meet all their expectations.

Grady Mangham made good progress setting up the WRC resettlement program, which also grew. He had strong contacts with CMA missionaries who had Vietnam experience, and soon they joined the WRC/CAMA team in Asia.

Jerry Ballard was perplexed. He felt he needed to have all funds come to Wheaton before going to the fields. We in CAMA always had the funds go directly to the field. The Europeans insisted on this, so Jerry finally gave in. WRC had been a guest under CAMA's legal registration in Asia. Since one could not easily register without some active history in the country, Jerry had to accede to that operational pattern. I noted these concerns and stayed busy with my part of the program.

Suddenly events transpired to tax all our resources. The Vietnamese had finally pushed the Khmer Rouge out of Cambodia. This is how we wrote about the experience in the January 9, 1980, Alliance Witness:

Like an aroused army, Christians around the world are responding to the desperate need of Cambodian refugees.

THE MIRACLE OF COMPASSION
By ANDREW E. BISHOP

I heard someone shout, "Don't put the dirt on them yet! I saw that one move."

Only quick action by one of the grave diggers spared the Cambodian refugee from being buried alive. She was on a cart being wheeled through the muddy throng of sick, weary refugees waiting for medical attention at the Sakaeo refugee camp in Thailand.

I grabbed a grass mat and pushed through the crowd to where the men were struggling with the cart. The woman looked awful: the gray pallor of death was on her face, and her hair and clothes were clotted with mud. And yet—yes, there was a heartbeat! Quickly we placed her on the mat and rolled up the corners until we had a stretcher. We made our way back through the crowd to the first of ten tent medical wards. Each of the tents contained close to 200 sick and dying people.

The French doctor looked at her and said, "She's too far gone to bother with. Take her away."

We moved to another tent. The Baptist doctor said, "Quick! Intravenous fluids. We'll try...I've found a vein, and the heartbeat is strong."

I bathed her face with a bucket of not-so-clean water. She was hot with fever and responded to the cool rag as the water ran down through her hair.

It was October 28, 1979.

Only a week before I had spoken in the American Church in Paris and celebrated my birthday with my wife, Bev, and son Matt. En route back to our home in northern Holland, we discussed the preparations under way for the expected refugee exodus from Cambodia into Thailand. In September I had attended a briefing by the Thai Military Supreme Command with Mr. Reginald Reimer, director of the combined activities in Southeast Asia of the World Relief Corporation (WRC) and CAMA Services, the relief agency of the Alliance.

The Thai Military had told us that famine was widespread in Cambodia, and this as well as the war situation would bring about 300,000 unwanted people into their country. They were concerned that the war would come to them also, and they were seeking assurance that we would continue to help in the way we had for the past four and a half years, and give additional assistance for the expected newcomers.

I had discussed some of the implications of the influx of refugees with Dr. L. L. King at the WRC board meeting in early October, and subsequently we had been fitting together the pieces necessary for program expansion.

God began preparations even earlier. Major Eva den Hartog, a famous Salvation Army disaster worker from Holland, had been commissioned by our Dutch fund raiser, ZOA, to evaluate CAMA's Service work in Hong Kong and Thailand.

This she did in September. Her conclusion: "The theme of 'soup, soap and salvation' is being fully implemented by WRC/CAMA Services in Southeast Asia." She also said to us: "If you need any help, I'll take leave and go."

On October 19 a consortium called the Christian Medical Team was formed in Holland. It would recruit a medical team of eight to twelve members that would be headed by Major den Hartog and be financed by WRC, CAMA Services, TEAR Fund, ZOA and the Salvation Army. They would all be seconded to Mr. Reimer during the impending Cambodia emergency. Their departure for Thailand would be in mid-November.

"Here and Now," the Dutch TV equivalent of "60 Minutes" in the United States, gave Eva den Hartog and the medical team eight minutes of coverage. Money began to come in immediately. We needed at least $600,000.

As Bev, Matt and I walked into our house in Holland, the phone was ringing. It was Jerry Ballard, director of WRC. "Andy, it's begun. Reg (Reimer) said they are pouring over the border. Can you go immediately and help? There is also a need to visit Hong Kong."

First I dialed Rev. John Fitzstevens in Hong Kong. Our conversation was quick. Only a few decisions had to be made, and then he would carry on in the beautiful way he and his wife, Esther, always do.

Next I telephoned Mr. Reimer in Bangkok. He was not yet over a bout with typhoid and sounded very tired. "Yes, they're coming ... Don't know exact numbers... We need food, medicines, and that medical team. And if you can come, come!

"We have half our mission staff in Thailand helping out on the border and over it. When Irene Brock found she was in Cambodia, she said, 'But I don't even have a visa for Cambodia!'

"They are hauling the sick and the starving out of the forest over the border. In one shelter I saw 100 people lying there, 20 of them already dead... Everyone is exhausted.

I then called Henk van der Velde of the Committee of Helping Southeast Asia, better known as ZOA. They have been the main source of relief funds for four and a half years of refugee work in Thailand. "Henk," I said, "the emergency we spoke of last Friday is now -- not next month."

"What shall we do?" he responded.

"Send Reg $100,000 and raise $500,000 more."

"OK," he said, "we'll do it."

Next I phoned Jan van Barneveld, of TEAR Fund Netherlands. "Jan," I said, "can you select the team and get Eva Den Hartog to Thailand next week?"

"With God's help, yes!"

A call to Rev. Donald Dirks, C&MA Board representative in Paris, followed. "Don, would you ask Norm (Rev. Norman) and Marie Ens (C&MA missionaries in France) and Ngyeth Thavy (a Christian Cambodian residing in France) if they can go to Thailand immediately? We must have the gospel preached."

"OK," he said. "I'll get it cleared and send them as quickly as possible."

Major den Hartog canceled her scheduled public appearances in England and returned to Holland on October 24. She selected her 11-member Thailand medical team from a group of 30 volunteers who had been assembled on very short notice. Among them were young, medically qualified C&MA missionary appointees brought by Rev. Clement Dreger, board representative in the Netherlands, and Adriaan Stringer, president of the Belgium Bible Institute.

Mr. Dirks called back that day to say that Ngyeth Thavy and the Enses were packing in Paris. Also that same day TEAR Fund shipped $52,000 worth of medicines to Thailand, and we ordered 200 tons of high protein biscuits. ZOA chartered a plane to send 32 tons of specialized foods, medicines and medical equipment -- that alone cost $260,000.

On Thursday, October 25, I was on my way. I slept soundly most of the 14 flying hours to Bangkok. The next day I met with three of the Thailand missionaries -- Reg Reimer, Dave Fitzstevens and Darlene Dreger -- and went through the list of things to do. A voluntary medical team from the Thailand Baptist Mission, augmented by C&MA Edna

Hooper and Peggy Gunther, was ready to start the CAMA Services medical program at Sakaeo.

Rev. and Mrs. Oliver Kaetzel and Donna Reimer were preparing the houses we were renting near the camp as an operating base. Two 15-passenger Toyota vans and a pickup truck were readied at the border. In addition Gary Johnston was everywhere, helping, hauling, and building. It was a magnificent team effort.

It all came together by God's grace, by His direction and from His great resources. Problems like customs clearance and visas, always formidable, were easily dealt with when the Dutch ambassador agreed to meet the medical team personally and receive the charter plane load of goods. In 14 days a half million dollars were donated in Holland for the work of the team.

Meanwhile WRC and C&MA were combing the world for doctors, nurses and Cambodian-speaking missionaries. In the United States Dr. Robert Beck, a former missionary doctor in Cambodia, borrowed $10,000 and left a just-purchased medical practice to help the people he had come to love. WRC flew in a doctor-and-nurse married couple who had taken a 45-day leave from their mission hospital in Brazil.

Franklin Graham of World Medical Missions arrived in Bangkok with his medical director. And so it has gone. God's people praying, giving and going when the need arises.

On November 2 Mr. and Mrs. Ens, accompanied by Ngyeth Thavy, arrived from Paris. Their first remark was, "When do we start?" Some who heard why they had come were apprehensive. "There are Khmer Rouge, the killers of Cambodia, in that camp," they said.

We knew that, but all we could see were tired, sick, lost people for whom Jesus had died. He was giving us a chance to reach them with the gospel for the first time in four and a half years. We also knew that not all of them were Communists. Some were slaves used to support the troops until they starved. We had to trust God for the right method, the right opening and let Him do the rest.

The next day I took Norm, Marie and Thavy to the camp. They were literally moved with compassion. In no time Norm was on his knees in the dirt, helping diagnose very sick Cambodians, and Marie was comforting some of the over 400 orphans and showing them the first real love they had had in a long time. Thavy moved down a line of patients with the doctors, helping them communicate.

That night the three said, "Send our clothes up from Bangkok. We can't leave here." Thavy's first night was a difficult one. Not having seen her people for eight years and having little idea what to expect, she was overwhelmed. But Major den Hartog prayed with her, and God's grace was sufficient.

Thavy and the Enses began to speak to the refugees of Jesus and slip tracts into interested hands. Marie introduced a lady to Jesus only hours before she went to meet Him. Then Norm and later Thavy, through helping in the time of physical need, led weary ones to Jesus. Soon refugees were coming to them and saying, "Please, tell me the story."

Marie was more excited about these new Christians than she was about being Rosalynn Carter's translator and appearing on the front page of newspapers around the world. And well she should be. This may be our only chance to tell people of Jesus' love and sacrifice for their sins. The Thai government plans to return them to Cambodia after the war is over.

When Norm crossed the Cambodian border recently to visit the anti-communist camp, he found Christians there, including the brother of the former director of Campus Crusade in Phnom Penh. Even more important, he was invited by the camp commander to return with the gospel. There are over 160,000 people in that camp. They may soon be in Thailand, too.

We have seen God supply so much for this huge new challenge, and we are encouraged to keep on praying, going and giving.

Who said there are no miracles in this twentieth century?

Drew and Heintz filming at Sakaeo

Cross border seed rice distribution

The lady pulled from the pit at Sakaeo refugee camp, Thailand

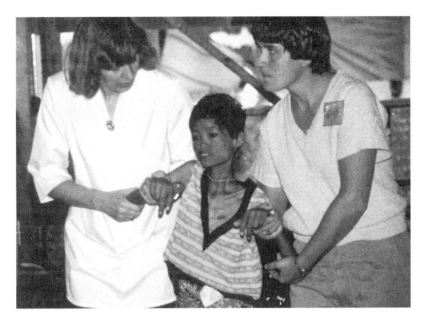

Ruth Ellison helping badly emaciated Cambodian lady in Sakaeo

The hospital where Marie Ens began to tell the story

Refugee stepped on a mine in Cambodia

Matt and Drew in Germany at the Black Forest Academy

Sue and Charlie Morton, constant friends

Refugee work, good news bad news

Chapter 10
Home & Abroad ~ Part 2

Chapter 10.
Home and Abroad ~ Part 2

One of the ongoing discussions at the time had been finding more places for refugees to settle permanently. People with the UNHCR and voluntary agencies met with heads of state and found some places. The French had resettled a group of Hmong in French Guyana, and because that went well, British Guyana was being considered. Franklin Graham became convinced that God wanted the Hmong to resettle in the infamous Jonestown, British Guyana, where more than 900 followers of Jim Jones had committed suicide. Jerry Ballard eagerly waited to see if we could join in and move several thousand Hmong there.

After lots of discussion with Reg Reimer, Wayne Persons, Dave Andrianoff, and the UNHCR, we had the shape of a plan. It involved having the Hmong prepare everything from tools to educational programs, charter a ship on which they could live, and build up a town on shore. Wayne Persons visited French Guyana and had mixed feelings about the colony the French government had placed there. They all missed family in the U.S. and Canada, and it was a lot different from the jungle they knew in Asia.

Franklin had a contact in British Guyana, Sir Lionel Luckoo, a clever lawyer who had become a believer. He said he could arrange the contacts with the government. After meeting with ZOA and TEAR Fund, I flew to New York, where Grady and I met with Bob Reed, the new area secretary for Asia, Dr. King, and Dr. Rambo, the new vice president for missions. Bob had years of Vietnam experience and had become the CAMA Services representative as well. We agreed that the Hmong should only go to Guyana if they were totally willing. Our research had indicated that British Guyana was a socialist government with ties to Cuba.

Our site investigative team included Grady Mangham, Allan Emery from the Graham organization, Percy Dean, Bev's dad and team architect, and Franklin Graham. In Georgetown, British Guyana, we had good talks with the government. Bjorn Johansson of the UNHCR brought Vue Mai, Xiong Leung, and Col. Hang Sao (all Hmong leaders) to see the place. The country fascinated them. They visited the zoo, asked which animals were good to eat, and then flew out to Jonestown by helicopter with us. While we conferred, Percy designed housing and checked on the availability of materials -- all vital concerns if we wanted to have a viable project.

It became clear to me that the socialist government was an obstacle for the Hmong. I couldn't blame them. They had become refugees because of the communist takeover of Laos, and it didn't make sense to move to the other side of the world just to be under a system like the one they had fled. We flew back to the States with mixed feelings. We had a lot of work ahead of us if we wanted the project to work out.

The Boat People project in Hong Kong was remarkable. Most of the team, which included John and Esther Fitzstevens, were CMA missionaries from Vietnam or Cambodia. As the dilapidated fishing boats struggled into Hong Kong harbor, the police boats herded them to a dock set aside for that purpose. Then they were moved onto the dock, where they sat while registration took place. John and Esther met them with the "Love Buckets," a key part of the program. Esther, born and raised in North Vietnam, spoke Vietnamese with a clear Hanoi accent. She always surprised the refugees with her language skills.

Once registered, the refugees moved to one of several huge warehouses where bed frames had been built to give them a place to live. They looked like huge bunk beds and gave each family a space of about seven by eight feet. With three or four levels, each warehouse held up to 7,000 refugees while they waited for some country to take them. Some found short-term work, but for the most part they stayed behind barbed wire fences until they could be sponsored to another nation.

Refugees were scattered all over Asia. Some lived on small islands in Malaysia and Indonesia, and new camps were built to accommodate them. The biggest was at Bataan in the Philippines. With UNHCR and voluntary agencies' help, refugees were brought from the outlying areas to the site for asylum, reunification, and onward movement to countries of final resettlement. The refugees (the boat people, Cambodians in SaKaeo, and the Hmong, who seemed to be facing extermination in Laos) all needed unprecedented attention.

At this time, I had occasion to speak with the Italian ambassador at a reception in Bangkok. The Italians had sent a naval ship to the South China Sea, where they rescued a group of refugees from Vietnam and took them to Italy for resettlement. When I complimented the ambassador for the rescue, he smiled and said, "We had no government at the moment, so we could do what we wanted."

We would do anything to get the job done, and we kept busy with new ideas and projects. I also learned about fund raising through various types of media. Bob Pierce used to gather his staff to pray over the piles of letters they sent out to report on their work and ask for money to do more. His motto was, "It's not by media or by mailings, but by My Spirit, says the Lord."

WRC made a movie about SaKaeo that introduced the work to a much wider range of people who could become donors. Demands for pictures and stories put pressure on everyone to feed the publicity machine. My new title became Vice President for International Ministries for World Relief Corporation, and that meant more conferences, meetings, and troubleshooting trips. People needed to be recruited, trained, and placed, plus new refugee moves had to be evaluated according to what help was needed.

My time in the Dutch village with Bev and Matt was never enough. Matt had a friend next door and loved to ride his bike with Bev on excursions to the shops three kilometers away. He also took swimming at the community swim center. We greatly missed Drew at home, but he continued to enjoy the Black Forest Academy. Bev's fortitude was remarkable as she taught Matt, spent time at our office, and entertained visitors as needed.

I went to Italy to look at a new WRC project in Ostia. Every year, 50,000 Jews arrived from Eastern Europe. Joel McElreath ran the center. He said the transit point in Vienna processed the people for onward travel to the States, Israel, and Canada. They were an interesting group of people, and I was happy we could help.

I stopped in Geneva, Switzerland, to meet with UNHCR officials. We talked to them about durable solutions. Our ideas included intervening earlier in war, famine, and natural disasters, which generated refugees, so that people wouldn't need to relocate. The UN felt that the only thing needed was to add money and all the problems would be solved.

Meanwhile, back in Beirut, the war went on. I visited the projects and the people, which always encouraged me. On this trip, I showed slides and told the church about the desperate situation at SaKaeo. The people felt moved to give more than $1,000 from their own pockets for the Cambodians. From their poverty they gave!

From Beirut, to Karachi, to Islamabad, Pakistan, took only a short time, but once on the road to Peshawar on the Afghan border, I had time to gather my thoughts about what needed to be done. The scenery made me feel as if I had stepped a hundred years into the past. The Russians stayed in Afghanistan, and hundreds of thousands of refugees fled. Rev. Noorakbar, a local pastor, met me, and we drove along the Indus River while discussing how to get the various mission groups to respond to the refugees in the name of Jesus. It was a tough challenge in the extreme Muslim country.

As we drove, we passed an old steam train headed for Islamabad. On it we saw people crowded into every opening, sitting on top of the cars and even on the front of the steam engine. Men passed chunks of wood to feed the engine boiler.

The refugee camps were bad. The people huddled in ragged tents or piles of twigs stacked up like a beaver's house against the cold wind. Children with runny noses and eyes scurried around barefoot. When the leaders were asked, "What is your need?" they responded, "Guns and munitions to kill Russians."

"But," I said, "your women and children are cold, sick, and hungry. We can help you with that."

The leaders replied, "We want them cold, sick, hungry, and mad so they will kill Russians!"

The number of hardhearted people amazed me. A few miles from the camp, the U.S. National Security Advisor, Zbigniew Brzezinski, waved a machine gun for the cameras and promised arms to kill Russians in Afghanistan. It was payback for Vietnam, to say the least, and fueled a ten-year war that finally drove the Russians out of Afghanistan, but the refugees it generated were a desperate lot.

I spent a few days there and then went to Lahore with Jim Tebbe. His father had been a long-time missionary in Pakistan and was one of the characters in James Michener's book Caravans. At a meeting at St. Andrew's Church in Lahore, a group of agency representatives assessed ways they could help. I was convinced that only missionaries with experience in the region could carry out any meaningful work, and this could gain them favor with the government. They agreed. I committed WRC to help with resources.

Back in Holland, things were going well, but there came a summons to the U.S. for more speaking and WRC staff meetings, as well as the annual meeting of the National Association of Evangelicals. Our WRC report had been the highlight of the convention. WRC grew rapidly and could be found in all the world's hotspots, with great results. Not only did the hungry get fed, the naked get clothed, and those in prison get helped, but thousands had also heard and seen the gospel enacted in their lives, and they followed Jesus.

My main concern was that our work be done in concert with churches and missions, because only then would the new believers be discipled. Whenever I could, I orchestrated visits and discussions with the CMA to be sure we stayed "on the same page" with our objective.

When Jerry Ballard began to urge us to move to Wheaton, we had mixed feelings. Drew wanted to complete his last year of high school with his friends at Black Forest Academy, and Matt enjoyed his life in Holland. ZOA was reluctant to see us go. They sent Henk van der Velde with me to the U.S. to talk to CAMA and then to WRC to make sure there would be representation in Holland. Henk also visited our family in Washington State. The size of the country and the fact that we all spoke the same language amazed him. Hollanders speak dozens of languages and have a little less than 13,000 square miles, about the size of Maryland.

Franklin Graham still insisted that Hmong refugees go to Guyana, and the government was open to having them come, so we made another visit. Lionel Luckoo was a great host, and the prime minister and other officials were supportive. Col. Hang Sao went along, but the result stayed the same. The refugees said, "No, we can't live under socialism."

When I returned to the U.S., I got a call from Good Morning America. They invited Hang Sao and me to talk about our project, and especially the Jonestown connection. David Hartman interviewed us, and we enjoyed talking with him. We made it clear that a final decision wouldn't be made until Hang Sao and the other Hmong leaders discussed it further with their people. While in New York, an old friend of Hang Sao's from the CIA contacted him and advised against the move. We flew to Bangkok for more discussions, and in the final analysis the refugees said no.

When I got back to Holland, I picked up Drew. Martin and Jean Hartog came for a visit in Holland, along with their two daughters. We had been considering Martin as our replacement in Holland, so we showed them around. Things were tight in Lebanon, but I felt he should go with me to get a clear picture of the work and the role he would be expected to fulfill if he took my job.

We sent Drew and Doug Dreger off to work at the Bataan refugee camp in the Philippines for the summer. They would finish their summer there, and then Drew would meet us in Wheaton, while Doug would return to his folks in Holland.

While Martin and I flew to Beirut, Jean and Bev began to pack our things for shipment to Wheaton. Matt put up a sign, "Feets te Koop." He wanted to sell his dirt bike, and it went quickly.

In Beirut, Sami and Fawzi (one of the elders) met us. They were subdued. Fighting had been taking place in scattered areas, and they expected more. They took us to the Hamra Street area, where we stayed with Harry and Miriam Taylor at the CMA church building. Things had quieted somewhat, and Martin, smelling the orange blossoms, wanted to go for a walk. I cautioned him that it was not a good idea, but he was determined, so I went with him. We had not gone far when a sniper opened fire. Martin shouted, "Where shall we run?"

"We don't, we step into this doorway," I said. "If you run, someone may shoot you. Watch the other people." I had learned this from past visits.

When the shooting stopped, we walked to the nearest corner and headed toward the church. Gunfire broke out again, so I guided Martin into a small grocery store as he trembled. Others had crowded into the store, too, and no one spoke. I bought some fruit. When the shooting stopped and people moved out to the street, we did as well. We got within half a block of the church when more shooting started. This time we stepped into a flower shop. I bought some flowers, and when the shooting stopped, we made a quick move to the church. Miriam

Taylor said, "How nice! With all that commotion, you still got us fruit and flowers."

Harry came in about then. He had been out for the mail. The sound of shooting and explosions of shells escalated. "Did you get the mail, Harry?" Miriam asked. Just then we heard a roar of explosions that shook the building.

"Yes," he said, "and the natives are pretty restless."

Miriam asked, "Was there mail from Nyack yet?"

"No," Harry responded.

More explosions and the rattle of AK-47s nearly drowned his reply. Martin, visibly shaken, listened as Miriam continued: "Why has no one been called to serve in Beirut? We are supposed to retire, and we must have a replacement."

More explosions as Harry reminisced, "Well, I guess they just don't make missionaries like they used to."

Martin and I gave a short presentation about our work at the Sunday service, and I told them how their money had helped the Cambodians. The fighting continued, and the so-called Christian militia began killing each other. One militia leader, his family, his servants, and even his dog had been butchered by the leaders of the other main militia. This locked them in fierce combat.

As we waited in Sami's car while stuck in a traffic jam one day, shells began to fall on our street. We saw one hit a building nearby. Traffic was grid locked. "What shall we do?" Martin asked, close to panic.

Sami gently said, "Get the tracts out of the glove box; this is a good time to hand them out."

We rolled down the windows, and people were eager to get them and pass them on to others. Shells continued to pass over us and explode nearby. Finally we got clear of the gridlock. Sami said, "This is a good time to go to the church for prayer."

He was absolutely right. We reviewed the projects and needs and then prayed. Because of the fighting, we spent the night at Sami's home. The next day we met with people from Tarshishe and heard of the progress of the repairs and their concerns as the fighting moved closer to their village. So we prayed some more.

As we stood in the ruins of a once-beautiful church in Hamra, Sami commented, "Well, they didn't damage their places of worship."

"This place doesn't look so good," I replied.

"Oh," he explained, "not this church, it's the banks they leave alone. They worship money!"

He was right; the banks were mostly unscathed.

We returned to the Taylors' home, and as fighting continued to rock the city, we checked for our flight departure. "The airport is closed due to the fighting," someone told us.

Martin questioned, "Can we go by boat, car, or bus?"

"No, all avenues of travel have been cut."

"We'll be like the Lebanese we serve and hunker down and trust the Lord," I said.

Sami reported that one of the church's families had gotten trapped on the fourth floor of their apartment building. The PLO had set fire to the ground floor and shot anyone who came out. The family requested prayer, and pray we did until very late that night. The shooting continued all night, but by morning it was quiet and sunny. We ventured out to check on the trapped family. The first floor of their building had been gutted, so we climbed the stairs. The walls of the second floor were still too hot to touch, but our people on the fourth floor were safe, and we praised the Lord together.

The family lived across from the Middle East Airline office, so we also checked on our flight. The airline agent seemed apologetic but said, "Try again tomorrow."

By now, poor Martin got really frustrated. "I have places I'm supposed to go!" he moaned.

We had another noisy night, but we made it to the airline office the next morning. "Tomorrow morning," they said, putting a stamp on our tickets, "go check in at the airport at 8:00 a.m., and be sure to follow all instructions."

The next morning, Sami drove us out to what appeared to be a mob scene. But after a nerve-rattling eight-hour bus ride from the Beirut airport to a Lebanese air force base, we finally got the last seats on a departing airliner. Martin stayed very quiet, and when the plane landed at Orly airport in Paris, he nearly kissed the ground. As we picked up our bags and went out to meet Don Dirks, Martin said, "Andy, don't ever ask me to go to Lebanon again. I'm not going!"

He never did. He became WRC's Holland representative, but he never again went to the Middle East.

Bev, Matt, and I flew to Seattle for some time with our families. We set up a mobile home at our place on the ranch near Quincy, Washington. After a few days, we loaded a truck with our stored belongings and headed for Wheaton, Illinois.

Romy Struckmeyer had been hired as my executive assistant. She had wide experience among the evangelical groups and knew the movers and shakers in that culture. I needed to know how to navigate in this new world, and she became my best chance for success. Then I hired Helen Iffland as my secretary. We had a great team and got right to work.

George Hoffman from TEAR Fund England and Franklin Graham from Samaritan's Purse came to Wheaton to discuss our various projects. They all required a lot of coordination. It wasn't long until I boarded a plane again, this time to Africa. I finished some UNHCR business at a stop in Geneva, then went to Nairobi. I was impressed with how modern Nairobi was compared to other African capitals. While there, I evaluated the needs of new refugees who had come to Kenya from Sudan and Uganda.

The next stop was Salisbury, Zimbabwe, via Blantyre-Limbe, Malawi. Surprise, the plane had a problem, so we had to stay overnight in Blantyre. Everyone wanted a "gift" for even the smallest service. It really depressed me. When we finally climbed onto the ongoing flight the next day, we were glad to be leaving. They had painted the South African Airlines plane a dull grey to foil ground-to-air missiles that rebels still fired, even though the war had supposedly ended.

We got into Salisbury, Zimbabwe, which had recently been Rhodesia. The missionary sent to meet me (an old hand in the country) drove me to Chicombedzi. We rumbled along an old gravel road for hours. Suddenly I said, "Hey, I think I saw a giraffe in that tree back there."

We had seen impala (African antelope), dik-dik (smaller antelopes), and other game as we drove through the buffalo range. Then I saw a giraffe in a tree! "Let's look," my host said.

We went back and saw a really tall giraffe eating leaves out of the top of the tree. "He's a big one," my companion said, "probably 19 feet from shoulder to head." Suddenly we saw several others eating from other trees, and then they glided away across the open country. They were breathtakingly beautiful.

When we arrived at the mission hospital, which had been damaged by the fighting, we discussed ways we could repair and restart it. Then we went on to Bulawayo for more discussions before I returned to Wheaton.

Drew flew to Chicago from Manila, Philippines. Since he had been in the refugee camps all summer and pretty much out of touch, we did not get his arrival time. He just knew we were in Wheaton. He had a WRC card, so he took a taxi from the airport and arrived early in the morning. At 7:30 a.m. I found him waiting for the office to open. He'd had a great adventure, and it came time to enroll at Wheaton High School as a senior. Matt enrolled as a sixth grader and began tae kwon do, and we experienced the Wheaton culture. Bev stayed busy. She attended our staff parties, and we joined the Blanchard Road CMA Church. She often told me she felt like a fish out of water. For one of Matt's school projects, he had to make a 3-D map of his favorite city. He chose Paris. He knew it well, as he had been our tour guide and a Cub Scout in one of the Paris scout packs. His teacher was skeptical. At our parent/teacher meeting she asked, "Did he do all those things? Africa, war in Cambodia, Beirut, Petra, and live in Holland, too?"

"Yes," we replied, "all of it."

I had been preoccupied with information gathering for budget planning and fund raising. This meant a lot of travel to places all over the world, including Haiti. I seemed to be on planes all the time and missed the smaller, slower life with CAMA Services. To be sure CAMA's programs continued to have priority in my work and in many of our field operations, CMA people became key workers. I also had an office in Washington, D.C., to visit. Bud Hancock was the man! He and his staff, including Cliff Frank, had good contacts with USAID and various government officials.

"This is Jim Whitmer, a photographer," Romy announced as she ushered him to my office door one day.

He was a pleasant fellow, and I enjoyed our meeting. Then I asked, "Do you have a passport? I'm going to Africa, and we need photos."

We traveled with Cliff Bjorklund, a board member, to see a relief project and work on the film Empty Bellies Have No Ears, as well as television footage for Paul Smith, a donor from Canada for WRC's Africa work. We met in Nairobi with Jerry and mission representatives and then flew out to a remote area of northern Kenya, landing at a rough dirt strip at Lodwar.

Paul Smith wanted "emotional footage" with which he could raise money on television. The Turkana region wasn't the end of the world, but as they say, "You could see it from there."

We spent the night at a fishing camp on Lake Turkana, where we heard stories about huge Nile perch weighing up to 900 pounds and 30-foot-long crocodiles that had eaten at least one missionary and several Africans in recent times. No one went swimming.

The next day we visited a Baptist missionary couple in Lodwar. The wife was almost in tears. She had cleaned her house to entertain us, but an hour of blowing sand had covered everything again—a common problem. We went to see the refugees who camped in the desert in huts of brush surrounded by walls of thorn brush to keep the lions out. The people looked pretty grim, but Paul Smith said, "I need emotion for my plea."

A ragged mother sat five feet from him, in the dust, cradling a dying child. I got angry. "What's wrong with them?" I asked, pointing to the desperate scene. "Give them our water and lunches," I directed Jim Whitmer, who was busy filming.

Paul Smith, not having noticed the mother and child, was overcome and made one of his better money pleas while crouching to give them water. The missionaries had done all they could, but they were in debt to the local Arab supplier and couldn't get any more food to distribute. We paid the bill and committed $50,000 to the famine relief project there. While Jerry and Paul Smith headed back to the U.S., I continued on to several other countries to review the work and get more photos. Jim's pictures of the Turkana refugees became a Sunday supplement in the Chicago Tribune.

Moise Napon took us to a village outside Ouagadougou that had opened to the gospel after they had been given a well. I loved seeing the lush gardens and hearing about how a clean water source had changed their lives. But the greatest thing of all was witnessing the change Christ had made in their lives. Dr. Bob Beck came along and seemed to enjoy his first visit to Africa. We had worked together in Cambodia and SaKaeo, and now he was helping with ideas and advice in Africa. As we walked in the central market in Ouagadougou, I looked above the meat section where fly-encrusted wares were hanging in the sun under a dozen or so huge vultures perched in a tree. Gazing up at the ugly birds, Bob remarked, "The old army advice 'Look alive and keep moving' suddenly has more meaning for me!"

After dinner we went to Moise's house. He had a lovely family with five children. As we enjoyed coffee, we heard a shout, "Fire!"

We all rushed out to the yard and saw a small, mud storage shed ablaze and a boy inside shouting for help. I leaped through the flames at the door, grabbed the teenager – one of Moise's sons – and jumped back out. The boy had been fueling a lamp, spilled the kerosene, and somehow set the shed on fire. After the fire got extinguished, we went back to finish our coffee. Moise did not have to get a haircut for his son for quite a while.

Moise met me later in Douala, Cameroon. There a lake had discharged gas from an underground volcanic source, and several hundred people had died, with several thousand more displaced. Moise went in for the early evaluation. He reported that things for the displaced villagers had gotten under control. He said that they had shelter, food, blankets, and so on, and that no crisis was evident. So I asked, "Should I go there?"

He didn't answer.

"I'm waiting for you, my African director, to tell me," I explained. "I'm listening."

A big smile was followed by, "Well, if your white face appears, then they will suddenly be in a huge crisis."

"Okay," I responded, "shall we visit the national church office here?"

"No," he quickly answered, "they, too, will have all kinds of wants that aren't needed."

"Okay, then what?" I asked.

He replied, "There is a small hospital in the south that has some valid needs. We should visit there."

We did just that and later sent them aid. Moise, the son of a Mossi chieftain, became a great partner.

The committee on durable solutions met in Geneva at the Palace of Nations, where the UNHCR was based. Jan van Barneveld and I had already met with one official to solve a problem with refugees in Djibouti, Africa. The UNHCR had shipped prefab refugee buildings to Djibouti, but they had no one to assemble them. Jan said he had a Dutch missionary engineer whom TEAR Fund would send to do the job. One problem solved!

We had been discussing the Fund for Durable Solutions for two days. Jan and I represented a group that had committed $1,000,000 to match the UN's contribution, but no one seemed to know how it would work. At lunch Shashi Tharoor, the aid to Kofi Annan who was eating with us, said quietly, "I'm sorry we are wasting your time. We won't be able to solve this because they won't agree which UN department will get the money."

We thanked him for his candor and went on to other things.

I made it home to attend Matt's tae kwon do demonstration. He was pretty good. Drew and I needed some time alone. He had given Bev some static while I was away. "What's the problem, Drew?" I asked.

Drew grimly answered, "Well, Dad, Mom acts like I'm a kid, and I'm not. It's 'clean your room, brush your teeth', etc., etc., etc."

"Drew," I said, "did you notice how my mom, your grandmother, treated me last time we were at the ranch? 'Are you well?' 'Are you getting enough rest?' 'Are you regular?'"

Drew laughed and said, "Yeah!"

"Well, that's Grandma's only way to say 'I love you.' It's the same for your mom. Asking those questions says 'I love you.' Try to see it that way."

"Yeah, okay," he answered with a smile.

He was a great kid.

Back in Thailand, at SaKaeo, I had some small problems to resolve. Eva den Hartog, the Dutch Salvation Army officer, had become persona non grata because of insulting the provincial governor. She needed a new visa. Col. Kamol advised me that I should not ask for her visa until she apologized. I always drilled my workers, explaining, "We are guests in these countries, so we must behave as guests."

Eva flatly refused to apologize, however, so her days in Thailand ended.

Ngyeth Thavy had gone to Thailand with CAMA and led nearly 100 women soldiers to Christ. Because they feared the killers (the Khmer Rouge had slipped into the camp), they met secretly in a large shower room. People all over the camp responded to Christ. It had begun when Marie Ens, a key translator for the medical program, worked in the bamboo thatch hospital that WRC/CAMA built in SaKaeo. As one lady close to death lay on a grass mat in the mud, she listened to Marie telling the story of Jesus. Later, as Marie came by, she raised her hand and weakly begged, "Tell me that story again."

This happened several times that day, and each time Marie told the story again and prayed with her. The next morning when Marie came by, she didn't see the lady on the mat. Her body had been placed in the communal burial pit. One of the other ladies lying there said, "Oh, please tell us that story. We want to know because when she died, she was not afraid."

People kept asking Norm, Thavy, and Marie, "Please tell me that story."

This pattern repeated itself hundreds of times in the totally Khmer Rouge communist camp. Hundreds found Christ.

Martin Luther once said, "I have held many things in my hands and lost them … but whatever I have placed in God's hands, that I always possess."

Our busy life had produced some very good things, but the feeling that I had become part of a business kept increasing. Jerry Ballard had a goal to become bigger than World Vision. I just wanted to serve the church regardless of the budget size. We seemed to be drifting away from our first love, the church. As Francis Schaeffer had pointed out, if Christ's gospel did not remain our first priority, we would lose our spiritual direction. We must keep God first.

Afghan refugees at Dir, Pakistan

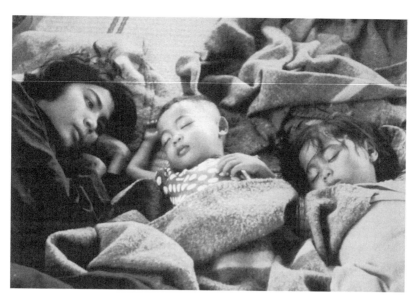

The refugees still come... but where to go?

Two brothers were the only survivors
in a family of four that fled Vietnam

Chapter 11
A Step Aside ~ Part 1

Chapter 11.
A Step Aside ~ Part 1

As I worked with various agencies and governments around the world, I always found it challenging to sort out all the players and their jobs. One day, for instance, I sat with Lionel Rosenblatt in his office at the U.S. embassy in Bangkok. He asked about progress on the resettlement projects we had gotten involved with, and we talked about the demise of the idea of sending refugees to British Guyana and other countries in Central and South America. The future of the Hmong concerned him, as well as other interests that needed to be considered. Suddenly, his office door opened and Jerry Daniels came in.

Lionel led the embassy's refugee programs, and due to his long personal involvement in Asia, he had become good at it. Henry Kissinger had decorated him for his valiant service in Vietnam. Jerry Daniels also had plenty of experience in Asia. He was a CIA case officer for the Hmong and quite active in various aspects of their lives, both in the camps and with their resistance efforts ongoing in Laos.

When I got up to leave, Lionel indicated I should stay. "No, thank you," I told him. "I know Mr. Daniels and respect his work, but I must keep well clear of this part of your work if I expect to maintain my credibility. See you around."

I saw an article about refugees in the New Yorker magazine; it mentioned both Lionel and me in a very positive way. However, I knew his role included involvement with the intelligence services.

During this period, CAMA/WRC got involved with the Land bridge project. With the chaos that came through the 1979 Vietnamese invasion of Cambodia, the delicate balance for food production that had been in place collapsed.

People could not get seed to plant even after the Vietnamese took Phnom Penh because the Khmer Rouge had much of the western rural territory under their control, though fighting still raged. CAMA/WRC explored all possible avenues for getting food and seed. UN and Red Cross officials went to Phnom Penh in 1979 to see what could be done.

The first efforts to send seed and food were unsuccessful, so we joined other nongovernment organizations and sent rice seed by barge from Singapore. It went through Vietnam up the Mekong River and reached Phnom Penh, but from there on west, no one had a reliable system to distribute rice to the countryside.

Finally, although the new government in Phnom Penh would not officially sanction it, a land operation into western Cambodia from Thailand had been worked out. One of the key workers who kept Land bridge functioning was Robert Ashe, with whom we had worked in helping the orphan kids in 1975. At the height of the Landbridge project, 3,000 Cambodian oxcarts came to a place called Nong Chan, where they lined up to receive 100 kilos of rice seed per family, plus rice to eat.

It was an amazing scene. Thousands of people with ancient big-wheeled carts pulled by oxen would arrive behind a fence on the border. After registration, the Cambodian farmers would line up behind a post with their number on it. There were over 20 posts. Twenty-five yards away, hundreds of tons of bagged rice were stacked in 20 rows. When the signal was given, the people streamed across the border to collect their rice. They then continued on to their carts. Once loaded with their rice allotment, they headed back into Cambodia. During that period, over 20,000 tons of rice seed, enough to plant 400,000 hectares, was sent into Cambodia and planted. It saved a generation from starvation in western Cambodia.

Reg Reimer was very active in Land bridge. He helped determine types of rice to send and where to send it. When politics threatened to put a stop to the program, he made sure the press heard about it and intervened with public opinion. He also developed several additional programs. One focused on animal health. The farmers' oxen were checked by CAMA/WRC veterinarians and vaccinated. The Thai government was really happy with this, as they knew the Khmer animals had not been vaccinated for many years. Reg's eyes and ears on the border were known as the border cowboys.

Dave Ens was a missionary kid we knew in Phnom Penh in 1975. His parents, Norm and Marie Ens, had served so heroically in Cambodia, France and Sakaeo invited him to join the efforts for the Cambodians in Thailand. Dave was a bit of a wild man, but he was single, able to speak Cambodian, and he fit the Wild West atmosphere at the border. He joined Gary Johnston, the man who did such a good job at Sakaeo, and from time to time other short-term "cowboys" joined them. They told Reg about the Cambodian farmers' needs as no one else could.

First, there were farm tools such as hoes and sickles to cut rice and so on. Some agencies felt these implements could be used as weapons, but we ignored the whining for what it was. The farmers needed them. If they were able to grow rice, they needed tools to cultivate and harvest it.

Another project Dave identified was the need for blacksmiths to repair oxcarts. The carts were often not strong enough to carry the loads back to Cambodia, so they were repaired and reinforced on the spot. One day Dave sat down in a circle of farmers and shared their tea. Opening a cloth bag he carried, he took out pliers, screwdrivers, files, a hammer, a saw, and other small hand tools. "If you had only this much money," he said, placing a small pile of coins on the ground by the tools, "which tools would you buy first?" After discussions that lasted for some time, Dave selected tools for the repair kits we made to give to the farmers. When Morton Abramowitz, the U.S. ambassador, visited the border camps, after all his briefings by military and refugee officials, he always asked for Dave Ens because, he said, "Dave knows what is really going on!"

I needed to know more about the situation in Cambodia. We were still praying for a day when we could go back to work in Indochina. I used to tell refugees who were in despair about ever seeing their land again to trust God and get training. When these countries began to rejoin the real world, they would need engineers, teachers, and others who could rebuild their nation. With our involvements in the rice shipments and hopes for the future, I needed to see all I could.

World Vision operated a cargo flight from Singapore, and after talking to some acquaintances we met in 1975, a place on the cargo plane was arranged. I wrote about the flight and visit in the following article in the September 2, 1981, The Alliance Witness.

I Visited Phnom Penh
By ANDREW E. BISHOP

The last C&MA worker out of Phnom Penh becomes the first to get back in

It was 6:00 A.M. as our old 1960 model Argosy cargo plane took off for Phnom Penh, Cambodia. I confess to mixed emotions as we rumbled across the southern Gulf of Thailand on the circuitous journey in.

Because of the political realities, you cannot just go direct to Phnom Penh. You must first fly to Ho Chi Minh City (Saigon) and get clearance to enter Cambodia.

As we ducked around storm clouds from a typhoon, I thought of the 1,500 "boat people" who had voted with their lives for freedom, landing in Hong Kong just the day before. The angry waves below us were a grim reminder that probably an equal number had died down there trying to find freedom.

The view on our approach over Viet Nam could have been that of any Asian country: rice paddies, plantations, small rural houses. But Saigon itself was not typical. Asian cities are filled with vehicles. But there was no traffic on the streets of Saigon. Few vehicles were in sight.

We circled low over abandoned compounds still crowded with rusting military equipment. A few ships were in port, including a Russian cruise ship.

The Tan Son Nhut airport in Saigon looked like a junk man's delight. There were hundreds of old planes in various states of repair, many of them still where they had parked six years ago! We also saw some Russian aircraft, and as we deplaned a Russian truck sputtered by, pulling a C-130 engine on a test stand. But for the most part the airport looked abandoned.

We were in the almost empty terminal building for an hour. The Vietnamese who met us were in threadbare clothing. Although they were friendly, they seemed sad. There was no joy on anyone's face.

Airborne once again, we soon crossed into Cambodia. Our approach to Phnom Penh took us over the city and past the hospital built by World Vision.

We again could see only a few vehicles, mostly animal-drawn carts. The airport was still littered with wrecks from 1975. Where rice and ammunition had once been off-loaded, Russian planes were parked.

The three old Cambodian Air Force cargo planes were still neatly lined up where they had been left in 1975. The tower was repaired. Its bunkers were gone, and it had a new paint job.

A military contingent seemed to be the only occupants of the town near the airport.

As we drove in Phnom Penh I could see the scars of war. We passed the spot where a rocket had landed in front of my car and old Chinese antiaircraft guns from the Pol Pot era.

There were more signs of life as we neared the city. Roadside markets. Bicycle repair stands. But no cars and only a few old U.S. army trucks and some new relief trucks.

Our first stop was at the hospital, where I had served in 1975. Under Pol Pot it had been used as a torture center. Now it is a children's hospital, as it was originally intended to be.

Dr. Marve Railey from North Carolina, along with Swiss and British nurses, are caring for over 100 very sick children.

"We get all the worst cases," Dr. Railey explained.

Marve is also teaching Khmer medical students. I asked if he needed help. "We could use two pediatricians for sure," was his response.

Phnom Penh was like any city that has been sacked and left for several years. Now it is being slowly brought back to life.

Our old C&MA mission house is a home for Vietnamese soldiers. The house I lived in is also in use. I did not stop to visit lest I cause problems for the present occupants.

I saw one street piled with cars, stacked eight or ten high. Some buildings were plowed under. There is no trace of the Catholic cathedral. Every stone has been removed.

The last time I had seen the Air France office, hundreds of people were standing in line trying to buy tickets to leave Cambodia. Now it is the home of one lone Cambodian family.

Some of the city is jungle, the result of six years of abandonment and tropical growth. On the riverfront, ships trapped there in 1975 lie beached and rusting.

Only the promenade by the river seemed like old times. A cache of bamboo poles waited to be used for scaffolding. Some fishing boats drifted by, and a river ferry was crossing. A few people were buying snacks from a street vendor.

Two million people lived in and around Phnom Penh in 1975. Now there are 50,000, and their existence is subsistence level. They are traumatized yet from the horrors of Pol Pot. The mass graves they continue to find only bring more shock.

The people are still in bondage. For instance, my translator's husband had been sent to Russia for five years of training. Until he returns, his wife must serve the state---or never see him again.

As I passed the army headquarters, I saw reminders of the phases the country had passed through in its way down: a French armored car, an American personnel carrier, a Chinese tank, a Russian fighter. They all gave a military air to the Cambodian army headquarters now occupied by the Vietnamese.

Phnom Penh is awaking from a five-year sleep, or more accurately, a five-year nightmare. In that time she has aged a century.

The free-enterprise system that made her flourish even in war is now stifled. The country lacks skilled people. True freedom is but a faint memory.

Recovery is likely to be slow.

The trip gave us hope, however, for CAMA to lead the CMA back to Cambodia one day.

WRC planned a series of meetings for worldwide staff to be held in Hong Kong. Among the guests was Claude Noel, president of the Haitian Association of Evangelicals. He tirelessly promoted Haiti's needs to everyone, and we became friends. It amazed him to see the work ethic in Hong Kong. Moise Napon, our African director, was there and at every meeting seemed to shoot hundreds of pictures. Finally I asked, "Moise, what are you going to do with all those photos?"

With a twinkle in his eye he said, "I'm going to take them to show the Africans all the white people."

We both had a good laugh while he whispered, "I'm seldom putting film in the camera."

Again I laughed and asked, "Is this how a Mossi prince behaves? What would your father say?"

"In the forest, the lion can walk any way he wants!" he said with a smile.

Bev's Dad, Percy, had come along to help plan a hospital in Bangladesh. Bob Beck, Claude Noel, and Percy went with me from Singapore to Dhaka, Bangladesh. Having been there before, WRC planned to help Paul Munchi design a projected hospital. He had already operated a boy's home with 50 boys. The men were amazed by the throngs of people working like bees. Everything seemed to be done by hand. We rode in a rickshaw pedaled by a hard-working man. One of Paul's projects actually produced the rickshaws that allowed the men to 'work to own' them, rather than being indentured for life to a large equipment owner.

Percy kept gazing at the tangled maze of wires strung haphazardly along the streets. Most of the wires that went into the shops were just hooked over the live main line without any safe connections. Finally Percy, a licensed electrician, said, "There's a wiring inspector in Seattle who should see this. If he did, he wouldn't criticize my work anymore!"

Next we visited a rice mill. The "mill" consisted of 40 or so women standing on one foot while pushing down on a long pole with their other foot. At the other end of the pole, which extended over a fulcrum, a block of wood was raised and then dropped into a hole to shatter rice husks. Children pushed rice in and pulled out handfuls of shelled rice, timing their moves between the rising and falling mill block. Thump… thump… The women chatted but did not miss a beat for hours at a time. The rice dried on the floor of the courtyard, plastered like the houses with cow manure. Some newly milled rice got put into a tin pot with a few grains of sugar and roasted. As we munched the tasty treat, Dr. Beck asked, "I wonder what makes it so tasty?"

"Probably the tang comes from the cow manure it's dried on," I responded.

"Ugh," Bob said, "I didn't think about that."

Next we visited a sawmill. Twenty-five teams of men, one up and one down in a pit with a long handsaw between them, sawed boards from big logs placed on a framework. As the sawdust fell into the pit, ladies scooped it into baskets, carried it half a mile, and dumped it over piles of newly formed bricks at a brickyard. Formed by hand, the bricks dried in the sun. Then, once covered by sawdust, the piles's were set on fire. As the fire burned, the bricks hardened enough to be put to use.

Once the heat cycle was completed, they loaded the bricks on 40-foot-long boats, where teams of men harnessed to the boats began the seven-day walk up the river to Dhaka. There they unloaded the bricks and took them to the site of the new road from the airport. At this site they carefully broke the bricks into small chunks to be mixed with tar to make the asphalt road! No gravel was available on the delta that is Bangladesh.

All the work we saw was done by hand. Finally Claude Noel, whose people, the poor Haitians, suffered so, said, "You know, if our Haitians would learn to work as hard as these people do, why, we would not be poor!"

"Claude," I said, "that realization was worth this whole trip."

Percy and Bob Beck remained in Bangladesh to work on blueprints for the hospital, and Paul went back to Haiti. I had to travel on to Honduras, where a meeting had been arranged by long-time missionary Donald Hawk. He and his family of sons operated a boys' farm named El Sembrador. They had been missionaries with World Gospel Mission and were deeply respected by the Honduran government and people. Refugees came in from El Salvador, and they wanted to help. They also had hopes that the government might make way for some Asian refugees to settle there. Jim and Mary Whitmer came along to take photos and prepare fund raising materials.

Col. Abraham Turcios became our contact man with the government. He wore a beat-up Stetson and walked and talked like John Wayne. He was thankful WRC would help. The UNHCR came, too, but a debate arose about some of the refugees' activities. Some were a part of the communist insurgents in El Salvador and came to the Honduran camps for "R & R" and to find recruits. The Hondurans were not happy about it.

From Tegucigalpa, the capital, we flew down to Mocoron. We saw shacks scattered all around with no windows and a couple of rudimentary trading posts that were easily more primitive than the ones I remembered from Africa. We didn't see any roads, except for a narrow track that came from Puerto Lempira 75 kilometers away. There wasn't an easy way to get supplies into the region.

A large building frame, about 40 by 60 feet, stood on the edge of the settlement. It didn't have a floor, walls, or roof, just the skeleton with a steeple and a bell. Beyond it, we saw an open field of about 300 acres. Five thousand Miskito Indians who had recently fled Nicaragua camped there. When the communists took over, they burned their villages, killed leaders, and tried to force them from their ancestral homes in the mountains down to the lowlands. Interestingly, they were predominantly Moravian Christians and spoke a dialect mostly using "old English." Some had blue eyes and fair hair. Curious about their heritage, I asked about their history. "Oh," an old man said, "we are descendants of English pirates of the Caribbean!"

The WRC worked with the World Gospel Mission and tried to help. The UNHCR had not yet declared them refugees because the communists claimed they were welcome to go back to Nicaragua. They would just have to go down to live in the lowlands and cut sugarcane. The situation reminded me of the plight of the Hmong back in Laos.

When the Sandinistas (communists) stayed in the mountains, the Miskitos gave them food and helped them. Once in power, however, the communists began to turn on them. They sent teachers in to indoctrinate the people in Marxism and then told them they would have to send their young people to the army or go to jail. After some of their leaders got killed, the Miskitos fled to Honduras.

With access to the nearest road some miles away, WRC had to be creative so that food could be hauled to Mocoron. Tom Hawk, along with his dad, Don, had floated a WRC Toyota pickup on two canoes to Puerto Lempira. It was the only vehicle that could navigate the rough track up from the port, but still a hard way to feed 5,000 people, and even that food had to come to Puerto Lempira in small fishing boats. Over a meal of eggs, polecat, and rice, we worked out the general details of a plan I needed to write up and get funded if the people were to survive.

I particularly enjoyed working with World Gospel Mission. My Uncle James Bishop had served with them in China and India; he'd even served as their president for a few years. The refugees prayed for a solution, and I believed God would once again supply an answer.

When I got back to Wheaton, I had an agreement with the Honduran government for ultimate resettlement and a budget covering food ($3 per person per week), health care ($4,000 per month), local workers ($1,270 month), and temporary housing (including canvas, tents, tools, and even sprayers and insecticide). This region of Honduras is known as the Miskito Plain, and it required all our ingenuity to succeed. We also needed staff, housing for ex-patriot workers, a bigger truck, one more pickup, and an outboard motor for a big cargo canoe. Transport for food alone cost $10,000 per month. Next we planned some air transport and even a water system. The project would cost $1.5 million for the first year, so we knew how much to pray for!

For several weeks I discussed our future with Bev, Dr. King, and Jerry Ballard. Drew prepared to graduate from Wheaton High School and wanted to join the U.S. Air Force. My service experience had been good…and I met Beverly while serving. So Drew agreed to my one request, that he spend a summer on the ranch. "You can understand me better if you spend a summer at our place next to your grandparents," I explained.

Bev was not too happy with life in Wheaton. She said that it had been the only year she suffered for the Lord. For me, several issues came to a head when, without much discussion, WRC signed an agreement with USAID that allowed it to set priorities for WRC rather than having mission and churches set our primary agenda. While the moves were good for WRC, as Jerry planned it, we had begun fulfilling Francis Schaeffer's prediction that if we didn't keep God first, we would become a social program like many others. One day during a discussion of these issues, Jerry said, "You're too much of a missionary for this work."

It was a wake-up call. I had considered doing further postgraduate studies from time to time, and this now seemed the right path to take and the right time to take it. Dr. King agreed to a study leave, and Jerry, relieved to find a way out, liked the idea, too. I would continue on salary as a consultant while studying, and we would live at the ranch in Quincy, Washington. I was so thankful for the Lord's leading in this. Bev told me I had spent more than 200 days of the past year away from home, and I felt it.

Bev and Matt packed. I bought an old Chevy step van, and Drew flew back to Wheaton to help me drive to Washington. Matt and Bev went ahead by air, Drew drove our Volvo, and I drove "Big Red." We had the truck so full that I had to reach through one of the kitchen chairs to shift gears! We had CB radios, and we "10-4ed" our way across the country in good shape, replacing tires from time to time and eating at truck stops.

After we arrived in Quincy and unloaded the truck, we used it as a camper for a couple of fishing trips. Drew was about to leave for the Air Force, so we did some fun stuff. Matt enrolled in the seventh grade in Quincy, and Bev went to work at the local 12-bed hospital. I bought a small camp trailer to set up as my "study center" and consulting office. I enrolled in an off-campus Ph.D. program from California and began to read books and write papers. It was great. I had time to hunt deer and pheasant and read in solitude. We lived in a remote area, over ten miles from town. Matt had a gun and a dog, as well as a Honda three-wheeler that he rode for more than a mile each morning to join his cousins and to ride two more miles to where the school bus picked them up.

The postgraduate committee accepted my proposal for the Ph.D. study. Dr. Thomas A. Neal, my advisor, found the subject rather exotic. I titled it "Managing Disaster Mitigation Operations." My degree would be in nonprofit management. I began in earnest to read approved books and build a body of research that would give the basis for a dissertation. I had piles of reports, magazines, and newspaper articles, plus years of experience, to draw from. The UNHCR even sent me material from Switzerland.

On September 29, 1981, Drew left for basic training at the Air Force base in San Antonio, Texas. I had taken my Air Force training back in 1956 at the same base. Drew did well; he wrote that "basic training is like boarding school, except they get a lot more upset here if I don't make my bed!"

In between my studies, I did some speaking engagements, hunting, and occasionally had consulting conversations with WRC and the CMA. It was great to have things so quiet. Bev worked nights, so I spent my days staying focused in the little camp trailer.

In late January 1982, Grady Mangham, who had taken over my old position at WRC, phoned to ask me to go back to Honduras. Since I had written the proposal and done most of the negotiations on that refugee situation, Jerry felt I should go back to move the project along. I accepted and made the trip, including the hair-raising descent to the Tegucigalpa airport. The final approach took you down the face of a steep hill and kept your mind focused until it screeched onto the short runway.

Don Hawk met me and brought me up to speed. The UNHCR still maintained that since the communists in Nicaragua claimed the Miskito could return, there was no need to treat them as refugees. When presented with the refugees' argument that leaders had been killed and villages burned, the local UNHCR official said they didn't have any photos to prove their story. "That's what you told the Cambodians until it was too late," I reminded them.

To Tom Hawk I suggested, "Let's go get the proof they need."

Tom replied, "I'll get an MAF flight set for Mocoron."

The airstrip there stayed in good shape, as Tom had bulldozed a longer strip to take in supplies and tents. So far, however, no one had agreed to fund the $1.5 million needed to do the complete project. Since Tom and I planned to enter a security zone, we let the U.S. embassy know our plan. "Check with us when you get back," they requested.

Once in Mocoron, we drove 50 kilometers to the village of Leimus on the Rio Coco (the border between Nicaragua and Honduras). We planned to go down the river to a point across from San Alberto, Nicaragua, from which the refugees assured us we could easily see the damaged town. The Honduran soldiers based in Leimus weren't too happy with our presence. "It's very dangerous here," they said.

They explained that the Sandinista army that had occupied the town on the other side of the river was only 100 yards away. We could see their machine gun posts, and the soldiers told us about a massacre in which over 30 people were executed as they tried to cross the river.

One man escaped to Leimus and died of his wounds. Another man who escaped got air lifted out and lost his arm. The soldiers also saw a number of bodies float down the river. The Sandinistas seemed bent on eliminating the Miskitos or enslaving them.

Tom translated all this and concluded, "They want us to go back to Mocoron."

"Tom," I suggested, "tell them to go to the cantina here and have a steak dinner on me, and we will come later."

After some further discussion in Spanish, Tom said, "They think you're challenging their macho, so they will go with us, but we must be careful. Last week the communists bombed some nuns in a canoe on the river."

We got into the pickup with soldiers hanging all over and drove about an hour to Suhi, then another hour on a trail to a farm near Buena Vista. From there we could go to a spot across from our target, the remains of the village of San Alberto. The refugees had told us about the killing that had destroyed their lives there. We piled into some canoes and, keeping under the overhanging brush, traveled rapidly up the river. We had to stop and hide when we heard patrol planes. The soldiers got very nervous. We finally parked the canoes and hiked another hour until we saw San Alberto. It looked like other war-torn villages. We saw burned buildings, dead animals, and remains of the refugees' lives – all the result of a scorched-earth policy, it was clear. The guide told us that many had died.

I used up a roll of film with my telephoto lens. Then we headed back to Suhi, a long, fast hike down the river. I remember it was nighttime and the jungle was very dark, but we finally got back to the pickup. As I paid for the soldiers' steak dinners, the lieutenant said something to Tom. They both laughed.

"What?" I asked.

"Oh, he says you move pretty good for an old gringo."

Old gringo? Well, I was going on 44.

We spent a few days at Mocoron waiting for the weather to clear so an MAF plane could come in, and then we flew to "Tegus." After getting cleaned up and getting the film developed, we went over to the UNHCR office. By seeing the photos of burned buildings, remains of animals, and so on, they had to agree with the refugees' point of view. The UNHCR official said, "We will contact our office in Geneva."

The desk officer at the U.S. embassy was glad to see us safely back. "Did you get the photos?" he inquired.

"You bet," I responded.

"Wait a moment," he said, picking up the phone.

Suddenly we found ourselves in Ambassador John Negroponte's office. He had a sharp, collected personality and had become quite aware of the Miskitos' plight. "Let me see what you have," he said.

I gave him the project plan and the photos. While he read, we drank coffee. "At last!" he said. "This is good. Where are you getting the $1.5 million?"

"We're still praying about that." I replied.

"The United Nations should do this," he said, tapping the pile of photos and the plan.

"I've been trying to convince them. Finally the main office in Geneva is considering the whole thing."

He thought for a moment, then said, "I'll help them," and grabbed the phone.

He quickly got the U.S. representative in Geneva on the line. Reminding him that the U.S. had just given the UNHCR several million dollars for refugees, he directed him to have them send $1.5 million to Honduras at once, earmarked for the Miskito Indian WRC project. He hung up. "Well, we have the money," he said simply. "What else do you need?"

I was stunned. What an answer not only to my prayer, but also to the prayers of the Miskito refugees!

"What else do we need?" he repeated.

"Well," I said, "we need a C-130 Hercules aircraft."

"What for?" he asked.

I quickly explained the need to get food to Puerto Lempira, where a six-wheel-drive truck could then haul it over the bad roads to Mocoron. "Mr. Ambassador," his assistant said, "we are already too involved in this."

Waving his hand dismissivley, he responded, "We will have a C-130 here next week. Can it land there?"

"Yes," I replied, "there's a gravel strip that DC-3s use, and having been in the Air Force, I'm sure the Hercules can land there, too."

He replied, "Okay … do you have the truck?"

I looked at Tom. "I know where we can get one," Tom said.

"If you need cash, there's a $25,000 emergency fund downstairs. Just have the truck at the airport next week."

The ambassador smiled and said, "You boys have just saved my butt. Senator Jesse Helms is coming here tomorrow, and the Miskito Indians are on the top of his agenda for action. Now it's done! By the way, would you like to attend the inauguration of the new Honduran president with us tomorrow?"

"Tom can," I replied, "but I've got to fly back to the U.S. tonight to continue my studies. I'm still a student."

He thanked me for the good work, and we left. Tom did meet Senator Helms, and they went to the inauguration together. (Eventually Tom went to work for USAID.)

While at the airport, we thanked God for the amazing answers to prayer. Not only was the ambassador to champion the Miskito project, but his wife for a time even became the project secretary. On my way home, I stopped in Wheaton to bring Grady Mangham up to speed, then headed back to Quincy.

Farmers head home to Cambodia with rice seed

Paul Bishop in the refugee camp in Hong Kong

The Landbridge rice seed

The oxen are vaccinated. The cart repaired and
the rice is loaded. Next stop is Cambodia

Chapter 12
A Step Aside ~ Part 2

Chapter 12.
A Step Aside ~ Part 2

Still a "full-time" student, I returned to my graduate studies. By March 1982, I had worked through phase two and was ready to begin the dissertation outline. Old friends in the UNHCR sent things like meeting minutes and documentation on negotiations that helped make my points regarding the road to effective, cooperative disaster response. They said they wanted a copy for their use after its completion. I also kept busy speaking in churches and places like Rotary Clubs, as well as giving several radio and newspaper interviews.

After finishing his basic Air Force training, Drew was assigned to Germany. He was happy to be back in Europe. Matt and Bev seemed to enjoy life off the fast track. Matt did well in school and was a good shot with his gun. He loved "off roading" on his three-wheeler.

Good reports came in from Honduras, and I helped find personnel to do the project. Zeke Reister, a smoke jumper from Ellensburg, Washington, signed on to be involved with logistics at Mocoron. He became known as the amazing Zeke! Another visit was needed so I went again for a couple of weeks.

Finishing the church building at Mocoron became a priority. I knew we would need food storage and that the church building would be perfect for it when done. When I asked the Moravian elder about it, he said they had work days where a tree got cut in the jungle and dragged to the site, and then the people cut boards by hand from it. At that rate, it would take years to complete the church.

"How about making a deal?" I asked him. "I will send the truck to the sawmill on the coast for boards and bring in tin for the roof. The refugees who are also Moravian will help finish the building. I'll use refugee funds for the materials that are to build food storage, and you will let us use the building for a year to store food."

The church elders set some limits on what could be carried out in the building, and it was done!

By mid-April I began my dissertation, but then came a summons to "consult" for WRC with USAID in Washington, D.C. Bud Hancock explained that others, mainly Tex Harris, an old agency operative, wanted to get their hands on the Miskito project money. Thankfully, after some discussion with Arthur "Gene" Dewey at the State Department, USAID was able to keep the funds in WRC's account. But at the UN's request, I had to make a trip to Honduras to supervise an airlift of materials and equipment from Tegucigalpa to Puerto Lempira.

A C-130 chartered by the UN was to airlift 200 tons of food and equipment to feed the refugees and build a new road to Mocoron. It took two weeks. We usually did two flights per day and even flew in dump trucks, a cement mixer, a road grader, pipe for the water system, and a D-6 bulldozer. We also took in a couple more Toyota pickups.

On one flight midway into the airlift, the plane suffered a prop failure, so after unloading it had to fly on three engines to Miami for repairs. The UN road engineer, a Swedish army officer, asked the pilot of the Southern Air Transport C-130 to try to find a road compactor (a machine with lots of wheels, used to pack the soil to make a firm road bed).

The next day, when the plane returned after an all-night repair job, out rolled the compactor. It had fit in the hold with two inches to spare! Zeke Reister moved all the materials up the 75 kilometers of bad road to Mocoron and was very happy that a good road would finally be built.

Mark Malloch Brown came from Geneva to inspect the project for the UNHCR. We had met at SaKaeo in 1979, where CAMA had done a major job setting up the hospital and water system for the camp and provided very effective refugee aid. He looked the situation over and pronounced it a success. However, he did question the "food storage unit" listed on the report. "I've never seen food storage with a steeple and a bell," he pointed out.

"Well, they can ring the bell for food distribution, and as an Anglican, you know what its 'end use in the community' will be," I said lightheartedly.

He laughed and agreed, but he thought he would try to get its photo without showing the steeple.

My CMA contact for CAMA Services had become Bob Reed. I enjoyed working with him, and he kept me abreast of CAMA's work in the various areas of the world. Jan van Barneveld phoned from time to time. "We miss you," he said. "Come back to us when you finish your studies."

⌒

In the summer of 1982, the Israelis had had enough of the PLO attacks on northern Israel and invaded Lebanon with swift and vicious attacks. Starting exactly 15 years to the day after the 1967 Six-Day War, "Operation Peace for Galilee" first swept the skies, destroying the Syrian air force and antiaircraft system. Then they fought through the mountains down to Sidon and up to Beirut. They drove the Syrians and Palestinians back and finally laid siege to the PLO trapped in Beirut.

During the fighting, the Israeli forces, known to the Christian Lebanese as the "Sons of David," captured enough arms to equip a 200,000-man army. Their swift action prevented a disaster! The Arabs and PLO had been planning a major attack on Israel.

Bob Reed asked if I could go help Sami assess the needs and plan how to help the Lebanese displaced by the war. In Amman, Jordan, Norm Camp confirmed that travel from Jordan to Beirut would not be possible, but Sami felt I could get there via Cyprus, which I did on a gun runners boat.

By the time I arrived, Sami's CAMA team had been busily passing out emergency food, blankets, and other essentials. They had also gotten a new supply of Bibles that they gave out, even to Israeli soldiers whenever they would take one.

The Russell Clarks, who had replaced the Taylors as CMA missionaries in Lebanon, stayed safe even though their area of Beirut had been hard hit. I spent a noisy night with them. In the evening, I went up the street to get some fruit. Walking back, I encountered a car parked on the sidewalk in front of a bank. I thought nothing of it, as people observed traffic laws as they pleased; there were no police at work.

I had walked a block farther and had just climbed the stairs to the Clarks' apartment in the church when, with a loud kaboom, the car I had squeezed by blew up! Pieces of metal buzzed through the air, and people began to scream and shout. Then AK-47s began to chatter. Just another night in Beirut. I breathed a prayer of thankful relief.

Sami told me that his 80-year-old mother had become a believer. One night the fighting in his sector of the city got fierce. For safety he took Joy and their two children, Paul and Anna, into the stairwell, along with their bedding. As the battle raged, bullets even passed through their apartment. At about 2:00 a.m., the phone rang. Sami did not want to go in to answer it, but it continued to ring. Finally, he crawled in and reached up for the phone.

"Sami, Sami, are you all right?" he heard. It was his mother. "I see there is a lot of shooting there!"

Living up in a village near Sidon, she could see Beirut.

"Yes, Mother," Sami said.

"Why did it take you so long to answer the phone, Sami?"

"Mother," he replied with the guns and explosions rattling the building, "we are sheltering in the stairwell."

"Why?" she said. "I thought you were trusting Jesus."

One day right after the car bomb, Sami picked his way through the debris from the latest fighting. The "Sons of David" had boxed the PLO into a small section of Beirut and kept the pressure on as we surveyed the needs for assistance.

We drove to Sidon and, after visiting Sami's mother, drove up into the mountains to visit Rmayleh, Jezine, and Kfarhouna. We saw the Israeli fire bases and observation points, as well as checkpoints along the roads. Near Damour, we saw a fire base equipped entirely with Russian rocket artillery captured from the PLO and being used to subdue them. We confirmed a plan to keep up the emergency aid and to start to repair the villages we had visited. Everywhere we went, we gave out not only material aid, but also tracts and Bibles, and everyone -- Muslims included -- gladly received them from Sami's team. Sami and his team had an amazing trust in God's care and energy in the face of such drastic danger.

After leaving Lebanon, again traveling by way of Cyprus, I stopped in Europe to bring donors up to date. I gave Jan van Barneveld a story I wrote about the trip, which got published in a major Dutch paper as well as in our paper in Ellensburg. ZOA, TEAR Fund, Wild Geese, and Word and Deed eagerly waited to participate with Sami in Lebanon and were pleased with the report and the plan for action.

Back in New York, I met with Bob Reed and Dr. King. The report pleased them as well, and the story got published in the Alliance Witness. When I finished all the discussions, reports, and meetings, I headed back to Quincy.

The morning after my return, sitting at the breakfast table, Matt said, "Dad, while you were gone, we voted. We voted to move to town."

"What?" I said. "How could you vote without me?"

Matt continued, "You would still lose. It would be two to one for moving!"

"Matt," I pleaded, "you have everything here, a dog, a gun, your three-wheeler, and cousins."

"We want to live where people are. We are town people," he said firmly.

"Okay," I replied, "we'll check it out."

Bev smiled and said, "We already have. There's a house available in Ellensburg."

We had been on the ranch for over a year and...well, their happiness was paramount, and I had nearly finished the first draft of my dissertation.

We had just settled into a routine in Ellensburg when Bob Reed informed me that we had been moved back to full-time CAMA status with "Coordinator for the Lebanon Relief Project" as my job title. The work could be done at a distance, so I could complete my Ph.D.

In this capacity, I made a trip to Beirut in late September 1982, entering Lebanon via Israel. Under international pressure, Israel had agreed to move out of Beirut to allow U.S., Italian, French, Swedish, and Dutch UN forces to move in and stabilize things. The Lebanese had welcomed the "Sons of David" as liberators who defeated the Syrians and the PLO. However, when they began to disarm everyone, the Lebanese of all factions had complained to the UN.

When I crossed into Lebanon at Metula, not far from the old Beaufort castle where so much fighting had taken place, the Israeli army had already begun redeploying south and setting up the South Lebanese Army under Major Haddad.

Ray Barnett of the High Adventure Group worked with their Lebanon Aid program. He said their Voice of Peace radio station had been approved by the Israelis, who also helped him with aid deliveries. While he had a very good program, with the changing political grounds, I advised him to separate his program from the military. When Israel finally did leave, unless they had a clear Lebanese aid program, they would be pushed out, too.

I drove to Beirut via Sidon. The fighting had been bitter and the devastation severe. When I got to Sami's, I found that Joy had gone to the hospital, so we decided that I would stay at the Clarks' apartment. We had a good time catching up on things there. They told me how Peter Garang, a Sudanese Christian student, had risked his life to keep the PLO from putting an antiaircraft gun on the roof of the church. That surely would have brought bombs. "The Lord was with me," he said, and he prevailed.

The situation continued to be tense. Blood feuds got mixed into the whole scene. After the assassination of Bashir Gemayel the year before, everyone watched the Franjieh clan leader closely. Gemayel's Phalangist militia had murdered Franjieh's son, daughter-in-law, granddaughter, and even the servants. Franjieh froze all the bodies, decreeing they would not be buried until the blood debt with the Gemayels got settled. Everyone watched when Bashir got assassinated, but none of the bodies of the Franjiehs had been buried, so no one considered them to be behind the murder. The bodies were said to be still in cold storage at the end of 1982.

We surveyed the area. The streets in the Hamra district were a jumble of wrecked shops and rows of burned cars, but in the midst of the mess a few small shops, like "Flowers of Spring," opened for business. One of the Christian families lived across the street from the Sabra and Shatila refugee camps, where Phalangists had massacred a lot of Palestinians as Israelis pulled back from the area.

Sami worked on a plan to provide aid to the refugee camps, but the area was still hot and not safe to work in. It was being cleared of mines and explosives, and some of the badly damaged houses were being demolished. There were lots of roadblocks, and we got searched everywhere we went. Sami gave out Bibles whenever he could.

I stopped at the beach near the airport where the U.S. Marines landed. It was quite a sight. The Marines were apprehensive as they moved into the surreal scene. Demolished houses, roads, and cars had all been covered with a coat of dust from explosions. As the soldiers swept their route for mines, they encountered people in fine clothes and lines of bumper-to-bumper luxury cars, punctuated by Israeli tanks, Jeeps, and sports cars. Offshore, an aircraft carrier deployed helicopters and warplanes amidst gun ships and landing craft headed for the beaches. On the beach, people sunned themselves and swam. Heat, dust, dirt, and even the stench of dead bodies not yet removed from some of the battle sites permeated the area. Lebanon, October 1982!

Once we toured accessible villages, we went through a series of meetings, wrote up reports, and finished developing the plan for the year ahead. It encouraged us to see how much work the church had done in spite of the continued fighting and dislocation. World Vision began using the CAMA project we developed in 1977 to do their village work. We were thankful the Lord had made it work. The U.S. embassy meeting went well, and Sami's team impressed them. Russell Clark and I heard encouraging comments about the work, which we hoped would result in funds at some point.

One village stood out. The people of Rmayleh near Sidon had already done their repairs even before Sami could get to them with funds!

The street in front of the Israeli command post in Sidon was a sight. To prevent car bomb attacks, the "Sons of David" had forbidden parking there. When their warnings went unheeded, they brought in a 25-ton Merkava tank. Placing one tread in the parking lane, they drove the length of the street, flattening the cars. Then they did the same to cars on the other side. Loaders removed the junk left behind and dumped it in a ravine. "No Parking" in Hebrew means no parking!

I met with Ray Barnett in Sidon, and he had blankets for CAMA. Ray took my advice and made an effort to separate his work from the Israelis. They even repackaged goods with Hebrew labels into packages labeled in Arabic. He also planned to get a Lebanese visa in Paris so he could move about outside the Israeli-controlled areas.

I crossed back into Israel during the time of the Feast of Booths. The army had set up little palm frond-covered structures for orthodox observances. It was quiet and beautiful as I drove along the Sea of Galilee on my way to Tel Aviv.

I had meetings in Paris and was pleased that the Lebanese donor consortium had come together so well. TEAR Fund England

and Holland, WRC Holland, CAMA, and Jan van Barneveld, who also represented our interests with the Dutch government, all came to Paris. Don Dirks hosted the meeting at his office. I reported on the trip, and they approved over $60,000 for Lebanon based on Sami's reports and our plan. As I left for home, Jan van Barneveld called and confirmed that the Dutch government had approved a $220,000 grant for Lebanon. God continued to answer prayer.

On November 2, 1982, Dr. Borden informed me that my dissertation had been accepted and that my defense of the dissertation would be scheduled for January 1983.

After all the reports and plans had been reviewed by those who gave to the work in Lebanon, they asked for a finalization of the plans and an audit of the books. So on December 6 I flew to Nyack for discussions, and on the 7th I went to Washington, D.C. Bud Hancock and Clint Frank, along with Dorothy Zbicz, were very helpful. Gene Dewey, now Under Secretary of State for Refugee Affairs, also had an interest in the Lebanese situation. I even saw Reg Reimer and Jerry Ballard. They all wanted a briefing on Lebanon, and CAMA happily gave it to them.

Bill Kerr, Andy Kerr's dad, wanted to send a suitcase to Andy and Marilyn in Beirut. They were back there in language study, having finished their seminary and home service and entering into their missionary career. I never did connect with the suitcase before leaving for Amsterdam, but KLM said they would find it and send it to me. In Holland, I met and talked to a lot of people about Lebanon. Since the Middle East was again in the news, people's interest and willingness to participate with CAMA grew.

On December 15th in Athens I met Jim Whitmer, who planned to go to Lebanon with me to get promotional photos for CAMA and WRC. The brown suitcase was there, too. KLM had done a good job, as usual. We went through a security check in Athens and had to get off the plane to identify our luggage. I didn't have a tag for the Kerr's suitcase, only a vague description of it, but by going slow on checking my bag, a brown bag stood out, and they put it on with us for Beirut. Andy and Marilyn had their Christmas gifts.

In Beirut we met Andy Kerr, Russell Clark, and Franklin Graham, who traveled with Guy Davidson, Roy Gustafson, and Russ Busby. Fawzi Saliby came, too. Old home week! We stopped in Sidon to look at the building Guy's church was financing for purchase by the Evangelical

Church of the Christian Alliance of Lebanon. It was a nice three-story building with a fence and garden. Over the years, it became a church and a clinic.

From there we drove up to El Aichieh and Kfarhouna. We had a number of homes under repair and did some surveys. I delivered money to an old lady who, having been heard of by a church in the U.S., received $30 from them to buy a winter coat. We prayed with an 80-year-old man with a broken leg. He sat by his stove in his newly repaired home. "I die happy here before I ever leave my home again," he said.

Eighty-four homes were under repair, and Jacob, our engineer, made sure the work got done right before advancing more money. He also led several Bible studies there in Aichieh, and 15 people drove each Sunday to Karantina for worship services.

A group of young people from a kibbutz in Israel came to town to clean up the remains of war and help with the home-repair work.

The mayor told us the work of the Karantina church team was wonderful.

In Kfarhouna, 46 houses were under repair. Everyone worked. Even the wife of a blind man busily repaired their home with CAMA help. Jim Whitmer got a lot of good photos, some of which newspapers back in the States used.

At the Sabra refugee camp, Andy Kerr and John bou Shebel, along with Simon Saliby and two young converted Muslims, stayed busy with food, shelter, and presenting the gospel. Six people had already accepted Christ. Down at Tyre and Sidon, both cities were under repair. After over 2,000 years of strife, they just kept rebuilding on the remains of the last war. People welcomed us everywhere as the "ones who care."

The international church in Ras Beirut was full. Nine countries were represented in the service, and afterward we stopped off to sing Christmas carols with some U.S. Marines.

We spent another day reviewing the books, writing reports, and making sure all the required audits were done. John bou Shebel came for lunch. He was so thankful for the opportunity to minister to the Palestinians. The Palestinians told him, "Who but you would care for us? The Arabs, the Europeans, even the PLO and the Russians are gone. We are left alone!"

"While the U.S. and UN do give some aid," John said, "the remaining Palestinians feel abandoned, but we will not abandon them."

The Lebanese CAMA program met and exceeded our expectations, and God got the glory. Sami's team had stepped up to the challenge, and the donors met their commitments.

In Amsterdam, I phoned the various consortium members and sent them packets with reports, audits, and plans for the future. With the work completed, I met up with Drew, who had some leave time from his base in Germany, and planned to fly back to Ellensburg. I had a nice time relaxing and enjoying the family during Christmas. We arrived home on Christmas Eve 1982.

Evading patrols on the Honduran border

A quiet moment in Beirut

Lebanese soccer club

Chapter 13
Back in the Saddle ~ Part 1

Chapter 13.
Back in the Saddle ~ Part 1

Everyone in Ellensburg was happy to see Drew home on leave. He had grown up in his experiences and enjoyed talking about life in the Air Force in Germany. He and Matt also talked about Matt's growing computer skills and hung out together.

In our conversations about Texas, where both Drew and I had taken basic training, I was reminded of my first relief operation while in tech school, after basic training. It snowed for hours one day in May, and the temperature fell below zero. The wind raced across the Texas panhandle, pushing the snow into gullies and in drifts against buildings and fences. Traffic couldn't move, especially from the town of Amarillo out to the base.

My buddy and I left the drive-in theater early, dropped our dates off, and returned our rental car. We followed some other GIs into a theater showing The Ten Commandments. We spent the night out of the cold, wondering, What do we do next? The theater closed at 6:00 a.m., and we hiked through the howling storm to the bus station. In the attached diner, we talked about how to get back to our base over ham and eggs with grits. Finally I called our first sergeant and explained that more than 30 of us had been waiting in the station, out of the howling blizzard, but there weren't any buses running. "Everyone stay in town till the storms blow through," he ordered. "I don't want anyone to freeze to death trying to get here. We'll extend your passes as needed."

What a relief! But we wondered where we could stay. Those with money had already gone to hotels, but what about the other 25 or so of us? Next, the bus station manager announced that they were closing due to the storm.

The radio played songs that the airmen loved, such as Elvis, the Everly Brothers, and Hank Snow. Suddenly I had a flash of God-given inspiration. With my remaining change, I phoned the radio station and explained our predicament. In moments, the disc jockey told Amarillo about our plight and asked for hospitality for the stranded GIs. It took only an hour as the people of Amarillo responded, and soon we all had a home for the duration of the storm. A retired Air Force captain who flew B-17s in World War II hosted my buddy and me. He regaled us with his exploits and fed us royally. Three days later, when buses began to operate again, we made it back to our base with great stories of how we survived the storm. There were still snowdrifts 15 feet deep on the base. Little did I realize that prompt action in crisis situations would become a way of life.

Drew's time at home had just about come to an end, so on Sunday evening we had a farewell party at Arnie Beckenhauer's place out in the country. The schedule included lots of food and fun. Arnie had a pond with a hill beside it, so we all decided to go ice skating and sledding. Unfortunately, as I made a couple of spins on the ice and a glide, my leg twisted and broke. I lay there thinking, This isn't happening. I just got back from yet another dangerous trip to Beirut, and now I broke my leg skating?

I had a double spiral fracture, so I had to be taken to Yakima to have pins put in my leg and a cast up to my thigh. I began to realize some plans would need changing.

The snow had not stopped, so Drew took a bus to Seattle to catch his flight back to Germany. After four days in the hospital, I got to go home.

I received a lot of phone calls and nice get-well cards. I also had some rescheduling to arrange. Bob Reed wrote, reminding me that trying to keep up with the kids could be hazardous to my health. A planned trip to California to defend my Ph.D. dissertation before my graduate committee had to be rearranged. When I explained my situation, Dr. Borden, the graduate school dean, said they would work something out and get back to me.

Before long, Dr. Borden phoned. The committee had decided I should do the defense in writing. They would send me a list of questions, and I had 24 hours to respond and mail it back. With Bev typing furiously as I wrote, we finished the defense in the allotted time. All I had to do now was wait for their reply. I sat in an easy chair by the fireplace with our cat, house rabbit, and dog, Snuffy, for company. It would be a long winter and spring.

With crutches I was reasonably mobile, but because our Volvo had a clutch and stick shift, Bev had to drive me when she wasn't working at the clinic or as a volunteer. I did have to do some repairs on the car and ended up with my cast in the air and my head under the dash. One of the missionaries on the CMA speaking tour in our district got sick, so by February of '83 I began speaking in churches with a fairly full schedule. When the pastor would ask, "How long will you want to speak?" I would reply, "Until my toes turn blue."

I discussed Lebanon with Bob Reed regularly by phone, as well as programs in Hong Kong, Thailand, and France. Having good staff in each country meant that they weren't having any problems. Cliff Westergren had become the director for CAMA Services in Thailand, and WRC began to pull out.

In March we went to Ketchikan, Alaska, to speak and fish. Gordon and Elisabeth McAlister hosted us. We had an excellent time, and during one discussion we learned that Gordon had created a telethon, a fund raising method popular at that time. His father, Jack McAlister, had used the method to raise money for Bibles in Canada. "How about doing one for CAMA Services?" I asked.

"No," he said sadly, "I never want to have anything to do with television again."

He explained his reasons, and that was that. But one day God would have the last word.

In late March, I flew to California to receive my diploma, a Ph.D. in managing disaster mitigation operations. I also met with Dr. Dave Thompson. His work at Bongolo, Gabon, progressed, and he had come back to get board certified in surgery. One of his long-range goals included a surgical training program for Gabon. He had been doing excellent work. While in California, I went to Sacramento to see my youngest brother, Paul. He was a deputy attorney general for the state and had visited our work in Thailand and Hong Kong, always encouraging us.

When I got back to Ellensburg, Bob Reed called to see when I could travel. I had been to the doctor and had the pins removed, so I could navigate pretty well with just a cast and a cane. Since it was the end of March, I agreed that a trip in early April would be possible.

I talked to our long-time friend and pastor, Tim Owen. "How about coming along to carry my suitcase?" I asked.

"Sounds great," he answered. "I'll ask the elders. They may get a one-way ticket, though."

"We'll fool them and buy a round-the-world ticket," I said with a laugh.

"Two weeks without Tim? Yes!" one of the elders joked.

So it was set. We would fly to Hong Kong on April 6, 1983, and just keep going.

"Bishop, why are they working on the engines?" Tim asked as we waited for takeoff.

The 747SP sat on the ramp. The engine cowlings were open, and the ground crew busily worked on them. Tim was apprehensive as we prepared for the 14-hour nonstop flight from San Francisco to Hong Kong. "Well," I replied, "it's easier to fix them while we're still on the ground."

Later, Tim woke me from sleep to say, "Bishop, it's been 14 hours and we're still flying."

I listened, and everything seemed to be working well. "Could be headwinds," I replied. "We seem to be flying okay, though."

Just then a voice came over the loudspeakers: "Your attention, please, ladies and gentlemen. This is your captain speaking. We have been bucking 200-mile-an-hour headwinds. It means we will need to land in Okinawa to refuel before continuing on to Hong Kong. We are sorry for the delay."

When we finally arrived in Hong Kong, Chuck Fowler and Tim Josephsen met us. While I reconfirmed our onward flights, Chuck took Tim to see the amazing CMA work there: refugee camps, roof-top schools, and churches. Tim was overwhelmed by the scope of the work and deeply impressed by the skill and energy of both the missionaries and the Chinese workers and their rapport with the Hong Kong government. Of course, he also loved the variety of food, from the San Francisco Steak House to the huge Chinese floating restaurant.

Field Director John Bechtel asked me to sit down for a confidential talk. He was nearing the end of his CMA role and moving on to serve with a large foundation. "How do you write projects, and what do you look for when evaluating them?" he asked.

"I look for how clear they are on their goals and whether their methods will achieve the desired outcomes," I explained.

We talked at length. We would meet again over the years in various parts of the world as he helped apply funds to solve Kingdom challenges.

My leg held up pretty well, so I had a good time in Thailand. After delivering a shortwave radio to Reg Reimer, we took a tour bus to Loei, where Wayne and Minnie Persons hosted us. Naree, their excellent cook, fed us one of her amazing Lao meals. The next day we drove to Ban Vanai, the huge Hmong refugee camp CAMA Services helped build. Debbie Vik from Seattle showed us the camp and the work. Tim preached and did well with the translator in spite of a cat who chased a lizard around the stage while he was making his main point. More than 550 Hmong attended and loved his message. We traveled part of the way with Romy Struckmeyer, my former assistant at WRC. She was a wealth of information and made the trip to conclude the WRC work in Thailand.

We visited with Jim Gustafson before going on to Aranyaprathet, where Dave Thompson had been doing some short-term medical work with the CAMA team on the border with Cambodia. Tim saw firsthand what Bev and I had been telling everyone about. CAMA Services is Matthew 25 in action. He was becoming a believer.

We had breakfast in Bangkok on April 13 with Reg and Cliff Westergren. As WRC left, we wanted to be sure all promises both to CAMA and the Christian Medical Team were kept. (Cliff had taken over this consortium called the Christian Medical Team [CMT], which had developed from the work we had done jointly at SaKaeo refugee camp in 1979.)

Next we stopped at Amman, Jordan, then flew to Beirut. Sami Dagher met our flight and kept us at his home. Tim was amazed at the casual way people seemed to deal with tensions and the shattered country. We saw the church at work in a war zone, but Tim did not care for the shooting that broke out in the night. We had good meals with the Kerrs, Clarks, and several Lebanese families. Tim's building experience gave him an appreciation for the reconstruction that CAMA and the Karantina church, with help from the Lebanon project supporters in Europe and the U.S., had completed.

Sami told us about a man in one of the villages who had lost an arm and leg to a mine in his field. It had been planted by the PLO to train and terrorize the people. Another man died in a snowstorm in the mountains near Kfarhouna.

We saw troops moving up to the Biqaa Valley, but the CAMA work kept on. Tim got introduced to the tiny, potent cups of Lebanese coffee. He was pretty wired by the end of the week. He especially enjoyed seeing Byblos and Sidon, as well as the third-century church on the site where they say the apostle Paul set sail. As it's located near the Dog River at the beginning of the road to Damascus, it just may be the place. Tim was quite moved after seeing the work among the Palestinians at the Sabra and Shatila camps. But tensions were high, and a few days after we left, a car bomb destroyed the U.S. embassy in Beirut.

On we went to Paris. Now Tim saw urban missions in post-Christian Europe. Don Dirks hosted us and gave him a thorough history of not only the country of France, but also the church there. Drew drove over from his base in Germany and took us touring down to Chartres and Velizy. He enjoyed the time with Tim and all too soon had to head back to duty. On Wednesday, April 20, we boarded Air France for New York.

Tim spoke to the staff chapel at the CMA headquarters in Nyack, New York. Fresh from his round-the-world trip, he was very enthusiastic about missions and especially CAMA Services. His testimony also impressed everyone at the CAMA Services board meeting that afternoon.

We arrived back in Ellensburg on Friday, April 22. Tim had 18 days of amazing scenes of God at work in ways he had not imagined possible. It had definitely been worth the trip, and the local newspaper did a good interview with him. While unpacking, he found one of his sermon tapes. "Well," he told me, "now I have a worldwide tape ministry!"

"Guess what?" I said to Bev and Matt. "We are being asked by CAMA Services to return to Thailand."

Based there, we would oversee CAMA Services and the CMT and continue to support programs in Lebanon, Europe, and other areas as needed. Dr. King had envisioned that CAMA would expand as needed and contract when not needed, but at the time, the needs dictated expansion. My CMA ID card still reads, "Overseas Representative for CAMA Services."

In Ellensburg, Matt had become a computer literate and skilled student. He was a member of the National Honor Society and even made A's in trigonometry, a subject I couldn't spell. He also became a member of the computer club in the eighth grade, and we bought him his first computer using the money I had earned as a consultant. Since I did not and still don't type, computers have always been rather exotic to me. "Matt," Bev and I said, "if you would like to stay in America while we're in Thailand, you may."

Several families had offered to keep him so he could continue his studies and friendships in Ellensburg. We felt we should give him the option. "Let me think about it," Matt said.

During supper a couple of days later, Matt said, "Dad, if I can go to school at Dalat my last four years, no matter where you and Mom get sent, I want to go to Thailand."

I was thankful he had decided to go with us. Our boss, Bob Reed, agreed to his request.

Drew was still in Germany, with two more years in the Air Force. He played soccer for the base team and planned to go to college after he finished his military service. Our move would have little impact on him.

By the end of May, I no longer needed my cast. Instead I wore a plastic removable brace. My leg was healing nicely. After I got the cast off, Bev massaged my leg daily, and no residual problems ever occurred.

May and June were filled with meetings and speaking engagements. We were excited about getting back to field work. We quickly cleaned out the house and packed for Thailand, then got on the road again.

We had a good flight on Thai Airways and arrived back in Asia on June 21. The moist heat of Bangkok enveloped us like a blanket. We spent a couple of days settling into our apartment at the CMA guest house where we would spend the next four years. Cliff Westergren had been the CAMA director for two years, and he and his wife, Marlene, were ready for furlough. Cliff had transitioned into the work as Reg Reimer left to start WRC in Canada. Cliff had done a good job of keeping CAMA's footing in the shifting situation with the refugees in Asia. The political circumstances dictated that planning had to begin to return some of the remaining refugees to their countries of origin.

Cliff drove me to the various CAMA work sites. Ban Nam Yao and Ban Vinai had mainly been Hmong sites. Ban Na Pho and Phanat Nikhom were Lao camps, Sikiew was a Vietnamese camp, and Khao I Dang was the main Cambodian camp. CAMA had churches in these camps and effective Bible training, leadership training, and assistance programs. CAMA medical teams worked in some dangerous places at the Cambodian border, such as Kok Tahan and Phnom Chat, which were primarily Khmer Rouge-controlled areas. Due to continued fighting, they required careful operation, but the people needed the Lord, so CAMA went.

CAMA was financially sound under Cliff's management, but some questions regarding WRC and ZOA commitments needed attention. CAMA Crafts, having done well, became our best example of a "micro enterprise."

At that time, the Royal Thai government had been in the process of reducing the number of nongovernment organizations (NGOs) operating in the refugee camps. This policy would decrease services for the refugees and give credence to their plans to terminate the programs, as well as send the remaining refugees back to where they came from. They needed to do this to improve relations with the neighboring communist countries. The Thai also fought communist insurgents in their own country.

The UN and others stayed busy in Laos, Cambodia, and Vietnam negotiating the refugees' return, but years passed before this actually happened. In the meantime, CAMA had been given permission to stay in most camps, based on our eight years of good performance.

Shortly after, I again became the chairman of the Committee for the Coordination of Services to Displaced Persons in Thailand. While most of the officials I had worked with in the past were no longer in the refugee program, Col. Kamol had become a provincial governor as well as Rotary governor and part of the National Security Council. He welcomed us back to Thailand enthusiastically and put us in touch with people behind the scenes who made things happen.

"Dad, I got a job!" Matt said happily one day.

He liked being back in Asia, and as a freshman in high school, he had just been hired by a store selling computers. He had the role of teaching Thai customers how to use the equipment, and he could work there during his vacations from Dalat.

Bev settled in well. She got some good experience with CAMA Crafts, which she helped start in 1975. She also filled in as a nurse when needed and helped organize office work. We had good staff. Bob Storms was the finance officer; his deputy was Kaek. She became one of the best workers and friends we had in Thailand. When we met her, she had been a believer for four years, led to Christ by her sister Dim. Later, they led both their parents to the Lord.

Not long after we got back to Thailand, ZOA began to ask for an accounting of $50,000. It was their money and had not shown up in Cliff's audit. For two months, Bob Storms and Kaek went through every account and scrap of paper, but they couldn't find it. The ZOA board had planned to come to Thailand for a meeting on the overall operations, and especially the CMT. They had appointed a Dutch doctor as "medical advisor" but wanted her to take over the medical program from CAMA. Their churches wanted to move out from under CAMA Services and be a separate NGO. However, they were not a registered NGO in Thailand, in spite of their financial participation. Like most of the other CMT members, they operated under CAMA's legal status.

On a deeper level, an issue arose because several of the ZOA workers did not meet CAMA's spiritual requirements, and we had already declined to renew a couple of contracts for ZOA medical people. That caused friction, and now there was the "missing" $50,000. It would be an interesting meeting, to say the least. I prayed for wisdom and grace.

We searched and prayed, and on the day the ZOA board arrived in Bangkok, a letter for WRC came from a bank in Singapore. It confirmed the transfer of $50,000 from Singapore to WRC's account in Toronto, Canada. Whew! Light at last. Bob Storm confirmed the money came from ZOA but had never gotten to CAMA's account in Bangkok.

When I sat down with the stony-faced ZOA board, I handed the bank slip to Jaap Tigchlelaar. "I think this is what we've been looking for," I said.

Amazed exclamations filled the room. "This is our account in Singapore!" someone said.

"Yes," I responded, "and as you can see, it never came to CAMA in Bangkok. You need to speak with WRC!"

The atmosphere thawed noticeably. However, the CMT agenda got manipulated by a few of the members from Europe who wanted to do the detailed operational management from there. I explained, "Since I answer to the Thai government for the people and the programs, I cannot accept this."

The executive committee of the CMT had become a bureaucracy, and it seemed they were determined to become the tail that wagged the dog. Jan van Barneveld, whose judgment and support I had counted on, had been maneuvered off the committee. I began to see that the relationship between CMT and CAMA had a limited future.

The ZOA people had a strong desire to control the CMT and CAMA. I prayed about this a lot. Our Cambodian border work had begun to close as the UN reduced the NGO presence in the border, and World Vision had given us a hospital at Ban Vinai.

I floated an idea. "What about ZOA getting registered, taking the lead in CMT, and operating the Ban Vinai hospital?"

"How could we do this?" a board member asked.

"I can make a case with the government that you have been CAMA's partner for eight years, and although not registered you have earned the status for registration," I explained. "Discuss it in Holland, and when I come for the meeting there in a couple of months, we will have already laid the groundwork."

Everyone agreed.

When I explained the situation to Bob Reed, he became understandably concerned. ZOA had been a major funding source and a partner from the early days. However, I pointed out that the questions of CAMA's program control, and especially the spiritual quality we demonstrated, were at stake, and we could not allow them to be compromised.

Later Dr. King visited us while on one of his administrative trips. He wanted to understand the behind-the-scenes issues in the changing situation. While he agreed we could not compromise on our spiritual requirements for workers, the possible loss of finances concerned him. I assured him that we had always trusted God for the resources, and He wouldn't leave us now. Although the WRC had been able to channel a lot of our European resources away from CAMA Services, I was confident we could count on God to replace them.

That evening, Dr. King preached a challenging sermon and gave an overview of CMA world missions, which he had always been good at. When he asked for questions or comments, Dr. Diny van Bruggen, the ZOA medical advisor, stood and said, "Well, all this Christian work is good, but we are here to just do good!"

Bingo! After the meeting, Dr. King took me aside. "Finish the disengagement from these people," he said. "I'll handle things in New York."

And he did. We had full support as we moved on to the meetings in Holland.

Ron Gifford, a friend from Wheaton and now a CMA pastor in Whiterock, B.C., along with his wife, Joan, and daughter Cindy, came to visit. He brought two other families, Ric and Gail Nesimiuk and Ed and Darlene Reed. We toured the camps and had great fellowship. Ron, a gifted speaker, taught us a lot, and with all the organizational turmoil we were working through, he was just what the doctor ordered. At the end of their visit, they and Matt went to Dalat, where Matt started high school. Ron was the special speaker at the opening ceremonies.

Charlie Morton, Dr. Schladerhof, Andy, Ben Kitti and Matt

Harry & Miriam, Taylor, Andy, Evelyn & Grady Mangham

H.R.H. Prince Ronariddh Sihanouk at Green Hill camp

Thai ranger security detail at Ban Vinai camp, Thailand

Debbie Vik, Ead, Tat, Kaek and Andy
with the CAMA team in Bangkok

"He's not heavy, he's my brother." Hmong in Ban Vinai, Thailand

Chapter 14
Back in the Saddle ~ Part 2

Chapter 14.
Back in the Saddle ~ Part 2

John Dean, the U.S. ambassador to Thailand, invited me to lunch. We had been acquainted since 1975 in Phnom Penh and had met again in Beirut and now Bangkok. I was interested in the U.S. attitude concerning aid to Vietnam. He expressed bitterness at the duplicity shown by their actions, but he said that if CAMA wanted an exemption from the U.S. restrictions on aid to that country, he would grant it. It brought us another step toward a return to those closed Indochinese countries, and due to recent typhoons, food aid would be provided.

In late August I flew to Europe via Amman, Jordan. I had a meeting with Norm Camp, and we made plans to visit Beirut after my meetings with ZOA and the CMT board in Holland. In Brussels, I had time to drive to Trier, Germany, to see Drew. We enjoyed a couple of days visiting Holland and Brussels, especially eating the moulles et frites in The Grand Place in Brussels, just as we had in 1970-71.

Henk van der Velde was leaving ZOA. New board members had come in and moved the old members out. It was sad. "We did some really good things together, Andy," he said.

"Yes," I replied, "and God is keeping the records. I'm going to miss our 'Moment Please Tours.'"

We had a good time remembering the previous eight years, but time marched on and the new board members eagerly anticipated change.

We didn't have many surprises at the meeting in Utrecht, Holland. Martin Hartog, Herbert de Ruiter, Dr. Diny's pastor, and Jaap Tigchelaar were clear: CMT would move to ZOA's control once they received their registration. I pledged that CAMA Services would support and assist the transition, but that any new medical work CAMA would take on would not be under the CMT. I was satisfied with the outcome and thanked them for the joint work we had been able to complete. They agreed to keep funding commitments made for several CAMA projects.

Turmoil stirred up again in Beirut. The only way in was by boat from Cyprus. In Larnaca, I boarded the Sun Boat for the trip to Jounieh just outside Beirut. Things were a mess. We arrived at midnight and found Sami out looking for Fawzi's son, who had been missing. Amidst a lot of fighting, a big building near Sami's home burned fiercely. There had been more massacres, so we spent our nights in Sami's basement bunker lined with cases of Bibles. Between explosions, we noted that we were literally hiding behind the Word.

In spite of all the turmoil, God was at work. Mahmoud, a young Palestinian, had found Christ. He said the PLO had sent him to Russia for four years of training. Then he had returned to Lebanon to train more fighters for the PLO. After the massacres in Sabra and Shatila, however, he had seen Christian love for the first time in his life, and he became a believer in Jesus. He began working with the CAMA Karantina relief team.

There were refugees who had fled their villages due to the widespread fighting, and Sami had up to 26 at his home for a while.

Everyone was tired. Fierce gun battles broke out at the drop of a hat. Even soccer games triggered angry outbursts of shooting between people not satisfied with the scores. However, people still repaired the villages. They even cleaned and repaired buildings in central Beirut that had been destroyed in 1975. A huge landfill near the harbor grew, as truckloads of debris from shattered buildings got dumped into the bay. Unfortunately, unidentified bodies, some dead from years past, got mixed into the debris and became part of the new land by the port.

One gutted building still had a sign advertising "Crisis Tours." You could pay a lot and see fighting up close. Leave it to the Lebanese to figure out how to make money from disaster!

We drove to Sidon on empty roads. Occasional shells landed nearby, but we kept on. The old Ferry Boat Liban, which I had once traveled on, lay on the beach. Sami said they had lost control while delivering arms and had to abandon it for the time being. It had not only delivered arms, but it had also served as a way to help refugees escape, including some of Sami's relatives, when Syrians had taken their village.

We stopped at Sami's home village near Sidon, Rmayleh. Heavily armed young men, several of them Sami's cousins, greeted us. We saw the debris of war everywhere: broken walls, smashed houses, pieces of broken equipment, and patches of blood. The Druz militia had fought with them through the night, "but we drove them off and killed a lot of them," they said.

They were dusty, dirty, and tired. They reeked of gunpowder yet stayed confident they could hold out in the defense of their homes.

In Sidon, refugees slept in the church. By phone we heard from Norm Camp in Beirut that Fady, Fawzi's son, had been found in a bunker in Deir Al Amar. What a relief! He had been trapped in the village by fighting and could not get out. Fawzi and Sami pulled strings and finally got him and the others released.

The church neighborhood in Karantina was being shelled. It was so loud and dangerous, yet when the shooting let up, more than 50 people came to worship. They told me that one time the shelling started during a service, and since the counter fire guns were near the church, it put them in grave danger. Sami and Fawzi discussed the situation. If Sami went out to seek help and the others got hurt, that would not do. If Fawzi got hurt going for help, it would be equally unacceptable. Sami finally said, "Fawzi, get your family in your car."

As they drove from the church, Sami walked ahead with his hands in the air, praying. As they reached the corner, a soldier swung a machine gun on them. But before he could fire, he recognized Sami. Sami had given him a Bible at a roadblock a few days earlier. Sami quickly explained the situation and got the soldier's cooperation. In the next few minutes, he led nine families out, walking ahead of each car with his hands raised, praising God for their deliverance.

Norm Camp had refugees sleeping in his office, too. After lunch we visited Achrafieh, a Beirut suburb. The people were still in bunkers. Seventeen shells had just landed. We talked with them and prayed before moving on to the international church near Hamra. Seven came to the evening service in spite of the turmoil, and all of them had grown wary of the future. Now both Syria and Iran were clearly involved with the fighting.

Norm, Sami, and I discussed an evacuation plan, if it become necessary. Usually the best thing was to sit tight until the shooting stopped. However, with the Syrians invading and the Iranian-backed Hesbollah growing, the situation became extremely unpredictable. The fighting continued through the night.

We toured a newly repaired apartment building. Twenty families lived above half a dozen busy shops. Each apartment was partitioned to provide a bathroom, cooking area, and a living/sleeping area. "Who owns the building?" I asked.

"Hmm," Sami demurred.

"Sami, are we fixing a building that these people will be forced to pay rent for?" I insisted.

"Ah," he explained, "this building belongs to a Druze businessman. The Druze seized these people's village, so when they give back the village, he gets back his building."

Given the way the fighting was going, each group grabbed as much territory as it could before a cease fire. The people would probably live in the apartments for years to come. I wired TEAR Fund for another $100,000 as soon as possible to cover emergency aid. There had been eight days of nonstop fighting. When it came time for me to leave, I boarded the boat for Cyprus, ready for a quiet night's sleep.

In Cyprus, I phoned Bonnie Camp in Jordan to report that her husband, Norm, and Roger Elbel were doing okay and did not feel they needed to leave yet. I flew to Amsterdam and spent a couple of days reporting to the Lebanon consortium for which I was still coordinator. Although anxious about the situation, they were pleased to see the spiritual and physical progress being made. I then flew on to Geneva to confer with our contacts at the UNHCR and discuss programs in both Lebanon and Thailand. Then I headed home to Bangkok.

By fall 1983, several of the refugee camps began to close. As we anticipated, someone notified CAMA Services that Samet South and Nong Samet, as well as Ta Priya, would no longer require our CMT services. Bob Storms and I had met with Col. Kittiampon, the head of Task Force 80, and were assured they would watch out for our interests in the area. We had continued access to the camps. The area was a smuggler's paradise. Every night people loaded tons of goods onto bicycles. Then they followed obscure trails to Cambodia's interior, where they traded the goods for gold and gemstones. This had also been a route we used to send Bibles into Cambodia. We had another load in our vehicle's trunk the very day we met with Col. Kittiampon.

The Vietnamese had used bicycles to defeat the U.S. in Vietnam, so the Cambodians used the same tactic against Vietnam. Some of the goods even made the trip all the way to Hanoi!

Our team had provided basic medical training in the region for Khmer workers, so we could see that even as we phased out of the area, if medicines could be supplied, medical care could continue. The UN moved toward using the International Red Cross in a greater role as a way to get leverage with the Khmer Rouge. From Aranyaprathet we drove north and then west, stopping at refugee camps along the way. All the discussions involved camp consolidation and eventual repatriation of the refugees. The Lao government was still getting used to the idea of the refugees returning and at that time had not agreed. The country was "overseen" by the Russians and the Vietnamese.

In one camp, the refugees' clothes needed some fixing, so we arranged to move CAMA Services supplied sewing machines from a closing camp to the ones remaining open. By supplying cloth and thread, we enabled the refugees to make their own clothing. Several camps used the high-protein biscuits we had supplied, and they repeatedly thanked us for office equipment and supplies that we gave. The biscuits were another reminder of the wonderful help we'd received from Jan van Barneveld in Holland.

"Can I buy the bakery equipment I've been using?" Yang Sao, a Hmong refugee, asked. "I am moving to another camp, and I want to make bread there, too."

His was one of the micro-enterprise projects CAMA had set up, and he had done well. "Yes," we told him and named a friendly price for the used pans and equipment.

At Na Pho, a tightly guarded Lao camp, they had good medical care, but an air of uncertainty pervaded, as it was one of the camps from which people would be sent back to Laos. CAMA worked to reassure the people, and we hoped we could somehow go back to Laos with them. We decided to plan projects that would help them go home with some new skills.

Insome, a Thai pastor, evangelist, and agriculturalist, rode up on his motorbike. He headed up a committee that did most of the CAMA work in Na Pho. Not only did they do relief work, but they also offered Bible training and even maintained a library. The group grew, and they ended up building a new church for 500 worshipers!

🖎

We met George and Elsie Wood in Udon. They moved there for ministry and continued to help with spiritual ministries at the Vietnamese camp at Sikiew, near Khorat. Soon Bev and Cydney Newman, the CAMA secretary, arrived by bus from Bangkok, and we enjoyed a birthday dinner for Elsie Wood. From Udon we drove to Loei for a picnic with Wayne and Minnie Persons. From Loei we went to Chiang Khan, where we spent the night with our CAMA team. I showed slides from Lebanon and discussed the CAMA Services' and CMT's future. The hospital we had received from World Vision had been undergoing repairs and needed work on its foundation so it would not slide off the hill on which it had been built.

We met with Mitch Carlson, the UNHCR representative in Ban Vinai, and reviewed CAMA Services' work. He also asked that we continue the program to help new arrivals. We agreed that the help would continue. Xiong-Ling, the Hmong leader who had traveled with us to Guyana a few years before, came by, and Mitch said, "This is a strange place. Xiong-Ling drives a better car than I do."

We sat by a smoking fire, drinking tea. Xiong-Ling stayed quiet as he thought about my question concerning the future.

"We did not go to Guyana for the many reasons we have discussed," he said, "but mainly because we want to go home to Laos. We still need aid for our resistance in Laos, but I think our chances for going back are better than they were four years ago. But while we are here, we must become literate, educated."

"CAMA Services will expand the school program," I assured him. "We will do all we can to make your return possible."

It was October, and we were preparing the 1984 budget, so it was a good time to make sure we knew the refugees' plans and needs.

We saw the vital Hmong refugee church meet spiritual and physical needs in every camp. We were also committed to find Thai church planters who could help maintain what had already begun and do more, as well as monitor the projects for meeting physical needs. The overall picture was good.

Back at Loei, we picked up Minnie Persons and loaded up the CAMA Crafts for the Bangkok Hill tribes Sale, then headed home.

A few days later, while in Nan, I went to a camp scheduled to close. Don Rulison and his wife were finishing up and preparing to leave Nan for furlough, so I flew there to help close CAMA's work and hand it off to another agency.

On an interesting side note, our check-cashing project started by Jerry Torgerson had shown a very good profit, and CAMA Crafts had just about become self-supported.

While walking in Nan, I misstepped and fell. "Not another break!" I prayed. We got bags of ice and packed the ankle. I flew back to Bangkok, where x-rays showed only a torn ligament, but Bev, my nurse, grounded me for two weeks.

Bill Essig, director of World Concern, began to worry about the manipulations by the CMT's executive committee in Holland. Like me, he wasn't happy with the power game they were attempting. I assured him that CMT or not, CAMA would maintain its working fellowship with him and World Concern. We had always enjoyed workers from his group who were committed believers and gave a high level of quality service. I wanted to continue that relationship.

David Moore, the CMA vice president for overseas ministry, came into Bangkok. Our progress pleased him very much, especially the church growth in the refugee camps. We discussed the future, and he indicated that CAMA Services had started to become a major subject in the churchs' discussions at home. The Lord had raised our cause with the CMA churches based on His results, as we had hoped.

In late October, I received a visitor from the government of Vietnam. He sought help for his country, which had been devastated by a huge typhoon. I promised to see what we could do. Later I called Bob Reed and discussed options. Dr. King, CMA president, came in on his way to Penang. Bev and I went there to see Matt and to hold discussions about CAMA Services' future with Dr. King. He was very complimentary and interested in how we planned to disengage from the ZOA/CMT program. "I expect we will complete the move in the coming year," I explained, "and we are sure the Lord will open new doors for CAMA Services."

He smiled and agreed with us.

Dr. Ineke Wolvort phoned me from Chiang Khan. "I think we have diphtheria at Ban Vinai," she reported. "We need vaccines and medications right away."

"I'll get things moving," I told her, "and we will pray for all of you!"

I called Dr. Diny of ZOA, who said she would get ready to go there. Then I phoned our contact at the UNHCR. They assured us they would have vaccines and medicines for us. Within two days, we found ourselves driving north into the coming night in a van loaded with the vaccines and medications.

I did not relish fighting the right traffic coming south. We faced huge trucks loaded with produce and supplies for the city, tour buses racing south, and lots of cars. All seemed to be in a NASCAR race to get to Bangkok ahead of the others, as they passed each other recklessly. Bandits and communist insurgents also lurked around certain areas of the road. We prayed as we drove. Twelve hours later, as the sun rose in the smoky fog over the Mekong, we began unloading the vaccines at the hospital in Ban Vinai. We were tired!

After a quick breakfast, Dave and Karen Fitzstevens and I headed back to Bangkok. Dave and Karen planned to spend the night there and, after a night's rest, drive back to Ban Vinai with another load of meds and vaccines. Even though a few children did die from diphtheria, our prompt action saved many lives.

At the meeting of the Committee for the Coordination of Services to Displaced Persons in Thailand (CCSDPT) on Friday, December 2, I got re-elected as chairman. The CMT executive committee had come to town, and most of the agencies that were part of the team's continuing program were on the executive committee. They had gotten ready to "take over" the medical work at Ban Vinai. We had transferred all the Cambodian border medical assets to Ban Vinai, and CAMA only had the Fitzstevenses on the medical team. The other CAMA Services staff at Ban Vinai, doing education and so on, lived in what we called the CAMA house that also served as the CAMA Crafts warehouse. We had long discussions, but as ZOA, WRC, and TEAR Fund were now free to run things their way, everyone needed to adjust to the new realities.

On December 13, Bev's parents arrived for the holidays. We enjoyed introducing them to Thailand and to our friends. Since Percy, her dad, was a skilled builder and architect, I had work for him. Bev and her mom, Wilene, shopped. The markets, bulging with goods and teeming with people, amazed her. After three days she said to Bev, "Well, hon, if I'd a-known about all this shopping, I'd a-come to see you a long time ago!"

We would soon be having a reunion with Matt coming in from Dalat, and his grandparents eagerly awaited his arrival.

After finishing meetings at Ban Vinai, Martin Hartog stopped in Bangkok on his way back to Holland. He had begun to wonder if he and his fellow CMT executive committee members had bitten off more than they could chew. The Dutch team members, a contentious lot to say the least, had presented him with a list of demands: more money, more holidays, and so forth. I smiled and said, "I'm sure you'll figure something out."

I was glad they had that group to deal with. Not long before the executive committee took over, World Vision had sent a gay doctor back to Hong Kong. He'd been caught abusing Hmong refugees. It was good they moved him out quickly, because the Hmong leaders would have killed him. However, some of the Dutch team had wanted to go on strike in protest. In Holland, homosexuality was considered normal. I'd told them, however, that if they went on strike, they would be on a plane to Holland the next day. So it had ended there. Now Martin and the executive committee had to deal with this medical group and all its personalities, albeit from a distance.

"Look at all the teak!" Percy said one day during his visit. He had never seen such a pile of teak logs.

We had been watching a steam-powered sawmill in Chiang Khan turn the logs into boards and posts. Some of the posts were being turned into newel post about four feet long. "How much for that newel post?" he asked.

Percy imagined a project. I talked to the proprietor and was told 130 baht, or about 5 dollars. "I'll buy it," Percy responded.

Back at the CAMA house, Wilene asked, "What are you going to do with that? How are you going to get it home?"

"It's going to become a pair of teak lamps," he said, grinning, "and when I cut it in two, it will fit into our suitcase."

Bev's mom looked unsure.

"Not to worry," I said. "Suitcases are cheap, and we can get you another one even bigger."

Another day found Percy studying the endangered hillside hospital. He measured the slippage below the structure and noted the cracks where the support posts had sunk as the hill subsided. "We can shore this up with a good retaining wall and jack the post level, then pour concrete pads with a wider support stance," he announced. "I'll draw the blueprints and specs."

The Hmong followed him and listened intently. "He is Bev's father," they said.

Everyone honored both him and her mom. People greeted them at the Sunday service and thanked Bev for her help, especially with CAMA Crafts. The expressions of gratitude really moved Bev's parents. Nine hundred Hmong attended that service.

Matt enjoyed showing his grandparents the sights of Bangkok. They rode canal boats and taxis and saw the palaces and temples. Col. Kamol hosted them at a lavish meal and expressed his thanks for Bev's work. He remembered the good banana bread she had served at the first meeting of the CCSDPT nearly nine years before.

My report to the board on the 1983 activities showed expenditures of $633,576. We had bought and delivered 10,000 school kits, 12,576 blankets, 2,000 tents, thousands of warm coats, and equipment and materials for making thousands of sets of clothing. In addition, medical services, language classes, literacy classes, and even a water system had been provided. The evangelism, literature, special meetings, and discipleship programs had harvested over 500 new believers. I enjoyed being able to explain all this to Percy and Wilene. It amazed them to see Beverly's range of activities and Matt's job with Nite Spot computers.

At the same time, we welcomed Leakhena, our "orphan" now grown up and working with Refugees International. She enjoyed some time with Ngyeth Thavy, the Cambodian girl who had come from Paris in 1979. It turned out that they had gone to the Lycée in Phnom Penh together before they both became refugees.

Percy and Wilene continued their touring, and between trips Percy built us a nice screened porch on the back of our apartment. When they left on January 11, they had given away most of their clothing but had bought extra bags. They stuffed them with their treasures from Thailand. The year 1984 started off well!

The nowhere people. 10 years in a refugee camp

Chapter 15
Up the Down Staircase ~ Part 1

Chapter 15.
Up the Down Staircase ~ Part 1

In between our travels and all the meetings, we loved spending time in the refugee camps. Sikiew, the Vietnamese camp, always encouraged us. I thought about Matthew 25:36, "I was in prison and you came to me," as we pulled up to the very-restricted-access camp.

I hadn't been to the camp for some time. The place had not only expanded, but camp administrators had also built higher walls, put up more barbed wire, and placed armed guards at the gate. The reduction of outside contacts demoralized the refugees, and they wrote home to tell their families not to come there. It had become part of the human deterrent policy to slow down the flow of refugees and encourage people in Vietnam, Laos, and Cambodia to accept their lot in life and stay home.

The voice on the guard's radio that day said, "Oh, CAMA? It's okay," and the gates swung open to admit our car. We drove down a long corridor and parked outside another fence and gate. We had entered a barbed-wire world. You could see it everywhere, in 10-foot-high fences with a strand every foot. The faces of children framed in barbed wire and cement posts took in the sight of foreigners, and then smiles came. "Oh, Americans!" they said.

Many recognized Bob Storm, our CAMA accountant, because he visited regularly.

We delivered boxes of supplies destined for various camp projects, and then a small delegation arrived from the church. "Service is under way," they told us. "Please come this way."

We saw a few open spaces. Most of the space had been covered with bamboo thatch and tin over rabbit-warren-like dens containing restaurants and shops. We also saw open patches filled with herbs and vegetables to supplement the UNHCR-provided food rations.

We quickly got seated as we entered the church, an open structure with narrow benches and a gravel floor. The service continued, then closed with Communion. After the service, we gathered with the church committee behind the platform to talk and drink lemonade. The pastors were mostly volunteers; some had Bible school training.

Kim Ngoc was the only ordained pastor. He went to a CMA Bible school and then became an Assembly of God pastor. He was quite morose. He had survived the sea with his 14-year-old daughter, only to have her kidnapped by Thai pirates just before coming ashore. CAMA stayed in touch with authorities, but no trace of her had been found at that time.

Nguyen Huu Nghia had studied in Vietnam at Nhatrang Bible School for two years. He knew many CMA missionaries and had been taught English by Reg Reimer while teaching Vietnamese to Reg. He served as a pastor for six years.

Nguyen Lien Luc had attended Bible school but got drafted during the war. He was in the diplomatic corps at the war's end and spent three years in re-education camps. His wife, fearing he would not come out, divorced him and fled with their two children to America. He was very depressed after two years in the camp.

Thai Binh An, the senior pastor, told me that his father, Muc-su Tran-xuan III, had been a well-known pastor in Vietnam. "The communists caught me and put me in prison three times," he said. "The last time was in the Delta. They were looking for me again, so I had a friend who took pity on me and offered me a place on his boat. I took my father's Bible and song book and held services on the boat every day for six days. God spared us. See," he said, holding up the battered Bible, "my father used it for 50 years. Now I preach from it.

"The second day we were boarded by Thai pirates. There were 41 Christians on the boat, and we prayed a lot. We knew about the robbery, rape, kidnapping, and murders these men committed regularly. Then I felt God's protection and said to the Thai skipper, 'Please, call your men and go.' The skipper hesitated and then called the men and left! Praise God!

"Then," he said, "a few days later we suddenly saw more Thai boats. Again we prayed, full of fear, as a Thai trawler headed our way. Praise be to God, the skipper recognized me, and I remembered him. We had been in the communist prison together. Oh! We were very happy. He gave us food and water and told us the way to Songkla, Thailand. Soon we were there, and all 41 of us got out of the boat and on the beach. We knelt and thanked God for sparing our lives and bringing us freedom."

Then he added, "Just like your pilgrims long ago."

I had been in CAMA relief work for nine years, but the tears still came as I fellowshiped with those folks who had survived by God's grace. The prison they'd been in had 8,200 people, each of whom had chosen to flee. I'm thankful the CMA, through CAMA Services, had been there to minister to them.

Our church there had more than 250 members. We had Bible classes three times a week. The need for literature and church repairs had been met because our Heavenly Father provided through the Dutch ZOA, the CMA, and WRC, to name a few. We could respond on the spot, as needed, with literature, a typewriter, cash, and a promise to return soon.

"When will George Wood come again?" they asked.

We explained his schedule for return from furlough. "Oh," they responded, "we will begin now to prepare for the celebration."

After a tour of their school of nearly 2,000 students, we shared lunch in a restaurant run by refugees. It had atmosphere. It was dark, and rain pounded on the tin so that conversation became a shouting contest. Bev laughed as a leak from the roof found her neck and then her soup. Children bathed in the cascades of water that poured from the roof, and smoky fires gave some light. The food was good and the conversation fascinating.

We argued over the check after lunch, and CAMA won. Then someone moved the car close so we wouldn't get too wet, and as we got in we said our good-byes.

As the tightly packed shacks, barbed-wire-and-steel gates, and mud of the way station to freedom fell away, we left discussing the vibrant church we'd found. It was led by aggressive Christians who brought God's light to such a dark place day after day, year after year, as they waited for some measure of earthly freedom. The CMA had been there with them through CAMA Services.

Jan Folsom, a fabric designer from Colorado, came to Bangkok soon after. She had come several times to advise the CAMA Crafts team on fabrics, colors, and styles that would improve our product for sales in other countries. Various tribal groups in the camps made the pieces. The Blue Hmong had special skills in batik, which was worked into their appliqué work. The White Hmong, who made up the largest clan among the hill tribes, did intricate cut work and embroidery. The Mien, or Yao, did traditional design embroidery and worked it into their elaborate costumes.

The Lao Isan Thailand wove fine scarves and did unique embroidery as well as crochet. These people were known as "affected Thai," a government term for Thai whose livelihood had been affected by the refugee flow. We incorporated their products into the CAMA Crafts project so they could earn a living, too. Jan Folsom helped expand our variety of products, which included oven mitts, toaster covers, hot pads, aprons, tea cozies, place mats, table runners, baby items, and even bedspreads. Bev and the team were always amazed at the wonderfully intricate patterns and swirls of color, and Jan helped devise the best-selling combinations.

Our customers came from Europe, Asia, Thailand, the U.S., Canada, New Zealand, and Australia. The monthly Hill tribe Sale in Bangkok was always exciting. One lady from Japan bought all ten of the bedspreads available that day at one time. Minnie Persons, who with Bev began CAMA Crafts in 1976, was the translator and cheerleader. Another key worker was Mai Txos. She, Cheryl Chauncey, and Tim Herman did a great job of getting products assigned, prepared, checked, and ready for shipment. Jan was horrified to see such a large number of aprons, oven mitts, and other items in browns, yellows, and oranges. "No one will buy this color combination," she exclaimed.

She knew the U.S. market, but all the items did in fact leave the warehouse and get sold in the ZOA shops in Holland! We also sold large consignments to the Mennonites, who marketed them through their various outlets in the U.S. and Canada. These efforts supplied cash for thousands of ladies and their families. The project was one of the first true micro-enterprise projects in the camps and had become a good example of a self-supporting activity, which was encouraged by both the Royal Thai government and the UNHCR. Marketing was a constant challenge, but with innovative ideas and the help of our church women's group, products sold and the work grew.

Grady Mangham and Martin Hartog of the WRC, Bob Reed of CMA, and Bill Essig of World Concern sat in the CMT meeting and asked for CAMA's continued assistance at the CMT hospital at Ban Vinai. Wayne Persons and I explained some of the problems they had been having in their relations with the Hmong. Wayne agreed to be a go-between when disputes arose, but he asked them to come to him regularly, before the trouble got too advanced. I told them about the repairs planned for the hospital and showed them the blueprints for Percy Dean's retaining wall.

"Can you come to Holland for a meeting?" Grady asked.

Grady was doing his best to keep the Ban Vinai hospital project on track, but working through the European executive committee wasn't easy. Bob Reed and I agreed to participate. Even though CAMA had stepped back from the CMT project, we wanted it to succeed, for the refugees' sake.

On the day Martin left for Holland, I had a call from David Morton, the director of the UN Border Relief Operation (UNBRO). He requested an immediate meeting, at which he soon came to the point. "I can't make a commitment now, nor do I want you to discuss this with anyone just now," he said, "but if you are offered the opportunity, would CAMA be willing to provide services south of Aranyaprathet?"

"What's the general time frame until you would need this help?" I asked.

He answered, "Probably in the next month or two, but this is off the record and unofficial at this point."

"Very well," I said, "I will be away for a week or so."

"I'll contact you in two weeks," he replied.

Wow…south of Aranyaprathet was Khmer Rouge country and very restricted.

The Vietnamese had recently pushed Pol Pot's armies into the Dong Rek and the Cardomom mountains to the south. In between, they held the Thai border by Aranyaprathet. They had destroyed many of the smugglers' camps at Nong Chan, Nong Samet, Phnom Chat, and some others, and held Poipet. The Thai held regular but unofficial meetings with the Vietnamese through Col. Kitti's Task Force 80.

From asking around quietly, I learned that the International Committee of the Red Cross (ICRC) was in conflict with the Khmer Rouge on several items, especially ICRC's demand for access to the Vietnamese prisoners of war. Pol Pot's people had no idea whatsoever about things like the Geneva Conventions. For ICRC, they were a stone wall. ICRC's only leverage was the medical services they supplied inside the Khmer Rouge border camps. Well, I had some time to think and pray, knowing that they would be tough people to deal with.

Jan van Barneveld welcomed me warmly as usual. He remained my best contact in Holland with the Inter Church Coordinating Office, the Dutch government channel for aid we used in Africa and Lebanon. "You know," Jan said, "we are going to miss Clem and Maddie Dreger when they move to Korea. He's such a warm, wonderful brother. Why, if Jesus had lived to His 60s, He'd be just like Clem!"

Jan was right, and as we discussed Dutch church agency politics, he said, "You know, if you have one Christian Dutchman, you have a church. If you have two, you have a denomination. But with three, you have a split!"

We laughed and agreed to keep in touch regularly, and we still do. We had meetings in Groningen, where our family had lived for a year. We discussed funding, and ZOA agreed that as CAMA helped them, they would continue to fund some CAMA projects.

The discussions with the agencies in the CMT went pretty well. They worked out a rotating chairmanship and detailed operating guides for the workers, as well as addressing their demands. I was glad that CAMA was no longer obligated, though I promised to remain available to answer questions or help with government negotiations.

At Dr. King's request, I flew to Copenhagen and on to Beringer, Norway. A group there wanted to affiliate with CMA, and I planned to talk with them about CAMA's work. Einer Pederson and his wife were very cordial, and their hospitality was superb.

Back in Paris, a telex from Bob Reed in New York advised me not to go to Beirut at the moment because things had gotten too hot. Instead I went to Amman, Jordan, where, at a picnic with Norm Camp, Andy Kerr, Betty Howard, and the Darrell Phenicies, we reviewed the work in Jordan and Lebanon. We worked out a plan to get more aid to CAMA Services in Lebanon.

Back in Bangkok after catching up on CAMA work, Bev and I

went to the airport to meet Don and Alice Dyk, a farm family from Ellensburg, Washington. They had been supporters from our first meeting in 1972. When things got hot in Phnom Penh, I would call them for encouragement and prayer. They ended up coming for a couple of weeks to build the retaining wall for the hospital at Ban Vinai and to get some holiday time.

With my discussion of the UNBRO need in my mind, I contacted a couple of pros whom I knew. One was Dr. Dee Garcia, my friend from Phnom Penh. She continued to serve on the Cambodian border, and if we planned to operate there, I would need her language, medical, and professional experience to build a team. I had no doubt about her commitment to following Christ. Without telling her why, I asked if she would consider working with CAMA.

"Yes," she responded.

Peter Benson, a Baptist journeyman worker, was another. He had experience in border operations and a good reputation as an administrator and a follower of Christ. Now I could only wait for official word from UNBRO.

Bev, the Dyks, and I drove to Khorat for the night. The next day we went on to Khon Kaen to visit the blind school. Prayat Punong-ong, the director, was a friend and a fine believer. It amazed us to see all he had accomplished, being blind. We saw kids without eyesight playing table tennis, learning to read braille, and gardening. Having gained support from the Canadian government, his program began to grow and had even come under sponsorship by the king of Thailand. His efforts eventually drew international interest, and for the first time ever he integrated blind children into Thai public schools, where they did well.

Driving on to Ban Vinai, Don and Alice were immediately accepted by the CAMA team. Don planned the retaining wall construction, and Alice joined in the CAMA Crafts and other projects. Bev and I drove back to Bangkok for a brief meeting with Franklin Graham. Then we put Jan Folsom on the plane to the U.S. Another CCSDP meeting reviewed fighting on the Cambodian border and in the mountains of northern Thailand.

David Morton phoned from UNBRO to say, "We need to talk again."

It was early March, and the story I heard from quiet sources was grim. When the ICRC got angry with the Khmer Rouge and threatened to stop all medical aid and even food, the Khmer Rouge invited them into Cambodia for "talks." While there the ICRC were "introduced" to the heads of the Vietnamese prisoners whom they had beheaded at a clearing in the forest. The ICRC lost the round and quit that area of the border in disgust. The only agency that would work there from then on was CAMA Services.

Mr. Morton and I discussed operations and the budget. He had some financial guidelines, so our contract with UNBRO for "Health Services, South Aranyaprathet" officially began on March 1, 1984. God had provided a new door to walk through. I called Ngyeth Thavy, who stayed in Thailand working with Youth with a Mission. When I told her what was happening and asked her opinion, she said, "Praise the Lord, that group of people really needs the gospel! I will pray for all of you."

Dr. Garcia and Peter Benson signed on, and a team began to take shape. Our plans and budget were comprehensive. We specifically planned to provide medical care, including medicine, outpatient care, maternal and child health, and emergency care. The patients who needed more-complicated care would be transferred to the larger facility at the Khao-I-Dang hospital, north of Aranyaprathet. The contract provided funds for two administrators, two doctors, five registered nurses, one laboratory technician, one medical assistant, three translators, five drivers, two cooks/maids, and the equipment and supplies required to support and maintain the program.

In our negotiations, UNBRO told us to lease vehicles because they didn't have any trucks or vans to provide us transportation. When I looked at their lease budget, I got an idea. Kaek and Bob looked at our cash on hand and the cost of new vehicles, and the result was "CAMA leasing." We purchased four new vehicles and redesignated one of our existing SUVs, and leased them to the UNBRO project, and by the year's end we had been repaid for the vehicles. UNBRO provided funds over the next few years for an expanded transport program based on the CAMA lease income.

The total project budget, with medicine and supplies, came to more than $300,000 per year. God had indeed opened a new door, complete with funding.

We then recruited more staff from CAMA contacts. Dr. Ineke Walvort signed on when her contract with the CMT at Ban Vinai was up. Several, including Dr. Garcia's niece Lydia, came from the Philippines.

Two medical people came from Burma, and one from India.

While in Aranyaprathet, we rented a new two-story home with enough bedrooms so that the nurses and doctors had plenty of space. Our cook had worked at the CMA guest house in Bangkok, so meals were delicious. We did our best to have deluxe living for the team, as their work sites were primitive and dangerous. We rented an older house across the street to serve as a warehouse.

For security, we were linked into the UN and Task Force 80 radio net. Our call sign was "Zebra," and each staffer had a Zebra number. Dr. Dee, medical director, was Zebra 1, Peter was Zebra 2, and so on. The work sites were all in Cambodia, but often only a few yards across the border. Some sites had been several kilometers into the forest and accessed by obscure trails on elephants! Imagine going to work carrying your supplies on an elephant.

With an official population of 43,000 to treat, we managed four basic bamboo-and-thatch hospitals and two outpatient facilities. Since they were simple roofs of thatch with primitive split bamboo beds and dirt floors, all medicines and equipment had to be taken to the camp and brought back to our compound each night.

Along with providing the primary medical care, we trained Khmer medical staff. We had already done this for some time in other camps, which had given us experience and prepared us for it. Next we added Doreen Blomstrand to the team. She was a friend of ours from Ellensburg and a skilled medical educator. We were soon up and running with a full team.

In addition to medical care, we supplied basic humanitarian relief supplies including food, clean water, shelter materials, blankets, mosquito nets, and clothing. We were told not to treat the refugees in such a way as to encourage more Cambodians to come to the area unnecessarily. This was sort of political, as severe fighting in western Cambodia between several Khmer armies and the Vietnamese continued.

The UN did not want us to engage in any religious activities. I interpreted this to mean that we could not use their funds for active witnessing activities and material, so we made sure to use only CAMA monies for tracts and Bibles. We had been operating for a while when the UNBRO summoned me to their office at the huge UN building in Bangkok. The subject was budget review, and the administrator went over our reports carefully. Finding no fault with our audits and narrative reports, he slid a Christian tract onto the table. "What is this?" he asked.

"Ah…it looks like a gospel tract in Cambodian," I replied.

"We do not condone religious activity in the camps," he said.

"Oh? Then what is the big Buddhist temple doing at Khao-I-Dang?" I asked.

It was built with UN funds, so I knew he had a double standard. I continued, "When I came into this building today, I saw a huge bronze tablet on the wall in the lobby. What is that?" I wondered."

Hesitantly he replied, "Umm…well, it's the Universal Declaration of Human Rights."

And I asked, "What does Article 18 of that Declaration specify?"

"Well, I'm not sure I've read it," he said.

"I have, and it guarantees everyone the right to assemble for religious purposes, to have access to religious materials, and the freedom to change religion at will. That's what the UN guarantees. Now, we are not using UN funds for either the materials or any religious activities, but we are making them freely available should the Khmer wish to take them. I expect this to be our last discussion of the provisions in Article 18, but if not, I'm acquainted with a senator named Helms who is a key decision maker on U.S. contributions to your budget. I'm sure if needed, he will find this discussion of interest."

It was quiet. I picked up the tract and put it in my file.

"Well," he said, "don't be too aggressive."

"No problem," I responded. "Come see us any time."

It was the last I ever heard from the UN on the subject.

Happy fisherman in Ilwaco, Washington. Charlie, Schlauderhut,
Kitti, Andy, State escort and Matt

Growing up refugees

Cambodian school girl gets a school kit at Green Hill camp, Thailand

Chapter 16
Up the Down Staircase ~ Part 2

Chapter 16.
Up the Down Staircase ~ Part 2

Janelle Martin and Linda Bowden on our Zebra team had a complaint: "We always get the blind elephant when we go into the jungle to our clinic. He walks under low limbs and nearly knocks us off! The good news is he smells the land mines, so we are pretty safe after all."

The daily routine for the Zebras started early with a good breakfast. After loading the trucks with metal cases containing medical supplies and making sure the water canteens and lunches were aboard, they saddled up for the drive to the work sites. Because we worked in a war zone, there were a number of heavily armed, sandbagged checkpoints to pass through, so the drive to the crossings into Cambodia took some time. The checkpoints were manned by experienced Thai army rangers, with whom we became friends.

While we didn't hold services in the camps, we did live the gospel. As the word got around, people started asking questions. We would leave boxes of Cambodian Bibles open in the bed of a pickup, and by the end of the day, they would be gone. They knew Dr. Ineke as the lady who dispensed medicines and told of Jesus.

A security nurse was designated each day, and she carried the main team radio and monitored the security channels. At Chrey, a footbridge crossed the stream into Cambodia and the Khmer Rouge refugee camp. It was the same at Tap Phrik and O'Sralau. All the camps had deep bunkers that were used when the sites were shelled. In these no-frills medical outposts, we treated people for a variety of diseases, including parasites, tuberculosis, and malaria. We also saw serious injuries from land mines and gunshot; those victims and any needing surgery were taken by ambulance to the large hospital at Khao-I-Dang. The hospital had a special project that helped make prosthetics for the many people who lost limbs, using bamboo and rubber tires.

Then there was maternal and child health. We delivered dozens of babies each month. Our patients showed much gratitude for any and all medical help we could provide. When the medicine did not seem to work, the staff would lay hands on the patients and pray, and it worked!

One such incident occurred when a lady named Madame Mai, who was 40 or so and losing her eyesight, came for help. The medical exam found that she had been suffering from years of abuse and malnutrition. She had been a Buddhist nun, so when Janelle, Dr. Ineke, and Valery Reed explained that her only hope lay in the hands of the Great Physician, she was receptive. They told her about Jesus and prayed with her. She came back for another treatment the next day. After two weeks, she announced that her eyesight was back!

The staff warned her to be quiet about it because the Khmer Rouge were still killing people to enforce their control. She didn't listen and loudly told everyone about how Jesus had healed her eyes. She got a Bible and read it aloud to anyone who would listen. Those who heard were amazed and wanted to put their trust in this Great Physician. In the years we operated this program, Madame Mai led more than 3,000 people to Jesus.

When the communists threatened to kill her if she didn't stop witnessing, she told them, "So kill me, then I'll be with Jesus in paradise!"

Mystified by her bold faith, they left her alone.

Dr. Dee caught up with Dr. Ineke one day. "Quick," she said, "I have a patient who wants to know Jesus, and I don't know all the words."

When the Vietnamese attacked and burned the camps, they allowed the people to cross into Thailand to a place called "Site 8." We built a better hospital there, with slightly better facilities as well as a good lab and a dental clinic. The Khmer eagerly waited for any kind of training, and the Zebra team was happy to provide it. Most of the trainees also became believers after some months of contact with the CAMA training team.

At the end of a meeting on border operations, a well-dressed Cambodian man asked me, "Would you come to visit our camp?" Then he introduced himself: "I am Prince Norodom Ranariddh Sihanouk."

I had heard of him and knew he had been teaching international law at Aix-en-Provence in France. "When would it be convenient?" I replied.

We talked about the various needs at his camp at Green Hill, and we became friends. A few days later, we met at Aranyaprathet.

We climbed into his deluxe van and, with heavily armed guards ahead and behind us, we drove north to Green Hill. There he monitored operations for his army, which had been fighting inside Cambodia. As we drove through the camp, I spotted a market. "Please stop," I requested. "I want to see what foods are for sale and what the prices are. This way I can help decide what the needs really are."

Looking a bit ill at ease, the prince complied. As we walked into the open-air market, a buzz of voices grew into exclamations: "The prince, the prince!"

People prostrated themselves and reached to touch his feet. It amazed me. "Oh, please take us home to Cambodia!" they cried. "We worshiped your father, the king. He is away. You are here. Please, royal one!"

Prince Ranariddh was visibly shaken. After a quick check on things, we got back into the van. People continued to cry out to him, and as we pulled from the worshiping crowd, he looked at me with tears in his eyes. Showing emotion is out of character in Asia, especially for royalty. When he could speak he said, "Thank you for taking me among my people. I have been so busy with military affairs that I forgot how they need and love me."

Over the years, CAMA provided a range of material help for his group, and his friendship helped us as well.

∽

By this time, Bev's injured left ear had become a serious medical problem. A fungus had invaded the bone and brought pain and infection. A Thai ear, nose, and throat specialist was very helpful. He had trained in Boston, so we were confident he knew his work. He finally scheduled Bev for surgery at the Chinese hospital.

Bev was awake and sandbagged so she wouldn't move. The doctor used a local anesthetic, but the one-hour surgery became three. She required a second surgery a few weeks later, which took six hours. By the end she was in shock, but God is good and she recovered well.

∽

We kept busy with management meetings, UN meetings, security meetings, staff meetings and reports, site visits, as well as phone conferences and long-distance recruiting.

Art Beals and Bill Essig of World Concern were pleased with their part of the border operation, and Linda Bowden, one of the nurses we received from them, did a wonderful job. They had become very comfortable with CAMA's management, and we felt comfortable with them because of their willingness to allow us full control of their personnel. It made a good, long-term working relationship.

In the midst of all this, we took a trip to Europe to provide reports and make sure our donors had a clear understanding of our activities. A trip to Lebanon confirmed that the work there was also progressing. In spite of the tensions in the hot zones of Lebanon, spending time with Sami Dagher and his faithful team always refreshed us.

En route back to Bangkok, I took a couple of days in Athens, where my brother Dave served in the U.S. Air Force. He was the European handball champion for the Air Force and enjoyed ocean sailing races, so I always had fun there with him and his family. I even tried handball. (My swollen hand took a week to recover.)

Back in Bangkok, I caught up on programs there. The border team functioned well, and operations in the other camps met and exceeded our expectations. Matt did well in school, and Bev stayed busy. The staff told me she had been filling in at one of the bamboo hospitals.

One day as Bev cared for patients in that border hospital, Vietnamese shells suddenly began landing nearby. As shrapnel buzzed through the thatch and bamboo roofs and walls, Bev continued working. She seemed unconcerned because she had heard guns before in Phnom Penh and Beirut. Finally, after a particularly close explosion, a Cambodian medic took her arm, saying, "Oh, Madame Bishop, we must go to the bunkers now! They are too close!"

Bev, surprised, said, "I thought that was your gun making all the noise."

Because of her being deaf in one ear, she couldn't tell the direction from which the noise came. They hustled her to the bunker, where everyone stayed until the shooting stopped.

A short time later, I received this report: "A crisis is growing in Africa. The church is requesting CAMA Services help. Five villages have no food at all, ten have some, but many others are in serious need. To complicate everything, Fula tribesmen with their cows have come down from the north. Their cows are eating the crops in some of the fields. One Fula was shot and killed, and others were attacked."

The report made it clear that Mali and Burkina Faso desperately needed help. As the overseas representative for CAMA Services, I needed to go. I headed for Paris via Singapore. While waiting to continue on, I had lunch with Jerry Ballard, president of WRC. When I filled him in on the African situation, he said, "Please let us know the details. We will try to help."

While in Paris, I got more details on Africa from Don Dirks. Next I went to the embassies of Mali and Burkina Faso for visas. I also phoned Jan van Barneveld to alert him to the upcoming project. He said that he would alert the various groups who funded our work and would be praying for me.

I flew next to Ouagadougou, where I got together with Moise Napon. He said there had been inadequate rain for six years. They expected some rain, but it would be too late to provide a useful crop. He also said he would get me detailed statistics on what they needed.

The next day in Bobo-Dioulasso, Dave Shady and Milt Pierce met me and told me that although the mission had bought and distributed grain, they just did not have the funds to do much more. Many of the people from their church struggled to find even one small meal a day. They felt we needed a plan, a budget, and a neutral outsider to implement it. They had given out 3,600 sacks of grain, mostly to widows and orphans. People named this type of aid the "Jesus Grain," and it opened many opportunities for the church.

We traveled about 200 kilometers over the rough gravel road to Tougan Circle. It wasn't the end of the world, but, as the saying goes, you could see it from there. Herb Nehlsen and his wife Jessie had a worker named Adama who had been a soldier in the French foreign legion in Vietnam. He had good administrative skills and had been in charge of the food distribution there. World Relief Canada had sent 800 tons of grain, which Herb and Adama carefully distributed. The district officer told Herb, "Without your Jesus Grain, we would not have survived!"

They eventually ended up running out of grain and supplies.

You could find the same story everywhere. No rain for years, wells drying up, people suffering. At one church, the pastor announced they would observe a day of prayer and fasting. They only had one small meal a day! Peter Colman preached on "What kind of branch are you?" He had a lot of good examples, including dry sticks, green stalks with no grain, and so on. Some people migrated to Ivory Coast, where they heard they could get food. However, it required money to go, and no one had much. Their needs were desperate!

Robert Overstreet drove me up to Koutiala, Mali, which was the CMA headquarters for the country. Jim and Judie Plumb welcomed me, and we worked out a plan for the coming days using Jim's district maps. The next day, we visited Rose Mary Nickel and Barbara Sorensen at Sanekuy. They were desperate. With tears, they told me they could not sleep or eat without feeling guilty. Their people were starving. I listened and prayed with them. "You must care for your health," I explained, "because when the food does come, you will need to be sure it gets distributed. I don't yet know exactly how or when, but God is somehow going to answer prayers, and you will be part of it!"

At Ntorosso and Yorosso, out of Mopti and Nouna, the people said, "The rain isn't enough, the wells are going dry, and the children are dying."

I saw a lot of really thin people, some suffering with kwashiorkor, a disease of severe malnutrition.

We discussed some food-for-work projects, but buying food got more difficult as even a close food source, the Ivory Coast, began restricting exports. At Kassan, I had a bit of a reunion with Dick and Lillian Phillips. We had met in Bangkok in 1975, when they were released by the Vietnamese after being prisoners on the Ho Chi Minh Trail and in Hanoi for seven months. They had taken reassignment to Africa and worked diligently on translating the Bible.

A plan began to take shape. We had already done some agricultural development in the region. One of the projects involved constructing rat-proof food-storage banks. People deposited grain and drew it out as needed. When we did get grain, the units proved ideal for storage and distribution.

It became clear that we would need a minimum of 8,000 tons of grain ASAP to avert even more deaths, and I needed a single French-speaking man with African experience to oversee the import, storage, and distribution. As I prayed, Robin Dirks often came to mind. In Paris, his mother had told me he had graduated from LeTourneau College, had a great job, and would one day marry and provide her with grandchildren. He had been a missionary kid, spending his early years in Gabon and then in France, where he finished high school. I committed the idea to the Lord and kept on working out the plan.

The Southern Baptists had also been doing a crop study, so when I arrived in Bamako, we got in touch with Norm Code, a "tent maker" in the Baptist mission. Loyal Bowman and I found that our figures came pretty close to theirs, and none of them were good news.

I visited the U.S. embassy, where Rich Newberg ran the U.S. Aid in Development (USAID) program. I had met him in 1972 in the Congo. He and his wife, Ginny, had also served at Imeloko in the late 1970s, and now they were in Bamako. Unfortunately, we could not get grain through USAID because we were a Christian agency owned by a church. We knew that God would supply some other way.

I stayed with Tim Steiner and wrote a better project outline. I also wrote a project to provide a pump for a church garden in Sanqui. As the big Air Afrique DC-8 roared off the Bamako runway at the end of my trip, pictures filled my head. I saw hungry people, dried-out fields, bad roads, as well as hopeful missionaries and national church pastors.

Don Dirks had meetings with various groups who eagerly waited to get accurate word on the terrible situation in the Sahel. I spoke with Dick Anderson of WRC by phone to his office in Dakar. WRC wanted to know details so they could get involved. I promised everyone a project plan just as soon as it was completed.

As I wrote I remembered conversations along the way, when they showed me fields with leaves but no grain. I had urged them to feed the leaves to their cows. When they said they had nothing to keep themselves healthy, I advised them to butcher the cows and dry the meat. When we talked about water, I remembered that the Dogon buried clay jars in watercourses and collected them when dry times came. Each idea was a departure from how it had always been done, but they needed a new way of doing things if they wanted to survive. We even had a hard time selling the idea of using short-season millet seed. "We don't like the taste," I heard often.

⌒

When Bev came to Paris from Bangkok, I was not feeling well and needed her help to move the project ahead. When laying out the problems and ways that CAMA could respond, we knew we needed to get grain to Mali and Burkina Faso as soon as possible, no later than early 1985.

In addition to the 8,000 tons of grain, which would cost $2 million if we had to purchase it, we needed staff, an office, vehicles, and operational funds. We also wanted an agriculturalist to help teach new farming techniques. We added follow-on projects, one called "Famine Prevention," which included farming tools, solar water pumps, and hand pumps for 20 villages. Our proposed budget also included cement, steel, and other supplies. The total, including grain purchases, came to $2,245,100!

Well, now we knew what to pray for. The whole program operated through the CMA church infrastructure. Bev and I stayed at the Hotel Olympic and had a good time seeing friends like David and Samuelle Soquier from our previous days in Paris. Bob Reed came in, and we had a positive review of CAMA and the plan for Africa.

One day as I read the mail Bev had brought from Bangkok, I noticed one return address and nearly shouted, "What's this?"

It was a letter from Robin Dirks. Talk about an answer to prayer! I had just finished writing the job description for the program director in Africa and was thinking he would be perfect. In his letter, said God had given him an education, a house, a job, a GTO, and a pickup, but he felt God might want him to be available for a short-term missions assignment. The letter closed, "If CAMA has one, contact me," and provided a phone number.

I grabbed the phone and dialed the number in Texas.

After a few rings, my call was answered with a groggy "Hello?"

"Robin," I shouted, "I got your letter!"

"Who is this?" he asked.

Suddenly I realized it was 2:00 a.m. in Texas. But I quickly outlined the African situation and our dire projections. "You are just the man to manage the distribution," I assured him. "Call me back when you have prayed about it, but time is short!"

Wow, I thought, is God great or what?

Suddenly, I was running a high fever and having diarrhea. Bev and Bob Reed said, "See a doctor ASAP!" I ended up being admitted to the hospital in Paris.

Dr. John Dax, an old friend, came into my room. I had an I.V. in my arm and felt lousy. He announced, "You have a severe malaria attack. You'll be here a few days."

My brain thought, I don't have time for this! My body, though, said that I did and I needed to rest! Then Bev came in, having finished typing up the project for my proofreading. She said that Robin had called back. "He will go to Africa," she reported, "but he needs to talk with you."

One of my prayers had been answered. Now we just needed grain and money.

The I.V. and medicines took hold. My fever came down, and I felt better. From my hospital bed, I got Robin on the phone and told him, "I need you in Paris in 30 days. You'll have a month here to meet all the donors, then a month in Africa before we start giving out grain."

It was October 15, 1984. "Andy," he said, "what do I do with all this stuff … my house, cars, and so forth?"

My reply was, "Make a list and put all the things that God needs to do on it, and then start praying. When you get to the bottom of the list, you'll be here! I have a list too... people, grain, money, and more. Now I'm crossing off your name. When I get to the bottom of my list, you will be in Africa passing out grain."

"Okay," Robin said, "pray."

I did!

I also called Jan van Barneveld. He was excited and wanted me to come to Holland at once. His government was very willing to help. I explained my situation, and he said he would call me back. Jennifer Evans of TEAR Fund England was glad to hear we had a plan for Africa. She knew Robin Dirks and agreed he would be ideal to oversee the work. "We need your plan here in London at once," she said.

I explained my hospitalization. "Bev is out getting the plan copied and bound," I said, "but I'll have her DHL it to you this afternoon."

"Fine," she said. "We are meeting in an hour. What do you need to get this program under way?"

"Well," I said, "$175,000 U.S."

The line was quiet for a moment, and then she said, "TEAR Fund will provide the money; let me know where to wire it."

With God at work, I could rest!

Jan van Barneveld phoned back and said, "Hans Blankenberg, the Dutch minister of foreign aid, is going to Mali tomorrow. Could you get a copy of the plan and supporting data to Charles de Gaulle Airport tomorrow morning and hand it to him while his KLM flight takes on passengers?"

I said Bev would take it out to him. Such an answer to prayer!

While Bev got the papers duplicated and bound, I used my hospital time to talk to donors. As copies of the project and supporting data were ready, they went to WRC, Zuid-Oost Azië, Jan van Barneveld, World Concern and Samaritan's Purse.

Don Dirks and Bev drove slowly to Charles de Gaulle Airport. The fog was thick, and they could barely see the taillights of the car ahead of them, even though it was less than a car length away. The KLM flight bearing Hans Blankenberg should have landed, but they still had several kilometers to go. Would they make it to the airport in time? Don drove and Bev prayed. Finally they arrived at the proper terminal and rushed to the boarding area, where they asked if the KLM flight to Bamako was still there. "Yes," the official said, "the fog is still too thick to depart."

Another answer to prayer! The packet was taken on board, and later the plan helped the Dutch government decide to assist CAMA with the famine relief program. They especially liked our follow-up Famine Prevention projects, as well as the precise data on the grain production shortfalls.

After five days, I left the hospital. Bob Reed agreed to expedite the paperwork to get Robin to Paris quickly. Then we heard that Canada might provide grain. While gaining strength, I visited donors and interested agencies in Europe. Bev and I took the train to Holland, where Jan van Barneveld hosted us and drove us to meet some government officials. Their high level of interest in Africa encouraged us. The Christian Broadcasting Network featured some CAMA work to help the ZOA and TEAR Funds raise money. People were happy to work through the CMA's grass-roots infrastructure.

"How are you feeling? Have you been resting?" Dr. Dax wanted to make sure I was ready to travel back to Thailand. I agreed to take it easy and listen to Nurse Beverly. So a few hours later, we were on Singapore Airlines headed home via Penang, where we planned to see Matt.

Matt was happy to see us back in Asia, and we enjoyed eating together and especially sharing ice cream. While there, we arranged for the Livingston's to come and speak at the Vietnamese refugee Christmas program. They were former missionaries to Vietnam who had worked at Dalat.

Back in Bangkok, the first order of business was to catch up with CAMA and a CCSDPT meeting. It had been quite a shift from hunger in Africa to the plenty of Thailand. It was November, and Ronald Reagan had just been elected U.S. president. I showed slides of Africa to our workers, and it gave them a feeling of partnership to know CAMA was busy not only in Europe and Lebanon, but also in Africa.

Don Dirks flew in from Paris to be the speaker at the CAMA team retreat, and we stayed at the Chomsurang Hotel in Khorat. We spent time swimming, playing games, relaxing, and hearing encouraging messages. We had taken Don to meet the team members at the various camps, so he had seen them in their work settings. They loved his messages and stories about resettlement in Europe. When Don boarded the plane for Paris, he had some encouraging observations for us.

A new group of refugees had become a problem for Thailand. The Karen hill tribes came from the mountains of Burma. Before the British left the country in the late 1950s, as the communists were taking over, they promised the Karen a homeland of their own. It never happened, however, so the Karen hill tribes fought the communists. After years of conflict, they were pinned to the northwest Thai border. The CCSDPT discussed ways they might help the refugees crossing into Thailand once the Thai military opened the area for travel.

After only three weeks in Thailand, I headed back to Beirut. Fortunately the airport was open, making it much easier to get there. We had a prayer meeting at the Karantina church, and when the people saw the slides on the African famine, they responded, "We have war, but we have food. We will pray faithfully for our African church family."

Sami and I reviewed the books. The finances were in good order, and we went to the U.S. embassy to get the reports notarized. Then we drove up to the orphanage at Mansourieh. Their van had taken a direct hit, but no one was hurt. However, they did need a new van. I took some photos and was able to get them to TEAR Fund in England, which provided the new van.

Sami told me about a visit from the Dutch government. Some in the Dutch parliament had questioned why so much money was given to CAMA in Lebanon when everyone knew there were lots of Muslims there, too. When Jan had told me of the upcoming government audit, I had recommended he show the man everything and try to answer all his questions. Later, when all the investigation and village visits were complete, the investigator said, "I am satisfied. We got our money's worth. You even help more Muslims than Christians. Your work is very good, but Sami, they say you talk about Jesus a lot."

"But sir," Sami responded, "I'm a pastor. I don't know drinking, dancing, smoking, or playing cards. I know Jesus. What else can I talk about?"

"Sami," the man said, "you just keep on doing what you do here. I'll take care of the parliament in Holland."

I watched Paul and Anna doing their homework. Sami was the faithful parent helping them with the details. What always amazed me was that they did everything, including math, science, and grammar, in three languages (English, French, Arabic). That means they did every assignment three times! "They are brilliant kids," I told Sami.

"Yes, but here everyone must learn at least three languages to get by," he replied.

oy, Sami's wife, had learned all three as well.

⌐

"Well, I made it," Robin Dirks announced.

His big smile said it all. He had checked off everything on his prayer list and was ready for Africa. We reviewed the details of the proposal and discussed implementation. By now, TEAR Fund England had sent the money to get equipment, rent a base, and prepare for the grain we needed to distribute.

In Paris we met General Mirambeau, head of SOS-Sahel. He was impressed with Robin's French and CAMA's plans. He said his agency would cooperate in any way it could. Then we headed off to Amsterdam, where we discussed the CAMA plan with TEAR Fund Holland, ICCO, and Jan van Barneveld. Jan thanked us for the excellent report and plan. The foreign minister had found our data accurate and of great assistance. "You see, Andy," Jan said, "I have always told you that information is money, and accurate, timely information is even more money."

CAMA received several hundred thousand dollars from Holland over the next few years.

From Holland we flew to London for time with TEAR Fund England. "Thank you so much for the timely gift to Africa," I told them. "I was on my back in the hospital and unsure what to do. You got things off to a great start, and now Robin Dirks is getting ready to leave for Bamako."

When I met with George Hoffman, the founding director of TEAR Fund, he said they were pleased to be working with CAMA in Africa. He was also very pleased with progress in Europe, Lebanon, and Thailand, and we made plans to meet on his next trip to Asia. Robin spent time reviewing their reporting expectations and pledged to be responsive to their needs. Again the strength of CAMA's system was confirmed. The money and feedback from Robin went directly from London to Africa and back. It was a winning formula and a great way to keep channels open for information and funds. We used the same system in Lebanon and Asia.

Robin and I talked with Bob Reed by phone. He had located a partner for Robin. Gary Schmidt, a Canadian, would become CAMA coordinator under Robin's supervision in Burkina Faso. After that, all we needed was grain. We knew what to pray for!

Matt beat me to Bangkok. He flew home from Penang for the Christmas holidays, so we fit him right into the Christmas program schedule. He still worked at Nite Spot computers, which kept him busy through the holidays, but he also made a number of refugee camp visits.

Peter Ferry, another missionary, invited us to Phuket, an island on the southwest coast of Thailand. It was considered "out of the way" but had wonderful beaches, and everything was so inexpensive. We had five lovely days of food and fun. We rented motorbikes, and even Bev joined in whizzing about the island. We returned to Bangkok refreshed!

The Alliance Witness

JANUARY 2, 1985

THAILAND
UPDATE

Seven Aids
for Life's Journey

Near Death at
Eskimo Point

Linda Bowden, Janelle Martin, driver and elephant
en route to Cambodia to deliver medical care

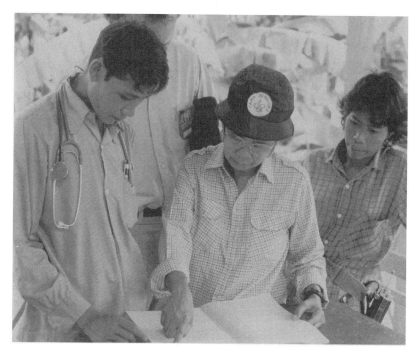

Dr Dee Garcia at Site 8 hospital, Thailand

The Phillips from Hanoi prison to Bible translation in Africa

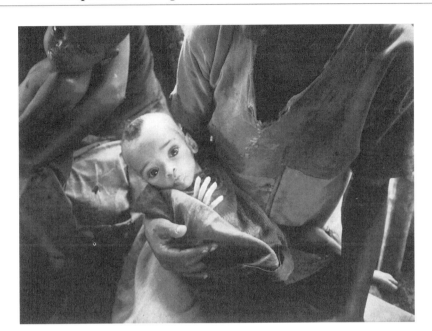

Hunger in Mali. The solution? Jesus grain

The used camel market in Timbuktu. Cash for clunkers

There's no AAA here... you improvise.
Moving the Jesus grain across Africa

Chapter 17
Up the Down Staircase ~ Part 3

Chapter 17.
Up the Down Staircase ~ Part 3

My next trip was set to begin with a flight to France. Suddenly I bent over with pain. I'd had a fever the night before, and since I had a few days' work upcoming in Paris, I hoped to get the problem checked there by Dr. Dax. My flight was that evening. Bob Storms and Bev insisted, however, that I go to the hospital in Bangkok. Perhaps that's best, I thought. I can take something for the pain to get me to Paris.

At the hospital, as I lay on my back in the examining area, the doctor poked my lower right abdomen. "Does that hurt?" he asked.

"Ouch! Yes!" I said. "Can you give me something for it? I need to go to Paris tonight."

"You're not going anywhere but to surgery," he replied. "You have a ruptured appendix."

Well, when they have you, they have you. Bev said, "Do it," and the shot for anesthesia began to kick in.

The surgery went well, and a few days later, as Cliff Westergren finished his visit to the camps and headed for Hong Kong, I headed for Paris via Copenhagen. After a couple of days of catching up on CAMA projects in Europe, Lebanon, and Africa, I flew to Nyack to report to the CAMA board meeting. The members of the board encouraged us by reading reports and asking questions. Everyone was amazed at what God was doing and the ways He was providing money, people, and opportunities.

In a later conversation, while asking a lot of questions about CAMA Services, Carol Johnston commented, "God promised when Roy and I married that we would become missionaries. So far we haven't made it to serve overseas."

Roy had been the one who screened Bev and me for service in Cambodia ten years before. He and Carol were both trained psychologists, and Roy held a Ph.D. in counseling. "Why don't you come to Thailand?" I suggested. "The Anderson's are going to retire, so they need a pastor at the international church, and you could be CAMA's chaplain. We have a great team, many of whom work in a war zone and deal with major trauma and stress daily. Since Carol is a nurse, she would be ideal as a counselor for them."

I was excited about the prospect. They could make a major contribution to the staff's emotional health, particularly to the Site 8 team.

Roy told me later that after praying with Carol about it, he went to Dr. L. L. King and said, "I've found a pastor for Bangkok. Carol and me!"

"But who will do your job?" Dr. King's assistant had asked, alarmed.

"Oh, God will provide."

Dr. King said, "If God's calling, go."

And they did.

Bob Reed arranged for me to talk with a couple. Their names were Stephen and Jacqui Bailey. They were young but well trained. Steve had already done a short term with CAMA, and Jacqui was a registered nurse. They had a clear testimony and a desire to serve with CAMA among the refugees. I felt clearly from the Lord that they would do a good job. "Come to work with us," I encouraged them.

And they did.

I phoned Drew and caught up on his news. He had been transferred from Germany to Michigan. I arranged to meet him in Wheaton, Illinois, at Jim Whitmer's, and we had a good time. We planned for him to visit Thailand later on. I also did some phone interviews with prospective CAMA workers. Joyce Johns in Spokane, Washington, seemed to be a good prospect for a year at Site 8. All these years later, she is still serving the Lord in Cambodia.

Kerry and Deb Schottelkorb were questioning where God wanted them to serve. They had been among the people who sent us off from Ellensburg to Cambodia, and Kerry had been a really good youth pastor, but over the years they had continued to pray and think about overseas ministry. "Why don't you come visit us in Thailand?" I asked. "I have a project in mind, and you could gather more information to help make future decisions."

Deb wanted details. I didn't have all of them, but CAMA was ten years old, and we had just been given permission to do some public relations activities. Deb got excited, and they decided to come and help launch some promotional materials for CAMA. In Ellensburg, I talked with Tim Owen and some of our friends at the church. We had been given the opportunity to take a short summer furlough, so our agenda included finding a place to live. He said the church would start looking for an apartment.

In Seattle, I had a good visit with Charlie Morton. He had recovered from some dangerous surgery and was becoming the new executive director for World Concern. We enjoyed remembering the help that he, as vice president of Pepsi Cola Asia, had given to CAMA Services in the beginning. His Cambodian son, Peter, one of our orphans, was in school. Another orphan, Leakhena, kept in touch with them as she did with Bev and me.

Back in Bangkok, I caught up on some work and had to revisit the cardiologist at Paolo Memorial Hospital. I needed new medicine for my hypertension and got stern advice from the doctor and Bev. Everyone said to avoid stress!

"Dave, I want Karen and you to move back to Bangkok," I said.

They were a neat couple. Dave, a red-haired missionary kid from Vietnam, was six foot two or so. We had worked with his parents in Hong Kong, and I met Dave in Washington, D.C. I hired him to work with Reg Reimer in Bangkok, and when the CMT moved to Ban Vinai, Dave and Karen became team administrators for the hospital. Karen had been a Korean orphan and, due to some childhood health complications, was not quite five feet tall. She had been raised in California and was a California girl with an outgoing personality. Dave was more Asian in his demeanor, quiet and introspective. He had good networking skills and soaked up information like a sponge.

I needed to open an office of information on Indochina, because we needed to begin gathering details that would help us plan to return to Cambodia, Laos, and Vietnam when the doors opened. Dave was reluctant at first. Doing full-time research was a new concept in missions, but I was determined to prepare for CAMA's return to Indochina with as much accurate information as possible. When they finally agreed to the move and got to Bangkok, we worked out the job description, and Dave joined the "Foreign Correspondents Club of Thailand" and began to ask questions and compile information. We saw the foundation that we had dreamed of being laid and the Lord providing answers.

A problem arose on my next trip to Africa. Arriving in Ouagadougou, Burkina Faso, I realized I didn't have Moise Napon's phone number with me and did not know his new address. I checked into the hotel and took a walk, during which I saw a small boy fishing by a pond. Ouagadougou was a city of several hundred thousand, but when I asked the boy if he would find Moise for me and explained all I knew of his general location in the city, he agreed to find him for the 100 CFA I offered. That's about 50 cents in the U.S. I gave him 50 CFA and promised the rest when he brought "Prince Moise."

Moise was amused. "When this small boy showed your card," he said later, "I was glad to know you were here. In Africa, we don't always get the word on people's travel schedules."

We attended the UN coordination meeting on famine response. They knew the need but were slow to respond. As usual, the church was ahead of them.

The next day, while in Bobo-Dioulasso, I heard good news. Grain from Canada was on the way thanks to farmers, the Canadian government, and World Relief Canada. Two thousand tons had arrived in Abidjan and were ready to begin the thousand-mile trip to the CAMA Services storage points for distribution. The Ballards drove in from Nouna. They enjoyed working with Gary Schmidt, who rode the countryside on a Honda dirt bike. Gary spent time improving his French and developing good relations with both missionaries and national pastors. He said that hundreds of kilometers on washboard roads had begun to wear him out.

Herb Nehlsen in Tougan had been ready, too. His team had used food for work to improve the roads and were ready for the grain. Robin Dirks came in from Mali. It turned out that Norm Code was willing to oversee the import and transportation to distribution sites for us. He had the import registration and was not listed as a Christian agency. We always joked that the Southern Baptists "laundered" the grain, and we distributed and reported on it. It was a great cooperative effort. Both Robin's and Gary's work exceeded expectations.

After reviewing the ongoing distribution, we were really encouraged by the progress in stopping the famine in areas where the CMA had churches. The meeting at the Jelibougou CMA church in Bamako was full of praise. They had prayed for food and rain, and God had been answering their prayers. They told me of how the Jesus Grain had not only saved lives, but had also opened new villages to the gospel. The food was given with no strings attached. The famine prevention work had begun as well, and farming tools, new types of seed, and even new methods of farming were introduced. It would take time and changes in tastes, but we had hope.

Back in Paris, I got some reports together and then did a couple of radio interviews. Franklin Graham of Samaritan's Purse requested a CAMA survey of food needs in Ethiopia, so I headed for Addis Ababa. Ethiopia had been under a communist government and had only recently allowed much in the way of outside involvement. The government was hard on the church, and even having a Bible at home was illegal.

I stayed at the Sudan Interior Mission (SIM) guest house and got a good overview of the situation from Alex Fellows. Thanks to communist inefficiency, things were a mess. Food coming into the port had been stored on the ground because holding facilities weren't available, and up to 8,000 tons had already spoiled. As many as 40 percent of the trucks in the country did not operate properly, and they also had a fuel shortage. Some airlift was going on, but the government made sure it went to areas under its control.

We bumped through the muddy streets. In the center of town, we saw a huge billboard with Marx, Lenin, and Engels extolling the joys of communism. Tefera, the driver, said, "When they put those men up, no one knew who they were. After a while, they knew about Marx and Lenin. But who is the third guy? The government made every group have a communist 'minder' to watch them and make sure they did not deviate from communist-approved ways. So the people decided the number three man, Engels, was Marx and Lenin's minder."

We had a good laugh.

A meeting of 36 nongovernment organizations (NGOs) gave me more insight. Modeled after CCSDPT in Thailand, they sought to share information and make sure the various regions got food. It had begun to rain, and as we traveled we saw crops being planted, but it would be 60 to 90 days until a crop could be harvested, so interim food was a must. Everyone prayed the rains would keep up until then.

Russian equipment could be seen everywhere. An-12 cargo planes shuttled food and troops, while fighter bombers flown by Russian, Cuban, and Ethiopian pilots roared overhead toward battles being fought in the north. A crashed Russian cargo plane lay off the end of the main runway. Russian and Chinese trucks rolled through the town, their low-quality diesel engines pouring black smoke. Some new Jeep Cherokees parked at the large foreign goods store intrigued me. Then I noticed a Chinese character on the rear door. They had been made in China. "Don't buy one," my Ethiopian escort recommended.

On the main road to a base south of Addis, I saw huge tanks and more modern fighter bombers, along with missiles and sophisticated radar equipment. Down a nearby road, donkey trains heading for the countryside patiently plodded along under their loads of goods. It had taken me a couple of days to get permission to travel, and even then the rules changed without notice, but we were on the road. We saw truckloads of students being taken to the "new regions" to help build houses at the government's direction. More than 350,000 people had been moved to areas under the government's control in spite of outcries from voluntary agencies. The NGO camps they had been in were burned, and the food sent there by voluntary agencies had been confiscated. The hard hand of fascism was not a pretty sight.

SIM had purchased 90 oxen to help with plowing and planting; it also provided plane loads of new farming tools. Its staff had set up feeding centers in Addis Ababa for those in particular need. It also brought in a number of retired missionaries to help operate its programs and did a fine job.

The Kale Heywet Church SIM had started was a good infrastructure in spite of government harassment. I enjoyed getting to know Dr. Mulatu Baffa, the church president. They had 2,500 churches and over a million members in Ethiopia, but the government kept them under surveillance and often closed churches while putting people in jail for their Christian witness. The church had been developing a department to deal with relief and development in coordination with SIM and other NGOs, a fact that really encouraged us.

Bruce Adams of SIM told me about a pastor who had been in jail. When the daughter of a high-ranking church leader died, he asked an Ethiopian pastor to hold a Christian funeral for her. This pastor asked his assistant pastor, "Do you want to preach or pray?"

Several thousand people came and heard the gospel.

They got arrested and jailed immediately for their faith. African prisons are grim, and in order to survive, you need family to bring food for you. Since many had known about what happened, the church people brought food. While in jail, the two pastors witnessed and held Bible studies. Soon a church was planted in the prison. More food came in, so they shared it among the others who needed it. They also sent a tithe of the food and supplies to the church poor fund outside the prison. People sent more than $150, and that, too, got sent out to the poor fund. Guards even become believers. The warden finally said, "This isn't working. Please leave and go home."

When they left, they sent another $150 to help other church families.

In my report to Samaritan's Purse, I urged them to work with the church and send funds for office equipment and supplies. Donors wanted reports and accountability, and they needed good equipment in order to do that. They also needed a warehouse, help for jailed pastors, and funds for Christian literature and encouragement from the church abroad.

It would not be my last trip to Ethiopia. Roy Gustafson and Guy Davidson came in. I had met Guy in Lebanon. They were happy for all the research I had done and promised to encourage Samaritan's Purse to increase its aid to the Ethiopian church.

After this, I headed for Bangkok via Bombay. Catching up on the work in Thailand went well. Cliff Westergren and his wife, Marlene, came in to be the speakers at our CAMA retreat. We had a picnic at a waterfall and some good spiritual refreshing together.

Steve and Jacqui Bailey had arrived and were in language study. Dave Moore, CMA vice president, spoke at one of our meetings. He, too, was becoming a CAMA convert.

Bev flew to Seattle to visit her family, get a medical checkup, and go to Ellensburg to set up an apartment for the summer. Matt and I followed once he got out of school.

CAMA Services had been asked to begin an opium detoxification program at Ban Vinai. The church leaders told us that opium had been widely used as a pacifier for kids, like aspirins for pain but very addicting. They told us that many church members were addicted. Steve and Jacqui did the research. Wayne Persons helped with the negotiations, insisting the church must assign people to help. Next CAMA built a closed compound complete with a kitchen and sleeping areas. When people signed in, Jacqui, a registered nurse, would carefully give them a physical exam. She coordinated findings with the hospital so that any tuberculosis, malaria, or other diseases masked by opium could be treated. Then the patients signed an agreement to cooperate until they were free of their opium addiction.

Addicts could not leave the program until the treatment ended. The patients drank water with Antabuse and progressively weaker amounts of opium. They went through pain and violent sickness, but at the end of two to four weeks, they were clean. Then the church followed up with them to help them avoid returning to opium. It became a model program extolled by both the UN and the Thai government.

"Dad, I can't sleep," Matt said. It was 1:00 a.m. in a Hong Kong hotel.

"Why?" I asked.

"I need a fan," he explained.

"But Matt, the hotel is air conditioned!"

"Yes," he agreed, "but I'm used to hearing an overhead fan so I can relax."

I wondered why we had not recorded "Dalat night sounds" so traveling missionary kids could sleep.

We had left Bangkok that morning, and Cathay Pacific Airlines was a great way to go. While waiting to leave, the purser had come to me. "How many boarding passes do you have?" he'd asked.

"Two," I'd replied.

"May I see them please?"

He had taken them and left. Returning a few minutes later, he'd said, "A tour group wants to sit together, so we have moved you and your son to first class!"

We had enjoyed steak and eggs for breakfast en route to Hong Kong.

After two days of shopping for computer stuff and eating great food, we headed to the U.S. We had been away for two busy years and welcomed a few weeks at Ellensburg.

We rented an apartment next door to Pastor Tim and Edie Owen and began a busy schedule of speaking engagements, barbecues, and good fellowship. Kerry and Deb Schottelkorb, who served in Bremerton, helped us find a '78 Volkswagen Rabbit, and we were set.

Col. Pranit of the Thai refugee office in Bangkok came on a state visit. He had told me he might visit, so I invited him to go fishing. Bev's dad had a nice summer home at Ilwaco, and when the U.S. Department of State escort called, we made a date for fishing. Charlie Morton, Matt, the handler, and I had a ball. We went out on the HoBo Charter boat at 4:00 a.m., and by that afternoon we had 12 fish between us. Col. Pranit packed a suitcase with canned salmon!

Later on, Daryl Brooks took Matt and me fishing at Campbell River, and we brought home more great salmon. By the end of the summer, we had a good supply of smoked and canned salmon to take back to Bangkok.

Matt's summer ended. On August 15, 1985, he flew back to Asia to start classes at Dalat. Some friends of his from the Ellensburg church had left a few days earlier to become missionary kids'. Their parents were to be teachers with the CMA in Indonesia. Our church's mission participation was growing.

Bev and I joined her dad at Ilwaco and caught more fish! Then on August 23, Drew arrived home from his four years in the Air Force. We had a great reunion and a few days to help him get ready to attend Central Washington University.

We made a whirlwind tour of meetings in churches and offices on the east coast and did some more interviews of prospective CAMA workers. On our return, Drew met us in Yakima. We signed the Volkswagen over to him and got ready to head back to Asia.

You ran over how many chickens? Andy,
Adama, Herb and Dave Shady

Robin Dirks refuels at the local gas station in Burkina Faso, Africa

African water system, water to drink and water gardens

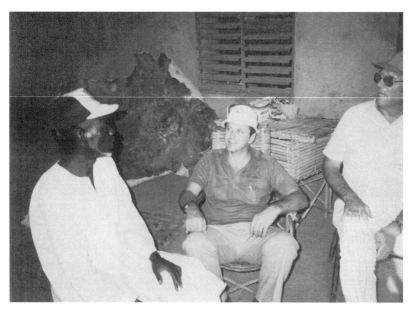

Adama, Andy and Herb Nehlsen review progress
on Jesus grain distribution in Burkina Faso

Chapter 18
Keeping On ~ Part 1

Chapter 18.
Keeping On ~ Part 1

Our Korean Air 747 descended into Seoul, Korea, through light fog. Clem and Maddie Dreger met us there and hosted us for a few days. Matt had already started at Dalat School in Malaysia, so Bev and I looked forward to a relaxed time, seeing the recently established CMA work in which Clem and Maddie participated. It was a fascinating introduction to a vibrant culture and a great church community.

As Clem, Maddie, Bev, and I walked on the teeming main streets of Seoul, sirens suddenly began to blare. Men with whistles, armbands, and batons started directing people into stairways leading to bomb shelters. Cars stopped, and their passengers jumped out and rushed to the shelters. It took only minutes for the city of millions to halt. Clem explained that it was an air raid drill. "With belligerent communist neighbors in North Korea and China, they have to keep alert," he said, "so on certain days of the month they hold the drills, and everyone must take part."

A few minutes later the siren blew again, and in a short time everything was going full blast once more.

Back home in Thailand, while at dinner with Pastor David Anderson, we talked about his upcoming return to Canada. We had left our shoes at the door, as always in Asia. Bev's feet got cold due to the air conditioning, so she found mine beneath the table and warmed hers on my calf. Suddenly Rev. Anderson stopped his conversation. His neck and face became crimson, and a look of confusion registered on his face.

Bev blurted, "Andy, are my feet on your leg?"

"No," I replied.

Bev had accidentally been warming her feet on Pastor Anderson's leg! We dissolved into gales of laughter.

Roy and Carol Johnston arrived from America to a joyous welcome. They planned to serve as the pastors of Soi 10 CMA International Church and counselors for the CAMA team. Our people worked long, hard days at remote and often dangerous sites. We were happy to have Roy and Carol's positive attitudes and professional skills in counseling, as well as Carol's training as a nurse.

Roy, being a pilot, wanted to know if he could fly in Thailand, and he knew of a Thai Airlines 747 captain who attended his church. The captain explained, however, that for various reasons, only members of the Thai Air Force reserve or members of a recognized flying club could pilot small aircraft in the country.

So Roy joined the Royal Thai Air Force reserve with Chokepichai's help. It all went well until Dr. Roy, the psychologist, flunked the psychological evaluation. It surprised Roy that he had flunked the very test he had given to thousands of people. When he asked why he had flunked, the man responded, "We can't tell you that."

However, when Roy explained that he had a doctorate in the subject, the tester said, "Oh, please, can you explain the test to me? We use it, but I don't understand it."

Roy was happy to enlighten the man, and he passed, of course, and became a lieutenant colonel in the Royal Thai Air Force reserve and finally got to fly. They did a great job as pastors and counselors and were even used by the U.S. embassy to help its staff deal with problems associated with overseas service. Today, even in "retirement," the Johnston's continue to maintain an effective international counseling service.

Pressure to conclude the refugee programs in Thailand continued. Ending them had been declared official policy by the Royal Thai government, but the implementation had become a serious challenge. I gave a speech in 1984 to the CCSDPT in Thailand's annual conference on Indochinese displaced persons. I told the story of the general asking the cadet why he crashed his plane. "Well," said the cadet, "I ran out of altitude, air speed, and ideas at the same time!"

Unlike the cadet, the CCSDPT had ideas. Both the CCSDPT and CAMA were ten years old, but they still came up with effective ideas to solve old problems. While the general population in the giving societies experienced things like memory loss and donor fatigue, we were still on the job. I reviewed the policies such as increased third-country resettlement and the yet-to-be-implemented voluntary return to the country of origin. It was easier to make a policy than to implement it.

I went on to review why people, as Vladimir Lenin said, "vote with their feet and become refugees." Unfortunately, crossing borders had become difficult. World strife and refugee accumulations in the camps like Thailand's had become more and more common. I used an old Beatles song title, Nowhere Man, to describe the nowhere people of our age. They had nowhere to go in their country of origin and nowhere en route to another country to stay. The only solution was to seek a durable peace that kept people at home, or else we would be handling refugee flows forever. As long as the groups in power accepted Mao's dictum that "power comes from the barrel of a gun," we would see refugees. Peace seldom follows guns; thus refugees, like the poor, will always be with us.

By the end of the summer of 1985, we had gained enough data through Dave Fitzstevens's research to begin thinking about how to stimulate voluntary return to places like Laos. We needed a plan, and as I talked with our CAMA staff and various UNHCR officials, it became clear that each country would have special criteria for deciding who would be most welcome. We already had micro enterprise activities in some camps, including bakeries, CAMA Crafts, literacy training, education, metalworking, and small businesses such as trading, animal husbandry, and gardening.

Next, then, we embarked on a project to equip the refugees at the Lao in Na Pho camp with marketable skills for their return to Laos. Bob Storms, who had been especially interested in the Lao people, was eager to help with the on-site management. Paul and Elena Stringer from Holland did the technical teaching. We got approval of the idea from the Royal Thai government and space for the center to be built in the camp. We planned to teach engine repair, woodworking, electrical wiring, and masonry. Women would be taught sewing. We just needed $100,000 to launch the project.

George Hoffman, founder and CEO of TEAR Fund, stood in the ashes of a section of the Na Pho camp just outside Nakorn Phanom, Thailand. Fires regularly threatened these camps made of bamboo and thatch. We had gone over the general situation in the refugee camps, and Sally Lambert, his deputy, liked the idea of the skills training center. "How much will it cost?" she asked.

George's mind went into high gear, because he saw the potential for both the education and the gospel. "Our project estimate is $100,000," I said, showing them our project outline.

"We will do it," George said firmly.

Sally agreed it fit the TEAR Fund criteria.

We began at once, and the building went up quickly. We got training materials from several companies, and even tools and a new engine on a test stand from Nissan Motors. Bob moved to Nakorn Phnom, and the Stringers came from Holland. They began learning Lao at once. Paul was excited and full of ideas. Elena set up the sewing classes.

Kaek came into my office one day soon thereafter. "We got money from TEAR Fund," she said.

"Oh, that's for the Na Pho training center," I responded. "It should be $100,000."

"Well," she said, "it's $175,000."

I was mystified, and then a thought struck me. I phoned George Hoffman in London. I gave him an update on the center and thanked him for the money. "However," I said, "it's too much. When I said $100,000, I meant U.S. dollars. I think you thought 100,000 British pounds!"

"Oh, my," George said. "Well, how much is the second year's operational estimate?"

"About $70,000 U.S."

"Well, then, use the extra for that and the $5,000 for something else."

"Thank you, brother!" I said. "I'll let you know the details once I determine what the special project is."

"Mr. Bishop, I think CAMA should get a computer," Kaek said, "We could do our financial work so much better with a computer."

"Can you use one?" I asked.

"Not yet, but the technical school is giving night classes, and I would like to get the training."

"Okay," I said, "CAMA will pay for the training, and I'll ask Matt for advice on which computer is best for our needs."

Our office secretary, Rindi Bowman, agreed with the idea. Now, I have never learned to type, to say nothing of using something like a computer. Today they would call me dyslexic. I just couldn't make my hand do the right thing and think creatively at the same time, but I knew CAMA needed a computer.

Not long after Kaek began her training, I was in Armonk, New York, speaking at a CMA church and attending a CAMA board meeting. Pastor Bush took me to lunch that Sunday at a parishioner's home. During dinner, the host, an executive with IBM, asked what kind of computer CAMA used. "Well," I said, "we're getting our staff trained, but as of yet we don't have one."

"I have one for you!" he exclaimed.

He returned from his study with a brand new IBM portable, the size of a small suitcase, so new it wasn't even on the market yet. CAMA had its first computer! When Kaek saw it, she was ecstatic. "It's even better than the one I learned on!" she exclaimed.

When Matt came from Dalat, he was amazed as well. Later, on a trip to Hong Kong, he had another PC built from scratch for us and bought a Winchester drive that he plugged into the IBM we already had. This allowed us to do everything on the computer. I used a good bit of George Hoffman's extra money to complete the CAMA computer system.

Once again I made a trip to #89 rue du Cherche Midi, the embassy of Mali in Paris. I needed a visa to visit the CAMA work there. Next I headed off to 159 Blvd. Haussmann to get a visa to Burkina Faso. My passport had extra pages and always drew comments from embassy and customs officials.

A short time later, my UTA Air flight dropped onto the hot, dusty runway at Bamako, Mali. Rich and Ginny Newberg hosted me, and

Robin Dirks came in to update me on the projects. He had written that he would like to stay beyond his two-year contract. I was all for it. God had supplied over 11,000 tons of grain for Mali and Burkina Faso. Robin had negotiated the delivery, storage, and distribution, kept good records, and accounted for all funds. Both the mission and the national church were very thankful.

The people of the country, including the president, knew about the Jesus Grain and its role in saving people from starvation. It had been instrumental in a significant response to the gospel. I heard one story that a senior Muslim official went to the president and recommended that he declare Mali a Muslim state. When the president asked why, the Muslim replied, "Khadaffi of Libya will give us a lot of money."

"Where was Khadaffi when we were starving?" the president responded. "It's the Christians who brought us Jesus Grain and saved our people's lives, and now they're helping us with better crops and farming equipment. No, we will not be a Muslim state."

Robin had written me about his work and added that he was being a "big brother" to the single missionary ladies. "I'm fixing cars, houses, roads, and I'm being a good guy," he reported.

But one station, Baramba, seemed to get a lot of help. Why? Well, an attractive, red-haired nurse named Donna Grubbs was stationed there, and...well...she needed more help than others. Jim and Judy Plumb said the whole field enjoyed the courtship. I had a good time hearing from everyone about their future in Mali, even if Robin wasn't a "real missionary." We heard that a lot in CAMA.

Gary Schmidt kept the distribution program moving with equally good results in Burkina Faso. He planned to finish his CAMA commitment and then go back to Canada to attend seminary before applying for full missionary status. I was so thankful for both men.

Back in Europe, I reported to our donors in France, Holland, and London. Then I flew to Cyprus, where I took the ship Empress to Jounieh, where Fawzi met me. Sami brought me up to date on work and finances, and I spent a day with him writing a status report for our donors in the U.S. and Europe.

"I'm going to be a medical missionary to Africa," said a young Lebanese man in Sami's youth group who had responded to the challenge to give his life for Christ's service. Young men all around them had given their lives for political gains, but the church youth began to see an eternal goal to commit their lives to. I always got a great blessing from these encounters.

After finishing our work, I boarded the Empress for Cyprus. It was by far a better way to go than the old cargo boats and gunrunners I had used from time to time in the past. The Beirut airport was closed, as was often the case.

Back in Paris, we had an encouraging staff meeting with the CAMA refugee team, and then I headed off to Amsterdam to meet with donors there. Jan van Barneveld took me to see an official at the Inter Church Coordinating Organization. We had met often as he signed off on funds for CAMA's work in Africa and Lebanon. He always grumbled that he gave CAMA more money for more "rice Christians"! I would give him a good-natured response and take the money. "The Dutch parliament has approved this," I would remind him.

Sean and Brenda Campbell from Calgary, Alberta, had joined the Site 8 team at Aranyaprathet to meet needs and share Christ. The team gave them a warm welcome. Brenda was a bit concerned by the rickety house on stilts that they would occupy, and when I killed a huge lizard on her wall…well, she was a good sport and fit in like a trouper.

The CCSDPT continued to keep me busy. The Cambodian border was especially dangerous. We constantly advised workers of all the agencies to be careful. "Don't let yourself get into a situation where a soldier may be injured or killed rescuing you," I would remind them.

One night, after a party at a restaurant outside Aranyaprathet, an intoxicated Red Cross nurse drove a van through a Thai rangers checkpoint without stopping. It was 2:00 a.m. in a hot war zone, and the rangers, not knowing if the van carried Vietnamese or arms, opened fire. The nurse was critically wounded and had to be air evacuated out.

One of her colleagues rose to demand an investigation and censorship of the Thai military at the following CCSDPT meeting. When he finished his diatribe, I brought the meeting to order. "As chairman of this body," I said, "I have warned all present of the dangers we face in border operations. If there is an investigation, we should find out who was responsible for this nurse and why she was drinking and driving at 2:00 a.m. in a war zone. We all know we must stop at military checkpoints and show our ID. We know the soldiers are in danger and have to react to provocations. They are not to blame. Her supervisor and she are to be censored if anyone is. We are guests here. Let's all review our operational directives to make sure this doesn't happen again."

Almost everyone nodded their heads in agreement.

Kerry and Debbie Schottelkorb, the former youth pastors from Ellensburg, visited Thailand to further investigate where God might be calling them. It amazed them to see the team's medical work and the spiritual results at Site 8. Dr. Ineke introduced them to Madame Mai, known as Joanna the Baptist. Whenever anyone converted to Christ, she took the person to a muddy pond in the camp to be baptized. After telling her story and being asked about her family, Madam Mai suddenly realized Kerry and Debbie were from California. "I have two children there!" she exclaimed, then ducked into her thatch hut and dug into the dirt floor.

She pulled out a small bundle and unwrapped two diamond rings. Holding them out to the Schottelkorbs with a slip of paper bearing her children's addresses, she said, "Give these to my children, and tell them to stop trying to take me to America. Tell them for me that serving Jesus is the most important thing in life, and my place of service is here in Site 8!"

CAMA was now over ten years old, and by permission from the CMA, we began to plan for some mass media exposure. Bob Reed intended to put "infomercials" in the Alliance Witness, our church magazine, and in Thailand we planned a brochure, a CAMA Crafts catalog, a calendar, and a slide show for missionaries to use on tour in the U.S. and Canada.

Karen Fitzstevens and Debbie Schottelkorb sat with me in the office as we tried to come up with a succinct motto to build our media around. Karen and Debbie bubbled with ideas and asked me questions. I wrote the answers on a whiteboard. "Well, we do relief, we do development, we do emergency assistance," I said. "Why? We want people to have hope and hear of Jesus, to see Jesus in our actions and believe …"

"Relief into Belief!" the ladies said in unison.

"I like it," I responded. The motto was born.

We first put together a brochure to introduce the concept and methodology. Then we made the cover, filling it with black-and-white photos of people we served, with the question, "What does it take to turn relief…" Then on the inside, we put a blaze of color photos of the same people and the rest of the question: "…into belief?"

The next fold read, "It takes people, long-term missionaries, short-term workers, and willing volunteers committed to communicating the love of God in tangible ways …" Below this, we included a line of color photos of CAMA workers. Under those photos, the text continued, "who draw from experience, 90+ years of evangelism and church planting, success stories among people who are today's Asian refugees, war ravished Lebanese, and famine-struck Africans." Under this we added a line of photos of people CAMA had helped. Then, "…and practice…10 plus years of recognizing Jesus in the face of the hungry we fed; the thirsty whom we gave something to drink; the stranger whom we invited in; the naked we clothed; the sick whom we treated; the imprisoned whom we visited; as well as the illiterate whom we taught and the unbeliever whom we witnessed to."

Finally, "Faith without works is dead" and "The proof of our love for God is how we love those whom He loves."

The last statement reiterated, "What does it take to turn relief into belief? The love of God shining through CAMA Services, the relief arm of the Christian and Missionary Alliance."

On the back we put a color photo of smiling Hmong children and the statement, "With your help, we can keep the smiles on these faces and hope in their eyes!"

We printed thousands of the brochures and sent them to the U.S. and Canada, and we received good initial responses. I still had some of George Hoffman's money left, so Karen, CAMA's media person, made a CAMA calendar for 1986. Bev became the editor of that project.

We used the same Relief into Belief motto, along with 2 Corinthians 9:13. The calendar contained photos from Asia, Africa, and Lebanon, and we mailed it to addresses all over the world. We had a strong response and gained a lot of new interest in CAMA Services, but the best was yet to come.

I contacted Gordon McAlister, a pastor in Clover Pass, Alaska. I said, "Gordon, will you come to Thailand for two weeks at CAMA's expense? I want you to review our work and help our photographer produce a slide show we can give to missionaries on tour. We are now cleared to do some reporting to all the churches. Our problem is that we're still a fairly unknown ministry in the CMA."

Gordon had seen our slide show "Around the World with CAMA Services" when we visited his church in Alaska and knew a bit about CAMA from that. "I'll come for two weeks in January," he agreed.

We had a busy time at the end of the year. Several of our CAMA teams finished their assignments, and new workers came. One couple was Doug and Kathinka Dreger. Doug had gone to Dalat and Black Forest Schools with Drew and Matt, and he had spent a summer working with Drew in the refugee camps in the Philippines. Matt welcomed them, and they headed for Chiang Khan to join CAMA Crafts.

Norm and Ruth Moy came to Chiang Khan from Orlando, Florida. Norm had been an executive assistant to Walt Meloon, president of Correct Craft Boats. Walt had become a good friend and faithful CAMA donor. Norm pitched in to help in the Ban Vinai camp. Ruth served as a cook and encourager. Ric and Gail Nesimiuk also joined us for a short term. They had visited before and felt God's prompting to consider CAMA as a ministry.

We spent some time at Pattaya, a nice break on the beach. Matt took scuba and para sailing lessons, and a group of us went out into the bay. We swam among the coral reefs and thousands of colorful fish. Janelle Martin and Evelyn Green spent some time there, too. They had been finishing their assignment and preparing to return to the U.S. We had a relaxing time and loved the food, as usual.

Robin Dirks and Gary Schmidt, the Africa relief team

Robin Dirks inspects a new well

Andy and Bev, Dr. & Mrs. Jun Vencer, Walt and Betty Meloon
at camp of the woods in New York

Jesus grain distribution from a 'grain bank'

Chapter 19
Keeping On ~ Part 2

Chapter 19.
Keeping On ~ Part 2

"Pat Robertson wants to get some film of CAMA's work on the Cambodian border," Bob Reed explained. "They will have a television crew in Asia to interview President Marcos in the Philippines, and they want to film at Site 8."

News of our war-front service had begun to spread. Site 8 was in a security area, and we had to get special permission from the National Security Council to take the TV crew there. I thought, Why not film some other areas of CAMA's work as well? When Bob Hatch of CBN phoned to set things up, I asked him, "Can you stay a full week?"

"I'll ask Rev. Robertson," he replied.

I thought, Boy, what an opportunity! I knew that a team and equipment like this cost up to $25,000 per day, and here a team had asked to come see us at no charge to us.

Usavadee Thongkiattikul worked in our office. She kept everyone's visa up to date and knew her way around the customs and immigration offices. Her mother had counseled the king, and Usavadee had gone to a university in India. She had good connections. I spoke with Governor Kamol Prachuabmoh on the National Security Council. He agreed to assist us with the necessary paperwork to secure passes and access. Rindi Bowman and Bev collected the required information. Bob Hatch called and said that his cameraman, Steve Kondracki, had asked Rev. Robertson for the extra days in Thailand. He said Rev. Robertson had told them, "If it's for the Christian and Missionary Alliance, you can stay and do the extra filming."

God is so good!

A lot had been going on at that time, and I almost forgot that Gordon McAlister was coming, and at the same time! Debbie Storlie had already arrived at Ban Vinai when I met Gordon at Don Muang Airport. I remembered his firm statement, "I never want to have anything to do with television ever again."

In the airport, I quickly explained what was happening. "I'd like you to go ahead of the TV crew, gain an impression of the work, and then help us be sure to get the right film for a CAMA video," I explained. "I didn't know they were coming when you agreed to help, but now we need you even more!"

Gordon stayed quiet. He looked like someone who had just walked into a trap. Then he smiled and said, "Okay, I'll help."

I put him in a car with one of the staff, Dave Fitzstevens, and off they went for a scouting trip, or "recce," as the photo people call it, to get an impression of what and how to film the subjects.

In the midst of all this, Bev had to go in for more surgery on her ear. Dr. L.L. King came through for a briefing. The Brooks Holidays tour stopped in, Bob Reed made a visit, and then there was the usual coming and going of staff from the work sites. Our guest room stayed pretty full, but we loved to minister to the team and the refugees, as well as the visitors.

We hired Usavadee's brother, an army major, to drive the van carrying the film team. Gordon was the "man with the plan," and they got on the road. First, Site 8 for 48 hours, then to Ban Vinai via Khorat and Loei. Due to time and other considerations, we did not include the project at Na Pho camp. We covered a lot of ground that week.

It all went well. Having an army major in the van and clearances signed by the chairman of the National Security Council got us into any place we needed to go. Gordon got fired up by what he saw and did a series of brilliant interviews with team members. He did my interview on the bank of the Mekong, with Laos in the background, and by the end of the week we had over 36 hours of film. I still didn't know how it would become a video, but the answers to prayer had been so overwhelming that I had no doubt something really good for CAMA would be the result. Gordon knew what to do to make sure God would be glorified when the video got completed.

We sent the CBN crew off with no problems. Everyone had done a thorough job on clearances, and I sent Gordon McAlister and Debbie Storlie off, too. Next we would wait and pray for good results.

Not that there wasn't enough to do. Bev ended up back in the hospital with a painful eye infection. Then we had the CAMA retreat in Chanthaburi. We had a great time with things like balloon tag, relay races, and lots of singing and good food. Steve Bailey's dad, Richard Bailey, the vice president of the CMA, spoke.

We saw a lot of progress. Paul and Elena Stringer operated the training school in Na Pho with a special touch. Whenever government officials or UN visitors came to see the camp, they always visited the school and were impressed by the program's quality. It had been the same with Jacqui Bailey's opium detox project in Ban Vinai. With the help of the Hmong church, especially in the area of follow-up, an unusually significant cure rate had been registered.

Daryl Brooks came for a visit, along with Ron Carlaw. He hosted Sean Campbell, Steve Bailey, and me for a great meal where we discussed CAMA's future and ways and means. Over the years, he became a good friend and a faithful donor. Today when I play golf, I still use the clubs Daryl gave me while in Thailand.

"Your father has suffered a stroke." The telex message was a surprise. My dad and mom had always encouraged our ministry choices and prayed regularly for us. We knew they prayed for us, and they sent letters full of information and spiritual counsel. My dad was 84 and had been in pretty good health. Now his voice on the phone reassured me. He said, "Don't interrupt your work to come home for this. I don't want you to see me like this anyway."

I responded, "I'm heading to the States in a few days. Bev needs some special care for an eye infection, but we're coming via Africa, so we won't be there for a couple of weeks."

"That's fine," Dad said. "If I'm still here I'll see you, but if not, I'll see you in heaven."

His advice reassured me, even though we were half a world apart, and I was comfortable with it. Those ended up being his last words to me.

Dr. Wendell Sprague, our Site 8 dentist, got sent to the hospital. The thought that he could have dengue fever scared us. Doreen Blomstrand was ill, too. We used the Paolo Hospital near the CMA guest house a lot. Fortunately, Dr. Sprague's ailment wasn't dengue and he responded to treatment, as did Doreen. We were thankful for good medical resources, but Bev needed a specialist's touch due to her medical history.

Gordon informed me that Greg Flessing, a friend in the video business, would make us a spectacular deal to turn Robertson's film into a video. Then Gordon asked, "What shall we call it?"

"Turning Relief into Belief," I replied.

We discussed the time it would require to be completed. "I will be in Nyack in a month; can we show something to the CAMA board by then?" I asked.

Gordon said, "Yes."

"Will you bring it to Nyack? They don't know about this yet."

"Okay," he agreed.

The die was cast -- good, bad, or whatever. I believed the Lord was in it and went about my daily work.

Bev got her medical records and the doctor's clearance to travel. She had a bandage over her eye, not unlike a pirate. We boarded Sabena Airlines for Paris. As we dozed in our seats while flying somewhere over India or Turkey, my dad went to be with the Lord he had loved and served so faithfully. He had been a pastor, teacher, artist, hunter, fisherman, rancher, husband, and father to seven children. The telex in Paris simply said, "Your father passed away late on March 15, 1986."

I phoned my mother, and she said, "Don't interrupt your trip to come. Your dad didn't want to have any embalming. He's already buried where he wanted to be, at the ranch."

I will see him in heaven, plan B. I'll meet him there.

We secured our visas and prepared to fly to Mali. We had lunch with Judie Plumb from Mali, and she reported that all had been going well with CAMA and with Robin and Donna Dirks. As we prepared to go to the airport, Bev suddenly needed to go to the hospital emergency room with severe pain in her eye. The doctor gave her some drops with a pain killer and more antibiotic, and we got ready to depart for Mali.

Don and Elma Dirks drove us to the airport. As we drove through the Bois de Boulogne, a woman in a long fur coat suddenly stepped out and flashed us. Bev shouted, "Don, did you see that?"

Laughing, Don replied, "Shall I drive around again?"

Paris!

In Abidjan, Ivory Coast, we hit a small snag. The plane needed repair, so we had a five-hour delay. We had all our papers rechecked in the terminal, but Bev didn't have her international shot record. They told us she could not re board the flight unless she got her shots. I asked what shots they would recommend. The official sent us to the airport infirmary. They asked about Bev's eye, our work, and our destination. Finally the medic gave her a tetanus shot and copied my shot record onto a new certificate for Bev. I gladly paid the five dollars, and we boarded our flight for Ouagadougou.

At dinner, we had a good time catching up with the Milton Pierces on the famine relief news. We also met with Titus Tineou. CAMA had been able to find funds for the Bible school he directed, and it pleased us to see the progress he had made.

As we sat at the dinner table, the missionary couple who hosted us explained to their son that he needed to give up his bedroom for the night. His mom reminded him of the Bible verse that says that by being hospitable to strangers, some will actually entertain angels. He didn't seem convinced, as he fixed his stare on Bev with her eye patch and blurted out, "Are you sure you're not really a pirate?"

At Tougan, Herb and Jessie Nehlsen entertained us royally. We heard about the successful food distribution, the food-for-work projects, and the good response to the gospel.

Peggy Drake and Jetty Souten showed us the mobile clinic CAMA had helped them get going in 1979. They had treated thousands of people and led many to Christ. They still had the little Sony shortwave radio I gave them. They had gotten a lot of good use from it. Jetty had been with us in Thailand for a short-term nursing assignment years before. Everyone in the country loved and respected both nurses. In Mali we traveled with Robin Dirks to see famine relief projects. We also saw a new clinic under construction by a Dutch CMA builder. His wife told us their toddler was recovering from a snakebite and that they couldn't be more thankful for Robin's help.

En route to Bamako, Robin drove a mission van that had been wrecked. We laughed a lot. He wore his motorcycle helmet and goggles because he didn't have a windshield, and a metal flap hanging loose on the roof kept hitting the helmet as he drove. When I took my turn driving I beat him to Bamako. Rich and Ginny Newberg hosted us, and we shared an Easter sunrise service with them. On a previous trip, I had prayed with them by the river and asked the Lord to give them a child. They ended up finding a child to adopt and were excited and thankful for the answered prayer.

From Africa we flew back to Paris and then took a train to Brussels. "There's where we lived in 1970, 16 years ago," I reminded Bev. "Who would have guessed all that has transpired in our lives since then?"

She agreed the Lord had showed us some wonderful things and granted us some great experiences, and we were confident more would come.

In Hilversum, Holland, we met with donors and the Christian television station fund raisers. They were pleased with the reports from Thailand and Africa. It was the same in London. Good reports cheered everyone and gained new funds for future work. Then it was on to America.

Bev and I parted in Boston. She flew on to Seattle to get treatment for her eye, while I headed for Nyack. I had attentive students in my seminar at Alliance Theological Seminary. CAMA had been a new concept in the CMA and was now a new ministry possibility for them. Their questions and responses were certainly different from the ones I had gotten in Colorado a few years earlier. Several of the students had even come from Ellensburg.

Gordon arrived with the video. "I've arranged to show it to the board of managers when they finish their meeting today," he said.

The leaders of the CMA, led by Dr. L.L. King, filed into the headquarters chapel. I went out into the hall to pray, "Lord, help them to see relief becoming belief."

Suddenly I heard applause. I ducked into the back of the chapel and watched the men stand and applaud. They had truly been moved by what they saw. Gordon stepped to the front and invited Dr. King to come up. "I want you, as president of the Christian and Missionary Alliance and CAMA Services, to have your own personal copy of Turning Relief into Belief," Gordon said as he handed over the video.

Dr. King smiled and responded, "Men, we've been debating the use of video in the Alliance for two years. Everyone had someone who they thought knew how. Well, this is good. This is what we want."

Looking at Gordon he said, "Get whoever did this; we want more."

Gordon's time in Alaska ended. He moved to Nyack, and the Alliance Video Magazine was born.

The headquarters staff saw the video the next day, and the CAMA board agreed that they should duplicate it and send it to all CMA churches. I thought about the conversation with Reg Reimer years before. "When God wants CAMA known to the CMA, He will provide the very best way."

In addition, the CMA got introduced to the latest method to communicate missions to the person in the pew.

"I would like to volunteer some time to CAMA Services." The speaker was Linda Leparillo, a young lawyer and a member of Long Hill Chapel, the big CMA church in Chatham, New Jersey. Being on the CAMA Services board, Pastor Paul Bubna always welcomed a CAMA presentation, and I had just spoken there again.

How to use her skills? After thinking for a minute I asked, "Could you come teach a course on civil law? Banking, rent, contracts -- things we all know but that refugees coming to America find confusing?"

She brightened immediately and replied, "Yes, I'll do it. I'll come in a month."

"The church will send her," Pastor Bubna said.

Bev's eye had improved greatly since she got the right diagnosis and correct medication. She also got excited about the video's acceptance. We showed it to the churches in Ellensburg and Seattle, and to all our friends who would watch it. We spent time with Drew, the college student, too. I phoned Greg Flessing to thank him for the excellent work and generous use of his facilities at half price. Not only did Flessing and Flessing do Turning Relief Into Belief, but for years after they also worked with Gordon McAlister to produce the video Alliance Magazine for CMA and "We Are His Hands!" for CAMA Services.

Near Quincy, Washington, we visited my father's grave at the ranch. He had set up a family graveyard, and he happened to be the first one there. His tombstone was a giant basalt crystal with a plaque giving his name and lifespan, E. Ray Bishop 1902-1986, and his epithet: "Daddy kept the faith."

"Bill! The boxes are floating!" Bonnie Carlsen said as she waded through the calf-deep water that covered the compound at the CMA guest house in Bangkok during one of the city's frequent floods. Since the city is only three inches above sea level, floods occur at least once a year.

Bill and Bonnie had served in Thailand most of their lives and had decided to retire. Bill had constructed the guest house and had also built some large teak containers in which they packed a lifetime of belongings. Now, stored in the carport of the compound, they began to float.

Bill called the staff and others who were staying at the guest house. Several of us went down from the CAMA office, and, by using bricks and levers, we got the boxes above the water by only a few inches.

The floods of Bangkok created a mess. Aran got flooded, too. Whenever they came, we waded through muck, water, and even snakes while the buses and taxis plowed along, sending waves into shops and houses. Finally the Thai government turned to the water experts, the Dutch, to plan dikes and pumping stations to keep the flooding under control. It was a tough challenge even for the Dutch, but they eventually became fairly successful.

Bev and I had flown back from the U.S. and gone to Penang. We brought Matt up to date on our travels, Bev's health, and the CAMA video. He was doing well in school and was pleased when we showed the video to a school assembly. After Penang, we went back to Thailand and visited Aranyaprathet. The team had been doing a good job as usual.

We also had another challenge. The Thai government had finally defeated the communists in the northern mountains. They fought them to a standstill in the jungle, then gave them an option: Lay down your arms and swear allegiance to the king and country, or die. Wayne Persons saw the hill tribe army march into Pua. The government expected 500 to come to the surrender ceremony, but over 5,000 marched out of the jungle and stacked arms like cord wood in the town's main street. The defeated soldiers and their families were then given land, tools, and small houses in resettlement areas of rural Thailand.

Our Aran team loved the video. We told them about the positive reaction in the States and promised to provide copies for them to use when they went home. Roy Johnston, our team chaplain and counselor, showed it to the international church as well.

Franklin Graham came in for a visit. He had seen the CAMA piece the 700 Club had done and wanted some film for Samaritan's Purse. He brought Dennis Agajanian along and Greg Flessing to film his movements. We visited Mae Sot, the town near the Burmess refugee camp where the Karen people had sent their families. I remembered earlier visits to the site that Drew, Matt, and I had made to take malaria medicines.

Since Drew was there to see us while he was still in the U.S. Air Force, we took photos of both Matt and Drew in Karen military hats and holding Chinese-made AK-47s. The Chinese had given the guns to the Khmer Rouge. They had sold them to Thai gunrunners, who had sold them to the Karen. What a world!

Next we took the Samaritan's Purse tour group there, and they filmed some interviews with the Karen. Then we went to Aranyaprathet. Our long-time friends Chuck and Midge Fowler came to visit, so they went along. In the camp at Site 8, they talked with the CAMA team and got into the bunkers used when the camp was shelled. We explained the political situation, and they interviewed a number of the nurses and Cambodian people.

We had just about completed our visit when…Bang! Sean Campbell shouted, "Evacuate!"

I pushed Chuck and Midge to the ground and tried to locate the site of the explosion. Franklin and Dennis cowered in a muddy ditch with several Khmer Rouge soldiers. No more explosions came. A siren went off, and our van came careening around the corner with Sean shouting, "Go! Go! Go!"

We piled into the van and headed for the camp exit. A pickup filled with heavily armed Thai rangers went the other way. We exited the camp quickly, followed by the CAMA team in their vehicles. The standard policy explained that all ex-patriots had to leave ASAP when any shooting started. We didn't have to be told.

As we untangled ourselves in the van, Dennis Agajanian shouted into his handheld cassette recorder, "Explosion close by! We smell gun smoke!"

"Aw, Dennis," Franklin said, "that's not gun smoke. Check your shorts!"

A short while later, we sat drinking tea and Cokes at a small store a mile or so from Site 8 while our hearts calmed down. We had always gathered there while waiting for word from the camp. Someone interviewed Valery Reed on camera. "So Valery," the questioner asked, "why would you be working in such a dangerous place?"

She didn't miss a beat. "As a nurse and a believer, the safest place for me is in the center of God's will," she said. "For me it's here."

The rest of the team murmured in agreement.

Word came from the camp that a Khmer Rouge soldier had accidentally set off a bottle grenade. It had shredded his lower extremities with glass and quarter-inch ball bearings. He was taken to Khao I Dang for surgery late in the day, so we all went back to the CAMA house for supper. Dennis entertained everyone with his music and guitar.

The Site 8 team delivered babies, treated wounds and infections, cured malaria and measles, and filled and pulled teeth. They also ran a place called "The Thin Room," where underweight children received special feedings of highly nutritious food. Children also got vaccines.

One day the team treated 1,500 kids in a huge tent in 100° heat! The needs seemed endless, the stresses severe, but the team soldiered on. Three doctors, eight nurses, a medical trainer, a lab technician, and some CAMA-trained Khmer that included dental techs, lab techs, and medics provided the care for more than 35,000 people. They did an amazing job. They worked 12-hour days, and yet they kept their balance by laughing and having fun. Commitment took on a new meaning for anyone who visited that work – or the CAMA team at any camp in any of the countries we served.

Rambo, a Laotian black gibbon, lived the life of leisure at the Site 8 compound in Aran. Doug Dreger bought him for me, and he lived on our back porch in Bangkok for a while. He loved to play, and visitors enjoyed seeing him cavort about the guest-house grounds. But he did not like Bev, and she didn't care much for him. After he trashed our back porch, sun room, and Bev's potted plants a couple of times, she decreed he must go. So I gave him to the cook at Aran. She spoiled him rotten. He would perch on her bike as she went to the market, eat ice cream bars everyone gave him, and lounge in his hammock in the shade. The team loved to play with him, too!

At Na Pho, we visited a group of students in the skills training center. For one of their projects, they had to take a derelict Land Rover and rebuild it using a Toyota engine. They had constructed a small building for the Thai officials and had gotten ready to employ their skills wherever they would be sent. Best of all, our Thai Pastor Insome had led most of them to the Lord. One small group of wood carvers asked me for carving tools. I bought them several sets. A few weeks later, they presented me with an amazing rosewood carving depicting life in Laos. The skills of the refugees never ceased to amaze me.

At Ban Vinai, we had graduated a large number of newly literate students, clean former opium addicts, and English Second Language (ESL) students. Some of them even set up their own ESL classes where, for a small fee, they coached those en route to America. CAMA Crafts thrived, and the Hmong blacksmith shop produced knives and gardening tools. They had gardens everywhere.

In talks with the UN and the Royal Thai government, the reality of returning significant numbers of people to their countries of origin was being planned. Negotiations with the home countries went forward.

The Thai also mandated that refugees could no longer get paid for working in the camps. While CAMA Services had only a few on anything like a salary, many of the agencies had significant numbers of people on their payrolls.

"CAMA will comply with this policy," I assured the refugee official. "However, we do not employ the refugees doing CAMA Crafts. They use Thai fabric to sew the crafts that we market for them. If you want this stopped, we would like some time to use up the stocks of cloth and tell our Thai suppliers not to order more."

"Well," he replied, "we can exempt CAMA Crafts from this order. Thank you for CAMA's good cooperation."

While eating lunch later with Gerald Walzer, the head of the UNHCR in Asia, he asked me, "Why did you risk the whole CAMA Crafts project that way?"

"We are guests here, as are you," I explained, "so I had nothing to lose by volunteering to do what we were being asked. As it stands, we won't lose anything. In fact, we're drafting plans to help refugees who will be sent back to their countries with tool kits and materials they can use to restart their lives when they go home."

"We need more thinking like this," he mused.

Matt came home from Dalat. He and Eddy Ford, another MK, went to work with CAMA at Aranyaprathet for the summer. Matt had refused to help the Nite Spot computer people unblock the codes on game and other software so they could pirate it, so they'd fired him. Bev and I were proud of him, though, and I happily gave him and Eddy work.

With all the activity, I could see that we and the staff needed to begin to plan long term for CAMA's future work in Indochina.

The CAMA Craft store in Bangkok.
Micro enterprise becomes macro

Jesus grain travels by bicycle

Chapter 20
You May Need A Plan

Chapter 20.
You May Need A Plan

In July 1986, the UN and the Royal Thai government officially announced the Khao I Dang refugee camp would close. A time frame had not been set, but with its being the largest of the Cambodian camps and the main medical center for Cambodian refugees, the announcement stimulated earnest discussions about the future.

One day Wayne Person and I were on that subject, and he observed, "The Lao won't take the Hmong as long as they keep the resistance going in the mountains there."

CAMA had been careful to stay clear of the men who went into Laos at night to supply the fighters. The Thai military habitually looked the other way and allowed groups, mainly from Europe and the U.S., to provide funding and arms. It wasn't until now, in 1986, that the Thai military began to discourage those activities. Because of this, we knew it might take a while to get the Hmong home to Laos, but we agreed that CAMA needed to take part in the process. While Wayne wasn't sure how to achieve this, he fully endorsed the concept. It was time to take the next step, a planning conference.

As mentioned before, our apartment at the CMA guest house in Bangkok was a Grand Central Station. Bev's nickname had become "Mamma CAMA" for how she cared for the team members who came our way. On one occasion, Carolyn Dean and Jacqui Bailey came by with dengue fever, as well as the nurses from Site 8. They all knew Bev was there for them!

Site 8 nurse Valery Reed was one of those with malaria, but she wanted to go to her sister's graduation from medical school in Manila. Bev wasn't able to persuade her not to go, so she flew to Manila. Due to her Indian passport, however, she couldn't enter without a visa. She was unceremoniously bundled back onto the plane and sent home to Bangkok.

"Val," I said when she returned to the guest house, "there's a story about a man on his front porch. A flood filled his yard, but his porch was dry. A truck came by. 'Come with us to safety,' the driver said, 'the water may rise.'

"'No,' the man replied, 'I'm trusting the Lord. I'll stay here.'

"The water rose higher, and the next day a boat came to the man, who was now looking out his second-story window. 'Come with me to safety,' the boater called.

"'Oh, no, I'm being a good example of trusting the Lord,' the man in the house said.

"The next day a helicopter hovered as the man, now on his roof and clinging to his chimney, once again refused rescue. The house suddenly lifted from its foundation and rolled over, and the man drowned. At the pearly gates he asked, 'What's going on? I'm down there being a good example, and you let me drown!'

"'Let's see,' said the record keeper, 'we heard your prayer. We sent a truck, a boat, and a helicopter. What were you expecting?'"

"That's not a very funny story just now," said Val, who was miserable, insulted, and very sick.

Bev bustled in with cold lemonade and shooed me out. "I think she's already learned a valuable lesson," Bev said. "Let her rest."

Life in CAMA Services was seldom dull.

Karen Gammelgard came from California to visit. We had served together in Africa back in 1971, at IMELOKO in the Congo, and she wanted to see our work in Thailand. She did some refugee camp nursing, filling in for Val while she was sick and while some others took a break.

In April, when the CAMA board met in Nyack, I presented CAMA's need to plan for the future. They agreed that in anticipation of the possible entry of CAMA Services into Laos, Vietnam, and Cambodia, CAMA Services Thailand should be authorized to:

a.   Contact UN representatives within these countries, seeking potential ministry opportunities;

b. Establish liaison with the embassies in Bangkok representing these countries;

c. Investigate the possibility of assisting compatible relief agencies now working in the areas;

d. Contact appropriate donor agencies interested in helping CAMA Services in these areas;

e. Assign personnel to an intensive study of the language of these countries, and approve in-country visits as opportunity permitted;

f. Submit proposed relief programs to the Division of Overseas Ministries for approval;

g. At a time deemed appropriate, meet with selected personnel with experience in Southeast Asia ministry for the purpose of developing long-term strategy.

The board sent these recommendations to the CMA Board of Managers, who approved it -- a huge vote of confidence. Gordon McAlister's presentation of the CAMA video had been crucial to these developments, and the vote of confidence for CAMA came at the right time. God's timing was perfect!

Dave Fitzstevens had been operating our Indochina information office for more than two years, so we already had good data. Reg Reimer had been to Vietnam, where CAMA joined in a relief effort to supply rice after a devastating typhoon, and I had met with Vietnamese officials in Bangkok. They had already shown us several projects that they wanted to help with, and we were ready to begin planning in earnest. One of our "compatible agencies" in Laos and another in Phnom Penh gave us inside information on needs and potential approaches.

In June 1986, I brought selected CAMA Services personnel to the Rama Hotel in Bangkok. Steve Bailey came to plan the Laotian efforts, Carolyn Dean was the Cambodia researcher, Dave Fitzstevens was the Vietnam guru, and Bev and I were CAMA Services donor contacts. We began to develop a working strategy for the coming decade. We wanted the Lord to help us dream dreams and gain a vision for the CMA's future work in Indochina. We used a simple planning template with Objective, Methodology, and Resource as our categories.

Our years of experience in the region confirmed that as the Indochinese countries struggled to recover from decades of war, they had become more receptive to aid from noncommunist sources. We wanted to help, but only if we could use it to gain presence in these countries. We understood the concept of witness through presence, so our objectives focused on seeking productive open doors. Through proclamation by presence, we sought to relieve suffering and help with a wide range of activities that would bring healing and recovery.

Our methodologies included education (especially English as a second language), medical care and training of medical personnel, micro-enterprise initiatives (such as small business loans), CAMA Crafts, and technical and agricultural assistance as opportunities presented themselves. All the activities would have sustainable self-sufficiency as a goal, so training of local people was a key component. Since CAMA had no empire-building intentions, working ourselves out of a job was a solid goal in the overall scheme of things.

Money, people, and tent makers such as we have with today's "International Fellowship of Alliance Professionals" were key to the success of the proposals. Discussions were lively and far ranging, even humorous. When CAMA Crafts as a piece of the plan for Laos was presented, Steve Bailey asked, "Would we need to change the name?"

"To what?" I asked.

"Well, they're communist there, so how about Commie Crafts?" he said with a smile.

Given our 12 years of refugee work and our worldwide contacts with specialists and donors, we felt comfortable working out scenarios. We knew what to pray for, and as the whiteboards filled with names, projects, resources, and timelines, we were excited about the future.

We also knew how to implement the dreams. We'd done it over and over. We were prepared for the open doors we believed were coming. We decided to step up the activities of our Southeast Asia planning office, where Dave and Karen Fitzstevens were already doing a good job. Visiting the countries became an important activity. Reg Reimer, a Canadian with WRC, had been to Vietnam. Since Sean Campbell was also Canadian, we decided he would be a tourist and see Vietnam. He would look for options for involvement there.

We wrote our proposals naming people we knew, donors we could approach, and projects we could implement. Most important was the need to stimulate groups to pray without knowing too many details. These countries had spies around, and we did not want to alarm them by being too loud about our overall intentions. We committed the whole plan to the Lord and began to act.

Steve Bailey increased his contacts with Lao sources, and Carolyn Dean and others were focused on Cambodia. We asked for increased prayer and recommended that the CMA designate funds for preparation and training equal to the 1974-75 Indochina missionary budget. We thought the coming two years would be a crucial time for preparation to enter these countries. We also knew that the first wave of CMA people would be tent makers and CAMA workers under CAMA Services.

This effort required seriousness of purpose and action if we were to expect God to bless and direct our return to Indochina. in 1922 R.A. Jaffray wrote of the establishment of the pioneer mission station for Indochina in Da Nang, Vietnam. King David had been told to listen for the sound of marching in the tops of the mulberry trees, the sure token of the going forth of the Lord's heavenly armies against His enemies. "We believe we can hear the sound of marching in connection with our Indochina work," he said. "God is on the march. Let us be ready to go forth with Him!"

What was true in 1922 was now true for Southeast Asia in 1986. Tens of thousands of refugees had become followers of Christ, and many were studying theological education by extension materials. They would be among those who would go back to their homelands when the camps finally closed, and today many are leading churches in their home countries, especially Cambodia. It's amazing when one realizes the church in Vietnam now approaches one million members, and the church in Laos has multiplied as well. Speaking of mulberries, our sericulture program in Laos depends on growing mulberry trees to feed silkworms for silk making. In some places, it has replaced opium growing as a cash crop.

Our son Matt and his friend Eddie Ford spent their vacation working with our Site 8 team. Bev and I also took Matt to Hong Kong and China on a short family break. After seeing China and buying a Mao hat, he said, "Well, Dad, I'm going to be a capitalist."

Gordon McAlister, the man who developed our Turning Relief into Belief video, was now director for the video Alliance Magazine, so we were glad to host him for some follow-up and planning for another CAMA video. Robin Dirks came in from Africa for input, as the subject was CAMA Africa. The title became CAMA Services, "We Are His Hands."

Both Gordon and Robin were amazed at the Thai program's progress in the refugee camps. We also talked about the Indochina initiatives we were proposing. We discussed the actions and methodologies, and I was happy for their input.

One very enjoyable experience that September of '86 was the wedding of Peter and Lydia Benson from our Site 8 team. The Benson's have continued as friends and supporters over the years as they served with groups such as CARE and the Peace Corps all over the world. The joy of their wedding was a nice break from the tragedy of the refugee camps. Dr. Dee Garcia, whom we met in Cambodia and worked at Site 8, was Lydia's aunt.

Ravi Zacharias and his wife, Margaret, came to visit. He had held public services in Vietnam and Cambodia in the 1970s and received a great response. Now he wanted to visit Site 8. Bev and I drove them to Aranyaprathet and south to Site 8. As we approached the camp, situated next to the border and at the foot of some spectacular cliffs extending into Cambodia, we met our team speeding out to the little noodle shop where they assembled during emergency evacuations. The camp was being shelled again.

We stopped and ordered coffee. Sitting at tin tables under a piece of canvas for shade, we listened to the excited team members tell about the attack. In the background we could hear the shells exploding. No one knew who was shooting. It could be the Vietnamese or, as sometimes happened, the Khmer Rouge might be "disciplining" the camp for its deviation from Marx's communist principles.

After a time with no explosions I said, "I'll go see if the shooting is over."

"I'm coming, too," said Ravi, jumping to his feet.

"No, you're not!" his wife said firmly.

We discussed the risk, and I assured her we would not go too close. Bev's look said, "Be sure you don't."

In a few minutes, from the shelter of a bamboo bus stop, we could see into the camp a couple of hundred yards away. People were still in bunkers, and the Thai special forces troops were hunkered down behind sandbags. A puff of dust and a bang told us the attack wasn't over and that we should not yet go down for a visit. Ravi agreed; he had seen enough.

That evening, we had a good meal with the team back at the CAMA house in Aranyaprathet. Ravi enjoyed the interaction with these young heroes who went to Site 8 daily. He was amazed to learn that more than a thousand former communists had already received Christ at Site 8.

I needed to visit Africa again to review the situation and help with planning for our next steps in that region. In Bamako, all the indicators pointed to a good year. The famine prevention projects had produced good crops. The food banks were full, and the food-for-work projects were building roads and schools, digging wells, and supporting other development activities. However, due to the rains, the roads were really bad. Robin and I got stuck in deep mud and bounced around a lot! In spite of the pain, I was thankful for all the good answers to prayer.

I did notice there were new armored cars at the Mali-Burkina Faso border, and everywhere the soldiers on both sides were in new uniforms and had new weapons. At the usual roadblocks, the soldiers were out by the road checking identity papers instead of sleeping under mango trees.

"Robin," I said, "this doesn't look right. They're on alert, I think."

"Libya has been active again," he replied, "but it won't amount to much."

When I mentioned it to Rich Newberg in Bamako, he was surprised he hadn't noticed it. Not long after, there was a short, sharp border war. Fortunately few were killed, and our missionaries were able to stay out of the way until the shooting stopped.

Back in Europe, after meetings with funding partners in Paris, Brussels, Holland and London, it was back to Bangkok and more meetings, this time with my boss, Bob Reed.

I had health issues that just did not go away. After the surgery for appendicitis, treatment for my high blood pressure was increased, but the aches, pain, and fatigue persisted. Finally, the doctor decided to remove my gall bladder. Recuperation took a long time -- too long for a fairly uncomplicated surgery. What was not made clear, due to the cultural resistance to giving anyone bad news, was that I'd had a serious heart attack during surgery. Looking back, I'm very thankful to have survived. For the next six weeks, I had to rest and not drive!

While I was recovering, George Hoffman from TEAR Fund England visited. We had just taken delivery of the CAMA calendars for 1987, which he helped pay for. They were a follow-up on our video report, and the response was very good. Annette DeBruyn took 500 to Canada to mail out. She had been an excellent nurse at Site 8, and now it was time for her to return home. She reported that the calendars were well received; the same was true in America.

Sean Campbell made his first trip to Vietnam as part of our probe for the CAMA plan. He went in early February 1987 and came back enthused about all he had seen. The potential for CAMA leading the CMA back to Indochina was looking good. John Ellison, Dave Fitzstevens, and I had lunch with Prince Norodom Ranariddh of Cambodia. He encouraged us to help reconstruct Cambodia. We were greatly encouraged to continue the process. He was always thankful for CAMA's faithful efforts to help his people.

Our CAMA Crafts program was continuing to grow now that we had added the Mennonites to our list of customers. This program was to be one of our flagship projects in Laos when we returned to that country. The government welcomed the hard currency it generated.

We enjoyed an outstanding CAMA retreat with Tim Owen as our speaker. It was great to see him back in Bangkok after his good response to our trip in 1983.

Events in Africa required another visit. Gary Schmidt had left to go to school. Robin Dirks had married Donna Grubbs, a nurse in Mali; Tim and Ruth Albright were taking over the CAMA work in Burkina Faso. Both Tim and Ruth were MKs, so they made perfect CAMA team members. I stopped in Holland to check on the status of project requests with various agencies. Now back in Africa, we reviewed the requests and rewrote some to reflect changes in the overall situation. I was so glad we had such a first-class team with a good vision for future work.

Back in Paris, I finished writing and filing reports and sent the rewritten projects to Holland and England. Dr. Chuck Folkestad was in Paris, studying French en route to ministry in Africa. I had not seen him much since our wild experiences in Phnom Penh in 1975. He told me a funny story about how they told their kids of the upcoming arrival of their new child. When Becky found out she was pregnant, Chuck told their son and daughters, "Tomorrow, do your chores, eat your meals, do well in school, and after supper we will have a surprise!"

The next day, the kids did everything they were asked to do. After supper, the kids looked expectantly at their dad. "You were great," he beamed, "and the surprise is that Mom is pregnant. We're going to have a new baby!"

Silence! And then their son burst into tears and ran from the table to his room. Chuck went to him. "You'll like this new baby," Chuck said. "It may be a brother for you."

"Well," said his son through his tears, "I thought we were going to have ice cream!"

From Paris and London, I flew to New York for a CAMA Services board meeting. It was good to sense their excitement about what God was doing through CAMA in so many ways and places. Next I flew to Seattle and then drove to Ellensburg to see Drew. He was doing well at the university, and since we were about to come home on furlough, he'd located a nice apartment for us. We were anticipating the respite after such a busy four years.

Following the visit with Drew, it was back to globe hopping. I flew from Seattle to Hong Kong, sleeping for most of the 14-hour trip. After some shopping and visits with the Fowlers, Schottelkorbs, and Sensmeiers, long-time friends, I headed on to Bangkok. I had just circled the globe for the umpteenth time. The TEAR Fund film team was again in Thailand, shooting Man of Compassion, a film about George Hoffman and the path he followed to develop TEAR, which had been such a great partner for groups like ours all over the world.

We sat having lunch at a small restaurant beside the Mekong River, across from Vientiane, Laos. Sally Lambert and John Muggleton listened to the ground rules for filming in the refugee camps. "Like it or not," I said, "we are guests here, and we must not try to embarrass the Royal Thai government." I went on to explain that some refugees were involved in drug running and arms smuggling; a few had even been killed. "We don't know all the details," I explained, "but the government is very sensitive about the situation."

John was eager to get some controversial information on film. I disagreed. "You may even get someone killed if you're not careful," I warned. His look did not reassure me. Then, looking down from the restaurant, I noticed a body floating down the river. "There," I pointed out as I directed his vision to the body, now only a few yards away, "is what I'm talking about." It was a Hmong man, his hands bound and his throat slit. The body floated, slowly turning in the river currents, on down out of sight.

The discussion was over. The film they made was a good one and devoid of politics.

May 1987 was a busy time. Our long-time friend Leakhena introduced us to her fiancé, Ralph Foelster. Once married, they kept in touch as he continued his career as an U.S. immigration officer. They now live in Washington, D.C., and have two nice kids.

Sean Campbell came in from Canada, where he had a good response to our Indochina initiative and his visit to Vietnam. People were excited about re-entry to the region. Dave Fitzstevens had been working on a trip to Vietnam under the auspices of AID RECIP, the group through which we had shipped rice into both Vietnam and Cambodia. "Will you go to Vietnam?" he asked. He was nervous and troubled. He knew we were packing for furlough.

"Yes," I responded.

He quickly got our visas from the Vietnamese embassy in Bangkok. We were soon shoehorned into the seats of an old Russian Tu-134 airliner used by Vietnamese Airlines, en route to Hanoi.

Our approach into Hanoi's airport took us over the Red River Valley. The Hanoi airport was guarded by a forest of antiaircraft guns. The Vietnamese were still having battles with the Chinese. The shabby terminal showed the signs of years at war, and the country was still in a difficult situation.

We were met by a government official who took us across the Long Bien Bridge to an ancient hotel on the shore of Hoan Kiem Lake in the city center. David began to calm down. He was suffering from some grim years as a MK in Vietnam during the war. That plus stories about the current situation, told by refugees who had risked their lives fleeing communism, filled him with apprehension. In spite of the drab, shabby look of this city with over 1,000 years of history, it was an amazing place to be. We were taken to a circus in a theater. Dave could understand some of what was going on and told me that several of the acts were performed by Cubans. There were Russians in the audience with us, too.

The time in Hanoi was fascinating. We visited the war museum and realized that this country had been in one struggle after another since the year 939! The city reminded me of Phnom Penh, with its French colonial architecture and wide, tree-lined streets. We rode the creaking, hundred-year-old tram, which the French had built and, in spite of wars, was still clunking along. Electricity was sporadic, but food was good and available. The hotel we finally stayed in was Russian-built, with a Cuban elevator. Not much worked, but the people were friendly and welcoming.

Dave began to relax, and at a noodle restaurant, while we listened to 1960s rock music, he asked if the staff would like to hear modern American music. Eagerly they put on the tape cassette he handed them, and the restaurant was filled with praise music. What a moment!

We visited the countryside. Colonel Le Van served as our helpful host. I figured out that our driver was security and listened to all we said, so it was no surprise when Colonel Le Van leaned close and quietly said, "I am glad you are here. We have to get away from the past and move ahead. My grandfather and father were soldiers fighting the Chinese, the French, the Japanese, and I fought the Americans. My children are fighting the Chinese and Cambodians. We should not be there. We must get out or my grandchildren will be at war there, too." It was an amazing statement after the years of seeing the results of the communist takeover and hearing all the triumphal rhetoric. Their victory was, after all, quite pyrrhic.

We walked through markets and bought souvenirs. Some were aluminum spoons made from melted American aircraft. We also visited Hoan Kiem Lake, which had an island connected to the shore by an ornate bridge. A small temple on the island housed a huge stuffed turtle. Their tradition surmised the world rested on the back of a huge turtle, which bore it through the cosmos.

On Sunday, May 24, 1987, we attended the CMA church in Hanoi. After we were seated, an old man came over and translated the sermon for us. It was good gospel. Later he told us he had been David's mother's language teacher and had known David's grandfather, the founder of that very church.

The pastor explained that after partition in 1954, he had met Ho Chi Minh and affirmed the fact that this was a Vietnamese national church. They were self-governing, self-supporting, and self-propagating, and as such, under Ho's nationalistic policies, they should be permitted to operate. Ho agreed, so the church was open all through the war. The pastor told Dave they had an informal Bible school and that some of the students were hills tribesmen from the mountains to the north, on the border with China. They were descendants of men his grandfather had evangelized so many years before. It was an emotional time for us, and especially for Dave.

Back in the countryside, on the Red River delta, the local government leader pointed from the veranda of a small clinic to a field where he said an American plane had crashed; the injured pilot had been given first aid in this very clinic. In the first room of the simple clinic, a medic in a well-used white coat stood smiling, a stethoscope hanging from her neck. It was the same scene in the next room: a simple iron cot, shabby bedding, few implements, and a smiling medic with a stethoscope. Between each room we got a short story about the area. By the third room, I realized the reason. While we talked, the equipment was handed out the window to the workers in the next room, who quickly donned the coat, laid out the instruments, and hung the stethoscope around his or her neck. All five rooms were the same. They really were poor and in need of aid, but they put on a good face.

Peter Conlan of the Operation Mobilization Logos Ships was now with us. He was negotiating for permission to bring their floating Christian library/evangelism base to Hanoi and Ho Chi Minh City (Saigon). We enjoyed his company. We'd seen the people's committee in Ha Bac Province, and the clinics and the hospitals all were basic and very needy. As we drove along, we saw coal-burning trains loaded with passengers bursting from doors and windows, clinging to steps and piled on top. We also saw unfinished agricultural projects abandoned by the Russians. All public transport was vastly overloaded. Clearly, the country was struggling to get back on its feet after so many years of war.

In Hanoi, we were given a farewell dinner hosted by Colonel Le Van. The menu was snails, dog, rice, birds, and other interesting things. The birds were deep fried, feathers and all. While we picked our way through these delicacies, Colonel Le Van cleared his throat. Suddenly everyone was silent.

"So David," he began, "you are of an age to have been here during the war." David was speechless.

I sensed where the conversation was going and spoke up. "David was raised as a missionary kid in Vietnam," I said. "His grandfather started the church we attended Sunday, and his mother grew up here. She speaks Vietnamese with a Hanoi accent. This is David's first visit since he was 16 years old."

There was a moment of silence. Colonel Le Van's face softened. Looking at David, he said, "Welcome home."

What a moment for all of us! It confirmed we were in fact hearing the "sounds of marching in the tops of the mulberry trees."

From Hanoi, the Russian IL-18 turbo prop droned its way south to Ho Chi Minh City. It was a shabby, old aircraft, and once when the crew came out of the cockpit for coffee, they locked themselves out. Quickly grabbing a butter knife from a stewardess, they slipped it into the crack between door and frame and lifted the latch!

In Ho Chi Minh City, we were met by some of Sean Campbell's contacts from the export company Artex. They put us in the Rex Hotel, and we set a schedule to see the various artisans for whom they exported.

The south was, compared to Hanoi, a beehive of activity. Although they were under the control of the communist north, the people were still energetic entrepreneurs, and it showed. There were new buildings and more electricity, and the bright colors were a sharp contrast to the dour, dowdy, colorless north.

On the street, as we walked near the ornate, old post office, we were suddenly accosted by a small group of boys. One of them pointed to Peter Conlan and shouted, "I know you, you're my father! My mother has your picture from the war!"

Peter was speechless, then indignantly said, "I beg your pardon! In all my life, I have never been in this country before."

His tone and Scotch-English accent caused the boy to back away, and then the whole bunch sprinted off amid screams of laughter. David and I were laughing, too. "Wait 'til your wife hears this," we said. Peter was not amused.

We knew about the Amerasian scams being played on visitors. Of course, by 1987, most of the mixed-race kids on the streets probably had Russian fathers.

I sank back into the Air France flight to Bangkok. It had been an amazing visit. How relieved I felt to be away from there, and yet I was excited to see that the future we dreamed of in returning to these war-ravaged countries was, in God's timing, coming to pass.

After reporting by phone to Bob Reed in Nyack, I had a meal with Colonel Kamol Prachuabmoh. He was pleased with what we said and pointed out that the only secure future for Asia was in peace and economic cooperation between all the countries. We agreed and added that practicing Christ's love was the only path to permanent peace.

I finished up the turnover of CAMA Services in Thailand to Sean Campbell, who was now interim CAMA Services director. Bev and I flew down to Dalat for Matt's graduation. It was a great ending to four years, and we enjoyed the flight home. Drew met us in Seattle with the church van. Little did we know that this was our last CAMA homecoming from Southeast Asia.

While the long-term future was unclear, the short term was a mission tour for both Bev and me. Matt had a full-scholarship offer to attend Worcester Polytechnic Institute in Massachusetts. They sent a recruiter to meet him in Seattle. He told of how good the school of computer engineering was and so on. Matt was noncommittal. After a couple of weeks he told me, "Dad, I don't want to go there."

Surprised, I asked, "Why not? It's a lot of money for school that I sure don't have just now."

He responded, "I just want to join the Marines. I've studied leaders in business, and most were former Marines."

"Well," I said, "I enjoyed my service years, and Drew did, too. For sure it's a mission field!"

However, after processing and testing, he failed the physical due to a hearing loss in one ear. My response was, "I know some senators who might be able to get you in on a waiver."

"No," Matt said philosophically, "if the Lord wanted me in the Marines, I'd be there without any waivers. I'd like to go to California, live with my roommates from Dalat, and do odd jobs for a year; then I'll go to college. I haven't lived in America for most of my life. I need time to get used to it." Bev and I left to attend the CMA missionary tour seminar in Nyack. It would be a busy, eventful year.

Elmer Kilburne with hill tribe Bible school,
graduates in Calcutta, India

Speaking to graduating students in Calcutta, India

Chapter 21
More New Experiences ~ Part 1

Chapter 21.
More New Experiences ~ Part 1

Bev's first full missions speaking tour began in the fall of 1987. She had always been content staying in the background and taking care of details, and when the boys were home, she was there for them. Suddenly, being part of a team of three, she had to speak and interact with people every day for eight to ten weeks. Being a bit shy, she was nervous, but she trusted the Lord.

She wrote out her personal story using Psalm 23 as a template. The "table prepared in the presence of my enemies" was the operating table used when she was injured in the car crash in 1965. The enemy was death. Having lived through and, by God's grace, prevailed over these grievous experiences, she offered a presentation powerfully used by Him to speak to both men and women.

We also prepared some slide sets, including "A Day in the Life of a Refugee Child" and "Round the World with CAMA Services." In addition, Bev showed :Turning Relief into Belief." She toured the eastern states with two other missionaries, and I toured the central states with my team. "Tour" included a series of church, community club, Rotary, and school presentations, as well as radio and TV interviews. Bev told me it was a bit unsettling when she told her personal story and saw the audience moved to tears. "It's God's way of reaching them through your determined, faithful obedience," I explained. "You never used your health to avoid service."

When we got back to Ellensburg, Drew introduced us to his girlfriend, Erin King. He had been doing well in his university studies and helped Matt while we were gone. After our fall missions tour, Matt was ready to head for California. He had spent one summer there a few years before, living in Sacramento with my brother Paul. While there he worked for Flessing and Flessing, the video people, to computerize their huge archives of footage.

Matt and I flew to Los Angeles and then drove to visit Dennis Agajanian in San Diego. We had met him when he traveled with Franklin Graham to Thailand. While there, we bought Matt an old Opel car and then set him up in Pasadena with his Dalat buddies. They were eager to start California living.

Once Matt got settled, I began my winter tour in San Francisco. One of my presentations included a story about the Marines fighting in Korea. They fought the Chinese, who kept retreating until they came to a place called the Punch Bowl around the Chosin Reservoir. Early in a cold and snowy morning, the executive officer woke General Lewis B. Puller and said, "Sir, those Chinese we have been chasing surrounded us last night."

"Good," responded General Puller, "they won't get away from us this time."

I used the analogy to emphasize CAMA's response to trouble in places like Lebanon, Africa, and Thailand. After the service in Fort Jones, California, a retired Marine colonel and his wife drove me to the next town for my evening presentation. "I like that story and the way you applied it," he told me. "I was the executive officer who woke General Puller that morning."

We always had interesting tours, because we got to meet and interact with so many unusual people.

In between the tour activities, we worked on the future of CAMA Services. We had discussions and wrote papers, and committees were convened. Someone told us we had been considered for a role based in Nyack, but the details seemed elusive. In April 1988, Drew and I flew to Europe en route to Africa to help film, "We Are His Hands" for African CAMA Services.

Drew worked out a "field experience for credit" at the university. He planned to write a paper on medical needs in the country of Guinea. In Brussels, we visited places we knew from our time there in 1970, and we ate moules et frites in the Grand Plas. Meetings took place in Holland that covered funding agencies and CAMA supporters.

One visit stands out in which a Dutch official who dispensed funds for us teased me about getting more money for "rice Christians." The Jesus Grain in Mali and Burkina Faso was a good example. He had recently visited Mali to see what was really happening. Out in the desert, he had spotted a small mud-brick house. An old man sat on the porch, and a Jesus Grain bag hung on the clothesline. The Dutch official had ordered his embassy driver to stop.

The old man had invited them onto the porch for tea. "I see you got grain," said the official.

"Yes, it was the Jesus Grain. We all got some, and it saved our lives."

"Did you have to do anything to get it?" questioned the official.

"No, we all got it with no conditions, whether Muslim or Christian."

"So," the official said, "you're a Muslim?"

"Not now," the old man responded.

The Dutch official said, "I was thinking aha! So I asked him, 'Why?'"

"Well," the man responded, "after we got the grain, the Christians prayed for rain, and it came. One day I saw a man pushing a bicycle loaded with 200 kilos of grain up the road in the rain and mud. I invited him in for tea and then saw he was the pastor from about five miles down the hill. 'Where are you taking this grain?' I asked. The pastor told me, 'Up the hill to the next village.' I was surprised and reminded him they were militant Muslims who even threw rocks at him when he rode by. He told me he knew that and hated to be stoned, but he had Jesus Grain from God's people and it was for that village, and as God's representative, it was his job to deliver it."

The old man paused and then said, "That was when I realized this was the true religion from the true God."

The Dutch official paused and lit a cigarette. "So," he said to me, "you keep doing what you do, and I will help."

It was a beautiful demonstration of God at work in word and deed.

Our Sabena flight to Conakry, Guinea was like old times. Mel Carter, another old friend, met us and took us to the guest house. The city was somewhat shabby, as were most African capitals of that era. Issac Keita, the national church president, was kind enough to give us a thorough update on conditions in Guinea. He answered questions for Drew's research. Drew toured the hospital there, and we met several government officials involved in health care. Years later, Drew and his family served in Guinea for eight years with CAMA Services.

Mel Carter took us to the airport early in the morning for our flight to Bamako, Mali. "You need to be sure to get your seats and pass customs early," he explained. "No one ever knows what may transpire in Africa."

Mel's language ability and acquaintance with the airport workers made the check-in and customs passage smooth, and soon we found ourselves drinking coffee in the boarding lounge.

Suddenly, well before departure time, an airline agent stepped up. "Please follow me," he said quietly.

We walked out onto the tarmac. We could see the Air Guinea Boeing 737 some distance away, but he took us to a smaller turbo prop aircraft with seats for about 40 people. "You must take this flight to Bamako," he said and left.

The plane filled rapidly, and then a soldier came on board and removed two passengers. The pilots, clearly agitated, shouted on the radio about the herd of people trying to get to the already loaded plane. The country's president had decided to take the 737 on a personal trip, thereby displacing the other 80 to 100 passengers who should have been going to Mali at that time. They wanted to riot, but soldiers held them back.

Suddenly, a man squeezed into the seats behind us that the soldiers had cleared for him. A young woman joined him. Still we didn't leave. Finally a limo pulled up and an official climbed aboard the plane. Walking up the aisle to the man behind us, he quietly said, "You must sign these before you leave."

Taking the stack of files from the official, the minister of something quickly unlimbered his Mont Blanc pen and signed his name to a stack of official documents for ten minutes. Finally we could leave. As we taxied away from the shouting, angry passengers who had no seats, I said to Drew, "C'est Afrique, n'est ce pas?"

"Oui!" he agreed, "West Africa wins again."

The air in Mali was still and hot! Our cameraman's wristwatch had a thermometer mode that registered 127° Fahrenheit. One of the retread tire caps melted from the Land Cruiser near Mopti. In spite of the oppressive heat, we got good footage of agriculture, wells, roads, grain banks, and other CAMA Services projects. Robin Dirks had done a great job of planning so that our time was used effectively. David Kennedy, our CMA assistant vice president, came along and gave good suggestions of subjects to be filmed. He had been raised in Mali as an MK and served there as an adult. Greg Flessing was the consummate professional as usual, shooting in the heat and dust, always with the artist's eye for telling the CAMA story.

After a few days I received a cryptic telegram: "Come home. Your mother's dying."

We had almost finished the filming and were on our way to Ouagadougou, Burkina Faso. "You go ahead, Andy," David Kennedy said. "I'll finish this project."

So Drew and I drove to Bobo-Dioulasso, Burkina Faso.

From Bobo-Dioulasso, we flew via Dakar to New York and Seattle, where we picked up a car to drive to our family's ranch near Quincy, Washington. We arrived at my sister Coarlie's home to find my four brothers and two sisters gathered there.

Mother had been in somewhat of a coma, unable to speak. It was the first time in several years that we had all been together, and as we talked about how to conduct the funeral, Mother opened her eyes. "Some tea," she whispered.

After drinking, she closed her eyes and got quiet. A couple of hours later she asked for some soup, then dropped off again. She roused a little later and, adjusting her hair and bedclothes, said, "My, it's nice to see all of you together, and I know why you're here, but I'm afraid I can't cooperate. I'm feeling better."

In six weeks she was out of bed, flying to Florida to visit my sister Audrey and friends. She lived nearly three more years.

In May 1988, the end of our furlough drew near. We still had no definite word on our future. CAMA's future had been in limbo, and leadership was not willing to modify my job description to allow any further work for us in CAMA Services. Then a job description arrived. CAMA Services wasn't mentioned. Bev and I prayed and talked and prayed and talked. Neither of us felt comfortable with the position being offered by the CMA. We prayed for God to "open another door"

so we could continue in the type of work He had equipped us for, or to make us comfortable with the job being offered.

Then Dennis Agajanian called and said, "Franklin Graham needs help. Would you be willing to talk to him?"

I had known Franklin since his first visit to Thailand with Bob Pierce in 1975. We had interacted on the Guyana project and several times when Samaritan's Purse had participated in CAMA projects. I had also made an evaluation of his mother's college in Montreat, North Carolina, and even appeared in one of his videos. I had traveled to Ethiopia in 1984 to do a relief and development survey for Samaritan's Purse. I still remember visiting Billy and Ruth Graham at their log home in Montreat with Franklin. Billy had been very warm and had answered my questions on how to maintain family balance with an extremely hectic schedule.

Samaritan's Purse seemed to be an opportunity opening to us. I knew Sean Campbell had joined Samaritan's Purse Canada, so we felt we should consider it.

I flew to Boone, North Carolina, to meet with Franklin. Bev and I had been there the year before to speak at the Boone CMA missions dinner, so there were some synergies at work. Franklin asked me to join his team.

After some discussion with Samaritan's Purse, we requested "special assignment" status with the CMA and moved to Boone. I became the Director for Projects for Samaritan's Purse. It seemed to be a good fit.

We found another culture there in the heart of Appalachia, and we happily accepted the work. We also found a good CMA church to join in Boone. We located a small apartment and settled in. Matt joined us as we transited California en route to North Carolina. He enrolled at Appalachian State University. Bev looked into returning to nursing.

At Samaritan's Purse, my first briefings were on Ethiopia and India. The projects needing attention included well drilling and agricultural development in Ethiopia, and mobility for pastors and construction of churches and related activities in India. In Africa, most of the action took place in the east, including Ethiopia, Kenya, Congo, and Tanzania. In the Middle East, they had projects in Jordan and Lebanon involving medicine and relief.

The John Fitzstevenses, David's parents, and Sean Campbell came to Boone. We had dinner and discussed our experiences with CAMA. We intended by whatever means to continue to partner and participate with CAMA as the Lord made it possible. The Fitzstevenses prepared to move to Vietnam to work with CAMA there.

My old friend Jan van Barneveld organized Samaritan's Purse Holland, and George Hoffman, a TEAR Fund England retiree, had been courted to start Samaritan's Purse there. Sally Lambert, George's long-time assistant, was brought to Boone to start a children's program. Her work laid the foundation for today's "shoebox" program that Samaritan's Purse operates.

I had not been in Boone long before I met Aart van Wingerden. He headed a huge empire of ornamental plant nurseries across the U.S. As a believer, he invested in agriculture-related developments in Africa and Haiti. He had a passion for drip irrigation and greenhouses to produce self-sustaining businesses for Africans and a big farm in Haiti.

The "tyranny of the urgent" came into play, as usual, and I suddenly found myself with a camera crew led by Greg Flessing on a plane to Jamaica to set up a relief response to Hurricane Gilbert. Matt went along as a helper for the crew. It was a devastating scene but a good opportunity to work with the local church people, some of whom I had met years before when I was vice president of WRC.

Soon containers of relief supplies were sent to Jamaica, equipment was assembled for well drilling in Ethiopia, and work teams were organized to rebuild housing in Jamaica. Everyone worked at a rapid pace. My secretary, Jackie Dodson, did a good job keeping all the details of communication and operations in balance. I could not have made things work without her. Pat Pilkington was another good member of the team.

A lot of networking needed to be developed. We knew some groups and agencies from our past work, and there were some new ones, like the Oriental Missions Society. I knew Elmer Kilburne had been the prime mover on the India work with which Samaritan's Purse partnered. World Gospel Mission (WGM) was another group from my past. My uncle Jim Bishop had been president of that mission at one time, and I worked on projects with their people in Honduras and Zimbabwe. Working with Gene Lewton of WGM in Kenya and others from Tanzania was really good! I loved meeting and working with men and women from all over the world.

By November, I headed back to London and Holland. I needed to meet with the suppliers and partners in the Ethiopian well-drilling program. We had already purchased two Mercedes trucks in Holland through TEAR Fund Holland and England. One truck went to Italy for installation of drilling equipment, and the other went to England to have drilling support equipment installed. The big compressor was being built in North Carolina. At the same time, drilling pipe and supplies were being bought, packed, and shipped to Addis Ababa, Ethiopia. Ken Isaacs, the driller from Boone, went overseas for the first time.

I spent the last part of November 1988 in Bangkok, Calcutta, and Mumbai. From there I flew to Addis Ababa, with a day in Nairobi, Kenya. At each stop, we met with people and partners who had been carrying out the various projects in those countries. Many good things were accomplished in God's name.

I got home in time for our staff Christmas party. Billy and Ruth Graham came, and we all had a lovely time. Bev decided to take a refresher course in nursing in Elizabethton, Tennessee, and Matt did well in university studies. He began a cleaning business, and for a time he became a night disc jockey on the local radio station. We made friends through the church and slowly became part of the community.

Drew and Erin got engaged, and she came to Boone to spend some time with us. We had a mix-up as she flew into Greenville, South Carolina. We had driven part way to Greensboro, North Carolina, before we discovered our error. Erin was very glad to see us when we finally got there! She became a great addition to our family.

The tempo of the work accelerated. One trip melded into another as Samaritan's Purse's income grew and new projects began.

One cool morning in New Delhi, Charles O'Brien, Elmer Kilburne, Sean Campbell, and I traveled with a group of donors to view church construction projects they had financed. We planned to meet Ezra Sargunam, president of the evangelical church in India, for a bus trip to dedicate a new church "just a short way" from New Delhi. Charles, the Samaritan's Purse coordinator for India, happily handed the responsibility to me. We also saw some other projects in India; however, Charles found work and travel in India difficult to endure.

At 5:00 a.m., we boarded an old school bus designed to carry 40 kids. I saw that the seats had been removed, and 2x6-inch planks spanning the width of the bus had been put in their place. Fifty-two people jammed into the space, and Charles, Elmer, and I made 55! The "short trip" took over seven hours. We clung to the boards and each other as the bus wove through cars, trucks, oxcarts, handcarts, and pedestrians. The dusty roads were punctuated by potholes and roadwork. This left our backsides numb and our spines sore.

When we finally arrived at the new church, we had a meal of curried goat and fruit. The trip left Charles so worn out that he didn't eat, and even Elmer's usual enthusiasm was subdued. We did have a good service attended by locals, including some Catholic nuns. Reluctantly, we boarded the bus for the return trip and endured the seven hour ride to New Delhi. Sean Campbell escaped the bus trip by taking a tour of New Delhi.

We went to Madras, a place my uncle had served many years before. From there we took the train to Vijayawada to dedicate three more churches. Fifty-one people got baptized as well. Our return train had been scheduled to leave at 11:00 p.m. I had never seen hundreds of people sleeping on the ground in the open and on the floor of the train platform as they do in India. At 11:00 p.m. the train roared in, the conductor shouted, "No places!" and away they went. It was the same at midnight and at 1:00 a.m. At 2:00 a.m., the station agent told us the 2:30 a.m. train had seats. It arrived at 3:00 a.m. They put the seven of us into six seats. Elmer and his helpers finally got on the 5:00 a.m. train. Back in Madras, a church with seating for 100 had been dedicated in memory of Franklin Graham's grandfather. Over 300 crowded in, and another 100 stood outside.

We got up at 3:00 a.m. to catch the 5:00 a.m. flight to Singapore. At the airport, they informed us that the flight had been delayed until 2:00 p.m. It finally departed at 5:00 p.m., and Air India put us up in Singapore for the night. I could well understand why Charles was happy to see the last of India.

One thing I recommended was that the church-building consortium in the States get a good audit to answer questions being raised. To do this, we first needed to buy computers, a copier, a fax machine, and other tools so the church could track contributions by the consortium and expenditures by the Indian church. Seeing their bookkeeping department for the first time amazed me. Twenty men tried to do accounts totally by hand, using small notebooks and pencils. They processed up to $1 million a year that way.

In the U.S. the consortium agreed, and after three months of work we had implemented the changes and the project got back on track. This pleased Ezra Sargunam, the church president. "We are the first denomination in India to have a computer," he told me.

In Bangkok, we enjoyed seeing CAMA's activities. Steve Bailey had made great progress in Laos. David Fitzstevens had gotten a shipment of Bibles to Hanoi, where his parents served. Site 8 was still a major CAMA operation, and Ollie Kaetzel did a great job as CAMA director. Political change became evident in that the Thai government was in negotiations with Vietnam, Laos, Cambodia, and Burma to lessen tensions and open up trade. They also wanted to get the last groups of refugees back home to their countries.

From Bangkok we went to Amman, Jordan, where we spent time at the Mufraq Hospital. Samaritan's Purse sent funds and staff there, as well as equipment and supplies. The beautiful new Alliance church in Amman had just about been completed. Later I helped Pastor Yousef Hashweh with pews and much-needed office equipment. I enjoyed having time with Andy and Marilyn Kerr, the folks who had worked so hard with CAMA in Lebanon in 1977.

The reconditioned medical equipment was outstanding. The people at the Christian Hospital supply foundation in Holland not only furnished equipment such as x-ray machines, but they also sent technicians to third-world locations to install it and give it a one-year warranty. Jan van Barnveld introduced me to them. They always went above and beyond to make sure things worked right.

We purchased one of the x-ray units and shipped it to Nyankunde in eastern Congo. When it arrived, we found that a piece had broken. The shipping insurance paid for most of the equipment and shipping, and the technicians who had been sent to install the unit took repair parts and installed them at no extra cost. Later, when the x-ray tube blew out through misuse, they replaced it and repaired other equipment as needed at no extra charge. In addition, the equipment was 220-volt, 50-cycle -- the prevailing power supply in Africa.

From Holland I went to London for more discussions with George Hoffman. After London, I went back to North Carolina. It had been a busy 17 days! Then between writing reports, I kept some speaking engagements in several states. I also went to several meetings with Franklin, often traveling in his Twin Beechcraft. He was a good pilot and careful to fly safely.

We also worked with the Operation Mobilization team operating the Logos ships. David Greenlee and Peter Conlan, whom I had met in Hanoi, came to Boone. We talked about their latest ship, and from experience I made suggestions on the layout for their ship-based clinic. We did the same for YWAM in Amsterdam when it overhauled its first Mercy Ship.

Another enjoyable aspect of the time at Samaritan's Purse was having occasional contact with Franklin's dad, Billy. At places like Boone, Montreat, and crusades held in places like Syracuse and Hong Kong, I had conversations with him.

In Ethiopia, I always enjoyed time with Dr. Malatu Baffa, president of the church there. He was a great man who led his church through the hard times under the communists with grace and perseverance. Aart van Wingerden worked on setting up a demonstration farm in an old volcano crater for them, and it drew a lot of attention from the government and nongovernment organizations. One day Dr. Baffa confided to me, "Billy Graham gave us money for a church where the farm is, but even though we have the blueprints drawn and materials purchased, we don't have anyone to make it into a building."

"I know just the man," I said.

Loyal Bowman, a CMA missionary, had grown up in Mali and was a good "bush builder." I had seen the churches he built in remote areas. I also knew he was semi-retired. He had lost his wife, and a job like this would be perfect for everyone. A few months later, we sent Loyal to Ethiopia, and he built them a lovely facility that could seat over 1,000 people. The communist repression had not diminished their faith in God; in fact, it made them stronger. War raged with Eritrea, and the communists slowly lost their grip on the country. Even though the war made things complicated, the church grew again.

Kenny Isaacs was in Addis Ababa, ready to drill wells. The equipment had been a challenge to assemble and ship, but we were finally ready – except for the fact that the big compressor wasn't there. I quickly called Ingersoll Rand's Swiss office. "We paid nearly a million dollars for all of this," I explained, "but where's our compressor?"

Finally they said, "Oops! It's still in Maxton, North Carolina" …100 miles from Boone!

I drove there at once, but no one seemed to know where the one and a half ton unit was. Finally a janitor said, "Ain't that the thing sitting out back?"

Sure enough, there it was. "A truck will pick it up tomorrow, and you can refund the shipping costs," I told them.

It was three inches too big to put on a 747 cargo plane, so we put it on a fast ship to Djibouti. From there we could ship it by rail to Addis. It would be about a one-month delay, but we were nearly operational.

A few weeks later, however, Kenny Isaacs was saying on the phone from Addis, "Andy, the war has closed the railroad, and our compressor is in Djibouti."

My mind raced for a solution. Then I remembered, "Ken, the Ethiopian Airlines just bought a C-130 Hercules. They also have access to Russian AN-12s, which are about the same size. See if you can rent one to fly the compressor to Addis."

"That may be expensive," he replied.

"What's the interest rate on $1 million these days?" I asked.

That's what was invested so far in the project, and we had yet to drill a well. "Okay," he said.

"Andy, you were right." It was Kenny again, and a day had gone past. "Their new plane was at the airport, and I rented it for $10,000. I sold $6,000 of space to the Southern Baptists and others who, like us, had shipments stranded. Now we're in Djibouti, loaded and ready to fly to Addis. However, I used my American Express card to pay for the plane. Could you call them and alert them to this charge on my card? I'm way over my limit."

My call to American Express was amusing. When I explained the incoming charge, they firmly told me that it was not possible and that Mr. Isaac had a $3,000 limit on his card. "Well," I told her, "the charge was made and the plane has flown. Let me speak to your supervisor."

Three supervisors later, I got someone who agreed to honor the charge. An offer to forward the $10,000 at once got declined. The charge did not come through for another three months, and by then we had begun drilling wells.

The World Medical Missions, part of the Samaritan's Purse organization in Kenya, had done a major overhaul at the hospital at Tenwick. They sent short- and long-term workers, as well as equipment and supplies. We began the same overhaul program for Nyankunde in Congo. Loyal Bowman finished in Ethiopia and went to oversee the new program, where his expertise was put to good use.

Back in India, we dedicated 100 bicycles and motorbikes for pastors and some more churches. Some dug wells in church courtyards and installed pumps. We welcomed everyone in the village to come for clean water and to hear of the Living Water. Franklin came in to visit the Indian site for a big evangelism conference. En route back to Boone, we stopped to do the same in London.

Andy, Dr. Joe Lucie and Aart van Wingerden
at Nyankunde, Congo Africa

Chapter 22
More New Experiences ~ Part 2

Chapter 22.
More New Experiences ~ Part 2

We enjoyed the peace and quiet of the ranch again in Quincy, Washington. Matt, Bev, and I attended Drew and Erin's wedding in Ellensburg. The ceremony was wonderful, and in keeping with the Ellensburg cowboy town theme, they left the church in a horse-drawn carriage. The motel marquee where the reception was held said, "CHECKMATE - BISHOP TAKES KING." We were thankful for both of them and enjoyed getting to know her brother Eric and her parents, Mike and Ann King. Best of all, Drew and Erin were determined to become missionaries.

Later, Drew and Erin drove to Boone, where we spent some good family time together. They described their plan to join World Concern and serve in Somalia. Later, when Somalia disintegrated into war, they spent some time in Kenya before moving to Ethiopia, where I saw them from time to time.

When George Johnson, vice president of Samaritan's Purse, passed away, my job description, signed by both Franklin and George, appeared in the office mail with Franklin's signature whited out. Guess that indicates the future here is not too long, I thought. But Guy Davidson, whom I had met in Lebanon and Arizona, came in as vice president, and he was a fine man and fun to work with. He had ordained Franklin a few years before, and he came on board to oversee the World Medical Missions and be a regular advisor. One of his best projects had been setting up training for hospital chaplains in third-world hospitals. He also trained chaplains for the anti-Sandinistas rebel army in Honduras and Nicaragua.

Hurricane Hugo gave me a good tour of the Caribbean. The area had been severely damaged, and again, containers got filled for shipment and repair teams were organized. Charleston, South Carolina, also had a lot of damage, and we decided to move trailer homes in to replace lost housing. Then the city announced it would not allow the trailers in and would stop them at the state line. It refused to give the needed building permits. One morning, Bill Deans, a local contractor, set up a meeting with local officials. We "negotiated" for a couple of hours. Finally I asked, "Where did you all sleep last night?"

They looked startled. Some had stayed in their homes, others in a posh hotel. I continued, "Well, the people we're helping slept on cardboard under a piece of plastic! The sad thing is that if you have police at the state line to stop the convoy of trailers, Franklin will have CNN, ABC, and CBS record this and tell everyone you don't want to help because most of the needy are poor blacks. I've worked in county government and know you have the power to grant a variance to the code requirements for a period long enough to build proper homes for these people."

Silence filled the room, and then the council chairman said, "Okay, get the building officials up here with some special permits."

As we helped out, several other organizations joined the project, providing new, dry mobile homes for many families. The program aired on national television with a positive comment for everyone, including the government. We even set up a day-care center in a trailer for the people in the damaged area.

November 1990 brought more travel to Kenya and Ethiopia, where good progress had been made on agriculture and church building, as well as the Nyankunde hospital overhaul. We had also installed solar pumps in some projects, and God blessed the efforts. My trip took me from Africa to Bangkok via Mumbai. The route had always been interesting to cover because you could smell the fires and garbage dumps at the edge of the city from a hundred miles away at an altitude of 25,000 feet. Calcutta was the same.

Lunch with Colonel Kamol Prachuabmoh in Bangkok was like a homecoming. "The king has awarded you a medal," he said. "You will be given the medal, The Royal Order of the White Elephant, tomorrow. Bring some friends. It's the highest civilian award given in Thailand."

This amazed me. We had never lost our concern for Thailand and still love to go there. The honor was for CAMA as much as for Bev and me. Our goal was to glorify God.

The ceremony was held at the Ministry of the Interior. Ollie and Winnie Kaetzel of CAMA and Colonel Kamol, who had become a provincial governor, were among others in attendance. The government clearly respected CAMA's help with Thailand's 14 years of refugee problems.

That evening, we had a good dinner with a number of the Thai missionaries and Governor and Mrs. Kamol at an old favorite spot, Neil's Tavern.

Berlin, 1989. The evening was electric as throngs of young people tore at the concrete slabs that made up the infamous wall. Communism in Germany had breathed its last. George Hoffman, Tony Neeves, and I walked through a gaping hole to the eastern side of the wall. People milled about into the darkness. Light from the west showed that the East German officers and soldiers had moved back to avoid any confrontation with the eager crowds.

President Ronald Reagan had challenged Mikhail Gorbachev to "tear down this wall," and it had finally happened.

People had mixed feelings. Some were angry that the communists had put East Germany 40 years behind Westerners. Others were delighted that Germany had been reunited at last. It amazed me to be there as history happened.

From Berlin I traveled to Vienna, then by bus to Prague. People were excited and pleased. I watched as Va'clav Havel led them around the parliament building holding candles, a symbol of what they called the "velvet revolution." They sang, "Peace at Last." It had been only a little over 20 years since Russian tanks crushed a previous attempt to gain freedom in Czechoslovakia.

One man said, "For the first time in 21 years, I can turn on television and hear the truth."

Another said, "For the first time in 40 years, we can visit Austria!"

I saw a line two blocks long of people exchanging local money for hard currency so they could travel and buy Western goods. Now they could visit the West and see friends and relatives on the free side of the border.

East German and Russian soldiers, along with others, wandered about Prague in shock. They could not believe the changes or the prices. At the border crossings, the soldiers had taken the clips from their AK-47s. It wasn't long until the mines, towers, and barbed wire began to come down as well. Graffiti on the walls of Prague said things like "72 years of communism – 72 years on the road to nowhere." People lined up in St. Wenceslaus Square to sign up for membership in the Public Forum, a new political party.

The fog was thick and pungent with the smell of burning low-grade coal. Sean Campbell and I had finally arrived in Bucharest, Romania, to deliver relief goods to Christian groups for distribution. Another communist domino had just fallen. The people had executed their dictator and his wife.

It was very dark at the airport. As we moved away from the 1950s-model Russian airliner we had traveled in from Belgrade, we wondered how anyone could drive us to the city in such thick fog. After clearing customs in the dark, dingy terminal, we found an old Dacia taxi. The driver informed us it was new. It was a '74 Renault 12 that they kept making in a local French-built factory. We crept through the dark streets.

Tanks and soldiers made shadowy forms along the road. They had overthrown the communists and seemed unsure what to do next. At midnight, we made it to our hotel. What a great relief to be there safely! We looked forward to meeting the pastors and people of Romania later in the day. I couldn't help but remember my time with Richard Wurmbrandt some years before. He had lived and suffered for the Lord in this country, as had many others, and they had finally become free of the communists, but a lot had to happen to bring them into the twentieth century.

First we checked on the truckloads of relief goods that we had sent from Canada via Europe. They had been in temporary storage, and we planned to distribute them as soon as we could. After coordinating their arrival, we planned the rest of the day. We met with the Canadian ambassador, Saul Grey, a cordial and helpful man. He described the changes and the challenge the Romanians faced in recovering from communism. He said the communists had not even published a phone book for nearly 20 years, so finding people would be hard for any outsiders. Newspapers suddenly became available, along with some information, but without street maps or addresses, we had to rely on word of mouth to find our contacts.

In the city we saw soldiers, tanks, and damaged buildings, some still smoldering from the conflict. We also saw small shrines in various places dedicated to people who had been killed at the site. Back at the warehouse, a line of cars and vans picked up the relief goods. We loaded our van to make a special delivery in the countryside, and as we traveled we saw people walking the roads, horse-drawn carts, and old, decrepit vehicles. Gas stations had long lines of people waiting to buy gas. One station had a shorter line, so we filled our loaded van. Gas prices stayed at only 50 cents per gallon.

We visited a village made up of gypsies who called themselves Pentecostal believers. They gave our load of aid a rousing welcome. We knew they had suffered. Their 78-year-old pastor, who had served the church for more than 50 years, greeted us. He said, "I have learned the privilege of suffering for Christ and to glory in it."

Looking at the poverty and malnutrition in the village, we were amazed at his perseverance.

We spent time surveying further needs, delivering clothes and medicines, and marveling at the "communist paradise." It amazed us to see hundreds of five-story apartment buildings. Each courtyard had a large multi person outhouse and a well, because they didn't have electricity or elevators. No wonder they hated the dictator. George Hoffman and Tony Neeves joined us and filmed interviews and distribution activities to be used in a fund raising film.

One meeting stands out in my memory. A group of Baptist pastors sat around a coffee shop table and spoke quietly about the situation and their needs. One objected to helping the gypsies. "They're not Romanians," he complained.

"But," I replied, "they are the most-needy people, precisely the ones Christ commands us to reach out to!"

As one of the pastors rose to leave, he whispered, "God bless all of you!"

Then he caught himself and added, "Why am I whispering? We're free now! God bless everyone!" he shouted.

We enjoyed a good laugh. "God bless you, too!" we replied.

Before they left, we all agreed to a model village project that they would implement even for those who weren't "Romanians."

Before leaving to go to Romania, I'd received a call from my brother Paul. He was a deputy attorney general for the state of California. He'd bought 100 computer workstations from a defunct travel agency and said I could have them at cost if they could be used in the work. Paul was always helpful and encouraging. He and his wife had visited the refugee work in Hong Kong and Thailand and kept up with our various travels.

Now, while talking to a Christian professor of computer systems at the university in Romania, I asked, "What equipment do you use?"

"We don't have any equipment," he said. "We can only teach theory."

"I have a something you might find useful."

When I explained about the work stations, he beamed, "Oh, that would be wonderful!"

Sean Campbell found a mainframe for them in Canada, and we shipped 100 workstations to the professor. It was a good project; they had a real computer system to learn on at last.

On the way home, we stopped in Holland to see Jan van Barneveld, who had been staying active as usual. He delivered medical equipment to the Logos II and sent containers of food to Angola and medical equipment and supplies to Nyankunde, Congo. He also helped the "small pastors and evangelists" he met at one time or another. I always enjoyed stopping there for fellowship. We worked out plans for him to ship food and survival biscuits to Romania.

David Greenlee of Operation Mobilization (OM) showed us through the Logos II. The clinic looked great, and the ship's overhaul had almost been finished. They recruited staff, and Russia became their first cruise destination.

After some meetings in London with Jennie Evans of TEAR Fund, I boarded my flight for home. As I rested on the plane, I couldn't help but remember the old Romanian pastor who, as we got ready to leave his village, pulled out his Bible and read 1 Thessalonians 5:23: "May the God of peace Himself keep you entirely pure and devoted to God; and may your spirit and soul and body be kept strong and blameless until that day when our Lord Jesus Christ comes back again."

Then he led the village in prayer for us. It was a blessed moment in the poverty-stricken village of the desperate country.

In mid-June 1990, at 87 years old, my mother began to fail. I sat with her for a few days before she moved on to heaven. We had a good send-off and buried her next to Dad on our ranch. Her tombstone was like Dad's, a huge multi-ton basalt crystal. Their plaques said, "Mother prayed" and "Daddy kept the faith." I am eternally blessed by having had them for parents.

After the funeral, we all enjoyed a meal at my sister Coralie's home. Someone asked, "Who wants Mother and Dad's little dog?"

My brother Dave blurted, "I don't want that dog. Everyone who gets that dog dies."

We had a good laugh, and my nephew ended up taking the dog.

The 1991 Gulf War opened up a new opportunity to respond in Christ's name in Jordan. Andy Kerr, Yousef Hashweh and Sami Dagher's team from Lebanon, as well as the clinic staff at the Mufraq Hospital, all worked together to provide food, water, shelter, and the gospel to people from Kuwait, Iraq, and several Asian and Middle Eastern countries. Many worked in the Gulf and fled the war. We were happy to meet their many needs.

Roy Gustafson, a long-time associate of Billy Graham and an excellent guide for Middle Eastern tours, came in to minister, along with many others. They carried out a wonderful joint effort in Jordan, and the Turning Relief into Belief strategy worked again.

When the shooting stopped, Sami Dagher took a team of workers and seven truckloads of relief goods from Lebanon, Holland, and Jordan up to Baghdad. There they worked with local Christians and government workers to get the aid to as many needy people as they could. They also gave aid to 6,000 orphans and worked out ways to continue to help. More than 60,000 people received food and clothes, and ten young men from churches in Baghdad were trained in relief work. The government even released some prisoners from jail to help with the distribution. They gave aid and Arabic New Testaments, and God blessed the efforts. One young man who believed went on to Bible school in Lebanon. Eventually Ghassan Thomas planted a CMA church in Baghdad.

Franklin and I were visiting Laos, and our Russian UAZ jeep chugged noisily into life. "Why does Steve have a Russian jeep?" Franklin grumbled.

"Because," I replied, "you bought it for him."

Smiling, Steve Bailey slowed for the Laotian soldiers at the Vientiane airport checkpoint. Dave Andrianoff, who now worked for World Concern, had his passengers and their luggage out of his Japanese SUV while soldiers looked in every nook and cranny for contraband. We got waved through without any questions. "They don't stop me," Steve said, "because they think only a Russian would drive this jeep."

Franklin smiled at the idea of putting one over on the communists. Dennis Agajanian chortled, "I gotta drive this ugly thing."

Steve, CAMA's representative in Laos, developed everything from CAMA Crafts and language classes to silk production. We discussed a new CAMA program to teach business English to the officials at the government bank, which would give us a great opportunity to get into all of Laos. Banks could be found all over the country. With this program, a wide range of new opportunities for outreach developed.

Bev stayed busy back in Boone. She joined Hospice and loved the work. She found it very satisfying to help people navigate the final days of life with gentleness and care, and as the opportunity presented itself, she also showed them the way to an eternity with Christ. Wanda Branch was her boss and a friend from the Alliance church where I served with her husband, Paul, as an elder. Matt kept busy with his cleaning company and university studies, and Drew and Erin stayed in Africa.

The old Cessna 206 station wagon pitched and bucked in the turbulence from the mountains of southeastern Turkey. Below us, we could see jagged, snow-spotted ridges and the clouds we had staggering through. Ice formed on the wings of the heavily loaded aircraft, and the up and down drafts made it seem as if we had gotten on an elevator gone mad. Franklin Graham rode up front with the pilot. Being a pilot himself, he wondered about the wisdom of his decision to charter the flight. Rick Auten, our cameraman and a Southern Baptist missionary who focused on the Kurds, came with us. In addition, our luggage and camera equipment made for a very full airplane. The air was not only turbulent, but also very cold. Frost built up inside the cabin, and the plane's alternator suddenly quit, forcing us to run on battery only. We held our breath and prayed.

I was not exactly following my doctor's advice. I had suffered a second heart attack. I had gone through a thorough work-up at the Cooper Clinic in Dallas, and everyone agreed I should take more medications, lose weight, and avoid stress. I prayed and wondered just how to avoid stress in the life I lived.

The trip to Turkey was to follow up on our Gulf War refugee work from the perspective of the Kurds who had fled yet another purge by Saddam Hussein to the mountaintops of eastern Turkey.

The situation was delicate. The Kurdish people once had a nation that included parts of eastern Turkey and northern Iraq, as well as northwestern Iran. They continued to agitate and fight to regain ground they had been losing since the time of Alexander the Great, more than 2,000 years before. Large numbers of them now perched in the high mountains of eastern Turkey. The Turkish government did not want them there, as it was a base for Kurdish rebels.

Finally we landed at Diyarbakir, Turkey. The Cessna's battery had nearly died. We crawled out and stood on shaky legs as our luggage was extracted. Julian Lidstone of OM met us. He had booked rooms in a small hotel in the badly overcrowded town. The streets were clogged with aid workers, Kurdish refugees who had money, and nervous Turks who were well aware of the already dangerous political situation now exacerbated by the influx of more Kurds.

The next day we drove the rough roads along the border with Syria, then north along the border with Iraq. Road checks by nervous soldiers on alert for more fighting with Kurdish separatists reminded us we were a long way from America and in a volatile region. Finally we turned into a rough track leading up into the high mountains where the Kurdish refugee camps were located, near the town of Uludere, Turkey.

After a couple of miles, we got out to walk another mile up to the camps. As I was short of breath, the others moved on up to the camp, and I came along slowly. We could see the huge Marine Chinook helicopters off loading food, blankets, and water. Someone told us that more than 80,000 refugees lived in the camp. Other refugees climbed to safety on other mountaintops. It was April 15, 1991, and still cold in the squalid camps.

The American troops did a magnificent job. They had been effective in war, and then they'd begun working out a safe place, including a no-fly zone above the 36th parallel in northern Iraq, to provide a safe haven for the Kurds. We came to see how we could help. They had many needs, especially for the gospel. I urged Julian to begin an OM project, as they had a number of workers in Turkey. I explained that the Turkish government would really welcome their help in spite of their Christian beliefs.

The next morning I sent a fax to President Bush, thanking him for using our troops in their excellent humanitarian effort. He wrote me a nice letter thanking me for our work as well. Since there weren't any flights back to Ankara, we made the 13-hour drive by bus. In Ankara I spoke with Sheppie Abramowitz, the wife of the U.S. ambassador to Turkey. I had met her and her husband while working with CAMA in Thailand. She was delighted with the firsthand report from the mountains and the fact we came to help.

Having seen the situation, Franklin was eager to get to Amman, Jordan; however, the only flights were from Istanbul. He seemed to be in a real hurry, so we hired a car and driver, making the trip in four hours. The driver drove over 100 M.P.H. most of the way and got a nice tip for his efforts!

In Amman we met with Yousef Hashweh, pastor of the CMA church; Darrell Phenicie, missionary with the CMA in Lebanon; and Sami Dagher. They gave us a good update on the refugee work that had begun to wind down in Jordan. The people could finally go home! Yousef reported that they'd started an Iraqi church, with services held in Amman each Sunday. Sami and Darrell taught a Bible school program that included some Iraqi students in Beirut. Relief was turning into belief. Later God used Sami's relief convoy to Baghdad to show the physical effects of His love for Iraq, which opened an opportunity for Sami in Syria.

After a couple of days of meetings, we drove to Jerusalem, and after some rest there we flew on to the States. Was there stress? Well, some for sure, but I loved the challenge. Today there are new church groups in Iraq, Syria, and Jordan.

We began to realize that at some point, I would need a change of pace if I wanted to stay well. So after talks with Guy Davidson, our pastor Roy King, and Geoff Griffith, I did some Bible review and passed a pastoral ordination exam. I was ordained at the Calvary Church in Charlotte, North Carolina. Perhaps someday I could serve as a pastor somewhere.

From Charlotte I flew back to Ankara, Turkey. Jim Whitmer, the photographer, joined me in Frankfurt, Germany. We talked about what we would see and do and how we would schedule the work. The big unknown was transportation, but we needed photos. I talked with George Verwer, president of OM, about the opportunities that helping the refugees presented. I explained that if properly done, it would open new doors for Christian service. He agreed and soon had over 30 OM workers in Turkey and Iraq.

In Ankara we met with Sheppie Abramowitz, now the embassy coordinator for refugee affairs. She welcomed us warmly and asked how she could assist. Donald C. Mullen, M.D., from World Medical Missions came with us, and with Sheppie's help, he soon went on his way to Zakho, Iraq, where a large NATO base and a big refugee camp had grown up. I also asked Sheppie for help in moving about northern Iraq; it was still officially a war zone. She smiled and made a phone call. Suddenly we had seats on a previously "fully booked" flight to Diyarbakir and got reservations at a hotel. Our party grew to three as Ken Isaacs joined the team.

We checked with the local U.S. embassy office in Diyarbakir and were told the ambassador had arranged helicopter transportation for the two days we would be in Iraq. What a way to go!

The Blackhawk helicopter roared through the canyons and over the plateaus at nearly 200 M.P.H. at 200 feet. "We fly combat operations here," the pilot explained as we whipped over the lip of a plateau, scattering people, sheep, chickens, and donkeys in a mud village. Leaving southeast Turkey, we were headed into Iraq.

When we reached the camp near Uludere, we saw an improved situation. We talked to refugees and aid workers. The refugees had an overall optimistic view that as the war damage and infrastructures destroyed by the Iraqi army got repaired, and as the Westerners provided security, they would go down from the mountains to their homes. That was our goal, too.

Down near Dohuk, Turkey, we met with Donald Mullen. He busily treated all kinds of ailments in a large tent. Thousands of tents had been erected, and a water supply system had been built for the returning Kurds.

We went to the huge military camp to spend the night. "You'll have to make your own bed," said the army sergeant, handing us folded cots and a blanket. He gave us a tent number and pointed toward the north of the camp, which was near the Iraqi town of Silopi. It was a long walk, but we found the tent with some empty spaces. As we wrestled with the cots, I wondered about our accommodations. Fortunately we weren't too far from the bath tent and toilets. The mess tent was nearby, too. We were very tired, but we had good, hot food.

Finally I was huddled in bed, dressed in all my clothes under my single army blanket. It got very cold, and we began to shiver. I had almost given up on sleep when a ranger patrol came in. An old sergeant saw my predicament. "Here," he said, handing me a padded sleeping bag liner.

It was a lifesaver, and I'm still grateful to him for the warm night's sleep.

After three days of reviewing the situation and getting some great photos, we caught an all-night bus to Ankara. It was a 14-hour ride, and along the way I picked up a great recipe for "Turkish Bus Stop Chicken" – chicken cooked with onions and lemon -- that I still use. They served it at every stop all night long.

Our trip had achieved all its goals. We had confirmed Dr. Mullen was set up, and we had reviewed the work in a variety of camps and projects. Jim Whitmer had taken great pictures as well. In Ankara we put Jim on the plane to Chicago, and I took Ken Isaacs to the embassy to get a new passport. He had lost his in one of the refugee camps. Again the embassy staff thanked us for our on-site evaluation.

Then I got good news. The previous February, I had accompanied my very pregnant daughter-in-law, Erin, on a flight from Addis Ababa, Ethiopia, to Germany. She had been on her way home to Ellensburg to have their first child. Drew had finished some work, and then, as the war closed in on Addis, he, too, had left for home. Now I got the word that I had become a grandfather! As soon as I got back to Carolina and did the reports and paperwork, Bev and I flew to meet Andrew III in Ellensburg.

A tree swayed gently in the warm October breeze. I had just enjoyed my 53rd birthday and become a grandfather. Robin Hayes, a friend I had made during the Hurricane Hugo effort, had invited me down to South Carolina to hunt deer on his private reserve, Salkehatchie, the great plantation. A squirrel chattered his protest to my intrusion into his territory. I had never hunted using a tree-climbing chair before and was up in the treetop, considering the realities of my situation. After three years and hundreds of trips to a wide variety of projects and countries, I was tired. I had discussed the situation with Bev and Matt, who still lived with us while he attended university. Our pastor, Roy King, Paul Branch, and the other elders listened and prayed with me as I decided to leave Samaritan's Purse. Guy Davidson encouraged me as well.

That morning in South Carolina, we had gone out at daybreak to set up our ambushes for deer. Robin came by at about 10:00 a.m. "Nothing is going to move now until evening," he called up to my nest, 40 feet above the ground. "Let's go to town."

I declined because it was restful up there. An hour later, I was reviewing future options when I heard "Crunch." I eased my dad's old Remington .270 around toward the sound and listened. More crunching. I heard something munching on hazelnuts that had fallen to the ground. Then I saw a movement...deer feet! They moved behind the brush and low branches, and then, from behind a tree about 100 yards away, a nose appeared. I looked through the scope and saw a nice buck. I concentrated, slipped off the safety, and shot him through the head. Meat!

Robin Hayes and the others came back from town at about noon, while I was skinning the deer. "I guess we quit hunting too soon!" Robin said with a grin.

I had gotten more than a deer. Up in the tree, a clearer picture of our future had begun to emerge. Although the decision to move on had been made a few weeks earlier, I had a better idea of how and where to go.

Matt with Greg Flessing filming hurricane
Gilbert relief work in Jamaica

Chapter 23
If We Knew Then What We Know Now ~ Part 1

Chapter 23.
If We Knew Then What
We Know Now ~ Part 1

Four of us eased a body bag onto the gurney from the funeral home. Next we took it through the house and down a long flight of stairs. The deceased was heavy, and the stairs were steep. The family stood silently, showing no emotion. One young man about 20 years old clutched a pistol that the dead man had kept under his pillow. Bev filled out papers with the coroner.

From time to time I was a hospice helper for Bev. The hill people of North Carolina liked her very much, as she would go anywhere at any time to help the dying. They often invited her to the wake, and always to the funeral. "We have to get another social life," I would say, but she smiled and we went.

I spent January 1992 developing Bishop Consulting Ltd., a personal venture. The work gave me the time we needed to rest and evaluate. I did a bit of travel to see clients and a lot of phone and fax work. I remember Charlie Morton's advice not to worry. He said, "If people don't follow advice, just make sure the check is good."

I could even turn down jobs.

Franklin Graham sent word, asking me to go to Russia. Guy Davidson advised against it, so I declined the offer. Then Peter Nanfelt called. I had already been to the CMA headquarters in Colorado Springs and discussed finding funds for some missions projects. Cliff Westergren became executive director for CAMA Services, so we also discussed finding funds for CAMA Services. "How about Christian and Missionary Alliance buying all your time and moving you here to Colorado?" Peter asked.

"It sounds good," I replied. "I'll pray about it and discuss it with Bev and call you back." Matt was a junior in the university and had just returned from a weekend with other MKs from his class at Dalat. They loved to meet spontaneously and fellowship wherever. We discussed the move. Bev loved her work, but perhaps she could join hospice in Colorado Springs.

We prepared to move and put our house up for sale. Matt was secure in school and could manage the house until it sold. I could easily do my work, especially since I would have only one client.

Bev and I flew to Colorado Springs. In a few short days, we signed a working agreement with the CMA, and Bev got hired by Hospice of Colorado Springs. We decided we would move in two stages. Bev would go out right away to start her work. As we drove across from North Carolina, we reviewed our lives and work and marveled at how God had sometimes led us into unusual situations, but always places where we were needed. We spent a day with my sister Audrey in Oklahoma City before driving on in Bev's four-wheel-drive Honda. Once she settled in Colorado, I returned to Boone to finish my current consulting contracts and pack for the move.

At the same time, I worked with CMA leaders to set up the first, by-invitation President's Briefing in Colorado Springs. I worked with names supplied by Duane Wheeland, vice president for finance and treasurer of the CMA -- people such as Walt Meloon, John Bechtel, Curt Anderson, Bill Chapin, Stanley Tam, and Scott Myers. They would hear firsthand from Dr. David Rambo, the CMA president; from vice presidents Duane Wheeland, Peter Nanfelt, and Richard Bailey; and from other staff about the goals of the CMA and how they were being pursued. At the end of the briefings and after lunch, a tour of the fairly new headquarters facility would be conducted. We planned a dinner in the evening and would encouraged the men to ask questions and give any advice they might have. All were CEOs and major CMA donors, and thus they could comment on their impressions as well as suggest ways to improve our management.

I charted a course in unknown waters for our CMA leaders. It involved a new level of openness and transparency. I was reminded more than once, "We never did something like this before."

That first President's Briefing was on February 25, 1992. As the presentations were made, it was clear that each of those participating was genuinely excited. At one point John Bechtel, a former CMA missionary and MK who now works for the DeMoss Foundation, reacted to Peter Nanfelt's presentation on ways he evaluated performance and measured the progress of the work and workers overseas with "Praise the Lord, it's about time!"

Following the dinner, we received a number of compliments on how we had been doing things. One guest wanted to know if Duane Wheeland would share his secret for making such good returns on investments. Probably the most-telling vindication of the briefing was made by Stanley Tam, president of United States Plastics. He said, "I've been in the Christian and Missionary Alliance 59 years. Each year I give my tithe and pay my missionary pledge. In addition, I give over $1 million to other missions because they invite me to speak and participate in their work. This is the first time I have ever been invited to even visit our CMA headquarters!"

Duane Wheeland, one of my supporters on this new venture, gave me a big smile.

When asked by one staffer, "When do we ask these guys for money?" I replied, "We don't; they've already given."

We did, however, give each man a list of current projects needing funds. All the men voluntarily repaid the CMA for their expenses, and several large checks came in for projects. Over the next few weeks, I followed up with letters and visits to the corporate offices of our guests. In spite of resistance from some of the headquarters staff, we scheduled another President's Briefing for July 17, 1992.

On July 13, one of my fellow elders in Boone, Dr. Gerald Parker, and I finished loading the moving van, sent it off to Colorado, and began the drive to the Springs. Dr. Parker taught at Appalachian State University and was a great friend and confidant. We talked as we made our way across the states. Once in Colorado, he, along with his nephew, attended the second President's Briefing. Like the first, it exceeded our expectations.

While I communicated with foundations in the U.S., Canada, and Europe regarding the funding of projects, Bev and I unpacked in our new apartment. She kept a busy schedule with the Hospice of Colorado Springs. Several interesting job offers surfaced from my consulting, but we happily stayed with the work for the CMA. We were both convinced that anything of lasting value in relief, development, and evangelism had to be done through the church. Duane Wheeland and I worked out an itinerary that would mean a long road trip to visit all the guests who had been at the President's Briefings and some other major donors who had not come.

~

I made one stop in Ohio to see Scott Myers and his brother Dana. Scott had gone to Colorado and enjoyed the briefing. He and Dana made a major gift to buy Jesus films and projectors for missionaries to use on several CMA fields. I had actually met them first when they were teenagers in Akron. I had stayed at their home while on missionary tour. When their dad passed away, they took over the multi-million-dollar S.D. Myers Company and directed significant profits to the Lord's work.

We sat in their boardroom and talked missions and strategies. I had already been to several donors, including Patricia Wynalda of the Wynalda Foundation. With the Myerses, a new subject came up. "What do you know about the new evangelism efforts in Russia?" Dana asked.

"Not much," I replied. "I've heard some things and that there are opportunities. I know the CMA is studying the situation for possible involvement there."

Dana responded, "Well, a group wants us to give them a million dollars for a program there, but we don't know if their efforts will include results like evangelism and church planting. Those are the results we want to see."

"So," I said, "send one of your staff with an outline of priorities and goals you want to achieve, and ask the questions there."

We discussed some general concepts and finished our meeting. I drove on to New York to see Dick Chapin in Watertown. His dad had patents on drip irrigation that Aart van Wingerden used all over the world. Their factory produced a major percentage of the drip systems, and Dick had come to the briefing. He, too, was excited about CAMA Services developments and opportunities to use their drip irrigation on our mission fields.

I had also made stops with John Bechtel in Pennsylvania and Stanley Tam in Ohio, plus a few others.

"Andy, you had a call from Scott Myers in Ohio," Bev said in a home-front briefing. We finished our conversation, and I returned Scott's call.

"Andy, we want you to go to Russia to do this evaluation for us," he said. "Paul Eshelman of Campus Crusade and head of the Jesus film project is going to visit the new project, and we want you to travel with him on September 12, 1992."

Surprised, I answered, "I'll ask my boss, Bob Reed, and get back to you."

My mind went into overdrive. Bev and I had been planning a getaway to a retreat in Durango, Colorado, owned by our friend Jim Neece from Ellensburg. Bev was about to celebrate her 53rd birthday and our 30th anniversary. Well, we would have a lot to talk about.

After some discussion, Bob Reed agreed to the trip. After all, it didn't cost the CMA anything except some of my time, and it would add to the research data the Alliance had been collecting on Russia. "Okay, Scott," I said, "I'll do it, but I want to know your expectations and the plan. Please fax it to me in Colorado. I'll be there soon."

Bev and I were both excited about the trip. My mother's parents had left Russia in 1900. They were Volga Germans who had fled the czar's pressures and pogroms. Mother never told us much, but I had heard stories about my grandfather's being a blacksmith at the Kremlin and Grandmother's sewing dresses for the ladies of the czar's court. I had already passed up an opportunity to do a job in Russia, but this one seemed to have a clear push from the Lord.

Over the next few weeks, I kept busy writing proposals for funding evangelism and development, plus holding meetings with donors to answer questions and urge their participation. Then I flew to North Carolina. Matt was doing a good job caring for the house, but we needed to find a buyer. The bank extended our note for a year, and at the realtor's suggestion, Matt prepared to move out so the house could be better shown and sold.

I told our former pastor there, Roy King, "Roy, I'd like you, Gerald Parker, and the other elders to pray for me. This trip to Russia seems to be more than just another consulting project."

Roy was not only one of the best Bible teachers I had known, but also a steadfast friend. Dr. Parker and Paul Branch were close friends, too.

"Well, Andy, let's go to Moscow," said Paul Eshelman. He was warm and excited about the project that had been named The CoMission. He had been showing the Jesus film all over Russia using a "Hollywood premiere"-type strategy to generate excitement and get high-ranking officials to attend. This went on during the final years of communism in the Soviet Union. The strategy and the film were well received.

In 1986, the Politburo of the communist party's Central Committee met to evaluate their situation. Communism was dying, bankrupt, and increasingly unable to govern. A special commission was sent out to find governments that worked. The Russian mind, being technical, felt they could simply decree a new path to control their decline and begin to recover. What the researchers found, however, created consternation among the leaders. The governments that worked and had their people's support were those founded on Judeo-Christian principles.

What to do? Communism denied the existence of God. The leaders concluded that, although it was too late for the older generation, they could teach their children and build a new order.

The minister of education was ordered to look into what to do. He began to seek information. How can atheists teach people about Christian morals and ethics? Years later Dr. Alexei Brudnov, the Russian director of alternative education, told a small group, "One evening I came home from a hard day at the office, flipped on the television, and saw the last few moments of the Jesus film. It so caught my attention that the next day I went to see it at a theater in Moscow." He paused and continued, "I have only cried two times in my life: Once when my father died, and once when they crucified Jesus. That night I became a believer."

He was a key to the Russian door's opening for The CoMission.

God had been at work. Many groups sought ways to take religion to Russia. They included groups like the Billy Graham team, but also groups such as the Mormons and the Moonies.

Paul Eshelman prayed for Russia as he attended a Mission 2000 Conference in Singapore. As he described the burden for Russia, a strategy evolved to evangelize and disciple teachers first and then reach students through them. During Paul's stopover in Mongolia, the Lord impressed upon him that he should stop in Moscow and seek a meeting with ministry of education officials. When he did so, he found that not only were they willing to meet with him, but they eagerly sought his help. They had come to the realization that a Christian morals and ethics curriculum must be added to the standard school curriculum as quickly as possible.

As our flight now cruised along to Russia, Paul told me that he was amazed and shaken by the enormity of the opportunity and the challenge it presented. He knew that up to 40 percent of the Russian population had seen the Jesus film and that more than 7,000 had written in, asking for follow-up literature on Christianity. Russian churches reported many times more contacts, but the lack of trained staff was acute. Now the opportunity was being presented to reach 130,000 schools! Paul had sought help from other Christian agencies.

He told me that a group of Christian educators already had the curriculum under development and that a number of Christian groups had joined together to form The CoMission. They included Campus Crusade, Walk Thru the Bible, the Navigators, the Association of Christian Schools International, and others. Before the project was done, 84 churches, missions, and para church groups would join in to implement this tremendous undertaking for the Lord.

Paul said they had been testing the concept and materials in Russia for a year and a half. They began with convocations at which American staff and teachers met with Russian educators to present the curriculum called "Character Development" or "Christian Ethics and Morality, a Foundation for Society." Although the curriculum and supporting materials were still under development, 14 convocations had been held with an average attendance of 400 teachers and administrators. The feedback showed that 48 percent of attendees had made decisions for Christ, 90 percent had promised to teach the materials, 96 percent had said they would show the Jesus film, and 80 percent had said they would attend follow-up Bible classes.

Paul was ecstatic about the results and the prospect of 40 more convocations that had been requested all over Russia and the Confederation of Independent States, the old Soviet Union. In addition, several groups, including Walk Thru the Bible, were busily translating materials for the video-based training program.

I told Paul about my Russian roots. At one point in our discussion he said, "Andy, you should be in Russia with this program."

"I'll see what the CMA decides," I replied.

It was a new idea for me.

At the airport, the long line of travelers inched its way through the dimly lit reception hall and down dark stairs to the passport control booths. Now and then someone cut into line and flashed something to the stern officers, who usually waved him through. As our passports slid into the slot for examination by the unsmiling officer, I thought, This is just like Checkpoint Charlie in Berlin over 20 years ago. Communism might have been on the decline, but the attitudes had yet to go.

We got our suitcases and passed the scrutiny of customs' officers who x-rayed everything, studied our declaration slips, and finally waved us on into the shabby reception area. A throng of cab drivers pressed in, offering their form of transportation. Brian Birdsall stepped out of the crowd and shouted, "Welcome to Moscow!"

His smile was the first we had seen since leaving the plane. He was a Campus Crusade team leader and had been overseeing the test phase of the program in the schools. He was also one of the key men setting up the convocations. He filled Paul in on the project's progress and soon had us in our hotel. I wrote notes for a while and thought, Russia, here I am. What's next?

We had a busy time visiting schools and talking to teachers where the curriculum was being tested. The materials, called New Life by Campus Crusade, generated real excitement. Fifteen teachers discussed their opinions at a follow-up conference. Some had traveled more than three hours by bus and subway to attend. That in itself said a lot to me.

Irina, principal of school #813, said that Christian thought has been a part of Russian history and culture for more than a thousand years. She was happy to return to Christian ethics and morality. She loved the teaching model and materials and said that teachers had to get more training. She knew that many facets of communism came from Christianity, but they excluded God, so it could not work. She said the society was in turmoil and short of finances, but she wanted her school to become a model for the others to see how the curriculum worked.

Natalie, one of the other teachers, said the teaching had made a change in her life and in her students. Marina, another teacher, had begun to read the Bible on her own, but the convocation showed her what it meant to her personally. She also told of changed attitudes among her students.

One principal said, "Years ago I decided there is a God; the convocation led me to know Him in my life. I knew I was worthless, but

God brought tears to my eyes. I told my husband I loved Jesus more than him. I lived so long without God, and I know I must teach the children about Him. The young must learn to believe; the teenagers are harder to convince."

Several schools had already shown the Jesus film. In one, more than a thousand children had seen it! All the teachers had been changed by their experience with the film and curriculum. Paul Eshelman promised to do the follow-up teaching as soon as people could be trained.

I was stunned by the open hunger for Jesus expressed by the Russian educators. This was the evil empire we had feared for so many Cold War years. They were people just like us, and they were eager for the truth that had been denied them during the 74 years of communism.

Andy and Bev Bishop

To Russia with Love. Suddenly being sent to
Siberia takes on a whole new meaning

Andrew III, Andrew II, Erin and Matt
in Ellenburg seeing us off for Russia

Harry and Mirian Taylor, Andy, Evelyn and
Grady Mangham. Suporters for our Russian work

Chapter 24
If We Knew Then What We Know Now ~ Part 2

Chapter 24.
If We Knew Then What
We Know Now ~ Part 2

Americans on their way to Orlyonok, a youth camp on the Black Sea, loaded themselves onto an old IL-62 Russian airliner. Paul Eshelman and I were going to a convocation. The American teachers who volunteered had raised $3,000 apiece and would spend two weeks in Russia, helping Russian teachers understand how to use the curriculum. Seventy-five of us got on the charter flight.

I noticed the airplane looked a bit ragged, not many seat belts worked, and several seat backs could not be latched in any position. The crew seemed unconcerned as they slammed the doors until they held, then fired up the engines and headed south.

The "camp" was on a beach, about three hours from the resort town of Sochi. Though not well maintained, the permanent facilities were adequate. Nearly 500 teachers, administrators, and government officials attended, and Dr. Alexander Asmolov, vice minister for education of the Russian Federation, led. One official was the director of the Moscow State University Teacher's Training Institute. Thirty-six of the 50 senior directors of school districts from across Russia came. Sixty of the group held Ph.D. degrees.

Group sessions were led by men such as Dr. Udo Middleman, Francis Schaeffer's son-in-law and director of the Francis Schaeffer Foundation. He was also a theologian at King's College. His presentations were everyone's favorites as he laid a clear foundation for concise Christian thought and Christianity as a foundation for a moral society. The attendees who heard him through one of Russia's best translators could not get enough of his discussions and answers to their questions.

Several of the government officials, including Dr. Asmolov, made presentations explaining the government's decision to add this Bible-based curriculum to the Russian school system. While stressing it was a voluntary subject for the schools, he left no doubt that Moscow strongly encouraged its use.

It was a tough crowd in some ways. Dr. Asmolov spoke about the "Soviet man" communism had created and the need for change. His statement on what they had created in the past was telling. He said that in separating church and state and teaching atheism, they had lost the compassion and mercy they must have for a just society. Studies had shown the effects of the indoctrination approach to education: "By age seven, children in Russian schools have lost their capacity for joy, and by age eight the qualities of compassion and giving. To recover from this situation," he said, "we must de-communize education and return basic humanity to our society. Christian Morals and Ethics is the place to start."

He was interrupted by stomping and shouts of, "We did what Moscow told us to do, now you tell us it's all wrong! What do you want us to do now?"

"Now," he responded, "we have democracy. You have to decide. Even this new curriculum is an option, as is the Christianity we are discussing!"

'Decisions' were a new option for Russians. Many told me they felt very uncomfortable making decisions.

As the week progressed and the truth of God's love penetrated people's minds, their comments changed. The teachers and officials made statements such as, "We have always been indoctrinated in the communist way. Change is hard, but the love and compassion shown this week by these professionals from America give us hope."

One person said, "We have much to learn, and Christian principles must be taught early and often. Our children are our future!"

An older man said, "We are seeing humanity versus ideology; we are seeing a new way to live. This week we have had deeply intellectual presentations, sparkling examples, and a level of personal concern we have not known before. I have taught atheism for 40 years. Your antimaterialistic information, given with love and example, shows me we need this curriculum in our schools if we are to achieve real change. We need Dr. Middleman's lectures to teach."

He got a round of applause as he sat back down.

"This was a wonderful time to be with my fellow administrators," said another, "and the family life sessions taught me to be a real husband. We became better people through this conference!"

Such comments reflected genuine change in attitudes and concepts, and by the weekend, after seeing the Jesus film, more than 200 expressed new faith in Christ. I have seen the Lord work in people in all kinds of venues -- refugee camps, mass evangelism, war zones, famine follow-up, and so on. I have never seen such eager response to the moving of the Holy Spirit as I saw in Russia.

An administrator from central Siberia said, in some closing remarks, "Just as a building is made of individual bricks, so are we as parts of society. We must become better. You taught us we are unique individual beings, not just a mass. We learned a new language, the language of love…. It is beautiful. When can you come to Siberia to teach us more?"

"We must continue to improve," said another attendee. "Thank you for the Christian patience to help us. For 70 years we were legally separated from God. Lenin's wife put the Bible on the banned book list, but we should not makes excuses for ourselves. Now we can choose!"

Many had not yet experienced the open, interactive teaching approach. They had all been using the indoctrination-by-rote-learning method, which as they explained was dehumanizing. Fortunately, Walk Thru the Bible translated a video, "Teaching with Style." It became one of the most widely used pieces of The CoMission program.

As the week wound down, Dr. Blair Cook, a convocation director, announced that the equipment and materials used there would equip the cultural center at the Orlyonok youth camp with the Christian Morals and Ethics program. It would be available to the more than 20,000 youth per year who came through the camp. The CoMission hoped to eventually equip all 63,000 cultural centers across Russia with the equipment and materials. People cheered!

An old soldier told us his story with tears in his eyes. He had been in the rocket forces, and during the fueling of his rocket situated on the Russian Pacific coast, an explosion was accidentally triggered. He lost both legs below the knee, one arm, and part of his remaining hand. He explained that they had been keeping American B-52s from entering to attack Russia. I assured him we had mainly been trying to get them to turn on their defensive radar so we could record their frequencies. Then if we did need to attack, we would know what frequencies to jam. It was an unusual moment because he had been in military service from 1956-60, the same time as I had.

The discussion turned to the here and now. Paul Eshelman had been invited by the old man's grandson, who said his grandfather was seeking answers. The old man rambled a bit: "What is happening to us? We did the best we could. Communism would have been successful if Stalin had killed more rich people!"

Paul explained Campus Crusade's four spiritual laws to him as he clutched a Bible he had gotten by writing to the Slavic Gospel Mission. "I've done too much wrong for God to forgive," he moaned. "Everything I believed, fought for, and even lost my limbs for is now wrong. I've wasted my whole life! How can God forgive this?"

He begged us to pray with him, and we did. After tea we prayed again. In tears his grandson begged us to come again to pray with him. There was no question that God's kairos moment for Russia had come.

As the Lufthansa flight to Germany lifted off from Moscow's Sheremetyevo airport, I looked down for my last glimpse of Russia. I had no way of knowing if or when I would see it again, but the experience of the days there had given me a burning desire to see the cry of the Russian heart for God satisfied. In my report to the CMA called "Operation Philip," I cited Acts 8:30-31, in which Philip asked the Ethiopian who read the Scripture out loud while riding in his chariot, "Do you understand what you are reading?"

The Ethiopian replied, "How can I unless someone explains it to me?"

I closed my report by urging the CMA leadership to join The CoMission as a sending agency and recruit teachers to go for the one-year experience as a first step in reaching Russia with the gospel.

While The CoMission had excellent educators and para church leaders, it clearly needed long-term follow-up. I reminded the CMA leaders that Alliance church planters were ideal to achieve the ultimate goal of the harvest. "When Marco Polo came back from his travels to China, he brought a request from Kublai Khan, grandson of Genghis Khan and ruler of China, that missionaries teach Christianity in China. The pope failed to respond, and the window of opportunity closed. When the U.S. occupied Japan after World War II, General MacArthur asked for thousands of missionaries to flood Japan to teach Christ and help heal the nation. Too little was done too late. In 1914, Czar Nicholas of Russia asked for missionaries. That, too, was an opportunity missed." We had now been given an opportunity in Russia again, and we must not fail.

On the way home, I stopped in Holland to see Jan van Barneveld and then went to visit the Help for Brothers Foundation in Stuttgart, Germany. We had good discussions about the project proposals for CMA work in various parts of the world. From there I flew to Paris, where I met with Bob Reed and David Kennedy. They were fascinated with what had transpired in Russia and cheered the $200,000 commitment from the Help for Brothers Foundation.

Bev typed my report and had a lot of good questions and thoughts. I made copies for the Myers brothers who had paid for the trip, then sent copies to the CMA leadership, including each member of the Board of Managers, our main governing body. They planned to hold a meeting soon after, and I hoped Russia would be on the agenda. Later I learned it had suddenly been added. A wide variety of people read and discussed the report.

Back in Colorado, I continued my work with donors and the travel it involved. I got some good feedback from Paul Eshelman and Brian Birdsall. Russia just kept coming up among the staff at Colorado Springs, and it was often on our minds.

"Andy," Bev said one morning, waking me for a "talk."

It was 2:00 a.m., and I was groggy. "What?" I responded.

Bev blurted, "I think we should go to Russia."

Shock? Well, surprise for sure. "But," I replied sleepily, "we just had our thirtieth anniversary, and you said 26 addresses in 30 years was enough! I thought you loved your hospice work."

"I do," she said, "but every time I pray, Russia is there. Your family has roots there. I think we need to go there, too."

"If CMA goes to Russia, we will need you here, helping raise the money," Peter Nanfelt said.

Peter, Vice President of Overseas Ministries, wrestled with the directive from the Board of Managers that the CMA go to Russia as soon as possible. I had just explained that Bev and I felt God's pull to Russia. Peter wanted us to reconsider. When I told Bev about our conversation, she was not satisfied. We had never felt we should just go off and do our own thing in Christian service. Some had urged us to start our own agency, but we were always drawn to the church, not only for support and encouragement, but also for the long-term follow-up for God's kingdom. We also appreciated the accountability and continuity that a church-based ministry provides. So we prayed some more.

The snow was deep and getting deeper. We were near Gunnison, Colorado, hunting deer and elk. Duane Wheeland and his dad, Gordon McAlister, and I stood by the roaring fire we had built to warm up. We had seen game and chased about, but with the snow falling, a safe shot was hard to come by. I enjoyed the time even without getting anything. We talked about things, and I got some good input on a possible course of action.

On November 2, 1992, Russia still had not left our minds. I'd had a second discussion with Peter Nanfelt, and we were told that the CMA planned to begin placing personnel in Russia within a year. Perhaps we could go then. Bev still wasn't satisfied, but I was hopeful. Now, as we men talked in the woods, I began to feel something was about to happen. It would be our last get-together for a while.

I made another road tour to consult and encourage donors, and then Bev's parents, Percy and Wilene Dean, came to spend Thanksgiving with us. Matt came in from Boone. Drew and his family, who worked for World Relief refugee services, couldn't join us.

We drove to Boone the first week of December 1992. Matt graduated December 6 with his bachelor's degree in business. We had good fellowship with Roy King, Gerald and Mary Parker, Paul and Wanda Branch, Ed and Becky Williams, and Ed's brother, J.D. Williams. They were close friends and offered prayer support and counsel as we continued to think about Russia.

As we began 1993, I wrote in my Day-Timer, "Lord, we do not know what to do. Our eyes are upon You!" The next day our phone rang. Roy

King, our pastor and friend from Boone, said, "Andy, we want you to meet us in Phoenix for a meeting with The CoMission. Gerald Parker and some of his family are going, and since you have been to Russia, we'd like your perspective."

On January 3, I drove to Phoenix through a lot of snow, but with a certain feeling of anticipation. Bev had to work, so she stayed in Colorado and prayed.

A large interdenominational group gathered in Phoenix. Dr. Asmolov of the Russian ministry of education came with another deputy, Dr. Olga Polykovskaya. Bruce Wilkinson, president and CEO of Walk Thru the Bible and chairman of The CoMission, came as well, and together they conducted the sessions. Their presentation explained the plan to take the Christian Morals and Ethics curriculum to Russia. Drs. Asmolov and Polykovskaya gave an urgent appeal to help Russia at this critical moment in its history. Their passion for their country was evident, especially when they likened their people to someone about to go over a waterfall and calling for the help that Christians in America could give.

Bruce Wilkinson was fired up. He told the crowd that he had come to feel like Elisha calling for a blessing from Elijah as the chariot took him to heaven. He said, "My coattails got caught in this chariot, and we as an organization are going to Russia. We will provide ten of our staff per year, continue to translate Walk Thru the Bible materials into Russian, and do all we can with God's help to make this effort succeed. How about you?"

Then he brought out a big whiteboard and began to write the names of organizations who had already joined The CoMission. "How many will you send this year?" he asked.

He exhorted the crowd. J.B. Crouse, president of Overseas Mission Society, called out a number, and Bruce wrote it down. Terry Taylor, president of the Navigators, called a number, and Bruce wrote it down. Bruce added the Walk Thru the Bible number, and so it went. By the time Bruce had finished, more than 900 people were committed to The CoMission in Russia. Excitement was high. Bruce called The CoMission executive board into a special session right then. They had work to do.

I was excited, too, but also tired from my long drive. After greeting Dr. Asmolov, whom I had met in Russia, and being introduced to Dr.

Polykovskaya, I went to the room I shared with Roy King to get some sleep. Not long after I closed my eyes, Roy came in and snapped on the light. "Andy, get up," he said. "We need to pray."

It was 11:00 p.m., and I was groggy. "What are we praying about?" I asked.

"Oh, we just need to pray," he answered evasively.

Suddenly I was wide awake, because I knew something was going on. "When Sami Dagher says that in Beirut, I know we're in trouble, Roy. Now, what are we praying about?"

He replied, "The CoMission leaders are challenged. They have all these people committed for Russia starting this summer, and there isn't anything in place to implement the program yet. In the morning, they're going to ask you and Bev to go to Russia to help make this happen!"

Wow! Now we knew what to pray for, and we did.

About midnight, I phoned Bev. When I explained what was happening, she didn't hesitate. "Let's do it," she said.

"We'll have to raise our support, get the CMA to assign us, and things like that, so you pray," I replied.

I didn't get much sleep after that. I met with the board for breakfast. After they described the job and the need to be in Russia in 90 days, I agreed with the caveat that I would have to get the CMA on board. We prayed, and I had that "things are about to change" feeling. We would go for the whole five years the project was set for. We needed to get five years of support committed and leave for Russia in 90 days with the Alliance's blessing.

God was already at work, as usual. In a few short hours, Peter Nanfelt had agreed to a special assignment, with CMA as our sending agency. We could put our donations through them and keep our CMA pension and health insurance intact.

What about our support? Where to start? I had just discussed these things with the Lord when Ronald Parker, Gerald's nephew, stopped me and said, "I'm so glad you and Bev are going to join The CoMission. We just gave Overseas Mission Society a half million dollar commitment on the strength of that."

"Well," I responded, "you'd better pray we find our support money; we've never raised personal funds before. I don't even know where to start."

He didn't miss a beat. "We will provide one quarter of your support for five years," he said with a smile.

Wow, God was busy! We needed to receive $40,000 each year, and it was happening.

Before long, a note from Patricia and Robert Wynalda added another $5,000 per year, and several others made pledges as well. Scott Myers invited me to Akron, Ohio, and his family committed $10,000 per year, plus gave me a check for $10,000 to help with the incidentals of getting moved to Russia. "You're the first missionary I've seen get a signing bonus," said Duane Wheeland as he went over the letters pledging our support. Five years of funding was committed.

I was so thankful for what God was doing. In February 1993, I stayed busy attending speaking engagements, planning the move, and helping Bev begin packing. We planned to store our stuff in Ellensburg. Our friends the Dyks and Onstots offered to truck the boxes and furniture to storage at Kathy Mee's home.

The CMA progressed, too. Fred Smith was appointed The CoMission coordinator for the Alliance, and Phil Skellie planned to move to Russia to be a CMA in-country team leader. He had been CAMA Services director in Thailand and did a great job there.

My boss on The CoMission board was Paul Johnson. A successful businessman from Detroit, he was also chairman of the board for Walk Thru the Bible. He organized a job description for the Arrangements Committee, which would handle the logistics of bringing teachers to Russia, supplying all their materials, supporting them, and getting them home again. This also involved negotiations with schools, government officials, and suppliers of a wide range of things from TV/VCRs and washing machines to water filters.

We would have logistical support from Mission Aviation Fellowship (MAF) and its partners, Transport for Christ. We met on February 9 in Detroit to move the plan along. Bob Gordon from MAF came, along with some others. We planned a quick trip to Moscow to find an office and get better acquainted with conditions there. Serge Duss, a friend from World Vision, came to help with contacts, and Paul Johnson said he would have my job description soon.

We titled our newsletter *'To Russia with Love'*, which let everyone in on the plan. We put a red stamp on the outside of the mailer that said, "Suddenly, being sent to Siberia has taken on a whole new meaning." Our supporters were as excited as we were. Volunteers for The CoMission multiplied. By March 7, 1992, we closed out our apartment and shipped our things to Ellensburg.

Our local church in Colorado Springs gave us a nice farewell and commissioning service, and we delivered our cars to buyers. We flew to Seattle to stay with Bev's parents while the final details were completed. We also had a full speaking schedule to keep up within the U.S. and Canada. Daryl Brooks, our long time Canadian friend, not only gave generously to our work, but he also pledged to handle any extra expenses we encountered. We even had a visit from David and Samuelle Soquier from Paris. They had just moved to Vancouver, British Columbia.

It was cold, and ice was everywhere. On March 21, 1992, I landed in Moscow to look for an office, talk with various organizations already working there, and prepare the way for our next step. I looked into the dimly lit arrival area for Vlad Gagaryshev, the man who was to drive me to the World Vision apartment in town. People kept muttering, "Taxi, taxi," and, failing to see my contact, I began to bargain with a fellow who spoke some English. Having been in Moscow before, I had an idea what the trip should cost, so we settled for $35, about half the opening bid, for the 45-minute drive.

Bob Gordon of MAF had already arrived. It surprised him that Vlad had not been there to meet me. Bob had met him while with MAF in Mozambique. Vlad had impressed Bob with his good attitude and initiative.

Suddenly the doorbell rang. I opened it to see a Russian man in his late forties. "Oh," he said, "you are here. I looked for you at the airport, but you were too fast coming through customs."

Vlad spoke excellent English, and we agreed to an early morning pick-up the next day to go looking for an office and meet people.

The next day I discovered that Peter Deyneka had left the country, but his wife, Anita, was very helpful. We had both gone to Seattle Pacific College and had Washington state in common. Brian Birdsall caught me up on the New Life and CoMission activities. He heard that the convocation office was being moved, so we made an appointment to see their old one on Monday. Sunday I enjoyed the international service at a church called The Rock. They had good music, a good message, and warm fellowship.

"Moscow has three seasons," Vlad explained, "summer, winter, and mud." It was still winter, but mud began to emerge.

The office we had been told about was on the twelfth floor of an 18-story apartment building at metro stop Konkova. It had been used for convocations for the last year. Jerry Franks, from the Association of Christian Schools International and the convocation's executive, arranged for us to pay three months' rent. We had an office! It also came with a phone, which was vital. Next came the mailing address. Serge Duss offered us coffee and Dunkin' Donuts! "It's a new service," he said, smiling. "You fax in an order by 4:00 p.m., and by 8:00 a.m. the next morning fresh Dunkin' Donuts are at the door."

I saw Russian entrepreneurs everywhere, offering every imaginable service.

At Serge's suggestion, we drove to an office that offered direct mail service through an address in New York. We signed up and now had The CoMission office, phone, and address in Moscow and New York! Over dinner with Serge and Donna Duss, I received a lot of good information and advice. They had been in Russia for a while and knew the ups and downs and what to watch for. However, they were being transferred to the World Vision office in Washington, D.C.

Since we would not have time for language study, I sought a good working partner. As Vlad and I traveled around, I found him to be ideal. His experience and wisdom, along with his sense of humor, were what we needed to make the project go. MAF had introduced us, so I knew they would have first call on his employment, but when I asked him, he said they used him only now and then for taxi service. As we drove to the airport a few days later, I said, "Vlad, think about working with me full-time when we come back next month."

"I will do that," he answered.

From Moscow I flew back to Boston, where I met Bev. We drove to New Hampshire, where our friend Peter Hoekstra hosted us at his church's mission conference. Between appearances, I finalized a report and a preliminary budget for The CoMission's Moscow office. We clearly saw God at work and knew we were going where He wanted us. What a ride!

Our apartment in Moscow is comfortable

Negotiating for CoMission teams to teach
in Russia. Lots of food and toasts.

Russian train travel is not for the faint of heart.
You never know who you'll 'room' with.

Bev at -40° f. Her breath freezes on her hair and fur hat.

Chapter 25
Russia

Chapter 25.
Russia

Bev and I were tired and thankful for the sofa we used as a bed. It was a common piece of Russian furniture that, like their easy chairs, folded down to become a bed. We had finished a whirlwind departure from America that included a few days in Boone with the Kings, Parkers, Williamses, Pilkingtons, Branches, O'Briens, and several others. Matt, who still lived there, assured us he would come to see us as his work allowed, and we flew off to Holland.

In Holland, our favorite country, we enjoyed time with Jan van Barneveld, Adriaan Stringer, and his son Paul, who had served with us in Thailand in the late 1980s (along with his wife, Elena). We even saw Henk van der Velde, our long-time friend and the founding president of ZOA -- Zuid Oost Azië, a relief organization in the Netherlands. Jan took us to SAREPTA, a purchasing and shipping company from which we purchased supplies to be shipped to us in Moscow.

We enjoyed a visit to Saaksumhuizen, where we lived for a year in 1979, and had breakfast with Janni Loman, who had been our secretary in Groningen. We ate at an old favorite restaurant for our boys, *Het Pannekoekenschip*, a pancake restaurant in an old canal boat.

Bev was nervous as we passed through the gloomy arrival hall in Moscow's Sheremetyevo airport, but Vladimir "Vlad" Gagaryshev was there and gave us a warm welcome. While driving to our temporary home -- a small flat belonging to Jerry Franks, the convocation executive – Vlad pointed out a huge sculpture. It commemorated where the Russians had halted the German army as it tried to take Moscow in World War II. We would see many such memorials of the "Great Patriotic War" during our five years in Russia.

The roads were pot holed and grimy with mud and slush from melting snow. Buildings were in poor repair, and even the newly constructed apartment towers had a worn, used look. Bev said that the country looked "distressed," as if the architects wanted even new structures to look old.

Jerry Franks's small two-room apartment was in a five-story building known as a Khrushevniki. The Khrushevnikis were erected by the thousands during Nikita Khrushchev's regime as temporary housing while "modern" high-rise structures were planned and built. Many were still in use 40 years later. Jerry's building did have a small elevator; it shuddered and creaked to our floor. We finally got our luggage inside and, after a snack of bread and cheese, tumbled into the sofa bed.

Boom! Pop! Pop! Pop! Flashes and more explosions shook our building. "What is that?" Bev asked, frightened.

I wasn't too happy either. "I hope we haven't moved into another war," I said as I slipped out of bed and crawled to the window.

Pop! Pop! Pop! Explosions followed by what sounded like small-arms fire continued, accompanied by multicolored flashes of light.

I peeped gingerly over the cement window ledge. What? Fireworks! In every direction, they rose above Moscow in the biggest fireworks display I had seen in a long time. Bev came over gingerly to look out with me. What a show! What a welcome to Russia! Vlad told us the next day that we had arrived on April 12, President's Day.

Bev was glad that she had just read Jeremiah 45, because she said she had some complaints for God, too. Our first walk in the neighborhood was not encouraging. We saw mud, broken sidewalks where there were sidewalks at all, and dimly lit stores. Some stores were concretions of shabby goods, and others were shipping containers with small windows through which shopkeepers handed your goods to you. Before receiving your goods, though, you had to wait in a long line at another counter to pay. Trucks sat with their back doors open, and cars with their trunk lids up displayed items for sale. The "gas stations" were usually fuel trucks of questionable origin, parked by the road.

Bev went out with Vlad our second day there and came home a bit baffled. She had found some boots but wasn't sure about purchasing them. Vlad had urged her to buy them, knowing they wouldn't be there long. Sure enough, when she went back later, they were gone.

We went out with Vlad for lunch. The restaurant scene was almost nonexistent. After we ordered something, the waiter would usually say, "We don't have that today."

Vlad suggested, "Just ask, what is good today?"

It worked, and if you didn't have preconceived ideas about what you had planned to eat, the food usually tasted okay. This meal, however, was at a hotel, so we had a nice multi course feast of sliced ham, bread, and olives, followed by coleslaw, vegetable soup, fried veggies, and Chicken Kiev. For dessert there was ice cream with sauce and strong coffee. Since it was the Moscow Radisson Hotel, the variety was better than at most hotel dining rooms or cafeterias.

One time about noon, when Vlad and I were out and about, we stopped at a restaurant. The sign said, "Closed for lunch!" When I asked what was going on, Vlad answered, "Oh, they won't open until the staff has eaten."

The reasons for the failure of communism were clearly emerging.

We did some "store browsing" to figure out just what was available. On my first visit in 1992 and again in March 1993, I noted that many things needed for daily living could be bought in Russia if one were persistent. This saved CoMissioners a lot of money. Bev bought an iron for pressing clothes for $6. The clerk plugged it in first to be sure it worked. This was a test we got used to. Even light bulbs were taken out of the box for a test before we paid for them. Their current was 220 volts, so it was better to use their electrical items than bring ours from America.

Bev got a hair dryer for $3, then an electric heater and other small appliances. They came with a two-year warranty, and more than once we found the warranty was good. When something malfunctioned, the clerk simply took back the unit, brought out another, checked it out, and handed it to us without comment.

Bev and I had a few Russian lessons and a handy language book. We learned the Cyrillic alphabet, and by the end of the first week we were using a map of their huge metro system and could travel about the city quite well.

The beauty and cleanliness of the underground stations impressed us the most. Each had statues, chandeliers, and murals in mosaics of history and valor by Russians. We accessed the metro by going through grubby entrances, which led to huge, long escalators that descended as far as 300 to 400 feet underground. We were told that the Moscow metro system moved two to three million people a day over 368 kilometers of underground tunnels. And move they did; some stations had strings of cars arriving and leaving every 30 to 40 seconds! They also had been designed as bomb shelters in case of war. Our metro stop was Konkovo on the southeastern orange line.

We began apartment hunting right away. We could smell urine in many building entrances. Drunks and pets used any spot handy when nature called, and because much of the maintenance system had broken down, the lobby was seldom scrubbed. We rejected several before we found one near The CoMission office, which was also at Konkovo. Though both the apartment and the office needed paint and wallpaper (a Russian touch we enjoyed), by the end of the first month we felt more confident that, with God's help, we could do the job.

Vlad finally connected Bev with some nice fur-lined boots for $18. We began to find the shopping less confusing. Bev learned that a system to control food had been put in place in the old government stores. When you got to the counter and indicated your choice, the clerk wrote the price on a slip of scrap paper. After that, you stood in another line to pay. Once you had the receipt, you got into a third line to exchange the receipt for the loaf of bread. Shoppers followed this system for each item they purchased. Bev's favorite was the heavy Russian black rye bread.

One time as Bev waited for meat, a shopping cart of sausages was rolled out of the storeroom. A string of smokies about one meter long hung over the side. Soon a cat emerged from under the fish counter and began to play with the dangling string of sausages, which amused the customers. Bev said to me, "Your health department in the U.S. would not approve!"

I guess the several cats that hung around the market were their rodent control. We were finding that just living would take a lot of time and effort!

The CoMission executive committee was a great group of men who were our representatives in the U.S. Bruce Wilkinson was chairman of The CoMission board, and Paul Eshelman was the vice chairman and chairman of the Sending Organizations Committee. Paul Kienel was vice chairman and executive director of the Association of Christian Schools International; he chaired the Curriculum and Teacher Training Committee. J.B. Crouse, president of Overseas Mission Society, chaired the Sending Organizations Committee. Peter Deyneka Jr., the president of Russian Ministries, chaired the Confederation of Independent States

Liaison Committee. Paul Johnson, president of Paul H. Johnson Inc. (a large construction and facilities management group), was chairman of the Arrangements Committee. He was also board chairman of Walk Thru the Bible and Moody Bible Institute.

John Kyle, executive director of Mission to the World (Presbyterian Church in America), was chairman of the Church Relations Committee. Joseph Stowell III, president of the Moody Bible Institute, was chairman of the Russian Church Coordinating Committee. Terry Taylor, U.S. director of the Navigators, chaired the Training and Materials Committee. Later, Mary Lance Sisk joined the board as chairman of the Prayer Committee. A prayer warrior herself, she organized a prayer support group that numbered over 200,000 who prayed for all of us daily, 24 hours a day for 5 years! And God answered!

I worked as the executive director of the Arrangements Committee in Moscow. My boss, Paul Johnson, became a good friend. Paul's job description for me included representing The CoMission and its members and being in charge of its office and operations in Moscow. This included: "leasing and maintaining the Moscow office, hiring Russian staff, coordinating the various activities of the other members of The CoMission Executive Committee, serving as an information center and source to each committee and its staff, helping to find housing, assisting with group purchasing, and local transportation as requested." I also assisted the Mission Aviation Fellowship (MAF) in locating, leasing, and operating a central warehouse, which received, stored, and distributed materials and equipment to CoMission teams all over Russia and the Commonwealth of Independent States.

My office was also to help keep statistics and provide updates for The CoMission handbook, A Guide to Successful Living in Russia and the Commonwealth of Independent States. Peter Deyneka, my local consultant and guide for any public or government interaction, was a fine friend, and we became a good team through the years.

The last line of my job description read, "Help anybody and everybody on The CoMission team in any way you can with logistics, information, contacts, networking, etc., etc." As Paul pointed out, "Anything required to get the job of CoMission successfully done!" Paul stood behind us in every way with prayer, advice, and funds and was a significant key to our success.

Vlad and I combed the city for material: washers, TVs, VCRs, water filters, and transformers for people unwilling to believe the Russian hair dryers really would dry their hair or run their radio-cassette units. Stores might display an item, but when we said, "We want 50 or 100," they backed away!

"This is for display only," they commonly responded.

Vlad once told me that everything, from services such as plumbers and electricians to cars, adapted to the new "free market." We stopped at an auto showroom, a space in a museum. They assured us that if we paid cash, we could get a car soon. Vlad said, "The old system required cash up front, followed by several years of waiting."

He told me a Russian joke. The Russian man sees a new car and is told, "Cash now and in only one year you can take delivery."

"One year from today," the man said incredulously.

"One year!" the salesman assured him.

"Morning or afternoon?" the buyer inquired.

In exasperation the salesman cried, "What difference does it make?"

"Well," the buyer responded, "I have a plumber coming in the morning."

We saw a Vesta washing machine. We had researched washers as much as we could and were told that Vesta was a joint venture with a western European manufacturer. They had a good production system and warranty and were among the new wave of products reaching the Russian market. "Sorry, it's for demonstration only," the salesman told us.

"But we want 100," we told him.

"Impossible," he said. "I don't know when we will get another one."

Supply had a long way to go if they were to meet demand. I convinced The CoMission that shipping the washers and other equipment from western Europe would be far too costly and would void any warranties. In addition, we would have to struggle with customs for every unit.

We moved into our apartment with all-Russian equipment, including a Vesta washer that cost $198. The cheapest import was over $800! Now we had to deliver. It was May, and our first group of CoMission teachers planned to arrive in August.

We had finally found a warehouse that MAF and a group called Transport for Christ (TFC) were preparing to receive and store printed materials and equipment for the teams. The Navigators struggled to get the printing done, and Walk Thru the Bible raced to translate and duplicate video teaching materials. Vlad and I scoured Moscow for the equipment.

We had yet to uncover a good supply source for anything. There were lots of showrooms that only displayed the things we needed. At one place the sign read, "Exposition by True Value, an American Hardware Store." They imported goods for "show only," but Vlad said that was a way to get through customs. None of the goods ever left Russia. So we bought their supply of transformers and a lockable cash box, as well as some folding chairs and a desk.

It was a start. Bev busily set up our apartment and unpacked our shipment from Holland. At first we were glad we had sent the food and supplies, but after a few months, we could find everything we needed during our scavenger-hunt shopping trips. More and more expositions and container stores appeared, each one having a unique range of goods and foods.

As time went on, open-air markets supplied by "Chelniki" grew. "Chelniki" were shuttle traders who were allowed to visit China, Turkey, India, Dubai, and other countries to buy up to $1,000 worth of goods, which were then sold for two or three times their cost. This financed another shuttle trading trip. It was an amazing system and greatly expanded the range of goods we could buy.

We still needed 100 washing machines. "Well, look here!" Vlad declared another day.

He had found an ad for Vesta washing machines in the trade paper we picked up in our travels. "And it's right down here in the same building on Ostrovityanova street where you live, about two blocks away," Vlad continued. "This store is the regional distributor for Vesta!"

"Finish your tea and we'll go find out," I urged him.

The ground-floor apartment had papers taped over the windows. When we knocked on the door, it was opened only a crack, through which a face peered out. "Stoh!" the man said sternly.

Vlad said, "Washing machines. We want to buy washing machines."

"What kind of money?" he asked.

"U.S. dollars," Vlad answered.

Opening the door farther, the man asked, "How many?"

When Vlad told him, he opened the door and invited us in.

We walked into a large, three-room apartment that was stacked from floor to ceiling with new Vesta washers. We reached a deal quickly and called MAF to have their truck transfer the washers to our newly leased warehouse.

The truck, a 2.5-ton GAZ V8, was another story.

When Bruce Prestige and Murray and Audrey Scott of TFC came with Bob Gordon of MAF to set up the trucking system for CoMission, they wanted to buy a used Mercedes from Finland. They brought a group of Mennonite farmers to see the program and invest in the truck, which already had a lot of miles on it.

For lunch we went to a small, newly opened restaurant, and all ordered solinka, a sour pickle soup. After listening for a while, Vlad said, "Why don't you buy a Russian truck? They are much less expensive, and you can get repairs anywhere here."

Bob Gordon replied, "I've heard they don't stand up to hard use and are poorly made."

One of the Mennonite farmers asked, "How much?"

When Vlad said it was only a fraction of the price of the used Mercedes, they all wanted to see one. Vlad said, "There's one near here."

It was blue and the right size. When asked the price, the seller said, "$3,300."

"Let's drive it," said the farmers.

"Come back in an hour," the seller replied. "I have the battery, carburetor, starter, and generator locked in a steel box so no one can steal them. I'll put them on and get some gas."

It ran well, and the farmers, counting their pocket money, bought it on the spot. Vlad found a driver mechanic (which was the Russian system) who would store, maintain, and operate the truck for us. Since it was essentially a 1957 Ford, it was a good, sturdy vehicle. Henry Ford built the first truck factory for Lenin in 1927 or so. Ford upgraded the factory in 1957, and they built them *Ruski-Ford tough*. The truck would haul washing machines and other CoMission cargo. The Mennonite farmers wanted to know if they could ship some of these trucks to Canada!

It was the same with TV/VCR units and VCRs. A trade show called "Global" set up a Western-style store. We bought dozens of units from them, and soon they became a full-fledged department store and our main supplier.

We still needed to find water filters. All kind of stories about Moscow's water flew around the ex-pat community, but I would tell them the Russians drank it. So we visited a "trade show" and found a locally manufactured ultraviolet unit. It was Russian and so was met with some distrust by our people.

I went to the Russian Epidemiological Institute and got data showing the water to be safe in Moscow but questionable in other regions. However, they assured me the ultraviolet filter unit was reliable and did kill pathogens. While this didn't satisfy all the skeptics, most were willing to use the Russian filters until something better came along.

The same was true of the U.S. hair dryers. Even with American transformers, the U.S. equipment tended to burn up, so a Russian dryer was purchased, and, wonder of wonders, it did the job! We learned the lesson that a variety of choices wasn't necessary. As Henry Ford told customers, "You can have the Model T in any color you want, as long as it's black."

We took whatever was offered as long as it did the job. Our clothes were washed and ironed with Russian appliances. Our coffee brewed in a Russian coffee maker, and our bread toasted in a Russian toaster. Bev even had a Russian mixer and space heater, necessary because our heat came from the city power plants. However, there was heat only from October to May. Hot water came regularly except for the month of August--just like France. The board was happy with our findings and experiences, as were most of the CoMissioners when they began to live their Russian lives.

We grew to love the Russian people. They were helpful and friendly and, with a few exceptions, glad we had come to their country. One day Bev had been gone for a long time. When I asked about it later, she said the store had just closed for its two-hour noon break when she arrived. "I found some ice cream and sat on a bench with a Russian lady," she explained.

"Did she speak English?" I asked.

"No," Bev replied, "but she had pictures and I had pictures, so we spoke 'grandmother.'"

We hired a lovely Russian girl as our secretary. Olga Krylova was just right for our work. She was always eager to help. One day she took Bev to a shoemaker to get my shoes repaired. When the repairman asked who we were, Olga explained The CoMission as she understood it. He was a believer and clearly told her about Jesus. He refused payment for his work, and Olga began to read her Bible and seek Jesus on her own.

Elena was our third worker. She had experience in the travel industry and was valuable as a tour guide for visitors and a ticket purchaser for travelers. She had spent time with the Moonies, but after a year she rejected their cult. Vlad joined in the spirit of things, too. He told me that he had been raised a heathen. His father was an engineer for the KGB, and although his mother was a Christian, she had to hide her faith once she married. "But," Vlad explained, "we buried her as a Christian."

Whenever we met with officials, Vlad took a Bible, explaining that we were bringing Russia what it needed to survive.

We settled into a routine. MAF had set up its office in the living room of our apartment/office. I had one room, there was a general administrative room where Bev and the secretaries worked, and we had a kitchen for our lunches and breaks. We served lunch, which included soup and sandwiches. The landlady, who was also a teacher, provided the soup, which was very good. We provided the bread, cold cuts, and mayonnaise for sandwiches, as well as endless pots of tea.

I spent a lot of time visiting future school sites for CoMission teams. In Moscow I usually went with Ron Kaiser, the Campus Crusade team leader. Outside Moscow, I usually went with Bev and Dr. Olga Polykovskaya from the ministry of education. In between there were more and more visitors to care for and show around. King Crow was hired as Bruce Wilkinson's deputy, so we saw him often.

I kept Bob Ehle, the purchasing agent for items bought outside Russia, informed. As he visited, he agreed that the only thing he needed to purchase in any large numbers in Europe were video projectors. These were purchased in Germany and handed to workers to bring to Russia as luggage. It was a good plan except for the fact that warranty service was not available in Russia. I kept Paul Johnson updated on everything from water filters to washing machines.

Whether talking with officials in the Russian White House or the Moscow city council, we always presented them with a Bible and the same explanation about Christian morals and ethics. Even with Orthodox priests and a couple of bishops, we held the same position and told them the same details. We explained, "We are a voluntary coalition. Each group is self-financing and self-governing, and we share strategy and materials."

"But who is in charge?" they would ask in disbelief.

"I can't do this for five years!" Bev seldom cried, but these tears were real.

"Why?" I asked.

"Hostess, hand-holder, now even my secretarial role is gone with the new help," she cried.

"Bev, God spoke to you first, and I believe He wants us here!" I replied. "I'm going to pray with you that His plan for you becomes clear, too."

So we prayed. We had an hour or two before taking delivery of a new Lada station wagon. It would be a combination ministry and personal car.

The next day we drove it around some, and Sunday morning we drove it to a riding stable where a Church of the Nazarene met. The arena smelled of horses, but that did not diminish the joy of the worship.

After the service, Bev talked with Carla Sunberg, the pastor's wife. She was a nurse, too, and Carla said she wanted to do for the Russian nurses what CoMission was doing for the teachers. Bev was electrified: Yes! There was a need!

On the way home, Bev was animated. "This is what I'm in Russia for!" she exclaimed. "I know what I'll do for the rest of the five years!"

She was to develop and implement a continuing education program for Russian nurses. After a few months, when Carla dropped out, Bev went on to establish ten two-week continuing education modules.

That night, the new car was stolen. It had gotten us to Bev's divine appointment and then disappeared. "Bev," I said, "we're going to have to find a less-expensive way for God to give you direction."

Fortunately, against the advice of the "old Moscow" hands, I had bought insurance. When told they would never pay, Vlad had said, "This is a joint venture company, so it should be good."

Two hundred fifty dollars for a year wasn't much, so with the car gone and the police report filed, we went to the insurance company. They paid 85 percent of the $6,000 cost--not bad under the circumstances.

"Vlad," I then said, "let me explain paying mileage to you. I'm not buying another car. We will use yours."

Vlad drove the rest of our time there and loved the American mileage deal.

Vlad's comments were cryptic and often humorous. One day as we drove by the KGB (now FSB) building at Dzerzhinsky Square, he quipped, "That's the highest building in the world."

"How do you figure that?" I responded. "It's only eight or ten stories above ground."

"Yes, but even from the basement you can see Siberia."

Russian humor with an edge.

Across from the Pushkin Square, the site of the big McDonalds in Moscow, was the Pushkin Theater. Restaurants and shops began filling its decks and basement, and umbrella-shaded tables appeared on its balcony. Vlad told me that his dad built it when he was a chief construction engineer. "Why did he do that when he was KGB?" I asked.

"Oh, they built all the theaters and controlled what was shown in them to protect the people," he explained.

What a system! As we drove on I asked, "What would your dad think of all of the developments to the theater now?"

"He would weep," Vlad replied. "He was a true believer in communism."

Bev's MPSE students in Krasnodar. "When do you
hit the patients?" A Russian question

Getting there is half the fun. Kazakhstan team ready to go.

Food being stored for the winter.

Chapter 26
The CoMission ~ Up and Running

Chapter 26.
The CoMission ~ Up and Running

A crisis visited our busy lives.

We were just two weeks from the arrival of the first large, one-year CoMission group in Moscow. Each sending organization was responsible for its people's support, but travel was handled by one group working through a U.S.-based agency. "Andy," Paul Johnson said on the phone, "all the in-country travel for over 400 people has collapsed. Can we help?"

I thought quickly and responded, "Yes, but within a few hours I need names, passport numbers, and destinations. We already have a lot of their materials and equipment in the warehouse, and more will come soon, but I need to know who goes where."

It wasn't long until my fax machine began to hum.

The next morning, I called the team together to let them know the challenge at hand. Elana, our travel agent, was out sick, and we needed her. We had devotions. I read the first chapter in James, and we asked God for direction and specific results, such as seats and tickets. We also prayed for Elana to get well quickly!

Just as we began to break down the work, Elana came in and said she had suddenly felt better. Vlad smiled and told her, "Oh, we just prayed for you. God is listening!"

We quickly broke out the list of people, destinations, and travel methods. The team fanned out to the various bus and train stations, cash in hand, to stand in lines and buy tickets. One group, however, needed a special arrangement. Two teams were going to have a very long train ride unless we chartered a plane. As each team had over five tons of washers, video equipment, and books, plus personal luggage, we chose to charter a plane.

The teams arrived on schedule. The MAF/TFC team met them with the truck for luggage and the buses we chartered. Everyone was taken to the Gorbachev Hotel and Convention Center for in-country briefings and preparation for travel. The Gorbachev Center was a "perk," as Vlad said, to the former Soviet president for being a "servant of the people."

The Gorbachev Center made us a good deal for our CoMissioners. Gorbachev had his offices there, too.

God had clearly answered prayer. We had tickets to every destination and a translator escort for each group. I elected to ride the charter flight to Novosibirsk and Alma Ata, Kazakhstan. The plane was a 1950s vintage Ilyushin-18.

The trip was interesting. We loaded a bus and two trucks with the teams' goods and luggage. Then we sat near the airport, out of sight, until about 11:30 p.m. Valentin Jarov, our charter agent, finally got us to the gate to the tarmac. After a few words with the gate guard, we were allowed to proceed to our aircraft and begin loading the cargo, and then the two CoMission teams boarded. At about midnight, some officials drove up and, after receiving a "gift" from Valentin, let us take off. It was after midnight, and the 19 CoMissioners settled in for the seven-hour flight. I found a nice office in the back of the plane, complete with a sofa. I spent my night sleeping.

In the morning, I asked the purser about the office. "Oh," he said, "this was President Yeltsin's personal plane when he headed the communist party in the Urals. We even took him to Seattle once on this plane."

To see whom? I wondered.

When Yeltsin got promoted, he gave the crew the plane, and they made their living flying groups like ours around Russia.

"Why are we not going to Kazakhstan?" I asked the crew as we sat on the ground in Novosibirsk after unloading the first team of ten CoMissioners.

"No fuel," they said.

When the government airline Aeroflot broke up, smaller airlines called "Mini flots" sprang up everywhere. They were often just one- or two-plane fleets that mayors or governors had seized for their own airlines -- never mind they couldn't operate or maintain them and the government no longer guaranteed fuel purchases. Fuel had to be paid for in cash at each stop. This resulted in chaos. Pilots had to carry huge sums of cash. Some chose to disappear with the money. Now here we were in mid-Siberia still with one team to take to Kazakhstan, and we needed fuel.

Valentin took a briefcase of cash and sauntered over to a fuel truck. The driver was asleep inside, so Valentin knocked on the window. The driver roused enough to shake his head no. Valentin opened the briefcase, and the driver sat up! After some quick bargaining, the truck rolled up to our plane to pump in the needed fuel.

As we refueled, a couple of officials drove over and made vague comments about flight clearance and so on, but we were soon airborne. On the radio, the flight controller complained about irregular paperwork, suggesting we could not cross Kazakhstan or land at Alma Ata. We droned on. I napped a bit and, after a few hours, went to the cockpit. The whole crew was asleep, the autopilot engaged. Air traffic called our flight over the radio, so I woke the navigator. He checked the time, answered the radio, and then woke the pilot and copilot. In a short time, we began our descent to Alma Ata.

The unloading went smoothly, even when airport officials came to us about our irregular situation. Everyone wanted a payoff, but we just smiled and thanked them for their hospitality.

Valentin appeared suddenly with a small group of people, including the crew, giving us clearance for our takeoff. He said the crew had been in the terminal, selling seats on our charter without our permission. We agreed to let the passengers join us. We let the crew keep the money and then we took off, leaving the Kazak officials sitting in their cars.

The next stop was Chelyabinsk, Russia, a nuclear research center. As we approached, I noticed perfectly round lakes scattered over miles of the steppes. I asked Valentin what they were. "Peaceful uses of atomic energy," he replied.

We left our charter there and flew on a commercial flight to Moscow.

The overloaded Yak-42 airliner bound for Domodevedo airport in Moscow took off at midnight. When our flight was announced, a stampede of passengers raced to the boarding ramp at the back of the plane. Their goal was to get a seat, because none had been assigned. As we climbed for altitude, some people wandered up and down the aisle. They hadn't found a seat, so they had to stand for the two-hour flight. I was really glad to see Vlad's smiling face when we landed at 2:00 a.m.

The next morning, our team had a time of thanksgiving at devotions. All the CoMissioners were where they were intended to be. God's arrangements were always the best.

Murray Scott and MAF did a wonderful job of shipping materials and equipment to all the sites. Bruce Prestige of TFC looked at the truck stops along the outer ring road of Moscow.

The trucks came from all over Russia and Europe. Once in Moscow, they had to wait to discharge their loads. The "stops" were mostly muddy fields. The drivers slept in their trucks and cooked on the ground beside their rigs. They were victimized by mafia, robbers, and prostitutes, and no one seemed concerned. Bruce and Murray said, "Why not do what we do in America? Let's set up a moving chapel in a semi-trailer and travel to their stops to minister to them." So they did. We helped equip the 40-foot semi as a chapel with a TV, VCR (to play CoMission and other Christian videos), Bibles, Christian books and other literature, and a huge samovar for tea.

When the two ministries shared their vision in the U.S. and Canada, the money came in. At one church, they were asked how much the three-axle Kamaz V8 diesel tractors to pull the trailer would cost. They replied, "Brand new, $16,000." The church promptly took up an offering and paid for the truck on the spot.

The venture was so well received in Russia that MAF/TFC began reporting new believers from all over, even Kazakhstan and Turkey! When a U.S.-style truck stop was finally built in Moscow, the Armenian investor came and asked for a permanent chapel "just like in America." They raised the funds for another trailer-mounted chapel, and we helped equip it. Murray told me it became permanent right away -- someone had stolen the wheels!

Others soon found our office to be a facilitator for the gospel. One was Daniel Lamb, a businessman from Denver, Colorado. He challenged wealthy friends to join his "Country Club" at $30-40,000 each, just like the clubs they joined to play golf and so on. Annual dues were $10,000, and each member would dedicate one or two weeks a year to teach at one of the several Bible schools he started in Asia and Russia.

We helped him with transport through Moscow and met some of the wonderful people who had joined his club. He invited me to teach in Omsk at a short-term Bible school.

It was a great trip. Omsk had a decidedly German flavor, as Stalin had deported a lot of Volga Germans to this Siberian city. We had 30 students who eagerly listened to and studied every aspect of my presentation. I had them join in small groups, pray each day for each other, and discuss barriers that would limit their effectiveness as disciples. The next day, they talked with the group and we all prayed together.

At the end of the week, they told us that each evening after their "homework," they went out into the streets to witness. They had 60 new believers to show for their efforts! What to do? On Sunday we took them to the local Baptist church and introduced them.

Flying back to Moscow with Daniel, I was amazed at how God works. These short-term Bible schools were very effective. On the flight we met a North Vietnamese man. He had just finished his two-year servitude in a Russian factory. He said that each year, 20,000 Vietnamese workers were sent to work off war debts the Vietnamese had incurred during the wars of Southeast Asia. It was news to me, but it did explain the growing Vietnamese community we saw in Moscow. In spite of the weather and distance, many workers elected to "pay to stay" and worked as traders in the markets selling clothes and whatever else they could find.

Back in Moscow, Bev did Daniel's laundry. Vlad took him to several appointments. After a couple of days, we put him on a flight to Hong Kong.

The next day, I got a call from Vagan Emin, our lawyer. "Andy," he said, "I'm afraid your friend Mr. Lamb did not get to Hong Kong. His flight crashed in Siberia last night."

After several calls confirming the awful facts, I called his wife, Grace, and told her about the tragedy. "Don't come here yet," I advised her. "I will go out to Novokusnetsk to identify him and arrange for his return."

I called the U.S. embassy, and they told me that no Americans were involved. When I gave them Daniel's passport number, they called back and said, "We will send an embassy escort with you to make the identification."

In Siberia, my embassy escort and I spent two days examining bodies, most of which had been burned badly, as well as jewelry and other artifacts from the crash. None of the bodies was Daniel. Only six or eight of the 76 people were found. The rest were totally gone. Most of the jewelry was stolen from the crash site by villagers, so even with dental records, we couldn't find him.

The Russian pathologist told us what had happened to the flight: The Russian pilots had been out of the cockpit of the brand-new Airbus. Their children had been in the cockpit seats, playing with the controls. At 39,000 feet, they had put the giant craft into a high-speed spin from which they did not recover. As we flew back to Moscow, I thought, Daniel is in heaven.

During this time, Bev stayed busy completing and supervising translation of her nursing courses. She was convinced that Medical Professional Skills Enhancement (MPSE) was the job God had for her in Russia. She taught Module 1 and corresponded with nurses in the States, encouraging them to come teach and help develop more modules.

She also helped out in The CoMission office as needed and even served as camp nurse for a group of 360 youth and 68 Americans at the Orlyonok Pioneer camp on the Black Sea. Dr. Olga Polykovskaya had been trying to get a good Christian program for the youth started there to replace the communism that had been taught in the past.

Bob and Cheryl Hosken contacted us from their mission in Izhevsk (western Siberia). Cheryl was a nurse who had heard of Bev's MPSE program. In fact, the news buzzed through the Russian medical community. Cheryl wanted Bev to teach her Russian nursing friends in Izhevsk.

While the travel wasn't too costly, the work by translators and the printing of the manuals got increasingly expensive. At first we dug into our personal funds to do the job, but eventually we needed more money to travel and expand the work. We prayed and decided Bev should go to Izhevsk. However, like Gideon in the Bible, she did put out a couple of fleeces. "Lord," Bev prayed, "if this is what You want me to do, I need help and I need money."

It was one of those activities we did even as we were in action, following the call of God.

Vlad and I took her to Domodevedo airport, southeast of Moscow. It was snowing, and we had to get back to Moscow for an important meeting. We got her checked in, paid the overweight charges for her books, manuals, Bibles, and stethoscopes, and then took her out to the cow-barn-like departure area. Since she wasn't good in the Russian language, we asked the lounge steward to please be sure she got on her Izhevsk flight. Then we prayed with her and headed back to the city.

She told me later that after we left, a group of Russian reporters appeared. They were going to Izhevsk to cover the event in which President Yeltsin was promoting Mr. Mikhail Kalashnikov (the rifle inventor) to the rank of general so that he would get more retirement pay. They were incredulous that this little, white-haired, American "babushka" was so far from her grandchildren, going to a place she had never seen, to meet people she did not know, to teach them about nursing and Christ. "We will keep you with us until you find your contacts in Izhevsk," they told her, and they did.

When she got home nearly three weeks later, she was elated and told me, "They loved the nursing courses, the Bibles, the stethoscopes, and the personal gifts. A Bible study has already been started, and Cheryl will do the follow-up. They want me to come back!"

"Well," I responded, "I sent the project proposal to some people. Walt Meloon of Correct Craft Boat Company sent you $10,000. Rob Martin of First Fruit Foundation said that if you raise $10,000, he will give you $10,000, so you have $20,000. I would say your fleece is quite wet! And," I continued, "a nurse has written to say she will come to help."

Fleece number two was good, too. In fact, during the next four years, more than 40 nurses came to teach, write modules, and help Bev prepare the modules about nursing. God's work indeed! During that five-year period, more than 3,000 nurses took the modules. Many of these were head nurses who taught the material to their subordinates. And there was Kingdom fruit. Numerous nurses accepted Christ as their Savior, and more than a dozen Bible study groups resulted from this MPSE effort by Bev and her friends.

The CMA, our sending agency and home church, was getting settled in Russia. Over dinner in our apartment one night, John and Ruth Harvey of the CMA advance team told us that the CMA had joined an indigenous Russian mission and was basing its work in Krasnodar, not far from the Black Sea. In a short while, Robin and Donna Dirks arrived from Africa to be the business managers for the CMA mission. They severely missed Africa that winter. Clem and Maddie Dreger came, too. What a crew! We got a nice thank you from Peter Nanfelt, Vice President of overseas ministries CMA, for the help we were able to give its missionaries.

The CoMission generated a lot of new ministries of various types. Judy Gwaltney sat in my office one day. Her year in Russia was almost up. She wanted to stay and had discovered a set of "Betty Lukens" flannelgraph that I had given to one of the cultural centers. She was animated as she described the children's and teachers' responses to her use of the materials as she taught. She was especially thankful for the way teachers of the deaf responded to it. "What if we could figure out a way to let you stay and use flannelgraph when your time is up?" I asked her.

Judy said, "I'm a widow. One day before coming here, I was having a pity party in a restaurant near a cemetery. Strangely, across the road by the cemetery, I saw a truck pulling a U-Haul trailer. The Lord cut through my self-induced misery, saying, 'You really can't take it with you.' So I signed up to come here with The CoMission. I'm a teacher, and I want to stay here and teach."

"Well," I responded, "let's pray and look to see what God wants to do with the flannelgraph idea."

I contacted Alice Dyk in Ellensburg. She committed to get a bulk price and ship more of the flannelgraph materials to Russia, and she did. At a convocation in Kislovodsk, Dr. Gerald Parker from Boone, North Carolina, not only delivered some flannelgraph sets from the Boone CMA church, but he also nearly wore off his fingers cutting out the figures for Judy.

Our son Drew and his wife, Erin, had their second baby. They named her Nicole. They were in Guinea, serving with CAMA Services, caring for refugees from Liberia and Sierra Leone. We decided we would pay them a visit in Africa as soon as we could.

Things were working well. We were able to handle the unscheduled crises and by God's grace managed to roll with each new challenge. We were in Finland for new visas when a coup attempt was made, but President Yeltsin led the troops who, until one of their own officers was shot by a sniper in the White House, were slow to respond. When the Alpha troops moved in, they blew the opposition hardliners away, and the communists were again turned back.

We had a great Thanksgiving. We found two turkeys, and I browned them by spraying Coke on them as they roasted. It was a trick that a Chinese visitor, Anita Leung, taught me. Twenty-three staff and family jammed into our apartment for a time of food, fellowship, and thanksgiving. God was truly answering our prayers.

Matt came to spend Christmas and New Year's with us. We took a road trip to try to find the home village of my maternal grandparents. When we told the Russians their names, they said, "Oh, they were Jews."

Later we found their village in southern Russia. When my sister Coralie and her husband, Tom, along with my brother Paul, came to visit, we went to the village. An old Russian-German lady told us all those who did not flee to the West were rounded up by Stalin and sent to Siberia in the late 1930s. Paul, noting the poor houses and muddy streets, quipped, "I sure am glad Grandpa caught the boat."

Matt flew back to Boone just before our second Christmas in Russia. January 7 is the Orthodox day for celebrating Jesus' birth. It was awesome to be in Red Square and see the choir file out of a small Orthodox church singing Christmas carols in the falling snow.

Speaking of snow, Russians don't plow the roads or clear the sidewalks. The closest they come is to sweep them with a truck-mounted rotary brush. The snow packs, and by spring a foot or more of ice covers the roads and sidewalks. Bev fell more than a dozen times before she learned to "walk like a penguin," taking small steps with her toes pointed in! She saw a statistic that more than 2,000 people are hospitalized due to falls on the ice each year just in Moscow.

🙠

Every four or five months, I flew to the U.S. to attend board meetings. The board appreciated our Russian perspective as they did their best to facilitate the teams who were coming every six months. One day when we were trying to understand the Russian mind on things, I suggested, "I'll bring Vlad to the next meeting. He understands our goals and could help us see things better through Russian eyes."

The board agreed.

Vlad flew with me to Seattle. The passport control was quick and polite. While we waited for our luggage, a custom's man with a beagle dog came sniffling along. The dog zeroed in on Vlad's hand carry bag. "Sir, we need to look inside the bag," the officer said.

"Oh! Yes," Vlad responded, opening the small, canvas bag.

The officer reached in and pulled out a waxed-paper-wrapped object. "Kolbasa! He's not sure we have food here," I explained to the officer.

With a smile, he gave Vlad back his food. We both laughed. We had just made the 11-hour nonstop flight over the North Pole from Moscow to Seattle. The Aeroflot IL-96 was new, and the trip was smooth. Bev and I made that flight several times during our five years in Russia.

Vlad asked, "Where should I keep my passport?"

"Oh, in your suitcase is fine," I replied.

"But if the police want to see it, what then?" he asked.

"Vlad, you are in America. They have cleared you to be here and stamped the passport. That's all, but if it will make you feel better, I'll ask a policeman to hassle you."

His smile was one of relief and amusement.

After going through the process of renting a car, we were handed the keys to a new Dodge. "Oh," said Vlad, "in Russia we would never give such a car back to the rental company!"

"Well, they have my credit card and will take the money daily until the car comes back."

"That's why Russians give so many fake credit cards," he mused.

We had a nice few days with Bev's folks and friends in Ellensburg. From Washington we drove to Colorado Springs. Along the way we saw deer, antelope, elk, and mountain sheep. "Wow," Vlad observed, "you have many wild animals. Russians shoot theirs."

"We do, too, but only in hunting season," I explained.

"We have hunting season, but we can shoot and pay off the game officers," he confided.

About then we saw a Montana road sign stating, "$2,500 reward for information leading to the arrest of poachers."

"We must find a poacher," Vlad said, "to pay for this trip."

The whole trip was a series of amazing revelations -- America through Russian eyes. Vlad had two college degrees and had traveled to India and Mozambique, but they always routed him through Soviet satellite countries. This truly was his first view of Western freedom.

The board loved his candid observations. When one member expressed fear of churches being planted, Vlad replied, "So call them Bible clubs. People want them."

He was right, and hundreds of church groups have formed in Russia and the CIS since those days.

On our drive back to Seattle, Vlad marveled at all the good roads and friendly people, but he said there were too many choices. Back home in Moscow he told everyone in Russia what he had seen.

Bev with teaching supplies arriving in Volgagrad

Bev and Dr. Cheryl Knight en route to teach MPSE.

Chapter 27
God at Work

Chapter 27.
God at Work

Bev and I finally made the trip to Conakry, Guinea, to see Drew, Erin, and our grand kids, Andrew and Nicole. After leaving snowy Moscow in 20 below zero weather, we deplaned in Conakry in 100 degree heat. We adjusted while flying down-country on -- you guessed it -- an old Russian airliner with Russian pilots. We brought 100 Russian Bibles for a CMA missionary reaching out to the Russians working in Guinea. We gave each pilot one, and they were very thankful.

The Africans were wonderful to be with. They treated us royally as Drew and Erin's parents. And, of course, seeing little Andrew and Nicole was amazing. The time went by quickly, and suddenly, we found ourselves back in the ice and snow.

Vlad met us and caught me up on the work. New schools were opening. Our CoMission board planned to come to Russia for a meeting, and another shipment of flannelgraph had arrived from Alice Dyk. Dr. Olga busily tried to get a foundation together to take on running the cultural centers. Now that communism was no longer taught, we could have the centers for a base to teach Christianity. It was a good idea, but it just never came together. We had too much to do in the short five years we were there.

Next I flew to Ulan-Ude and met with Pastor Nicolay Markin. From there we drove to Ust Barguzin. Nicolay and his wife, Olga, asked that Bev come to teach in the small town of log homes on the eastern shore of Lake Baikal. They wanted Bev to bring MPSE to their nurses, so I made the advance trip to make sure all was ready. The Markins had become Christians while at Moscow State University, thus their teaching assignment was in Siberia. They taught English and started a church there.

We went there several times. On one trip, they took me out in an old, clunky Mil MI-2 helicopter for a trip up Lake Baikal to a hot springs by a bay filled with icebergs. It was always beautiful and starkly remote. The people were mainly Buriyat, Mongolian descent and Buddhist or animist. When teaching Bev would often ask, "When do you tell patients they are dying?"

The usual response was, "We don't, because they will lose hope."

Bev would respond, "What if they have hope beyond death?"

Then she would tell them about Jesus and our hope in Him.

After the session, one Buriyat doctor said, "We must talk about this hope. I have a patient who needs it." Pastor Markin soon had an active Bible study going with the medical people.

"You're going to Siberia!" I told Judy Gwaltney.

Judy had been busy using flannelgraph to train teachers of the deaf, cultural center directors, and Sunday school personnel in how to tell Bible stories with it. They loved it. We planned to send her to Ust Barguzin. She was excited about the new project and the overwhelming response she received. One group of 46 kindergartens wanted all 1,000 teachers and 10,000 students to have the teaching. They needed 70 sets of flannelgraphs to do that job. Alice Dyk and others in Boone kept them coming, and the Siberians loved Judy and her teaching. The requests for her grew.

The old Izh car bumped over Moscow's rutted roads. Spring had arrived, and the ice season began turning to mud and slush. Margaret Bridges was in the front seat with Pastor Oleg Zjidulov of the Second Baptist Church of Moscow. Margaret was the wife of a U.S. pastor and also the founder of the Tabernacle School in Concord, California. The Lord had laid Eastern Europe on her heart, so, working with groups such as the Association of Christian Schools International, she founded Christian schools in France, Poland, Romania, and now Russia. She was born in Britain and became a busy conference speaker and fund raiser for God's work. She joined The CoMission board as chairman of the Cultural Exchange Committee and was one of the key people who urged Bruce Wilkinson to join. We always enjoyed her visits.

"Andy," she now said, "I can see the road through the floor of this car. I'm getting splashed!"

Her British diction was such that I had to laugh.

"When I get home," she added, "I will find the money and get Pastor Zjidulov a new car!"

And she did. When he bought another Izh, I asked why. "They continue to build them the same," he said, "so the parts of the old fit on the new one, too."

When The CoMission board met in Russia, we always experienced challenges. On one trip, they decided to have part of the meeting in Odessa, Ukraine, and part in Moscow. They also traveled to see CoMission teams in the field. We never lost anyone, but I do remember the Odessa visit well. Our private charter back to Moscow turned out to be a 35-year-old Antonov AN-24 looking worse for the wear. Small puddles of fuel and oil had formed under the engines, and the tires were bald, with cord showing in places. Paul Kienel, a pilot himself, muttered, "We're all gonna die, but at least we'll die in good company."

Our suitcases were stacked by the plane, and the surly baggage men refused to load them without a big tip. "We'll load our own," said Bruce Wilkinson as he began to pitch bags to Joe Stowell, who stacked them in the plane. The others prayed and climbed aboard.

The crew arrived and casually entered the plane. The pilot wore a brown leather jacket and red scarf. He smiled from the cabin door and announced, "The Red Baron."

As we droned on to Moscow, people relaxed, and Paul Kienel even went into the cockpit to view the antique equipment. After three hours, we landed in Moscow. Valentin had a nice new Mercedes bus take us to our hotel. We got everyone through the experience in good style.

The Russians never did figure out how such a diverse group as CoMission could function on such an ad hoc basis. They firmly believed that someone besides God was in charge. I finally bought a $3 rubber stamp in a stationery shop in America. It said CoMission in Russian, with a fancy edge around the outside. All papers and documents had to have a stamp. The government only issued stamps after a lengthy, costly process, but my $3 stamp was never questioned.

One day Dr. Olga came in all flustered. "I want to go to America," she said, "and I have a letter of invitation from Dr. Paul Eshelman, but the ministry of education said the document must have a stamp!"

"No problem," I replied.

Pulling out my $3 stamp with a flourish, I stamped Paul's letter and scribbled an illegible scrawl across it. Voila! An acceptable stamped and signed document appeared. Olga got her exit visa.

We received team after team and shipped them with their goods to the far corners of the former Soviet Union. We also handled emergencies and always saw God answer prayer.

The fishing was great. Vlad, Oleg (Dr. Olga's husband and our van driver), and I were in eastern Siberia at Magadan, a port city on the Sea of Okhotsk, by the Kamchatka Peninsula. We were told that it was an old Gulag city built by prisoners from the Russo-Japanese war in 1904. After it was set up, the prisoners were executed, as well as thousands of Russian "enemies of the people" under Stalin. A hulking maximum-security prison still stood near the airport.

We went there to visit teachers who wanted our program and to help with their cultural center program. We saw their art, heard their music, and met their officials in both Magadan and Palatka, 80 kilometers to the west.

One meeting was amazing. The lady in charge was the head of the Communist Teachers' Union. She welcomed us, eager to tell her story. "I am a history teacher," she said, "and a few years ago, when we could begin to read more books, I remembered that I had always wondered about the Bible."

The books we saw in homes were all the same, works by Lenin and others of like mind. Vlad explained that each time the communists published a new book that was politically correct, you had to buy it and display it in your bookcase. If the KGB heard that you did not have that book, you could be in trouble or even disappear! So everyone had shelves of politically correct books they had never opened.

The communist teacher told us she had begun to read unapproved books, and as she saw the Bible having historical content, she began to teach that, too. Then she saw "principles for good living" in the New Testament, so she made up crossword puzzles of the Beatitudes and other verses for her students to memorize. I was astounded. "I am going to send someone here to teach you the full meaning of this book," I promised.

Judy had another Siberian adventure ahead of her.

We caught a lot of salmon, drove into the outback taiga in an old six-wheel-drive army truck to catch more fish, and enjoyed being out of Moscow for a while. It was something to meet so many prisoners of the Gulag system. When I asked the teacher from whom we rented a room in Palatka why she didn't go to Moscow, where her husband (a medical doctor) and their two children had been transferred, she said, "Oh, I'm not allowed to travel. I'm a child of the 'enemies of the people.'"

"How is that?" I asked.

She explained, "While they were in the university, my mother and father were denounced by someone, arrested, and taken in boxcars to Siberia. In Vladivostok, they were put on a ship and sent here. When they arrived, the women were marched to a factory to work, and because there were too many already, the men were marched to a lake and shot. My father, though wounded, escaped. A friend helped him and got papers that gave him a sentence of 25 years of hard labor. During that time, he met my mother and they married. I was born a prisoner and may never leave!"

Vlad was almost in tears. "But," he cried, "that's all over now. You may go at any time!"

"They say it is," she replied somberly, "but I know they're watching, and when I do try to leave, they'll arrest me!"

Later Vlad told me she waited two more years before joining her family.

I heard from one of the people in Palatka, "At last we have an Orthodox priest."

When asked if he was a good one, the person replied, "Well, he knows us. He was the KGB chief here for years."

Both Bev and I read books by Aleksandr Solzhenitsyn and Fyodor Dostoyevsky. Their pictures of the life in Russia before and after the revolution were stark reminders of what had gone on in the country and shaped their world. One day Bev asked our young secretary, Olga Krylova, "Was it as bad here as Solzhenitsyn writes?"

"Oh, you know how writers are," Olga responded. "They make things seem worse than they were."

"No," Vlad said from the corner of the room, "things were far worse here than anyone could ever write!"

"Judy, you have a new assignment," I told her one day. "It's back to Siberia for you."

She laughed and, after a family visit in the States, packed yet another flannelgraph set. Then she flew to Magadan from Alaska. Later she told us the communist history teacher cried when she met Judy. She said, "Everyone who has visited us made promises. You are the only promise that was kept."

When Judy explained that she hoped to teach the Bible with flannelgraph, the teacher quickly arranged to have the classes last several hours a day and be televised!

We got to see Drew and Erin from time to time, first in Africa, then in Holland when they came through Europe. We had to go there to get new visas for Russia, a common occurrence in those days.

Drew and family finally came for a visit in Russia. The kids loved riding the metro, and little Nicole always recognized our metro stop when the train pulled into Konkovo. We toured Moscow, and they saw the sights: Red Square, Saint Basil's Cathedral, the Kremlin, and the big GUM store -- places Drew's great grandfather saw. Then we all flew Aeroflot over the pole to Seattle. Andrew Eugene Bishop III, whom I nicknamed A3, sported a scar on his forehead from a close encounter with a bush taxi. He was thrown a ways but had only a small cut. Eventually he let me know he didn't like his nickname.

People praying for us kept things going along well, even when it didn't seem like it. One phone call came to my office at 4:30 p.m. "You must come to the ministry of education now!" I was told.

The caller was Dr. Olga, and she was insistent. "Andy, you must come now!"

It was a cold, slushy February day in 1995, and we were about to go home for the weekend. Vlad was already in his fur hat, coat, and boots.

As we drove through the evening slush, mud, and traffic, Vlad said, "This is just like the old days. You will get bad news. They always tell you at the end of the Friday so you cannot do anything about it; by Monday it's too late."

At the ministry, a stern-faced Dr. Olga had me sign a letter telling us The CoMission protocol had been suspended! Politics and the Chechen war had caused a stir, and some Orthodox officials, never happy with CoMission's work, got the State Duma (the Russian parliament) to put pressure on the ministry of education to do something about us. After I signed, we relaxed, and I asked if we should evacuate our teams and shut down all our operations immediately.

"Oh, no," Olga replied, "not that!"

"Well, then," I probed, "can we keep on with the local agreements?" I needed to know what was possible.

"Yes, you can make local agreements." She seemed relieved at this option.

We discussed some other things, and as we were about to leave, Dr. Olga said, "We must send this decree to all our administrative officials in Russia. The copier you gave us needs paper. We are out."

"Vlad will bring you a case of copy paper Monday," I said.

She thanked us for being so understanding.

"Well," Vlad asked afterward, "bad news?"

"No," I responded, "now we are free of the part in the protocol that discourages church planting."

It was a clear case of others meaning something for evil, but God meaning it for good!

There was another blessing in disguise. The next week, a lady from the ministry of education came to my office asking for $25,000 for a video project. I said, "I'm sorry, but the protocol has been suspended. Legally, I can't help you."

CoMission was never hindered by this lack of protocol, however. Later, my report of the episode to the board was met with silence. Then Dr. Joe Stowell, president of Moody Bible Institute, said, "Andy, I'm glad you were there, not me. I'm not sure I would have had the grace to send her the case of paper."

Bev's MPSE program grew. More nurses came to teach and help write the modules, and more cities were visited. They always gave a positive response to the teaching. One time in a class of 20 nurses, Bev began talking about knowing Jesus. Her translator, a Christian doctor, said, "Let me tell them my story."

When she got to her conversion she said, "When I prayed that prayer, I was forgiven. My life changed. My relationships with my husband, my children, and my work all got so much better!"

One nurse jumped up, saying, "We must pray that prayer too!"

Bev had the doctor go through her conversion explanation again, then instructed, "If they want to pray and accept Jesus, have them bow their heads."

"This is Russia; they must stand," replied the doctor, and 19 of the 20 nurses stood. A Bible study began the next day.

One day as Bev entered the clinic, the chief doctor was by the door. "So," he said, "you are studying the Bible with our nurses."

"Yes," replied Bev in a startled voice.

"Well," he said, "why aren't you doing a study for the doctors?"

Bev asked, "When can you meet?"

After one module in Siberia, a lady responded to the gift of a Bible and the gospel by saying, "If only I had been given this teaching a long time ago, my husband would not have committed suicide!"

Others would say, "Thank you for the Bibles, but who will come to teach us the Word?"

At a seminar for 600 nurses, someone asked Bev, "So in America, when do you hit your patients?"

Fortunately, Bev had heard of this practice. An American nurse friend had visited an elderly lady in a hospital with her Russian neighbor. When they arrived, they saw that the poor old lady had wet her bed. The Russian, who was the old lady's niece, marched up to the head nurse and scolded her for the shabby care given to her aunt. The head nurse then marched over to the patient's nurse, slapped her across the face, and said, "You have a patient in a wet bed."

That nurse marched into the patient's room, shouted "Don't ever wet your bed!" and slapped the old aunt across the face!

In response to the question, Bev asked, "Why do you slap a patient?"

The Russian nurse replied, "We do it when they don't do what we tell them."

Bev responded, "We're here to teach you how to show patients that you love and care for them. When they feel this, they will want to learn from you, and you won't need to slap them."

We got into the relief area of our work by sending school kits for Russian kids. Ralph Plumb, the president of International Aid, and Margaret Bridges organized everything. The supplies made a lot of teachers and children very happy. Seeing other needs, Ralph sent medical equipment and then a 40-foot container of relief goods for children in Chechnya. I flew down to Stavropol to work with Brett Clark, the local CoMission team leader. We had a good reception from the officials and made arrangements to get things on to Grozny. We sent 8,000 Russian/English Bibles to a pastor in Grozny, too.

We also helped buy two Lada Niva all-wheel-drive vehicles for a Swiss group called MedAir, for war-zone work. Oleg Kozin drove one of them all the way to Grozny. Sadly, when the rebels began to kill relief workers, the project ended. One of the Nivas, with a young German driver and three Russian workers, was accidentally crushed by a tank, killing all four occupants. It was a dangerous place.

Politics were never quiet. President Yeltsin just kept the course to a free market and ignored the Duma. When they got obnoxious, he dissolved them and began new elections. When the communists marched, demanding a return to the old days, Yeltsin suggested, on television, that perhaps it was time to remove all the dead bodies from Red Square, where Lenin's mummy lay. The communists suddenly quieted down. We joked that Yeltsin was holding Lenin's corpse hostage. He let people think he was an oaf, but he cannily got his way over and over. Given the politics in America at the time, President Clinton may have wondered how one dissolves a congress.

Inflation confronted us often. The ruble would be 100 to the U.S. dollar, so eggs and bread would be 50 to 70 one week and 500 to 1,000 the next. We could always tell what inflation was by the price of Snickers bars! Everyone loved them, and their price was always pegged to the daily ruble rate. When the ruble got to 10,000 to the U.S. dollar, the government decreed the last three zeroes would be struck. I had a few bills with a bar stamped over the last three zeroes.

It was good that we were able to open and maintain a U.S. dollar account at the big Inkombank. Of course it meant trips for me and Vlad. We had to carry stacks of $100 bills to pay for things. There weren't any checks, credit, or Internet bill paying available in the early days. For a while, we even served as a bank used by a number of CoMissioners until they got their own accounts set up.

This cash economy caused problems. We often heard of administrators collecting cash to pay bills and workers, then disappearing with the money. Finally the government began to issue credit cards to the workers. Each month they could go to the bank, the only place the card was valid, and collect their salary in cash. Teachers and nurses were paid $100-$150 per month, while metro drivers got $400. It was a convoluted system, to say the least. Your salary depended on the productivity of the people you served.

Crime was always a problem as well, but thank the Lord it seldom touched any of us in The CoMission. The "wild west" atmosphere of the get-rich-quick "new Russians" made for colorful stories, but even in Moscow, with shootings to solve business disputes, there were fewer drive-by shootings than in Los Angeles. We traveled freely, though carefully, the entire five years.

Judy Gwaltney became Judy Rentschler. She had met Bill during a Josh McDowell trip, and he, a widower, became a supporter.

Bill told her "my calling is Africa,." Judy replied. God wants me in Russia teaching with flannelgraph.

After some discussion, Bill renegotiated his mission calling from Africa to Russia. They received flannelgraph sets from Alice Dyk in Ellensburg and Gerald Parker in Boone. We even got a flannelgraph grant for $6,000 from Jan Van Barnevelde in Holland. Bill and Judy covered hundreds of thousands of kilometers, teaching and delivering flannelgraph sets across Russia..

Matt announced his engagement to Sara Pawelek. He had hired her as a traveling occupational therapist for his company and fallen in love on the phone. Drew and Erin went home, taking a vacation from Africa, and Bev and I flew to Seattle to join in their wedding on September 16, 1995, in Bellingham, Washington. They were and are a lovely couple. They were married on the bow of Sara's dad's sailboat. Bev's dad Percy Dean did the ceremony As in Africa, Matt had bargained for her for 30 cows, which he paid with cream pitchers, salt and pepper shakers, and a painting of a milk maid with a herd of cows. He gave everything to Sara's parents, Fred and Mary, at the wedding. Mary said, "He overpaid."

When Drew and Erin came home for a few months, we spent some time with them. Nicole came into my room the first day. "Grandpa," she asked, "can we turn the generator on and watch a video?"

"No problem," I explained, "the generator is always on in America."

Before we left for town, Andrew showed concerned about security. "Who will guard the house?" he asked.

"We don't need a guard like in Africa," his mother replied.

He disappeared for a minute and returned carrying his "*people* pillow" that his Grandma Bev had made for him. "*Peop*le will guard the house," he announced, propping him against a cupboard by the door.

Soon we needed to fly back to Russia with Drew, Erin, and the kids on Aeroflot. It was a route Bev and I used often, but this time "air maybe" failed to deliver; a "broken plane" caused a three-day delay. Bev had planned for nurses to come teach the MPSE modules in Russia, so she felt pressured to get back.

Drew and family were to come in "a couple of days." Not! Their 11 boxes of baggage were on our flight, so I got them stored in the customs holding room. The family, however, did not get seats for five more days. They lived in a motel by the Seattle airport for a week. Even though Aeroflot paid, it wasn't fun. When they finally arrived, we put them in the Moscow Novotel and got ready for their 2:00 a.m. departure the next morning. As Drew made sure all 11 boxes were put on their Conakry flight, he was told, "Sorry, no seats! Maybe next week."

Then an agent said, "Oh, there are so many people needing to go. Check at 9:00 a.m. Perhaps we will send another airplane to Conakry tomorrow."

The next morning the agent said, "No, no, we don't put on another flight."

An angry Indian businessman remonstrated with the agent over the shoddy service. "What's your problem?" the agent responded. "Africa will always be there! The next flight is next week, and it's oversold, too!"

Then we discovered that all of Drew and Erin's things were en route to Conakry on the plane with no available seats. We quickly faxed a copy of all the baggage tags to the mission there, and they secured their goods when they unloaded in Conakry. Now what to do? We checked every possible option, but finally we had to book them on KLM to get them home.

After all that mess, Drew and family were en route from Conakry to their home in Guéckédou, Guinea, when a big gas truck hit Andrew and his driver's SUV head on. Their driver, André, died later in the hospital, and Andrew had severe cuts to his head, but God was good and he survived. A few weeks after he recovered, he pointed to a picture of an angel on a magazine and told his mother, "That's the angel that saved us."

Erin replied, "I think Jesus saved you."

"No," Andrew said, "Jesus sent two angels to save us, one for me and one for Andre'." He told Erin the exact details of the wreck even though he had been unconscious. It was great to be reminded that God is always at work for us.

Russian MPSE students

Developing MPSE in Izhevsk

Chapter 28
Last Days for The CoMission

Chapter 28.
Last Days for The CoMission

Bruce Wilkinson sent a new set of videos titled "A Biblical Portrait of Marriage." It generated a lot of interest. Teaching on marriage in Russia and in the churches was decidedly lacking. The state managed the marriage system under communism, and dissolution of a marriage was a simple bureaucratic procedure.

Bruce's plan was to launch the videos in Moscow. We printed 2,500 tickets and rented a 1,000-seat auditorium at the huge Izmailovo Olympic hotel complex. Dr. Olga and others were nervous. They didn't know if Russians would come to such a presentation, but I believed they would. It was a much-needed program.

When Bruce and a Walk Thru the Bible donor group arrived, we were ready to begin. We had gotten all the tickets out, prepared the booklets, and had copies of the videos. Sure enough, the presentation drew a standing-room-only crowd. People were overcome by the words and concepts Bruce presented. The video set comprised 12 sessions, and as Bruce spoke on topics such as leaving parents, cleaving to your spouse, helping, submitting, leading, loving, romance, sex, communication, and loyalty, we heard murmurs of agreement and saw tears. Later we heard, "No one ever told us these things before. They are in the Bible, and they are saving our marriage!"

Peter Deyneka printed Pastor's Libraries in Russian about this time. He translated commentaries, concordances, and books by authors such as A.W. Tozer and Billy Graham. As I traveled, he sent cases of these libraries to pastors in cities all over Russia. The CoMission team in Alma-Ata, Kazakhstan, asked that A Biblical Portrait of Marriage be presented, and for a couple of Pastor's Libraries.

I flew down and spent a few days setting things up. I still remember the museum with "Golden Man," a 2,500-year-old suit of armor made of pure gold, dug up from a tomb there. About 300 young couples came to the meeting. As I began playing the videos, the electricity went out – as usual. So, as I told him later, I used my best Bruce Wilkinson voice and did the one-day seminar from the workbooks and my Bible. They loved it.

I met one pastor who had been an Olympic wrestler. While in prison in Bishkek, Kyrgyzstan, he had noticed a quiet man reading in the corner of the large cell holding more than 20 prisoners. "What is that book?" he demanded. He continued, "I was king of the cell; no one resisted me."

The man quietly said, "Only real men can read this book."

Stunned, the wrestler went away, but he could not keep from asking again. Again he was told, "This book is only for real men."

A few nights later, he dreamed of a book out of which flowed clear water, milk, and honey. He awoke convinced it was the book this prisoner had, and he demanded to read that book. "It was the Bible," he told me, "and soon I was a real man in Christ."

He took a copy of A Biblical Portrait of Marriage back with him to Tajikistan.

Bill and Judy Rentschler soldiered on with the flannelgraph project. They had trained hundreds of teachers, ridden hundreds of trains and planes, and even traveled to the most northeastern tip of Siberia, almost to Alaska. They were received with open arms everywhere. They reported that they could easily use 200 sets of flannelgraph each year! Their Russian translator, Evelina Bits, even went to Izhevsk, where Bev taught nursing, to do the flannelgraph seminar herself.

Evelina, Jim and Eleanor Hinckle from Ellensburg, and I went to visit Saratov and Norka, the home of my grandparents. Their families came from there, too. When we showed the old German lady we had met on the previous trip some photos of their families from the old days, she squinted. I gave her my reading glasses. "Oh! So!" she exclaimed, and named them all. I left the glasses with her.

Bev began to study for her masters degree so she could feel more qualified to carry out her program. She used module 1, "Health, Health Team, and Physical Assessment of a Healthy Adult," as her project and spent hours reading books and writing papers. When a group of graduate nursing students from the University of North Dakota came, the professor offered to help her. Bev took statistics from there. What a challenge! Her main program was under Dr. Kenneth Briggs of Central

Washington University in Ellensburg, where in one summer quarter in 1996 she took 20 on-campus hours.

In addition, she kept up a busy MPSE (Medical Professional Skills Enhancement) schedule. On one trip to Krasnodar, Char Stemple told me that on the first morning they went to teach, the police stopped their taxi, which was loaded with books and supplies, and arrested the driver. Bev didn't miss a beat. She quickly flagged down another taxi, loaded the supplies and everyone in, and made it to the hospital in time for class. They called her "super nurse."

One time on a trip to Ulaanbaatar, Mongolia, I was carrying a video projector, CoMission videos and books, as well as a Pastor's Library for the new seminary there. I stayed with Dave and Jean Andrianoff friends from our CAMA days in Thailand. They went to Mongolia with World Concern, helping the seminary and working in community development. On the way there, I sat beside a Chinese fellow who was continuing on to Beijing. I noticed that his carry-on sport bag kept moving. He spoke English, so I pointed to the bag and asked, "Lunch?"

He laughed and said, "No."

He opened the bag and showed me four or five cute Pekingese puppies. "In China," he explained, "the communists did not allow pets. Now we can have them, and everyone wants a Chinese dog. The Russians breed the best dogs available, so I go to Moscow. These cost me $500 each, but in Beijing they are already sold for over $2,000 each!"

When I told Dave the story, he laughed and showed me a variety of dog-fur coats in the market.

I checked with the medical people in Ulaanbaatar about Bev's teaching the MPSE modules there, and because they still educated the nurses in the Russian language, they were very interested.

We got word from Africa that Andrew was using his "nine lives" at an alarming rate. He had recovered well from the car crash, but one day as he sat on Erin's lap, talking on the phone to Nana King, the line got hit by lightning. Both were severely shocked. The force knocked Andrew off Erin's lap and into the wall. He had first-degree burns on his face. His guardian angel was working overtime.

In September 1996, we discussed having another board meeting in Kiev, Ukraine, that November. Bev had just returned from her long study summer in Ellensburg. She got four A's and two B's, so I owed her good grade money. She was only home for three days before she left with three nurses to teach and do research in Izhevsk. Among other things there, she had a session with more than 1,000 doctors and nurses. The medical school asked her to move there to help set up a graduate school for nurses.

Then Bill and Judy returned. They had 16 huge bags filled with flannelgraph sets. Getting those through customs was a hoot. They couldn't get the 70-pound bags through the x-ray, so Judy just charmed their way through. Vlad had to hire an extra taxi to carry all the stuff. They had more than 80 sets of flannelgraphs. Their apartment was on the fifth floor of an old Khrushevki building, and by the time Vlad, Bill, and I got everything up to their apartment, I wasn't feeling good. I was taking more nitro than ever to control my angina, but we just kept on.

A Biblical Portrait of Marriage seminar was arranged for the Ukraine. Bev sold 25 sets of module 1, complete with video and workbooks, to U.S.A.I.D for their Russian medical projects. A foundation for the deaf agreed to fund Bill and Judy's seminars for deaf schools, and the TFC mobile chapel stayed busy. When the police stopped them, they asked only for Christian literature.

CoMission was about to begin its final year. We were busier than ever, and suddenly I was lying flat on my back. Heart attack number three began on the metro. The pain was intense, and the nitro didn't work. I staggered home and collapsed in the apartment. Fortunately, Bev was home and called an American doctor ministering in Russia. Dr. Bill Becknell lectured me about being in Russia with such a heart condition and gave me some Nefedipine. It helped. "You're totally grounded for ten days," he said, "and then we'll see."

"Why are all these people here?" I asked Bev.

I still wasn't feeling good and didn't need the noise.

"Surprise!"

Suddenly I saw Robin and Donna Dirks, Vlad and Larissa, Bill and Judy, Olga and Anton Krylovo, and Dr. Olga and her husband, Oleg. "It's your birthday," Bev said, "and we're celebrating the fact you're here to enjoy it."

I was 58!

Judy Rentschler said, "You know I own that heart attack. It was those bags of flannelgraph that did it."

I couldn't disagree.

By mid November, moving gingerly, I was in Kiev, ready to meet The CoMission board. Vlad had stepped in to carry the workload while I recovered. He made contacts, bought plane tickets, and, after three weeks of working half days, I was on the road again.

Two days before the executive committee arrived, I left my briefcase in a taxi. Money and all the committee's air tickets were in it. I prayed and phoned Vlad. He rushed to the airline, cancelled the old tickets, got new ones, and put Irina Sundikova on the train to Kiev with tickets and what was needed for the meeting.

I was told again by "old hands," "You'll never see any of that again." But praise the Lord, I got a call from the taxi company saying, "Please come pick up your briefcase." When I did, everything was intact.

The board meetings were a success. More than 1,000 people took the marriage seminar, and we flew commercial to Moscow; no more charters.

Even though I was a bit slow due to the heart problem, everything went well. However, the Moscow meetings ended with everyone's being ordered out of the hotel. It was commandeered by the Russian government for an emergency. Vlad and I got everyone into the Novotel at the airport, and, in spite of its budget-busting price, the men and women were pleased with our quick arrangements.

The next day we sent everyone, including a Walk Thru the Bible tour group, off on their flight. Well, we thought we did. John Hoover, the tour group leader, soon called in a panic. One member of his group was carrying $6,000 of the tour's cash. He had not put it on the customs form, and during a search, he got arrested with the undeclared cash.

We raced to the airport customs office. Vlad finally convinced the officials to let the man go, and we booked John and him on a later flight. We were about to send them off when John slipped a package into my pocket. "It's $6,000 more that I was carrying," he whispered.

"We'll work it out," I said.

So they got on the plane. The customs guys were $6,000 wealthier, and I had $6,000 toward my budget. No stress here, eh?

Bev had E-mailed my medical situation to Keith Lundberg, a senior administrator at the Virginia Mason Hospital in Seattle. After talking to cardiologist Dr. John Holmes, we were told to come as soon as we could.

Bev had finished the requirements for her master's degree, and I was notified that I was to be the Alumnus of the Year at Seattle Pacific University (SPU), from which I had graduated in 1966. We had a busy year ahead of us.

In my year-end report for 1996, we showed that more than 1,500 U.S. teachers had taught in more than 2,000 Russian schools. Seven and a half million children had been taught the Christian morals and ethics curriculum by Russian teachers. Six and a half million pieces of literature and books had been given out. Forty-two thousand teachers had been trained at convocations. All this plus MPSE, flannelgraphs, and the TFC mobile chapels were reaping a spiritual harvest.

"On furlough, in the 1850s, in England, Hudson Taylor was speaking. Suddenly he bowed his head for a few moments. When he spoke again he said he'd seen a vision. In the vision he saw a great war that would encompass the whole world. This he said would recess only to be followed by another world war, actually being two wars. After this, much unrest and revolts would affect many nations. There would be spiritual awakenings in some places. In Russia there would be a general, all encompassing, national spiritual awakening, so great there would never be another like it. From Russia, awakening would spread to many European countries followed by an all- out awakening, after which Christ would return." This passage from the book Awakenings was amazing.

In Russia, we saw some of that vision come to pass.

At the end of January 1997, Aeroflot got us to Seattle on schedule. Bev's brother Les Dean met us, and we drove to Ellensburg to attend Bev's oral presentation for her master's in health education. She did a brilliant job with maps, materials, and videos of the lessons being translated into Russian and taught to their nurses. As she began to leave, the dean of the graduate school called her aside and said, "I've been following your career for years. Yours is the best graduate project we've ever been involved with."

Praise God!

Dr. John Holmes was serious as he told me, "We've done all the tests, and your problem is grave. I understand you're having a big week at the university. Enjoy it! We'll do a triple bypass on Monday. You can't go back to Russia without it!"

The week flew by with speeches and the big homecoming game. I used the theme in 1 John 2:15: "Being in the world but not of the world." I had a hard time concentrating, knowing what I would face on Monday, but a great group of friends surrounded me for prayer at the final ceremony. After three Sunday services at the Bremerton CMA Church, Bev and I drove back to Seattle. We prayed and agreed that no matter how the surgery went, she needed to be back in Russia in two weeks for the nurses who were coming to teach.

We claimed Psalm 55:22 and cast our cares on the Lord. Keith Lundberg told me, "The university brought you back here at just the right time."

The Lord's timing is always best. While I checked in, Bev busily recruited Sandi Tidwell, my cardiac nurse, for teaching MPSE. She was an SPU grad and supported a teacher with CoMission.

The surgery went well, praise God. While I lay in the recovery room, barely conscious, a nurse brought a phone, saying, "You have a call from Moscow, Russia!"

It was Vlad. "Are you okay?" his anxious voice said.

"I'm better off than Yeltsin," I quipped. (The Russian president had just survived bypass surgery and was recovering slowly.)

I was out of the hospital in a week. Bev flew back to Russia as planned, and I spent the next seven weeks in rehab before flying back. En route, I stopped in Washington, D.C., and stayed a couple of days with Matt and Sara. Matt and I attended Easter service at the beautiful Washington Cathedral.

We had agreed to the request for help from the medical school in Izhevsk. The move there was set for late May, so I took the 23-hour train trip out and found with help from our local MPSE folk a tiny but clean and newly painted apartment. It was on Ulitsa Karl Marx 275, and though old, it had a new, U.S.-style bathroom. Unlike many Russians, we didn't have to share it with our neighbor. The apartment probably wasn't more than 400 square feet, but it was cozy, with windows to the sun.

Move number 28 in 35 years of marriage went well. Vlad got set up at the new MAF office in the complex that Peter Deyneka and Campus Crusade had leased in a new building. The future was looking good. Vlad, Dave Bochman of MAF, Robin Dirks and Ron Priest of CMA loaded the truck. My brother Paul and his wife, Marion, came to visit. They toured St. Petersburg and even helped us pack. When Marion flew back to the States, Paul joined me on a trip to Lake Baikal. I still couldn't lift much, but I didn't need to with such good friends to help. We had been in our Moscow apartment for more than four years -- the longest we had ever stayed at one address.

As the train to Izhevsk rolled across the Russian steppes through the taiga, we passed through dilapidated log villages with carefully tended fields. They were more than scenery. Russia is an experience, and the 23 hours on the train went by too quickly. Just as with Abraham, God once again told us, "Move out." So we put on our shoes and headed for Siberia.

I had been asked to serve as team leader for the last CMA CoMission teams coming to Russia in the summer of 1997 and spring of 1998. We agreed, as long as one of the CMA comission sites was Izhevsk. Fred Smith and I did a ten-day train, plane, and auto trip to assess the sites for the coming teams. We had a busy year ahead of us. We barely got unpacked, set up Bev's office at a large hospital, and got acquainted with the people before it was time to travel to the States again. Our Russian friends loaded us down with fresh fruit, vegetables, and love. My recovery went well, too.

Vlad and Larissa flew to the U.S. with us. From Seattle we drove across our own country. Each morning we had devotions with Vlad and Larissa. After a few days Larissa said, "I will pray, too," and she did every day thereafter.

We stopped in Missouri to see Bill and Judy Rentschler, who were vacationing there, and then headed off to Kankakee, Illinois, for the final CoMission training program. There we met with our CMA teams for Russia. Paul Johnson treated Vlad and Larissa royally, as did the other board members. There had been many discussions about a CoMission extension, but as Bruce Wilkinson reminded everyone, "Our goal of five years is being met. If we go beyond that, we risk starting a new agency. Anyone who wants to continue may as individual agencies, but CoMission as we know it ends with these teams."

He reminded us often that our joint effort worked because God made it work. "There is one Donor," he would say, "and as long as we please Him, we have all we need to do His work."

Our CMA teams would work in Astrakhan, Penza, Taganrog, Volgagrad, and Izhevsk. Vlad planned to hold down the CoMission office in Moscow, and I would be his backup in Russia while living in Izhevsk. We all flew to Moscow, and our Russian guides took the teams on to their cities. I planned to visit each team within a few weeks.

In September, Bev was invited to present MPSE at the Billy Graham School of Evangelism's meeting on medical evangelism in Wheaton, Illinois. I went with her to Moscow, and we enjoyed some of Moscow's 850-year celebrations. Then she flew to Wheaton, and I took $50,000 cash in an old briefcase and headed out to visit our teams and leave money for their operations. It took 87 hours on the train and two flights on planes before I got back to Izhevsk. What a marathon! Everyone however was happy and busy, I made that trip several times that year.

While in Izhevsk, we bought another Lada station wagon. Peter, the husband of one of the Russian nurses, was our driver. I had Yuri

Korchaginy as my translator, and Bev used his girlfriend, Stacey, for hers. Our previous translator from Izhevsk, Helen, and Andre Ivanov, our Moscow translator, went on scholarships to do their graduate studies at SPU. Most of my travel in Izhevsk was on foot, for exercise, or on what we called the "Toonerville Trolley."

Soon we all began teaching. I had a group of English teachers at the Agricultural Institute each week. They loved the Seven Laws of the Learner video curriculum. Bruce Wilkinson's enthusiastic delivery and interactive teaching method excited their imaginations. One teacher, Olga, said, "My father was a communist, and so is my husband."

"That's okay," I told her, "you are welcome to take the class."

At the end of the seven sessions, when Bruce presented the reality of salvation as a key to being the best teacher possible, we got to the part in the workbook where they could sign their name if they accepted Jesus as Savior. They all sat still. Then Olga began to sign, as did the other six or seven teachers. I gave them each a pin that Bev had made for the nurses that said, "Jesus loves you." Olga pinned hers on. The next week, she came to class wearing her pin again. She marched up to me and said, "Oh, it's so good to be loved!"

We had a lot of interaction going on. The husband of one nurse was an official at the prison. He invited Tim Keib and me to present the gospel and hand out Bibles there. It was amazing to see their work. Using primitive tools, they made motorcycle wheels and cut up missiles that had been banned by the START treaty with the U.S. I still have a beautiful knife they gave me made from the special steel.

We were offered television time. Rick, one of the missionaries with Pioneers in Izhevsk, took on the project of writing 20-minute plays based on the Bible parables. Yuri and Stacey acted, as did others. They did so well that our shows were aired twice a week with good response. We called the program "Notes from the Master Teacher." We also showed Focus on the Family's Sex, Lies and the Truth, which Bev had been allowed to translate into Russian for MPSE. All that TV time was made available for $200 (U.S.) per month by a "businessman" who traveled with bodyguards. He told me I believe the programs are good for the people.

Matt and Sara came for Christmas. We showed them around and took them out to Tchaikovsky's home. They were able to participate in a Christmas party at an orphanage where Olga Tensina, Luda Dineko, and Natasha Kiselyova (part of our CoMission team) worked part-time.

Roy and Carol Johnston flew in with their daughter Becky from Quito, Ecuador. They were now school counselors at the Alliance Academy International in Quito, but they also served as counselors for our CMA CoMission teams in Russia.

We took the teams to Sochi for their Christmas break. CoMissioners usually went to Switzerland, but the hassle with travel and visas, plus the expense, seemed extravagant when compared with the Russian teachers' lives and income. Our team of 29 people, including Vlad and Larissa, agreed to use the money that we saved to fly to the Black Sea and stay at the Radisson SAS Lazurnaya Hotel. We had a great time of fun and fellowship. We had been there two days when Luda came up and asked, "Are we still in Russia? Everyone is so nice to us here!"

While there, we had a real wedding shower for Yuri and Stacey, and they loved it. Carol Johnston even brought some specialties from Ecuador for the party. Everyone enjoyed the time there, and one of the translators even accepted Christ.

They then spent a few days with us in Izhevsk. Carol loved being with the nurses, but she drew the line at a banya with them. "But Carol," Bev said, "it's cultural and it's relaxing."

"Bev," Carol firmly responded, "I'm CMA from western Pennsylvania, and I cannot get naked with other women in a steam room!"

At last! Vlad had come to Christ! For four years he had attended Bible studies, asked questions, and given Bibles to everyone. At an executive meeting during a break, while Paul Johnson and I prayed, Bruce Wilkinson answered his final questions and prayed with him. When we heard Bruce exclaim "Yes!" we went into the office.

"Tell them, Vlad," Bruce said.

"Well," Vlad replied, "it seems now that I have eternal life!"

He became a fine friend and a brother in Christ, which is how he signs his letters today. He began setting up his own business to facilitate missionaries coming to Russia. He worked for CMA as well, doing visas and transport.

As our time in Russia came to a close, I worked out distribution of the equipment, furniture, and supplies. Don Plummer, a CMA team member in Astrakhan, agreed to stay and help get things to their final destinations. A number of team members, including the Murleys from Taganrog, Carolyn Hawkes from Astrakhan, and the Hines family from Penza, all planned to return. Each city reported new believers, and the Christian Mission Union sent a pastor to Taganrog. The strategy was working!

I gave the book "Chicken Soup for the Soul" to my group of teachers. Later they told me through tears, "This book is so wonderful. We read it and weep. No one in Russia says such kind things."

I had a hard time leaving them. I had met their boss Valeri(the dean of the agricultural school) when he came to "check on" the class. When I offered him a Bible, he said, "I already have one."

Opening his briefcase, he showed me that he did!

We worked on a couple of small projects together. At his request, Don Dyk, the farmer from Ellensburg, Washington, whose wife sent so many flannelgraph sets, sent funds to publish Valeri Kromtchenov's book on replenishing dairy herds in Russia. In another project, Don sent 150 doses of frozen bull sperm. Gordon Kelly, a long-time friend and supporter from Ellensburg, brought the canister to Izhevsk. Valeri needed the Hereford sperm to cross with Siberian beef cattle to improve their herds. That project worked well, too. Gordon, Director of Environmental Health in Ellensburg, gave some lectures and visited the Russian their environmental programs in Izhevsk.

Bev busily helped finish her part in the new graduate school program for Russian nurses. She did not want to leave Russia. In spite of the bitter cold winter, she had accomplished a lot. When the director for Russian nursing education in Moscow heard she was to leave, she sent word from Moscow by Dr. Ida Bykova, saying, "Don't leave us. You have changed the way we do nursing in Russia! If you need money, we will get it for you."

But our five years were about up. Peter Nanfelt wrote, offering new assignments in China, Cambodia, and Mongolia. Because of MPSE we considered Mongolia, even though I had endured all the winter I would need for a lifetime. The 40-degrees-below-zero weeks made walking hazardous for my health, but we survived and thrived, and we would miss the warm friendships.

Bill and Judy were finishing up, too. In their four years, they had done an amazing job. They were leaving thousands of kids trained by hundreds of teachers using flannelgraph to teach the Bible. On their next stop, they planned to teach flannelgraph in Israel to the Russian immigrant churches there.

Audrey and Murray Scott of TFC came out and then traveled back to Moscow on the train. Even the train crew wished us well. We had spent so many days on the train that it seemed like part of our home, and the crew had gotten to know us. One time Bev left her computer on the train, and the car conductress returned it to her a few days later, safe and sound.

We did have a hot trip that time to Moscow. We couldn't open the window, and the air conditioner didn't work. We still remember the trip clearly, especially the time we saw an old man steering a plow pulled by two women in one of the villages. The Scotts joined when Vlad met us at the early-morning train and took us for breakfast at the Starlight Diner, our favorite U.S. fixture built "behind Lenin's back" in Oktober Square.

Finally Carl and Dr. Patricia Giurgevich came to Izhevsk. Patricia, a nurse who had been there to teach an MPSE module and do research with Bev, helped pack, and Carl did a final audit on our books. All the teams had gone to St. Petersburg for their final celebration, and then on to America. Bev also welcomed Olga Tensina back to Izhevsk from training in addiction counseling and promised to find someone in the States to help her do a program for addicts there.

We packed, attended farewell parties, gave stuff away, and cleaned out the apartment. Being so small, it didn't take long. Then Carl and Pat took the train back to Moscow with us. A large crowd of nurses and friends came to see us off at the station. They gave us hugs and kisses, then sent us on our way. We couldn't have been more thankful for their friendship. We still miss them.

We had spent five wonderful years in Russia. All our expectations had been more than met. The CoMission turned out to be the largest interagency, interdenominational Christian effort in modern church history. Eighty-four churches, missions, and parachurch groups had formed a cooperative, using the same materials, training, and strategy to introduce the Russians and CIS countries to a society based on Christian morals and ethics. And they practiced what they preached through the harmony they exhibited.

It blessed us to be part of the effort. The inconveniences never deterred us from giving the work all we had. Dr. Bruce Wilkinson wrote us, "Each time I am in Russia, I am reminded afresh of the tremendous challenges for those in the West. Doing without conveniences and dealing with shortages is bearable for a ten-day trip. But you all are coping day in and day out with incredible inconveniences and often actual hardships. I want you to know that you have my deep admiration and appreciation. Your upbeat spirit and injection of colorful humor into a monochromatic cultural environment bring variety and style to a tedious task. Thank you for setting the pace in so many ways for the Moscow team."

Well, it was a shot in the arm to get such encouraging feedback. Dr. Wilkinson was a God-sent leader and cheerleader for everyone. We could write a whole book about our time in Russia. Maybe someday we will. It's a place you never forget.

Carol Johnston with Andy at the
winter carnival in Izhevsk, Russia.

Andy with Gordon Kelly in Moscow. This ain't Ellensburg.... Toto

Visiting Tchaikovsky museum with Helen.

Chapter 29
The End in View

Chapter 29.
The End in View

We left Russia feeling unsettled because we really liked the life, work, and people there. Normally when we came back to America, we didn't feel a part of what was happening. However, we always enjoyed the welcome by friends and family, as well as the time spent fellowshiping while catching up on personal news. We had even gotten used to questions like, "So when are you going away again?"

Within a couple of months, people were back in their comfort zones, which usually unwittingly excluded transients like Bev and me. We have few close friends even today, partially because of those years away.

En route to the U.S., we had a nice week in Holland visiting old friends and eating Dutch food. We got home in time for Bev's dad Percy's eighty-seventh birthday. Matt and Sara, who had been living in Seattle, met our plane and helped us get to Ellensburg after the party.

We had discussed our next assignment with Peter Nanfelt, the CMA vice president for overseas ministries, and things changed. To follow up on our earlier discussions and correspondence, we received a letter while still in Izhevski, March 1998 in which he wrote:

Our top two choices are (now) Mongolia and Bosnia, but we need a little more time to see which of these locations will present the greatest needs and opportunities for your skills.

Assuming you would be prepared to accept one of these overseas assignments in the summer of 1999, we would like to invite you to come on board as missionary associates beginning July 1, 1998. You would be appointed for a four-year term. If you agree to this proposal, it would be with the understanding that you would both go on missionary tours in the fall of 1998 and winter/spring of 1999. With this in mind, we would like you to attend the Home Assignment Ministries Seminar in Colorado Springs August 1-6, 1998.

Please be in prayer about this and then respond as soon as possible so we can make appropriate arrangements. We are sincerely pleased about the prospect of your serving more closely with the Christian and Missionary Alliance and the Division of Overseas Ministries in the future. I look forward to hearing from you soon.

I answered his letter on April 23. There had been a lot of tough news from Colorado. Our CMA president, Paul Bubna, died while playing tennis. At about the same time, Cliff Westergren, who had just retired as the CAMA Services executive director, died the same way. Both had heart attacks.

I apologized for the delay in answering, explaining that his letter took 30 days to reach us in Izhevsk, Russia. Then I wrote, "Yes, we will accept the plan as presented."

I added, "Mongolia continues to be our first choice, but we will serve as needed. I would like to request that the Medical Professional Skills Enhancement and its fund be kept in place, as it will be a good door opener in either country. I've booked our homeward travel, and we should arrive in Seattle on July 1. With that lead time, we will be able to attend the home assignment seminar."

Still not sure which direction we would go, we planned our mission presentations on Russia and our previous CAMA Services work. Phil Skellie became the executive director for CAMA Services and was getting his footing in the new role. He was an excellent choice and had been with CAMA in Thailand as the director before going to Russia. He had a good feel for all the work ahead of him.

Now it was back to work. The next few weeks were busy. We found a house to rent for the year, picked up a "missionary car," and spent some time cleaning out Bev's brother Ed's home. A fire had burned it down and killed his wife.

Helen, a graduate student at Seattle Pacific and Bev's former translator in the early visits to Izhevsk, spent some time with us before flying back to Russia for a summer. We also spent time in contact with nurses and others who had taught an MPSE module in Russia. I noted that Bev had become so effective since the MPSE program that many people began recognizing her. When people met me they would often say, "Oh, yes, you're Bev's husband."

It had a nice ring to it, and she had earned it. Thousands of hours in demanding, 20-hour days resulted in changing the lives and practices of thousands of nurses.

We spent time fixing up the house we rented from long-time friend Kathy Mee, and I painted the 40-foot container for our belongings that sat in the pasture of Erin's parents, Mike and Ann King. We had work to do at the ranch, too, and the few weeks at home flew by too quickly. Of course there were the usual "coming home physicals." Bev was alerted to the possibility of osteoporosis. Well, we were getting older. I was about to turn 60 and Bev 59.

Then we were off to speaking engagements and the seminar and meetings in Colorado with Phil Skellie, Duane Wheeland, Peter Nanfelt, and a few others. We visited California to see my brother Paul and his family, Margaret Bridges of CoMission days, Karen Gammelgard, and several others.

Matt and Sara came to Ellensburg to camp by a stream out of town a ways. We spent a nice afternoon relaxing, and I even caught a trout. Then Matt said, "Okay, we camped! Now let's go to town for dinner and a movie."

Sara gave in reluctantly. They enjoyed their time even though a bear visited them that night. A few years later, Matt solved his problem with tents by buying Sara a Volkswagen camper as a present when she finished her master's degree in occupational therapy.

On September 19, 1999, I went to the East Coast to begin my speaking tour, and Bev went to the Midwest. One of my talks was from Jeremiah 29: "I know the plans I have for you."

I was glad God knew, because as the tour passed and we spoke in meeting after meeting, I still did not know whether we should go to Bosnia or Mongolia.

My tour was interrupted on October 6 when a huge hurricane roared through the Dominican Republic, where we had a lot of CMA work, and it swept on to Haiti and Puerto Rico. Dick Colenso, who also had relief experience, flew to Santo Domingo with a team of CMA workers. The field leaders, Bruce and Rebecca Dyk, had already begun a rapid response effort, delivering rice, oil, beans, and other needed staples.

The sugarcane-producing area where CMA had a number of churches was hardest hit. The fields and village were in shambles. It looked as if a huge mower had been used on the countryside. The sugarcane was salvaged by workers using machetes and hauling the cane onto large, wooden-wheeled wagons pulled by oxen. They took the cane to a mill that turned it into sugar. The people were so poor, we could have just as well been in the Congo more than 20 years before.

One pastor told me about the night of the storm. "The wind blew so hard we thought we were gone," he said. "Then when the eye came and it was quiet, I ran to the village nearby. It was a mess. The only building left was the CMA church. Men from the CMA in America had just been there and reinforced the structure using clench nails to secure the new metal roof. For once, everyone in town was in church and safe. Then I ran home. I arrived as the other wall of wind arrived. As I entered, the roof of my house began to lift. My wife jumped up and grabbed it, shouting, 'Lord, this roof belongs to one of Your children!' It still tried to blow away, so I grabbed it, too. She shouted, 'Lord, this is one of Your children who pays her tithes!' Still the roof tried to go. She added, 'And Lord, if this roof goes…well, I'll still pay my tithes!'"

"Then," the pastor recounted, "the roof settled in place."

We met with the missionaries. They were tired, yet optimistic about the future. We worked out a supply of food and a plan for more Alliance work teams to come and help.

Dick Colenso and some others left to check on things in Haiti, and I flew to San Juan, Puerto Rico. There I met with church leaders and several CMA volunteers. Some churches got flooded with mud and water, and a few had broken roofs and windows. Several towns had nearly been washed away, but, due to much experience, the church leaders were organized and did a good job. CAMA Services could help by sending money, food, and work teams.

Back in New York I rejoined my tour. Usually Bev and I didn't see each other for eight to ten weeks, which is what the missionaries called the "Alliance trial separation program," but Dick Chapin in Watertown, New York, arranged my schedule so I could rent a car and drive to Burlington, Vermont, where Bev's team was presenting its programs. It was a nice break.

Bev told me a funny story about her tour leader and lead speaker, Darrell Phenicie. He opened the mission celebrations, and as the other two arrived he would move on to the next stop. After finishing in the Midwest, they headed to Connecticut. Darrell was engrossed in reading a book while waiting for his flight at the Chicago airport. Two men sitting beside him were going to the same place. Suddenly he realized the men were gone. Looking up, he saw people disappearing through a boarding gate. Grabbing his bags, he sprinted through the gate and onto the plane. He settled into the seat and began to read again.

The plane had been flying a while when the flight attendant announced they would land soon and the temperature at their destination was 87 degrees. Eighty-seven! Suddenly Darrell was awake -- that was way too warm for Connecticut in November!

His seat mate was asleep, but he could see her boarding pass sticking out of the seat pocket. Quietly, he slid it up far enough to read…Dallas, Texas! He frantically called the flight attendant and explained his situation.

"Well," she told him, "you made one mistake, but we made two. We will get you to your destination on schedule." And they did.

It was 3:00 a.m. by the time he got to the town where he planned to speak. At 8:00 a.m., he began three back-to-back services. A few days later, as I was changing planes in Washington, D.C., there came Darrell down the jet way … reading a book. "So, Darrell, do you know where you're going today?" I asked.

He looked startled and replied, "I don't suppose I'll ever hear the end of that, will I?"

"No," I said with a laugh, "you've entered the missionary tour hall of fame."

Bev and I arranged to meet in Chicago at the end of our tour. We were both tired, but I insisted that we visit and thank all the people who had made major contributions to our five years in Russia, including Pat and Robert Wynalda, the Myers brothers, Walt Meloon, and others. It was an extra week, but considering that we would soon be going overseas again, it was the right thing to do. While in Orlando,

I got to check on two containers of relief goods being assembled at Correct Craft (Walt Meloon's factory) for shipment to Haiti and the Dominican Republic.

Phil Skellie informed us that Bosnia was our most-likely destination. The war there had been going on for more than eight years and had recently spread to Kosovo. CAMA Services researched the best route to bring relief and to open doors for missionaries who might go there. We began to understand what to pray for.

The 1998/99 winter/spring tour was in the west, from California to Alaska. Bev spoke in Idaho, Washington, and Oregon. She was excited about an invitation to present the MPSE program at the first international nursing conference in Beirut, Lebanon, that coming June. She had dozens of speaking engagements in between, and she also learned that she would need surgery to remove a tumor on her parathyroid; it had been found during her osteoporosis exam.

I prayed about everything with a lot of concern. We were about to go to another new place with people we didn't know and a language we didn't speak, all in an active war zone. Then there was the matter of raising several hundred thousand dollars for the work. We would not know a lot until we got there, but like Gideon, we just kept showing up for work, and God did the rest.

The Lord knew and understood our concerns, of course, just as He knew we would be on the plane to Bosnia at the appointed time. And in His special way, He gave us an encourager. Phil Skellie was on the phone from the CAMA office in Colorado Springs. "What did you tell the Wynaldas?" he asked.

"Let's see…I told them we were going out again to either Bosnia or Mongolia. That's all I knew."

"Well," he said, "they just sent money to your personal work special account. It's $100,000."

"Praise the Lord! Boy, that will get things going wherever we go," I responded.

Only God knew our ultimate destination, and before we even arrived, He had begun providing what we needed.

∽

In April, Dr. Wechter scheduled Bev for surgery. "It won't take long, perhaps an hour," she assured us.

 So the day after Easter, Bev went to the Virginia Mason Hospital. Unfortunately, things did not go exactly as planned. The surgery took over five hours! The next day, as she left the hospital, Phil Skellie phoned and asked me to join him on a survey trip to Kosovo and Macedonia. The bombing in Kosovo was going full force, and he needed to decide what CAMA Services should do.

I got Bev settled with Patricia and Carl Giurgevich before flying to Kodiak, Alaska, for a speaking engagement. I stayed in Alaska for four weeks. Bev was making a good recovery and proceeding with her plans to go to Beirut with Pat Giurgevich to present MPSE at the International Nursing conference.

On May 5, 1999, I met Phil in Cincinnati, and we flew to Zurich, Switzerland, where we met with Steve Goodwin, the CMA point man for the Balkans. Based in Budapest and able to speak German, he had a lot of good connections in the region. He knew pastors and missionaries all through the Balkans, so as we flew from Zurich, he told us about the status of churches in the area.

Getting to Tiranë, Albania, proved a challenge. On the flight from Zurich, the pilot told us that there was too much air traffic, which meant there were NATO bombers in the area, so we detoured around the Balkans and landed in Thessalonica, Greece.

We drove three hours from Thessalonica to the Albanian border crossing. Then, in a few minutes and $45 later, we arrived in Albania. The customs building was grimy, didn't have any windows, and was only partly finished. Beside it, a small group of nondescript, grubby, unshaven men warmed themselves around a fire. One offered a taxi. Steve bargained for a ride to Korcé, Albania, where we could get a bus to Tiranë, and we were on our way in an old Russian Lada.

The frontier was awash with small cement domes -- two-man pillboxes. Occasionally, one as big as a house appeared with doors and a cannon. The regime convinced everyone that they might be invaded any day, so they needed all the fortified defense points. They should have put the cement in the rutted and pot holed roads. Our careening taxi shared the road with donkey carts and heavily laden women.

The Chinese influence was everywhere. Large derelict factories, partially finished public works, and rusting equipment made the scene pretty dismal.

Albania followed Tito, the Yugoslav leader, into communism after World War II. When Tito broke away from Stalin, the Albanians invited the Russian communists in. When Khrushchev announced the move away from hard-line communism, Albania invited Mao's Red Guards from China and had its own "cultural revolution." After communism died in 1990, anarchy soon prevailed, and the people raided the military weapons stores. Now they struggled with the realities of freedom and the thousands of refugees from the war in Kosovo.

We packed ourselves inside the minivan taxi for a six-hour drive to Tiranë. Steve took us to the Stephen Center first, which was a joint agency office used by church groups and Christian voluntary organizations. We stayed with Dave Fyock, a CMAer who worked with MAF. He said MAF no longer flew there because everyone had an AK-47 and liked to shoot at planes. They began doing communications and logistics just as they had in Russia. We found that even Tiranë, the Albanian capital, was in a primitive state. I found it hard to comprehend the third-world situation, with modern Europe just an hour's flight away.

Ingrid, a facilitator with Stephen Center, arranged for a van, and we headed off at daybreak to Kukës, the border crossing to Kosovo, where Steve knew some missionaries to whom CAMA had sent refugee funds. It took over seven hours to climb the 135 miles of twisting and often badly deteriorated roads. We met huge trucks, armed NATO convoys, and Italian engineers valiantly trying to keep what remained of the road from sliding off the steep mountainsides.

As we drove into Kukës, which was nestled against the mountains that were the frontier with Kosovo, we saw a U.S. C-130 lifting off the recently upgraded MAF airstrip. The crew was helping the UNHCR as it struggled to keep up with the needs of more than 100,000 refugees. About 1,000 refugees still crossed the border daily.

We contacted Mathias and Martina Schriber, German missionaries cooperating with the Albanian Evangelical Church program. Their maternal and child health programs included a baby washing in which 800-1,000 babies were bathed and given clean clothes, food, and vitamins each day. They evangelized through the project and trained new believers to help. Their church services had mostly young, enthusiastic people. They hoped to send the trainees as missionaries to Kosovo once the fighting stopped. We were very impressed with their work and plans.

⌁

We watched people at the border as they struggled out of Kosovo, past Serbian soldiers. They ran a gauntlet of television cameramen who pounced on refugees for their stories. The rush of attention by the news people eager for photos frightened one man pushing an old woman in a wheelbarrow. In the midst of it all were voluntary agency workers with signs and hats with their logos, also trying to be on television doing "their thing."

"Looks like these refugees are pretty well cared for," I told Phil Skellie as we toured neat rows of tents in the huge tent suburb that had sprung up.

Thousands of refugees with money stayed in rooms that cost up to $1,000 a month, and 15 to 20 people crowded into each room. Although Albanian, the Kosovars represented a cash windfall for the rest of the Albanians.

Suddenly, we looked up and saw a pair of U.S. B-52s setting a course to launch cruise missiles into Kosovo. We heard gunfire in the distance and were told that the Kosovo army had a camp near Kukës that the Serbs shelled every now and then. We spent the night on the floor of the church, amidst sacks of clothes, cases of food, and bundles of diapers. The church freely worked among the refugees, turning relief into belief, and they did it well.

The next day we had another rough trip, this time down the mountain to Tiranë.

We picked up all the information we could on the needs and work by Christian agencies in Albania. Everyone compared it to a "wild west" situation. The Albanians robbed agencies and workers, and when stolen vehicles got reported to the police, they shrugged and said, "Well, they have bigger guns than we do."

Not too encouraging, but the Christians found that both the Albanians and the Kosovar refugees were open to the gospel. All the churches came together and cared for about 60,000 of the 600,000 refugees in Albania at that time. They had plenty of volunteer workers from Europe and the U.S., which seemed to keep them ahead of any problems. It was time to move next door to Macedonia.

The trip to the Macedonian border was quick – it took three hours by taxi, plus a short walk across the frontier, as we made the transition from the third world back to Europe. The customs people were friendly, and when they learned that we were humanitarian workers, they gave us our visas for free. A few minutes later, we found ourselves in a nice Mercedes taxi, speeding to Skopje, the capital. En route we met a British armed convoy loaded with road-building equipment, headed for Albania. Good luck, I thought.

I noticed right away that the road signs were Cyrillic. Just like Russia, I mused. Maybe this will be a good place to work from.

Our time in Macedonia went quickly. Pastor Mirco Andreev, president of the Evangelical Church of Macedonia, and the Macedonian Mission to the Balkans directed the relief work called AGAPE.

Yugoslavia had broken up, but Macedonia remained a major friend and trading partner for Serbia. With the war and NATO-enforced embargo in place, the Macedonian unemployment rate had reached 60 percent. Rather than complain, the Christians set to work caring for the Kosovar, Albanian, and Serbian refugees who flooded into the country. The best estimates counted more than 200,000 people living in camps, apartments, or with their relatives.

We visited some of the Macedonian and Albanian towns. Skopje, the capital, was beautiful; it sits in a bowl surrounded by mountains. A plain scattered with streams flowing down to the Vardar River which bisects the town. That river flows on down south and east to Greece, where it becomes the Axios River. Scattered across the plain are villages, some Serbian, some Macedonian, and some Albanian. The latter are marked by the spires from the mosques.

Sredno Konjare village is Albanian. The Macedonian government placed 50 families (more than 350 people) in the town, mostly with relatives. They felt it was better than a refugee camp, especially if they planned to be there a while.

When we arrived, we were invited in and served strong Albanian tea. I noticed the absence of furniture right away. Everyone sat on mats and mattresses on the floor. Up to 20 people packed into each room. They offered us cigarettes along with the tea, and a place to sit. We each took a cup and sat down. I knew there would not be room to move about when everyone lay down to sleep. As we spoke, we could hear planes overhead from time to time as they flew over to bomb Kosovo. One man said, "The Serbs bombed us because they hate us. NATO bombed us because they love us. What shall we do?"

When asked about when they might go back to Kosovo, they replied, "When it's safe."

Eventually the conversation stopped.

In the next room, a 90-year-old woman lay dying. A 13-year-old, probably a great nephew, sat forlornly by her mat. The old lady would not see Kosovo again.

The headman announced that they were ready to unload our truck full of food and other supplies. Their warehouse was a mosque. "The Turks built it with Saudi money, but we don't use it. Store the food there," he said.

The Albanians converted to Islam after Ottoman armies defeated Christian armies on the fields of Kosovo in 1384. Although conversion to Islam for then was a good political move, they didn't become very fervent in their beliefs. They resisted most of the rituals and requirements, such as no alcohol, even with Saudi Islamic missionaries. However, the women were pretty well subjugated in keeping with Muslim culture.

The main refugee camp was two miles from the border with Kosovo and spread out around an old, unused airport. Surrounded by barbed wire and NATO armed vehicles, it housed more than 100,000 Albanians. I was told that the fence was put there for their protection. They had a soccer field, a food distribution center, and even phone service. A CNN reporter showed up to get the latest rumors for the evening satellite feed to America. Mrs. Clinton visited the camp the following day. There was a lot going on, and NATO bombed on, day and night.

Pastor Mirco and his team really impressed me. They had set up a couple of warehouses to receive aid goods from European churches. We helped off load a large semi from Ireland. The churches viewed the situation as time to help the needy, get acquainted with the refugees, and pre-evangelize. When the refugees went home, they planned to follow with aid and evangelism. With this in mind, they registered more than 1,500 families comprising more than 15,000 people. They saw them biweekly and provided food boxes, clothing, and a listening ear. We visited several other groups doing similar aid, but AGAPE's (the Macedonian evangelical church) work seemed the best managed and had the most-coherent long-term plan.

We stayed in one of three apartments the church had rented for the many volunteer teams who came from all over Europe to help. On our second day there, a meeting of voluntary agencies was held in the church office. There we met Lars-Eric Lundgren with the Pentecostal Missionary Union of Sweden; we quickly found that we shared a common understanding on working together with AGAPE. A man from Germany said, "I want to help now. We can bring food from Germany."

Mirco said, "Our farmers are in trouble. They can't ship their crops to Serbia, so we buy all the food we can here."

It was hot in Macedonia -- 90 degrees, with high humidity and no air conditioning. "They need fresh food like watermelons," Mirco explained.

Before the German man left, he purchased 700 tons of watermelons. AGAPE delivered them to the Skopje camp and the one in Tetovo. AGAPE became identified by the refugees as "the watermelon church."

We looked at some apartments. They came fully furnished, just like in Russia. In talking with one of the owners, a comment was made regarding a rumor that Milosevic, the Serbian leader, had fled to South Africa. Then the man asked us, "Where will Will Clinton go?"

We were learning where the cultural and political mine fields were very active.

Once we completed our survey, we caught an early-morning flight on an old Russian TU154 of Macedonian Airlines. As we lifted off and headed out, we could see the sprawling refugee camp, the hills, the valleys, and even some smoke from the fighting in Kosovo. In my mind I heard Pastor Mirco's invitation, "Come over to Macedonia and help us."

It seemed like a good idea.

I met Bev in Spokane, and from mid-May on we crisscrossed the States and went up and down the West Coast, speaking in churches and getting ready to go to the Balkans. Her first night back from Lebanon I rolled over in the middle of the night and put my arm around her. It was good to have her home from Lebanon. She and Pat Giurgevich had traveled there for her to present the MPSE program to the first International Nursing Conference. It had been quite an experience, especially weathering an Israeli air strike on a power plant about a kilometer from Sami Dagher's home, where they had stayed. They loved Lebanon and had fun in London.

That first night Bev stiffened and said, "Pat, I'm not Carl!"

I hugged her tighter.

"Pat," she repeated, "I'm not your husband!"

"Well, I am," I said.

Suddenly she awoke. "Oh, I'm always uncomfortable sharing a bed with a woman!" she said. "I was dreaming I was in Lebanon."

We had a good laugh and I told her, "I'm going to have to speak with Pat about this."

Unloading relief goods in Skopje, Macedonia.

Kosovar refugees make do in a camp at Kukes, Albania.

Staying busy in the camp. Later this handcraft joined CAMA Craft.

Chapter 30
On to Macedonia

Chapter 30.
On to Macedonia

While at a CMA council meeting in Portland, Oregon, we received our official Macedonian call. We were at a breakfast with Phil Skellie, a CAMA Services director, and John Harvey from our Russian days; he had become the regional director for the Balkans. We had already discussed taking the "CAMA Services Eurasia Regional Coordinator" role. We would go to Sarajevo, Bosnia, to research, implement, supervise, and raise funds for the relief and development projects in Eurasia, including the Balkans, Commonwealth of Independent States (CIS), and Turkey, as a complement to CMA church-planting efforts.

The activity included working with AGAPE in Macedonia and the evangelical church in Bosnia. I planned to visit Turkey and Russia and develop more relationships with European donors when needed. I would also recruit workers as needed, arrange pastoral care for CAMA Services workers, and report to Phil Skellie quarterly. The chain of command was to Phil, all the other CMA team leaders, and project directors in the region. On paper, it was set up to try to please everyone, but in reality, I worked for Phil. So calls in Portland were made to Kosovo and Macedonia first, and then to the uttermost parts of the Balkans and Eurasia.

Bev was ready to go to another country that she didn't know, whose people were new to her, and whose language she didn't speak. She wouldn't know much until she got there, but she was ready to start MPSE in a new nation. We had the usual flurry of meetings, family get-togethers, and farewells, and then we traveled with the Byrom family, who were headed for Bosnia. We planned to travel together as far as Vienna, Austria. Bev was able to help them with their young children from Seattle to New York. It looked to be a long night over the Atlantic with some very active kids.

We traveled on Bev's sixtieth birthday, so I asked Dave Lundblad (our friend from Africa) for a cake or something on the flight. In New York, the agent called us up to the counter of Austrian Airlines. She took our boarding passes and gave me two more. I didn't examine them because I was helping the Byroms prepare their kids for the nine-hour flight to Vienna. When boarding the plane, the steward examined our passes and redirected us to -- you guessed it -- first class! "Happy birthday, Bev," I said. "Honey, from now on we travel on your birthday!"

We left the Byroms in Vienna and flew on to Skopje, Macedonia. I told Bev all I could, especially that the language had a lot of Russian words and that the Cyrillic alphabet was not only in use, but had been developed there in Macedonia more than 1,000 years earlier. Cyrill and Methodius did the work at Lake Ohrid University in the ninth century, using Latin, Greek, and Hebrew. Then they translated the Bible into Slavic.

The heat hit us hard. Someone said the temperature had reached 113 degrees that day, plus the humidity was high. David Aderholdt, a missionary who had just arrived, and Kosta Milkov met us with the church van. In a short while, we began unloading everything into our apartment right next to a fairly modern shopping complex called Beverly Hills. We had finally arrived in Macedonia, our new home!

The next day was our thirty-seventh wedding anniversary.

In our first newsletter from Skopje, we wrote, "A funny thing happened on our way to Bosnia…" The letter went on to tell about our time with family, including Drew and Erin, who arrived home for a break from Africa just before we left. We told folks about Bev's Lebanon adventure and then outlined our plans for Macedonia and Kosovo. CAMA Services planned to work with AGAPE, helping rehabilitation efforts in Kosovo, and Bev sought an MPSE continuing education program in Macedonia. We would also care for those still displaced in Macedonia.

The people of AGAPE and the evangelical church gave us a heartwarming welcome. Even Macedonians in the street, though expressing dislike for our President Clinton, welcomed our intention to help them deal with their crisis.

We sat in the "old town" section of Skopje, originally the Hellenic

Jewish part of the city. When the Nazis came, the Muslims joined them in killing the Jews and took over that part of the city. One could still see the Star of David carved on doorways. As we drank wee cups of Albanian tea, Bev and I agreed that Macedonia was a mixture of Lebanon, Greece, and perhaps Belgium. The people were Slavic and Albanian, with a few of Greek or Turkish descent, but the atmosphere was fairly laid back compared to Europe or Russia. We liked the food -- meat, salads, and a wide range of spices and fresh vegetables.

We could walk in most places, but I bought a very red Skoda for long-distance travel. It was built in Czekia (Czech Republic), in a joint venture factory with Skoda and Audi. It was a great car, and Pastor Mirco loved to drive it as much as I did. It was in his name and the church's, as the old Soviet laws complicated ownership by foreigners.

I returned from my first visit to Kosovo, the NATO bombing ended in July, and while the UN, NATO, the European Union, and Vol-Ags worked on a two-year plan to slowly return the refugees to Kosovo, the refugees en masse went back on their own. They not only took back their homes, but they drove out most of the Serbian families as well. They seized homes, businesses, and factories, and armed Albanians carried out their own form of ethnic cleansing right in front of everyone. Payback! NATO was powerless to stop them. More than 100,000 Serbs were driven out in just a few weeks.

Mirco took a group of us in the AGAPE van to look at what needed to be done. We got out a map of Kosovo and grouped the refugee families AGAPE had registered by village, then marked the village of origin. The majority of the people we helped were from an area in southeastern Kosovo. Crossing the border from Macedonia took a while, as long convoys of NATO military equipment and semis loaded with trade goods and relief materials lined up to enter Kosovo. An orderly procedure had yet to be established. Crossing the border would be problematic for a couple of years.

When the bombing stopped, the NATO armies rushed in. The British beat the U.S. military onto the one good road that would take them north to Pristina, the capital. The Russians, their "cousins," came south through Serbia and got to the Pristina airport first. When NATO commander General Wesley Clark ordered the British general to expel the Russians from the airport, he responded, "I'm not starting World War III over this godforsaken piece of real estate."

Once the Russians secured the airport, the side of a hill close by opened up, and the Serbian Air Force flew its MiGs out to Belgrade. The Dayton Peace Accords allowed the Serbs to keep Kosovo as part of the remainder of Yugoslavia, along with Montenegro and any military assets they still could use.

There is still no real peace there, even all these years later.

When we drove into the village of Kačanik, about 25 miles inside Kosovo, where the main road exits the mountains and the plains of Kosovo begin, the people rushed out of the shops calling, "AGAPE! You've come to help us!"

Thus began our rehabilitation work in Kosovo. They were Muslim, and the area had been a stronghold of the Albanian resistance, so they had a strong prejudice against the Macedonians. They also knew that we were Christians, but what they really remembered was AGAPE food, clothes, and watermelons.

"Mirco, I need to hire a partner for Kosovo," I told him. "I can pay him directly or through AGAPE at the rate you recommend, but he needs to be able to speak Albanian."

Mirco didn't hesitate in replying, "I have just the man for you: Risto Petrovski. And here he is."

Risto was medium height, had dark hair, looked about 32 years old, and he could work for me full-time. "Good," I said, "do you have your passport handy?"

Looking a bit startled, he said, "Yes."

"Well, let's go to Kosovo."

And we did.

Because of the border congestion, Risto and I decided to take a taxi to the border crossing, walk three quarters of a mile, and then hire a taxi in Kosovo. We hired an Albanian driver and spent the day visiting possible work sites in and around Kaçanik, Ferizaj, and other villages in the region. The roads were bad and crowded with civilian and military vehicles. After a stop at a Swiss church project site, we headed back toward the border, where we encountered a roadblock. Wondering how long it would be, I got out of the car and walked to an armored vehicle and ambulance where a Swedish soldier stood. There's no road rage in these situations. Their cannon was big, and people did as they were told. "How long might this take?" I inquired.

"Oh, not long," he said. "They found a big mine by the Russian base here, and they're working on it."

I turned to go back to the car. Keeping next to a stone wall, I had gotten about halfway when ker-blam! The mine exploded! I was momentarily stunned. Shades of Cambodia and Lebanon! "I'm getting kind of old for this," I mumbled to myself.

Risto's eyes were very big as I climbed back into the taxi.

When we got back to Skopje, I got my hands on a KFOR (Kosovo FORces) map that showed routes and mine fields. KFOR was the name given to the peacekeeping effort in Kosovo, and we became well acquainted with its maps and personnel.

Bev was busy getting her MPSE program going. She first discussed the idea of offering classes to the nurses with Mirco. "Oh," he said, "my wife, Nada, trained as a nurse before she went to seminary. I'm sure she will want to work with you."

When Bev explained the program to Nada Andreeva, she was enthusiastic. "When do we start?" she wanted to know.

Bev responded, "We need to find someone in authority or in a nurses' association."

Suddenly Nada remembered that she had seen a hospital nurse with a pin that said, "Kindest Nurse of the Year."

"Let's find her and ask who gave her the pin," Bev said.

Soon after, they met with Velka Lukic, the president of the newly formed Macedonia Nursing Association. After listening to Bev, Velka said, "We are about to have our first Macedonian Nurses Association meeting. You must come. It's at Lake Ohrid."

In a short time, MPSE made a donation to the Macedonia Nursing Association, and we were driving to the three-day meeting in the red Skoda.

Bev had been praying about how to let the nurses know what she wanted to teach, and the Lord answered. The opening speaker was the country's leading forensic pathologist. He spoke of the great need to improve their medical care delivery and said the basics must be attitudes found in the Bible, specifically 1 Corinthians 13. "Wow!" Bev said to Margarita Milenkoska, a Christian nurse who was translating for her, "so he's a Christian!"

"No," said Margarita, "he's my uncle; he does not go to church, but he knows the truth."

Bev was amazed and felt that if the opportunity came, this was a good opening for her to explain the MPSE program. On the last evening, Velka said to Bev, "Tomorrow you will present MPSE at the closing session."

Bev prayed; she worried because she didn't have any brochures, handouts, overheads, or videos. The next day, in her speech to the 600 nurses, she quoted the words from 1 Corinthians 13 used by the opening speaker and said, "I would like to teach you patient care based on Christian love and western skills."

She was a hit, and God opened the door for MPSE in Macedonia. In a short while, she hired a translator and began to translate the modules. She sent out an SOS to American nurses to answer the Macedonian call to teach an MPSE module, and she also visited clinics and hospitals with Nada to find places to teach.

We moved to another apartment soon after arriving in Skopje. We needed space for visitors and offices for MPSE and for Risto and me. It was on a quiet street, which was a pleasant change. Half a block away was Sveta Petka, a historic Orthodox church. We enjoyed the bells and the choir. Our first apartment was at a park, and the Macedonians loved to socialize and party in the park, right beneath our bedroom window, until 1:00 or 2:00 a.m. Now we had two floors, four sleeping rooms, two baths, two offices, a living and dining room, and a nice kitchen. We also had two balconies where we could sit and eat meals. We loved the place.

We hadn't been there long when one day I began to smell wood smoke and something aromatic cooking. I went onto the balcony and saw our neighbors below in their courtyard, stirring a large pan on a small, wood burning stove with a spoon about four feet long. They were cooking a red sauce. I got my camera and called down to ask if they minded my taking a photo. "Not at all," they replied. "Come down and have some."

The sauce, called ajvar sauce, was made from sweet red peppers. It was a fall tradition we came to enjoy with them. One time Bev even went with Nada to her childhood village near Strumica, Macedonia, to help make the sauce and to harvest peanuts. She made a big hit as a "peasant woman," and when Mirco and I drove down to get her, we feasted on homemade bread, boiled potatoes, trout, and ajvar sauce.

Our guest house was a favorite with the incoming regional director, John Corby, and John Harvey. They came in for a tour of the work and reviewed our strategy. The CMA did not plan to plant CMA churches in the Balkans; they wanted to help the churches already there. The men were pleased with the Macedonian evangelical church and AGAPE connections. They fully understood CAMA's role and rationale for living in Macedonia, especially since MPSE had begun educating nurses. After nearly five hours of waiting to cross the border, they knew why we planned to commute to Kosovo rather than live in Pristina. After staying with us, they recommended that Trent Thornton, the Balkan CMA team leader for CMA get a guest house in Mostar, Bosnia, too.

Dianna Ullrich arrived in Macedonia to begin language study. We had first met her in Portland, Oregon, at CMA Council, and knew she wanted to study Albanian and work in Kosovo. Risto and I took Di on her first trip. Eshref Shehu, our regular taxi driver, took us to Pristina and then to some of the houses under repair that CAMA/AGAPE financed.

We began the repair program by meeting with families we had on record from their previous time in the camps. When we offered to supply materials for the repair, the first response was, "Who will pay us?"

"Whose house is it?" I asked.

"Ours," they responded.

"Who built it in the first place?" I asked.

"We did," they answered.

"So build it again. We will give you the materials," I said.

"But the fighting did this," they responded.

"You were fighting too," I replied.

At that time NATO, the UN, the European Union, and several large Vol-Ags debated how to proceed with rebuilding Kosovo. About 100,000 houses had significant damage. Major buildings in the cities were smashed, and the infrastructure was in shambles. Each organization wanted the rebuilding to be done according to its country's building codes. Kosovo had been built without using any codes. They had built sturdy houses of cement, clay tile, and timber with terra-cotta roof tiles, and they wanted to rebuild in the same way.

Picking up my papers, I told the group in that launch meeting, "Well, if you want to live in tents for a couple of years while they work out the bureaucracy, okay. I'll go to the next village."

"Oh, wait, we will do the work," they said.

I explained the plan further. We would have a Macedonian engineering team help decide what materials to give and supervise their flow. I also committed to providing food boxes for the first year because all their gardens had been destroyed. We would provide clothing and blankets as well. We selected ten homes with an estimated cost of $9,000 per home, and the work began. Lars-Eric Lundberg of Pentecostal Missionary Union (PMU) moved to Macedonia to join AGAPE with his wife, Elisabeth, and their children, Petrus and Matilda. They donated a heavy Volvo truck with a hydraulic arm so we could move materials, and we were under way.

Dianna Ullrich wanted to move to Kosovo right away, but her supervisor said, "It's too dangerous. Study the Albanian language in Macedonia." With Macedonia being at least 25 percent Albanian, this worked well for her.

We had weekly relief and development meetings, and AGAPE ministered to more than 7,000 families in Kosovo and Macedonia. The meetings usually consisted of Risto, Mirco, Lars-Eric, Marino Mojtic (Mirco's assistant), and me. Bev, Nada, and Elisabeth often came, too. We discussed the work's progress and needs, prayed for each other, and gave updates on developments in other work in the region.

Mirco told us about a Macedonian missionary to Croatia. He had saved money to buy a car and was en route to Skopje, where Mirco could help him find a good one. While at a roadblock, however, soldiers stole most of his money. He was sad because money was hard to save on his meager salary, and he really needed a car.

After Mirco dismissed the meeting, I pulled him aside and said, "I know you just got a one-year-old Skoda. How about this? You sell him your car for whatever money he still has, and I'll sell you my new red Skoda for that amount. Please don't tell anyone, even him, what we're doing."

Mirco's eyes widened. "You would do this?" he asked.

"Yes," I replied, "the Lord provided the car in the first place, and you drive it more than I do. It's already in your name anyway."

We sent a very happy missionary in a nearly new car back to Croatia, and Mirco, with a smile that nearly matched his great size, loved the red car. I contacted Daryl Brooks in Canada, and he immediately sent funds to replace the Skoda.

AGAPE had full registration with KFOR, and that gave us the privilege to cross the border and buy vehicles. I ordered a new Ford Ranger diesel four-wheel-drive, crew-cab pickup. Marino Mojtic and I flew to Copenhagen, Denmark, and had a nice drive across Europe on our way back.

Two days after I returned, Trent Thornton and I used tire chains and four-wheel drive to cross the mountains from Kosovo. We were in a snowstorm, so I used the Jazince crossing that took us home via Tetovo. New political tensions complicated our work. The Kosovar Albanians grew unhappier all of the time over the Dayton peace agreement. The more-militant ones ambushed NATO soldiers and attacked Serbian enclaves that remained in Kosovo. It made our work and travel more dangerous.

In February 2000, Bev began teaching MPSE in Macedonia. A nurse came from Seattle, and the program began. She hired Marija, a

Macedonian social worker who spoke very good English, as a secretary-translator. With Nada as Bev's deputy, they did the visits and slowly gained the confidence of the medical community.

While speaking in the U.S., Bev recruited nurses whenever she could. She also looked for someone to help with MPSE in Russia, and especially the substance-abuse project that Olga Tensina had there. Finally, at her last tour stop, she linked up with Jane Wolf in Salem, Oregon. Jane ran an extremely effective substance Abuse treatment program for the Salem CMA church. They helped up to 100 addicts recover each year through their adaptation of the 12-step program. Bev invited Jane to go to Russia to help develop Olga's program.

In October 1999, Bev and Jane Wolf had gone to Izhevsk, Russia, where they educated pastors on how the churches could work together to reach addicts in their community. By the time Jane left, the churches adopted the concept that "it takes a church family to fully recover an addict." Jane had also arranged for the Tensinas to be supported full-time through the recovery group of the CMA in Salem. It was an amazing answer to prayer! Mainly funded by the recovered addicts in Salem, it continues today.

Bev really began to feel at home in Macedonia. We had good neighbors and colleagues. She considered driving but told me, "Traffic here is kind of like square dancing, and I don't totally understand the rhythm."

"Part of the problem," I agreed, "is that not everyone dances to the same song."

Eventually, she did drive there.

At Christmas, Bev flew back to Seattle. She finalized the agreement with the Washington State Nurses' Association and got approval for MPSE modules for Macedonia. She also convened a family meeting with her brothers, because her parents' health was failing. Her dad, who had cancer, was trying to care for her mom, who had Alzheimer's. When she got back in January 2000, she told me that we needed to monitor the situation and take a two- or three-month furlough the coming year.

Soon modules were being taught in several clinics in Skopje, as well as in other cities. Bev got requests from cities in the Balkans, especially Bosnia. She needed full-time help and realized that someone should be identified as her eventual replacement. By getting help soon, she could train the person for the future leadership of MPSE.

"How can I pray for you folks?"

We were enjoying lunch on the main square in Skopje with Captain Douglas Prentice, a CMA chaplain with the U.S. Army's 101st Airborne Division. We had become friends and even visited him at Camp Bondsteel, the main U.S. base in Kosovo.

"Well," Bev said, "pray I find a helper. I need a nurse to eventually replace me."

He started to make a note of her request and then said, "Wait, I know who she is! In my church in Akron, Ohio, there's a very-well-trained nurse. She has done all her qualifications for missions, and she's ready for her assignment. Her name is Cynthia Swanson, and I think she's teaching at Cedarville College right now."

We prayed and immediately requested Phil Skellie to expedite her appointment to MPSE in Macedonia. Another answer to prayer, hers and ours!

Things developed well in Kosovo. Lars-Eric Lundgren invited some Swedish officials to see our house reconstruction project. They were impressed with the "food for work" aspect and the overall progress. "All the bureaucrats are still arguing over how to do this," the Swedes said. "Where did you learn how?"

"In Beirut," I replied.

In a short time, the Swedish government approved $1 million to rebuild 100 homes and began to process a follow-on program for another $1.5 million.

We rented a storage yard for building materials from Eshref's cousin. The PMU not only managed the rebuilding, but they also had their offices and equipment there. We received semi loads of brick, cement, steel, lumber, and so on at the yard. We also stored food boxes for the food-for-work and emergency needs. We bought 20 semi loads of building materials each month.

Getting things across the border was a full-time job for an expediter. On one trip with me, Bev counted 500 trucks waiting to cross from Macedonia to Kosovo. The heavy traffic broke a strategic bridge over a gorge, forcing officials to build a detour up and down its steep sides. There was always something to adjust to.

During the first year, we sent more than 1,000 tons of food to Kosovo. Mirco and the team agreed that we needed to plant seeds when spring arrived to reduce the need for imports. Considering the altitude and climate, we needed to find seeds that would grow in Kosovo. The UN and World Food Program were again at odds, this time over what kind of seed to buy. The Irish said they had the best potatoes, but so did the Germans and French. Meanwhile, the planting season was coming fast.

Mirco and I agreed that Macedonian seed from the high altitudes in their mountains would be best. We purchased 27 tons of potato seeds, 7 tons of onion seeds, and 3 tons of garlic. In addition, we found seed packets from one of the Vol-Ags and made up 12,000 garden kits. When the season came, they could plant their own food.

One request came that year from the director of the Red Cross in the enclave of Strpce, Kosovo: "We need paprika," he implored. The sweet, red peppers were the key ingredient in Ajvar sauce. "Ajvar sauce," he said, searching for the right analogy, "is to us like…ah…Viagra is to the rest of the world!"

We sent him 20 tons, and I sent Phil a photo of the "Serbian Viagra."

While the Macedonian church had well-trained pastors and could function effectively and cooperatively, the Bosnians did not have much training and had little in the way of cohesive leadership. This made forming an AGAPE-type agency complicated. Peter Kuzmic came up with the name when the Croatian president asked him to form an aid program for war-torn Croatia. "You can work with CARITAS," the

Catholic program, the president suggested.

"I don't think so," Peter told him. "We are evangelicals, and to get others to work here, we need our own name. Since evangelicals don't use Latin much, we'll use Greek and call ours AGAPE. They mean the same thing."

President Tudzman agreed, and so in Croatia, the Balkans, and Macedonia, the evangelical church aid work used the name AGAPE, or "love in action."

As new needs arose, God supplied. Elisabeth Lundgren saw a great need to deal with children traumatized by the war. She brought the idea to our weekly aid meeting at the church in Skopje. Mirco agreed, and CAMA Services pledged money to help. She met with school officials in Kačanik first. They had a lot of needs, and we agreed to help with school repairs, books, and even computers. KFOR took our school-repair estimates, their soldiers brought the materials, and the Albanians did the work.

The school director agreed with the plan for the traumatized kids. First Elisabeth and Dianna Ullrich held classes for the teachers so they could understand trauma in children, which they observed in both their socialization and action. People there instilled hatred in the children early. The kids had trading cards with photos of the rebels and their body counts from killing Serbs. Some kids lost their ability to socialize or concentrate on studying. Vengeance was instilled in the children by the adults at every opportunity.

Once the community and the teachers were trained, Elisabeth enlisted the help of short-term workers to put on a 'Dream Day' in Kačanik. Supervised games, contests, races, food, and just plain joyous fun helped get the kids out of their depression. We had "Dream Day" in Macedonia, too. In Sredno Konjare, Lars-Eric and I roasted 300 hot dogs for the kids. We loved the "Dream Days" as well.

Mirco invited a few of us to drive to Rostushe, a small village with a unique history. Under the Ottoman Empire, not only had the Albanians converted to Islam, but some of the Macedonians did, too. When Macedonia sent the Turks back to Turkey in 1956, they also sent a significant number of Macedonian Muslims. They formed an enclave in Turkey in which the people still speak Macedonian. Not everyone in Rostushe got sent out of Macedonia, and our church wanted to reach them.

We met the officials, who said their schools needed help. We also toured the beautiful village, which was perched on a steep mountainside above a deep valley, and where the ancient Saint Jovan Bigorski church and monastery sat. In the winter they had deep snow. At a small restaurant, we sat by a swimming pool filled with big trout, some of whose former family members we were now eating!

"Are the bears a problem here?" I asked. I'd seen a silver gray skin on the principal's floor.

"Oh, yes, they eat the livestock."

"Do you hunt them?"

"No," he said, "they are protected here. But if they eat a goat or cow, we can sue the bear in court."

I laughed and queried, "If the bear loses, what then?"

"We can shoot him," he explained, "but the bear never loses. Bears do, however, have accidents."

Over the next weeks, we provided them with books and school furniture, and a great "Dream Day" was done by students from Simpson College in Redding, California. Mirco also planned a concert and a showing of the Jesus film.

Nada told Bev their evangelism strategy was "inching people along to the gospel." When a nurse passed a module, she was given a professional gift, a personal gift, and a Bible or Christian book. Approximately one-quarter of the nurses were Muslims. One administrator did not allow Bev and Nada to give them a Bible. He did agree we could leave a box of Bibles in the classroom, and on their own initiative most of the nurses took one.

In one class a nurse asked, "Who finances these modules? There are many costs: salaries, treats, translators, notebooks, gifts, airfare for nurses coming to teach a module, and so on. Who pays for this?"

When Bev responded that nurses and friends provided the money, she wanted to know what kind of nurses and friends would do this. Bev answered that they were Christian nurses and friends, and she wanted to know why? Bev told her they were following Jesus' example. With this, she wanted to know more about Jesus.

Nada and Bev decided to put on retreats for the nurses who had taken the modules. Bev would invite 20 nurses and have professional workshops and games, but the main thrust would be a speaker presenting four talks on Jesus and making the gospel as clear as possible.

The first retreat was at a resort high in the mountains at Mavrovo. The theme was "Who Is on Your Health Team?" It grew from the teamwork model of all the MPSE modules. It was beautiful there. The hotel was a Swiss chalet style, with pool, hot tub, and sauna, as well as hiking and winter skiing. The 27 nurses who went were wild about the retreat. Bev was able to bring Peggy Gunther, a nurse we had known from 1975, as the speaker. Her church paid all costs for the retreat

Bev and Nada decided that retreats, as the Lord provided, would be a regular feature of the MPSE project. There was no objection to presenting the gospel in this manner.

Our place in Skopje, Macedonia.
We drove many miles in this Ford

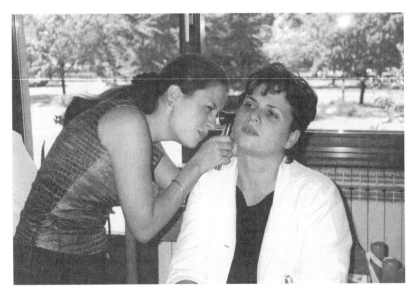

MPSE in Skopje, Macedonia

A new CAMA Craft product line grows in Kosovo.
The lady lost both legs at the knee.

Sonja with her gypsy class

Cindy Tolmachev and Bev representing MPSE in Macedonia

Eric and Andy prepare lunch for 300 kids at Dream Day

Sara and Matt visited us in Russia and Macedonia

Chapter 31
Preparing to Move On

Chapter 31.
Preparing to Move On

Risto and I were tired. We'd been to Prizen, then to Pec, and finally over to Pristina, and now fighting had blocked us from crossing the border. We got the only hotel room left and found we would have to share the only bed. We laughed a lot, and then Risto told me his story.

When he was young, he got into drugs. "I was a mess," he said. "My drug use got me kicked out of the Serbian army, and I spent my time on the streets like your hippies. One day I was in Skopje and came upon a crowd. Two young Swedish guys were talking, so I stopped. When I heard them mention Jesus, I said 'This is not for me' and started to leave.

"A girl I know said, 'Oh, Risto, you know English, please stay and translate for us.' She was pretty, so I said, 'Okay.' When they were done, the Swedish young people came up and asked me to do translation for them. They were nice people, and I said, 'Okay.' The next day, we were about to finish when one of them said, 'This truth is for you, too, Risto.'

"I had a beard and long hair and was pretty dirty. I told them I have a rotten life. If God can change that, I'm interested. We prayed, and God changed my life. They convinced me to go to a Bible school in Tiranë, Albania. I went and improved my Albanian language, but I soon found they were pretty shallow.

"About then I was invited to go to Sweden to work. I stayed two years and learned Swedish. When I got back to Skopje, Mirco said, 'Oh, Risto, we have a job for you. A gypsy family have come to Christ. We want you to go over and lead a Bible study with them. You know Romy [the gypsy language], and they know Macedonian.'

"They lived in the gypsy section and were a very nice family. At the end of the lesson, a young woman came out to serve coffee. I was melting inside; she was beautiful! On my way home I told myself, 'Risto, you go there for Bible study…nothing else!' But every week she was there, and I had to tell myself the same thing. I did this for three years!

"One day she was standing outside the church when I came out.

"'So Risto,' she said, 'when will you marry, and who will you marry?'

"Without thinking I said, 'How about you?' and before she could answer, I bolted for the car to help with an afternoon service across town. On the way back I asked Pastor Mirco, 'What do you think if I were to marry Nena?'

"He gave me his big pastor's smile and said, 'She is a fine sister in Christ. She has a seven-year-old son from an 'arranged marriage' when she was 13 or so. When she became pregnant, the husband gave her back. All that happened before she met Jesus, so the church has no problems with her, but you must know you are marrying into another culture.'

"When we got to the pastor's house for supper, he said to his wife, Nada, 'Guess what?' Nada said, 'I know. Nena has been here already.'

"We were married three months later," Risto concluded.

Nena's son, Michael, had been praying for a daddy for years. Risto adopted him, and together he and Nena had a daughter, Sarah. I was so thankful the Lord had brought Risto to CAMA Services. We traveled all over the Balkans, and he always knew a local language to do the work.

The church was always open to help anyone in need. In Kochani, Macedonia, the local pastor made a deal with a restaurant that was closing: Provide a good meal a day for the destitute and elderly, and we will pay the restaurant price for the meals you serve. More than 100 people each day were enjoying the food, fellowship, and simple gospel presentations from time to time. The restaurant workers were able to keep their jobs, and the town elders took notice. A similar project was done in Bosnia.

In Skopje, the church did a similar program at the time of the Orthodox Christmas on January 9. Tickets were printed, and invitations were sent and handed out to the needy. A closed restaurant was reopened for the occasion, and more than 600 people were served a simple meal, with Christmas singing by the church band. We even sent meals to a gypsy village near our rented warehouse. More than 40 families lived there in squalor. We helped with food, clothes, and firewood, and we hired them from time to time to load and unload trucks.

When the gypsy chief asked me to divide the firewood on one occasion, I said, "You're the chief."

"Yes," he said sadly, "but if anyone gets one stick more than the others, there will be a fight, and I'll be attacked!"

So I did the work instead.

We also put in a water system for them and started a school to teach the kids to read and write Macedonian. Without basic Macedonian, they could not attend public schools. In the church we had a special education teacher, Sonja Sazdanovska. We hired her to run the program, and she was very successful. She even taught them to cook one good meal each Friday, which they got to enjoy if they had done all their lessons that week.

One girl was so determined to learn that when her parents tried to marry her off when she was 13, she put up such a fight that they gave in and let her continue her education. By the end of the year, she had caught up with the rest of the students in regular Macedonian public schools.

We continued a youth work program and helped them with their homework. After the whole village saw the Jesus film, one young man believed and became a regular church attendee.

In June 2000, Bev and I flew to Thailand to attend an international CAMA Services conference. It was held at Khao Yai. We had a great group there. We played golf and had good food and fellowship. The speaker used the subject wholism, a total integration of faith and action. It was our heartbeat and had been for years. In Macedonia the people were often puzzled at the Western notion of separating the two artificially, which was so contrary to Scripture. Bev and I marveled at what CAMA Services had become, and we loved time with Kaek and her husband, Verdon, and their two children. The Bailey family had grown, as had the Albrights and the Dirks. Carolyn Dean was now Dr. Carolyn Dean, and there were many new faces. We also saw Colonel Kamol and his wife, Oiy.

We returned to Macedonia via the U.S. We spent some good time with our family. Matt and Drew were both in graduate school; Drew at Central Washington State for a masters in organizational development. Matthew at Seattle University for a masters in software design. I had a checkup at Virginia Mason, as did Bev. All was well, so we flew on to

Edinburgh, Scotland, where we met Nada, Mirco, and Margareta. An International Christian Nurses conference was being held there.

I stayed a day or so, then continued to Macedonia. A team from Simpson College was just finishing its summer with CAMA Services. The students had handled 127 tons of vegetables, put on several "Dream Days," and survived being attacked by some skinheads in Strpce, Kosovo. All in all they'd had a good experience, and we were thankful for their service.

AGAPE finally got its full registration with the Macedonian government. Under the old socialist rules, there was no work category for pastors, especially evangelicals, so to get social services, they had to be listed as unemployed tradesmen. With AGAPE now registered, they could be listed as employed humanitarian workers. This was partly the result of the election of Boris (Kiril) Trajkovski, a clearly evangelical believer, as Macedonia's president. The new laws began to break down barriers for the church. Near Strumica, the first evangelical church in 100 years was being built. More new churches were being planted, too. It was great to see God acting through prayer and hard work.

The church in Skopje had to expand; they had no room for all the new believers. In the backyard they had put up a "tent." Its metal structure was covered by rubberized canvas. "Mirco," I suggested, "we could seat 100 people out there year round if we put up an aluminum roof and temporary walls."

It had to be temporary, as no building permit was possible. So CAMA Services helped and threw in a Pergo floor. Bev and I purchased 120 chairs, and the church grew again until you had to come early to get a seat. Soon it was 120 sitting and 100 standing for the two-hour worship service.

They began an outreach called the Alpha Course. Our neighbor Mimi attended. When she got home at 1:30 a.m. one night, her phone rang. "Mimi," her older sister demanded, "where have you been? I've been calling you!"

"Oh," Mimi replied, "I was at work, then went to the Alpha Course at church."

"What's that?"

"Well, we have a nice meal and talk about life's problems, then we look for answers in the Bible. We talk and pray until we're through."

Her sister interjected, "Well, I'm coming to this Alpha!"

"You know you can't," Mimi replied.

"Why not?" her sister asked.

Mimi responded, "You know you're an atheist. You don't believe in God."

"I'm an atheist because the Orthodox don't have answers," her sister said. "If you're getting answers, I'm coming to Alpha!"

In August 2000, Cindy Swanson arrived. She was sharp and well trained. She not only had two master's degrees, but she was also a certified midwife. Bev was delighted. She had a partner and a potential successor. Cindy was on a two-year appointment, but said she would consider a longer assignment. She'd begun the language school and quickly adapted to the new culture.

A few days after she arrived, we were having a meal at a restaurant. Looking at me, she asked, "Do you remember me?"

"Umm, no, I don't think so," I answered.

"I was nine years old," she said, "and you brought slides of CAMA Services to our Christian school in Akron, Ohio. I decided that day to be a missionary with CAMA Services."

What a wonderful answer to prayer and commitment! Cindy is now the MPSE regional coordinator in Europe. She married Aleksandar (Atse) Tolmachev, one of the young men in the church. After seminary in Croatia they returned to Macedonia where they serve the church and MPSE

Shahadia Shehu wanted us to expand our AGAPE project. More women wanted to earn money through crochet, and we wanted to help them. She had been working with AGAPE in Kosovo from the first. She had worked in a bank before the war and knew everyone in the region. I hired her to keep records and help us know who really needed help. Her English was okay, and her executive skills were excellent. More than once she marked an aid application in a way that I knew we needed to help someone else.

Eshref was her cousin, and being Muslim, he frowned on her working, but she would not be held back by the growing Muslim pressures to go back to the old ways. She was trained in economics.

She first suggested the crochet project when we were trying to come up with a way for widows, especially those with children, to earn money. One lady was particularly sad. She was from a small village high in the hills. She had a son, and when her husband was killed in the ongoing fighting, she was pressured to move to his family's village and become another wife to her father-in-law. When she refused, his family came and took her son. We were happy to be able to help her use her crochet skills to earn some money.

Soon there were others. Bev patterned the work like the CAMA crafts program she'd helped start in the Thai refugee camps. In Kosovo she worked with Shahadia Shehu to explain the required quality, and once the handcrafts began to sell in the U.S., CAMA developed a catalog of the favorites. We would buy the items, which ranged from doilies to tablecloths, ship them to the sellers in the U.S., and after they sold get the money back to the widows. Erin, our daughter-in-law, sold $15,000 worth in her first year at crochet parties.

The program kept 40 women employed. Shahadia wanted to add 20 more, and up in Bosnia some ladies were beginning production, too. We worked out a way to grow with Dianna Ullrich, known to the ladies as "Lady Di," overseeing the project. She had moved to Kosovo along with several other CMA language students and was now joining the CAMA Services team.

In September, Matt and Sara came for a visit. They loved the blend of cultures that make up the Balkans. They found the time in Kosovo, visiting the enclave of Strpce, fascinating. It's made up of 10 to 15 Serbian villages surrounded by hostile Albanians. Their main protectors are the U.S. army and the Ukrainian army, which patrol and maintain heavily armed roadblocks. It's always tense traveling there, as one passes several sites where bloody ambushes have taken place. After they saw Macedonia, we drove them down to Greece, and they went on to Athens.

In October, I met Phil Skellie in Mostar. We were doing several micro-enterprise projects after having held seminars on small business in both Macedonia and Bosnia. We reviewed the projects and discussed ways to press home the gospel message through the relief and development context. It was a constant battle. In Bosnia, the small business loans were not performing, partly because we had no one there to follow up consistently. Bev had even gone to Bosnia to teach, but although the ministry of health endorsed MPSE, when she held a seminar in Zenica, no follow-up could be arranged. The Bosnians had the idea that once they got the Christians' money, they did not have to repay. We had work to do.

Phil and I flew on to Turkey. In Istanbul, we visited some tent makers and talked about ways to increase their number. I'll never forget visiting the Blue Mosque, a tenth-century church. Inside, crusaders had carved graffiti. In the main room under the huge dome, each pillar had a 60-foot mosaic of a seraphim inlaid over a thousand years ago, before the church, now a museum, was turned into a mosque.

From Turkey we went to Russia. Vlad was his usual cheerful self. He chauffeured us about and sent us on our way to Krasnodar. We looked at the seminary and discussed CAMA's opportunities with the Russian mission director, Douglas Tiessen. Doug Wicks caught us up on his project to develop Russian Christian writers, and we took the long train trip to Astrakhan.

In Astrakhan, Don Plummer was church planting and showing the Russians how to use drip irrigation. He had challenged the director of the agricultural school to see who grew the best plants. He used drip irrigation, and in the arid land he grew three times as much as the normal Russian methods. The school entered the results in a national agricultural fair and won a gold medal. Phil and I congratulated him and enjoyed the tour of the school. They were, among other things, training young camels to pull a plow.

Back in Macedonia, we had a great Thanksgiving. Our international dinner, which included U.S. turkeys, Swedish dishes, and of course Macedonian dishes, was delicious. Nine of Bev's nurses attended. Following Mirco's sermon on thankfulness, people stood up to tell wha they were thankful for. The nurses got up and presented Bev with a ni bottle of wine, saying, "We are thankful for Bev and Nada teaching us the modules of MPSE."

One of our many CAMA short-termers was Tineke Broedersz, a Dutch CMAer. Her husband was an air force general in charge of th Dutch contingent in Bosnia. I tasked her with trying to bring som order to the micro-enterprise project in Bosnia. Based in Zenica, she held Bible studies and tried to explain why they should pay their debts. But although some money came in, there was no long-term follow-up. She was successful in starting a craft project among the gypsies. So many clothes were donated from all over the world that some were burned to warm the gypsy homes. Tineke taught them to make patchwork quilts from the excess clothing and then set up a way to market them in Europe. She did a great job.

Fighting flared up on the border with Kosovo. Terrorists just could not accept the status of Kosovo and wanted to carve out a Muslim area in Macedonia as well. Fighting was fierce, and for a while, Dianna and the other missionaries left Kosovo for safety. With the borders closed, we shifted our relief efforts to those in Macedonia displaced by the new fighting. We gave them food, medicine, and clothing.

When terrorists blew up the water line for Kumanovo, a city of 100,000, AGAPE swung into action, delivering bottled water and Scripture portions to both Muslims and Christians. When asked on national television why the Macedonians would help, even though some of these people were enemies, they reminded everyone that the Bible ays, "Love your enemies and do good to those who despitefully use u."

At Metanoia, the new Christian bookstore, coffee shop, and net café, weekly evening discussions on Christian topics and t affairs were held. One night the topic was "Who is my enemy, w should I love him?" It was held even while the terrorists were lacedonians and was so well received that it was shown on elevision. They also showed the Focus on the Family film Sex, e Truth, which Bev had translated into Macedonian. It was requested not only on television, but also in every school Macedonia.

e had completed more than 300 homes in Kosovo, and cheduled. The Swedish Pentecostal Mission Union ng the ball on this, and I did a range of other things. g the water systems in villages. I got a water test kit ople the need for cleaner water. One day as Risto ook at the water source for the village of Banista, ndering about a field following the headman. why we are going in circles here when the water he hillside?"

After a conversation in Albanian, Risto replied, "He says we're in a minefield, and he is being careful."

I urged Risto to tell him to take his time. "I was thirsty, and you gave me something to drink" took on new meaning there.

Dianna Ullrich was teaching English to the Muslim police. She also was doing occupational therapy and the handcraft project. We got funds for her to open a women's center in Kačanik. There were always new ways to help people and witness for Christ.

Risto became the pastor of the small Volkovo church. The evangelical church bought a small house, expanded the building, and began children's work. Risto and Nena were perfect for the small community, some of whom were refugees from Serbia. Risto told me, "I didn't plan to be a pastor."

"Then," I replied, "you should not have married a pastor's wife. Nena loves the people, and they love her."

Volkovo was close to the fighting between the Macedonian army and the Albanian terrorists. David Aderholdt, Trent Thornton, Risto, and I were sipping Turkish coffee one day and admiring the newly built AGAPE warehouse next to the church. (We had found that with the money spent for three months' rent at the old warehouse, we could instead put up our own on the Volkovo church property.) Just then, Bang! a mortar shell landed close by. The guys spilled their coffee.

"Let's go!" someone said.

"No," I advised, "let's wait to see where they're shooting from. That way we won't run into them." A couple of explosions later, we finished our coffee and exited the area.

"You have to come see this on TV. Either it's a bad show about New York or there is bad trouble in America."

The speaker was our upstairs neighbor, and she was shaken. Bev and I had just returned from a summer furlough. We'd confirmed Bev's parents' medical needs. Her dad had about six months to live, and her mom's Alzheimer's was advancing. Her dad had gone on his last fishing trip and caught a 29-pound salmon, which we'd enjoyed at his ninetieth birthday party. Our boys were doing well in school, and we had spent a week with Lars-Eric and Elisabeth Lundgren in Sweden on our way back. It was now September 11, 2001, and the U.S. had been attacked by Al-Qaeda. In addition, we could hear the shooting not far away between the Macedonian army and the Albanian terrorists. NATO was trying to find a workable solution, but so far it had left people even more discouraged. I was reminded of Sami Dagher's response to a visitor's query, "When will there be peace in the Middle East?"

Smiling, he had replied, "Right after Christ returns."

That's how we felt about the Balkans, too. Now we were dealing with the bad news of September 11.

I had recently spent some time in Israel, reviewing CAMA Services work with Roger and Ellen Elbel. They'd served in Lebanon and now in Israel. We had seen village development and driven to Rmayleh. This village had been wired by CAMA Services for electricity. In another project, we had added rooms to their school. Near Mount Moriah, we had passed through a small village above Rmayleh. A man dressed in a peculiar maroon robe had stepped out of a gate. Roger had said, "That's a Samaritan high priest. I know him; he's a good man. He's retiring soon. There are very few Samaritans left, and up there on Mount Moriah, that structure is their temple under reconstruction."

I had enjoyed Jerusalem as always, especially the Arab CMA church inside the old city. Like Skopje, it had been standing room only. At the Church of the Nativity in Bethlehem, a Palestinian guard had asked, "How can we get more tourists to come here?"

"You could stop killing each other," I had suggested.

So on that September 11 evening in Macedonia, I thought, Things will not be the same. The next day, Risto and I drove to Sarajevo via Serbia. The soldiers at the roadblock, often in sight of buildings destroyed by NATO bombs, were always professional. On this trip they handed back my passport with condolences and remarked, "That should not happen to America. They do not deserve this!"

President Bush's new orders included rounding up the foreign Muslim fighters in Kosovo and Bosnia. We saw a few bus loads of men cross the border en route to the Middle East. Sensing a new policy where Muslims were concerned, the Albanian terrorists began to settle while they could.

John, Marija's husband who is a Jordanian pharmacist, wanted to go to graduate school. He needed help. His former boss had kept some of his documents, and he needed them to get back to work or go to school. "Ask Mirco," I suggested.

"But he's a Macedonian," John replied.

"Ah, yes, but he's also a pastor, and he's been kind to you," I reminded him.

When we explained the problem, Mirco said, "The minister of labor is from my village." Picking up the phone, he called him and, after some pleasantries, told him about John's problem. Mirco hung up and told John, "Go to his office at 1:00 p.m. He will have your papers for you!"

John was amazed that the church cared for him. I brought him a Jesus film and some Bible study books in Arabic. He began to understand what Jesus taught.

Jennie Evans of TEAR Fund England had visited the work, and now they were sending money. The micro-credit project was financing cows, grain mills, and a couple of small businesses. CAMA Services even made a video, 'Your Hands to a Hurting World.' Suddenly it seemed as if it was becoming time for Bev and me to go. Everyone was trained and motivated. Cindy was full of new ideas to grow MPSE, and Risto was not only ready to carry on, but he had even enrolled in a master of ministries program online from the CMA in Colorado Springs.

We were having tea with Shahadia Shehu one day in Kačanik. "Risto cannot come to our home anymore," she said sadly.

We had gone there often, had tea and meals with the family, and when an emergency medical need arose, Risto had braved war and snow to get medicine to them.

"But why?" I asked.

"He is Macedonian, and my brother has joined the rebels fighting Macedonia," she said. "He will make trouble if Risto comes again."

She was very apologetic, but I knew the terrorists would kill even someone like Risto just to make their point. "Well," I said, "you can still work at the PMU office, and we will talk to you there. I won't be able to come to your house without Risto."

On the way back to Macedonia, Risto's attitude was good, and he pledged to carry on the work in spite of the danger.

We had a great Thanksgiving 2001. We bought 20 small barbecued turkeys. There were more than 100 nurses and clinic administrators, and the church family was another 60 or so. Mirco preached a brilliant sermon on being thankful, and everyone was.

Our neighbor Mimi, Katarina, her daughter, and her son, Jordan, were sad to see us go, as were all our friends. We had a great farewell service in December. We moved in for a couple of nights at the U.S. embassy consulate's home. Eleanor Nagy, deputy chief of mission, hosted a fine farewell party there. She was very kind to us and an encourager for the church.

On December 1, 2001, Bev and I were walking through a beautiful snowfall in Skopje. It was our last night there. Bev was recovering from a nasty fall, which had left her head badly bruised, and we were packed and ready to go. "Do you think we will fit in back in America?" she asked.

I thought a bit and replied, "I hope not too well. We won't really know until we get there."

The next morning, at the international airport in Skopje, the whole AGAPE crew, along with Cindy, Nada, and Marija, joined us for an early breakfast as we waited to go through customs. Vanco, Mirco's brother, looked around. He had been on the Kosovo team through some hard times. Risto was wearing a shirt I gave him, Vanco a coat I had given him, Mirco my shoes, and Atse my hat. Vanco suddenly said, "Look, we're all wearing the Andy collection!"

Oh, by the way, we flunked retirement.

Micro Andreev, Bev, Andy, Nada Andreeva and daughters.
The farewell at Mavrovo, Macedonia

Sonja with Phil Skellie, director of CAMA services at the gypsy school

Phil Skellie, director of CAMA with Andy and Bev
at the AGAPE church in Skopje, Macedonia

Kosovo road scene. Tanks have right of way... Always

Hundreds of homes were repaired in Kosovo

Andy's Life Message

Dr. Timothy Owen, Billings Montana

Faith, the Great Commission, the Great Compassion

As we consider the life and ministry of Bev and Andy Bishop we are inspired to live the life of faith in Christ and commit our lives fully to the Kingdom of God by living the Great Commandment and accomplishing the Great Commission.

Bev and Andy lived the life of faith as described in Hebrew 11. They are not living their lives for This Age, but for the Age to Come.

It may be true that some people engaged in the vocation of ministry are doing so because they couldn't do anything else, but that is not true of Andy and Bev. I came to know Andy and Bev when they moved to Ellensburg in the early seventies. Andy was hired to be the Director of Public Health for Kittitas County in the state of Washington. He took the county by storm. He was not the quiet bureaucrat ensconced in the back office. He was a leader. He brought reform and enforcement to all matters health-related in the county. He was highly respected and was very influential.

We were in Kiwanis Club together. When he wasn't around, club members would remark on how effective and influential he was and that he was heading for "the top." They said that if he ran for public office, he would be elected. As his pastor I observed his career from the sidelines. As he became involved in State level leadership among public health directors he emerged as a leader. I could see he was not to be long in Ellensburg.

He often says that I remarked that the town was not big enough for both of us. In fact what I said was that the town or the county was not big enough for him. More rightly it was true that the town and county were not big enough for what God had planned for Bev and Andy.

Andy was an elder in the Ellensburg CMA Church. At one meeting he recommended we set the goal of God calling twelve people from our congregation into missions. We passed that motion. Did Andy know he and Bev would be the first two to go?

While I was observing his secular career from the sidelines Chuck Fowler was the speaker one winter at our annual Missions Conference. He inspired and challenged us to take up our part in fulfilling the Great Commission. The Sunday evening following the conference Andy and I drove Chuck the 35 miles to the Yakima airport. I drove up to the curb in front of the small, unsecured airport and said to Chuck that he should check in. Andy and I would park and come in to see him off.

As Chuck was standing on the curb with the car door ajar, Andy looked at him and said, "No, he doesn't need us to see him off, let's just get out of here!" Chuck said that was right, gave us God's blessings and was on his way.

As we pulled away from the curb I said to Andy, "That was kind of rude. I know Chuck can find his way to the plane. I was just trying to be a good host! What's with you?"

Andy replied, "Tim, if I hear that airplane, I'm on it!"

I asked, "What do you mean?"

He replied, "Well, I have just been sensing lately that God wants something different for Bev and me. Does the Alliance have any opportunities in missions that we could take?"

I said, "I just received a flyer from National Office asking for help in finding a director for a pediatrics hospital in Cambodia. Would you be qualified for that position?"

He said, "Yes, I earned my masters degree in Health Care Delivery Systems!"

Well, wonderful story abbreviated, he and Bev took that one on. You have read about it in his story.

Like Bev and Andy, we are called to be people of faith. What is faith? It is to believe *"The assurance of things hoped for, the conviction of things not seen."* HEBREWS 11:1 *It is to believe that God will reward those who seek him.* HEBREWS 11:6 Like Abraham, Bev and Andy "Obeyed when he was called to go out to a place that he was to receive as an inheritance.

And he went out, not knowing where he was going." (Note the title of this book!) At this point Andy would joke and say, "That's right! I never have known where I was going!!" But in his humor he is serious. Like the sage advice says, he takes God seriously, but not himself.

This faith in God who rewards eternally forsakes the world as a destination and acknowledges that we *"are strangers and exiles on earth"* HEBREWS 11:13. They desired a *"better country that is a heavenly one"* HEBREWS 11:16.

What are the pieces of this faith? First it is the knowledge that God is supreme. Christ is King and alone deserves to be served. His kingdom shall reign forever and ever. So we do well to serve him and his kingdom rather than the kingdom of this world that will fade away. Andy was not sophisticated in this strong belief. He quoted the cliché "Only one life will soon be passed; only what's done for Christ will last." Cliché was not cliché because it was wholesale commitment of life and every breath.

Second it is the understanding that the kingdom of God is made up of subjects, people who turn to Christ as savior and Lord. Andy and Bev were always about winning the lost to Christ. Andy was always witnessing. Often during a Kiwanis meeting a speaker would hold forth on the problems of youth in our day. During the discussion time Andy would say, "Well I know from my own life and from when I served as a probation officer for Whatcom County that the only hope for these young people and for all of us is to know Jesus Christ as savior." The men around the tables would either nod their heads in agreement or take note of what he spoke. He never hesitated to witness. He was not ashamed of the gospel of Christ.

A few days after that ordained trip to the airport in Yakima we were having lunch at the Hi-Way Grille talking about missions in the Alliance. CAMA Services hadn't been formally established yet but the Alliance did relief and development ministries in various places around the globe. The pediatrics hospital in Cambodia was an example of that kind of ministry. I pointed out to Andy that unlike some mercy ministry organizations the Alliance always combined the proclamation of the gospel and the establishment of churches with mercy ministries. He said "Good, I won't work for a mission that doesn't proclaim the gospel!"

If you want to get Andy to tear up, listen to him tell stories until he tells one about someone coming to Christ. It is then that his voice thickens and his speech is slurred. He is under the influence of souls saved. *"Therefore God is not ashamed to be called their God, for he has prepared for them a city."* HEBREWS 11:16B

Third, that faith is confident in God and not afraid of man. *"By faith he left Egypt, not being afraid of the anger of the king, for he endured as seeing him who is invisible."* HEBREWS 11:27-28 Our eyes should always be on the prize, bold in him who will give it to us for his glory. Andy was easy to work with as long as you did not represent an obstacle to getting God's job done. He was flexible (some would say messy) in some administrative detail, empowering others to clear the path, and he was strong in assessing the disaster situation, formulating a plan to respond, recruiting the providers of help, getting them pointed in the right direction and then turning it over to a person he put in charge. If in his pursuit of responding to a disaster you proved to be a help, you liked working with Andy. If you got in the way, you didn't. Whether it was confronting county officials in South Carolina, or persuading high level officials in Thailand, Andy had such confidence in God he moved with courage, simplicity, clarity, boldness and faith. One opines that had he been in charge of FEMA when hurricane Katrina hit, George Bush would have looked like a hero.

Fourth, our pursuit of goals and objectives must be guided by compassion, mercy: In short, Love. The Great Commandment is the central priority in the Great Commission. The two ought not to oppose each other. In fact, it is good to note that Christ by implication called the Commandment Great. We have called the Commission Great. Not that the commission is not a great one, but it is to be guided and inspired by the Great Commandment. Andy was a lover of God and people.

His first love was Bev. Years after the accident that nearly took Bev's life, and they had moved to Ellensburg, Andy tells this in his story. Andy and Bev providentially reconnected with an important person in their lives. She was/is Linda Lundy. Linda was Bev's nurse in the hospital neurological ward during her convalescence. Their reunion was a happy one. Later, Linda and her husband Dave became a part of our church. As we came to know them Linda testified, "We nurses saw lots of women severely injured by accident and noted with grief and frustration many of the husbands abandoning their wives during the time of trauma. Andy was faithful to Bev; in fact, devoted to her. We nurses saw him bounding into the ward every day like a sunbeam to spend time with Bev! She was badly damaged and he was full of enthusiasm, sharp, handsome and was totally devoted to his injured wife! I knew they were Christians and I wanted what they had. I was a Christian, and was drawn as to a magnet to have what they had."

Love will also lead us to being servant, not leader. When Andy and Bev lived in Russia and Andy had The CoMission up and running and not needing much of his time, energy and creativity, he turned to assisting Bev. He used to say, "I'm the house husband! I do the cooking, cleaning and running errands for Bev!" And he did. He could fill the glory role or the behind the scenes humble role equally unawares. He could serve as well as lead. Why? Because he had faith in God that it was not the notice of people he sought, but of God and he knew God was pleased. *"For I have learned in whatever situation I am to be content. I know how to be brought low, and I know how to abound. In any and every circumstance, I have learned the secret of facing plenty and hunger, abundance and need. I can do all things through him who strengthens me."* Philippians 4:11b-13

Andy was a "can do" man, no doubt. And what he could do was whatever God put in front of him to do.

And Bev was the same. With little self awareness and much awareness of God and great human need, she served Andy in his ministry pursuits. Later it was her turn to shine and his to serve.

The lesson we learn from their story is the one of faith in God who is supreme, is worthy of service, willing and able to work wonders and empowers those like the faithful of old *"...who through faith conquered kingdoms, enforced justice, obtained promises, stopped the mouths of lions, quenched the power of fire, escaped the edge of the sword, were made strong out of weakness, became mighty in war, put foreign armies to flight. Women received back their dead by resurrection. Some were tortured, refusing to accept release, so that they might rise again to a better life. Others suffered mocking and flogging, and even chains and imprisonment. They were stoned, they were sawn in two, they were killed with the sword. They went about in skins of sheep and goats, destitute, afflicted, mistreated— of whom the world was not worthy—wandering about in deserts and mountains, and in dens and caves of the earth."* Hebrews 11:32-38

And these lessons of faith are to us who are fallen, being redeemed, called and empowered by the Father, Son and Holy Spirit. We are far from perfect. We are sinners saved by grace and being sanctified,

"pressing on towards to the goal of the upward call in Christ Jesus." PHIL 3:14
The heroes of the faith whose stories are told in the Bible were sinners
too and God chose to use them heroically. Abraham, Moses, David,
Peter, and Paul all were saved sinners being sanctified. They could not
hide behind their inadequacies and sins and thus avoid God's call on
their lives. Neither can we! Neither did Andy and Bev. They went out
under the atoning blood of Christ and the power of the Gospel and
the Holy Spirit. They would not, and certainly we do not say they were
flawless. What we do say is that God chose to use them as imperfect and
willing servants to accomplish great things for God and his kingdom.

So as many great leaders have asked, "How should we then live?"
The author of Hebrews, inspired by God, says it best:

"Wherefore seeing we also are compassed about with so great a cloud of
witnesses, let us lay aside every weight, and the sin which doth so easily beset
us, and let us run with patience the race that is set before us, Looking unto
Jesus the author and finisher of our faith; who for the joy that was set before
him endured the cross, despising the shame, and is set down at the right hand
of the throne of God. For consider him that endured such contradiction of
sinners against himself, lest ye be wearied and faint in your minds."
HEBREWS 12:1-3.

Solo Gloria Deo